DSA CALIFORNIA
GUIDE TO THE DSA CODE KNOWLEDGE EXAMS
DIVISION OF STATE ARCHITECT

by Khurt A. Geisse and Stephen Payte

Printed and Distributed By:

Builder's Book, Inc.
CONTRACTOR'S BOOK CENTER
BOOKSTORE • PUBLISHER

8001 Canoga Ave.
Canoga Park, CA 91304

1-800-273-7375 — www.buildersbook.com
ISBN 1-889892-38-6
Copyright © 2005 Builder's Book, Inc.

Copyright © 2005 by
Builder's Books, Inc.
8001 Canoga Avenue
Canoga Park, California 91304

All rights reserved. No part of this book may be reproduced in any form or by any means, without permission in writing from the copyright owner, except that purchasers of this book may reproduce any forms for use in the internal operations of the purchasing organization, provided that such forms may not be sold.

"This publication is designed to provide accurate and authoritative information in regard to the subject matter covered. It is sold with the understanding that neither the publisher nor author are engaged in rendering legal, accounting, or other professional service. If legal advice or other expert assistance is required, the services of a competent professional person should be sought."

. . From the Declaration of Principles jointly adopted by a Committee of the American Bar Association and a Committee of Publishers and Associations.

Library of Congress Cataloging-in-Publication Data

California Guide To The DSA Code Knowledge Exams Division of State Architect
    p. cm.

ISBN 1-889892-38-6

1. California Guide To The DSA Code Knowledge Exams. I. Title

© 2005 Builder's Book, Inc.

TABLE OF CONTENTS

CHAPTER 1	Lesson 1.1	What is DSA and the Application Process	pg. 1 - 7
CHAPTER 2	Lesson 2.1	This Guide and How it Works	pg. 8 - 12
CHAPTER 3	Lesson 3.1	Building Codes and How They Work	pg. 13 - 19
CHAPTER 4	Lesson 4.1	Administrative Code	pg. 20 - 31
CHAPTER 5	Lesson 5.1	Occupancy	pg. 32 - 38
	Lesson 5.2	General Building Limitations	pg. 39 - 42
	Lesson 5.3	Types of Construction	pg. 43 - 46
	Lesson 5.4	Fire Resistive Construction	pg. 47 - 52
	Lesson 5.5	Interior Finishes	pg. 53 - 55
	Lesson 5.6	Fire Protection Systems	pg. 56 - 59
	Lesson 5.7	Egress	pg. 60 - 64
CHAPTER 6	Lesson 6.1	Structural Design Provisions	pg. 65 - 75
	Lesson 6.2	Structural Tests and Inspections	pg. 76 - 79
CHAPTER 7	Lesson 7.1	Concrete Background Information	pg. 80 - 95
	Lesson 7.2	Foundations and Retaining Walls	pg. 96 - 100
	Lesson 7.3	Concrete (1901A-1906A)	pg. 101 – 106
	Lesson 7.4	Concrete (1907A-1929A)	pg. 107 – 117
CHAPTER 8	Lesson 8.1	Masonry Background Information	pg. 118 – 136
	Lesson 8.2	Masonry	pg. 137 – 142
CHAPTER 9	Lesson 9.1	Steel Background Information	pg. 143 – 155
	Lesson 9.2	Structural Steel (2201A-2231A)	pg. 156 – 161
	Lesson 9.3	AISC ASD (Steel Manual)	pg. 162 – 189
CHAPTER 10	Lesson 10.1	Wood Background Information	pg. 190 – 209
	Lesson 10.2	Wood (2301A-3504A)	pg. 210 – 224
	Lesson 10.4	Wood (WCLIG "Standard 17" Lumber Grading)	pg. 226 – 235
CHAPTER 11	Lesson 11.1	Electrical	pg. 236 – 239
	Lesson 11.2	Plumbing	pg. 240 - 243
	Lesson 11.3	Mechanical	pg. 244 – 245
CHAPTER 12	Lesson 12.1	Access Compliance	pg. 246 – 265
CHAPTER 13	Lesson 13.1	Suspended Ceilings	pg. 266 – 279
APPENDIX # 1		DSA Certified Inspector Exam Application Package	
APPENDIX #2		IR A-8 Inspector Duties and Performance Rating by DSA	

© Professional Study Inc. 2003

Chapter 1
What is DSA and the Application Process

DSA

DSA (Division of the State Architect) is a California State Government Division or agency that has been given the task of regulating the construction of public schools throughout the state of California. This is the result of an act of the State Legislature. They are the building department for public schools. DSA has their headquarters in Sacramento and it also has a number of "Field Offices" mainly in the large population centers that do most of the work.

School Districts that want to build new schools, or remodel and add to existing ones are required to apply for construction permits through DSA. As a part of that regulatory process DSA requires that a DSA Certified building inspector or assistant inspector continuously observe all aspects of the construction process. Therefore unlike most other jurisdictions such as L.A. City or Orange County where construction is only required to be inspected at certain times, DSA requires that an inspector be onsite continuously to provide inspection.

Once the plans are approved and the funding has been worked out for a project construction commences. DSA Project Inspector works under the direction of the project architect/engineer and is supposed to be onsite until the project is completed. DSA provides a 'Field Engineer' who is a DSA state employee that comes to the jobsite on a regular basis and verifies that the inspection process is taking place per DSA regulations. The School Districts are required to pay for the services of the Project Inspector.

Inspector Certification Process

DSA regulates how the project inspectors are to be certified and how they will be used on school projects. As a result of this whole certification requirement DSA developed a state wide certification process which has a number of aspects.

1. First in order to be considered to take a DSA certification exam the candidate must fulfill some specific experience requirements, and be accepted to sit for the Class 1,2,3, or 4 exam.

2. Once those requirements are met then the candidate must pass the certification exam for the appropriate Class of certification. Each exam is a two part multiple choice exam, Part 1 (Plan Reading), and Part 2 (Code Knowledge).

3. After passing the exam the inspector must be approved by DSA, The Architect, and of course The School District for the specific project for which he is to be hired.

Project Inspector Classifications:

1. **Class 1 Project Inspector**: This is the highest classification of project inspector. With this classification you are supposed to be qualified to inspect any type of school building.

2. **Class 2 Project Inspector:** This is the second highest class of project inspector. With this certification you can inspect buildings over 2000 square feet up to $8 million valuation and with wood lateral force resisting structural systems.

3. **Class 3 Project Inspector:** With this certification you are eligible to inspect single story wood frame buildings with primarily wood shear walls. The work must be under 2000 square feet have only isolated steel or concrete structural members. This certification is generally limited to renovation work or modifications.

4. **Class 4 Project Inspector:** This certification is limited to relocatable building inspections. The market for this type of inspector is very limited and often a wasted effort.

5. **Assistant Inspector:** Assistant inspectors are not considered certified inspectors so therefore the approval process is a bit different. However the assistant inspector program allows assistants to work under the direct direction of a Class 1 inspector. Assistants are limited to work on modifications or highly supervised work under Class 1 inspectors. Their approval is also up to the discretion of the DSA Field Engineer.

6. **DSA Masonry Inspector**: This DSA Certification entitles the holder to work as a masonry special inspector on DSA projects. The application process and requirements for this work are completely separate from the Class 1-4 project inspector certifications.

© Professional Study Inc. 2003

Experience Requirement

In order to qualify for DSA Certification an individual must satisfy an experience requirement. DSA refers to this experience as "Qualifying Experience".

This means that the candidate must have at least 3 years of experience working on projects similar to those which they would be inspecting as a DSA Project Inspector.

Question: How does DSA determine what projects are similar?

This is the big question, and it requires a complicated answer. We recommend that you read the DSA Exam application material carefully. In general terms DSA looks at the kinds of materials used for the lateral resisting structure, the size of the project (valuation), and the square footage to determine the class that the project would qualify as.

Question: What type of Experience do you need?

DSA has a rather complicated way of determining what type of experience they will count towards your three years of "Qualifying Experience". We have included a DSA Project Inspector Exam application which does a good job of explaining what the experience requirements are. Read through the application and pay particular attention to the matrix of experience limitations. The type of work that you have done on a construction project will determine how much credit DSA will allow you to count toward your qualifying experience. For example, if you were an electrician for twenty years on large commercial work DSA will let you count all twenty years toward a Class 3 certification but only 12 months toward a Class 2. Read the application carefully.

© Professional Study Inc. 2003

Certification Exams

DSA administers a certification exam for project inspectors every three months. The exams consist of (2) three hour parts.

- Part 1 (Class 1) consists of a 45 multiple choice questions "Plan Reading" exam

- Part 2 (Class 1) is a 90 multiple choice question, open book, "Code Knowledge" exam.

- For the Class 2 and 3 exams the number of questions is reduced by approximately 5 questions for plan reading and code knowledge.

The Plan Reading Exam (Part 1)

For the plan reading you are provided with a set of plans depicting a project that is typical for the Class of certification you are seeking. You must answer 45 questions in the span of 3 hours (180 minutes) which allows you 4 minutes per question.

For the 2004 exams DSA has added a new wrinkle. The plan reading exams are now divided into sections (Structural, Architectural, Mech/Elec/Plumb). The candidate will be required to obtain a minimum grade of 55% on each "Section". In addition they have raised the overall passing grade from 60% overall to 65% overall.

Code Knowledge Exam (Part 2)

The "Code Knowledge" exam has also been change from 2003. The Code Knowledge part has also been divided into sections (Structural, Architectural, Mech/Elec/Plumb, Administrative). Notice that the Code Knowledge includes an Administrative section. The candidate must obtain a score of 55% on each section. The overall passing grade has been raised from 60% to 65%.

© Professional Study Inc. 2003

This Guide to DSA Cerification

This guide is intended for construction professionals that are adept at reading plans and have only a general understanding of building codes. We do not recommend this guide to those who do not have experience in construction or who do not qualify for any of the DSA exams under the established criteria.

For the code portion have included the materials that we believe you need to know in order to successfully complete exam. We also provide a structure and practice that simulates the actual exam which will help you assess and improve your skill in preparation for the real exam. It is up to you as the candidate to learn the materials.

This guide is not intended as preparation for the Plan Reading part of the DSA exams. In order to prepare for the Plan Reading part of the Exam we recommend our plan reading course that can be taken entirely online. Refer to

DSACertification.com

Appendix 1 is a copy of the DSA Certified Inspector Examination package. In order to apply for the DSA exam you will need to file this application. Read the instructions carefully and provide detailed information with regard to the structural aspects of the projects you worked on and your (preferably hands on) participation.

DSA EXPERIENCE CHART

Study the following flowchart and use it to determine what Class of inspector exam your experience qualifies you for. Remember that the important things are the type of lateral system, the overall budget, and the square footage of the construction.

Start at the left and follow the arrows according to the criteria in the boxes. Follow the arrows to the right until you arrive at a classification for the type of construction projects that you have participated in. This chart provides you with a rough idea of what your experience should qualify you for. Remember that DSA has the final word so be prepared to argue your case.

Also remember that when you apply you may have to lobby the DSA staff for admission to the appropriate exam. DSA's interpretation of the class criteria is sometimes cloudy, therefore it is important that you have a good understanding of this information in order to plead your case.

PROJECT CLASS CRITERIA

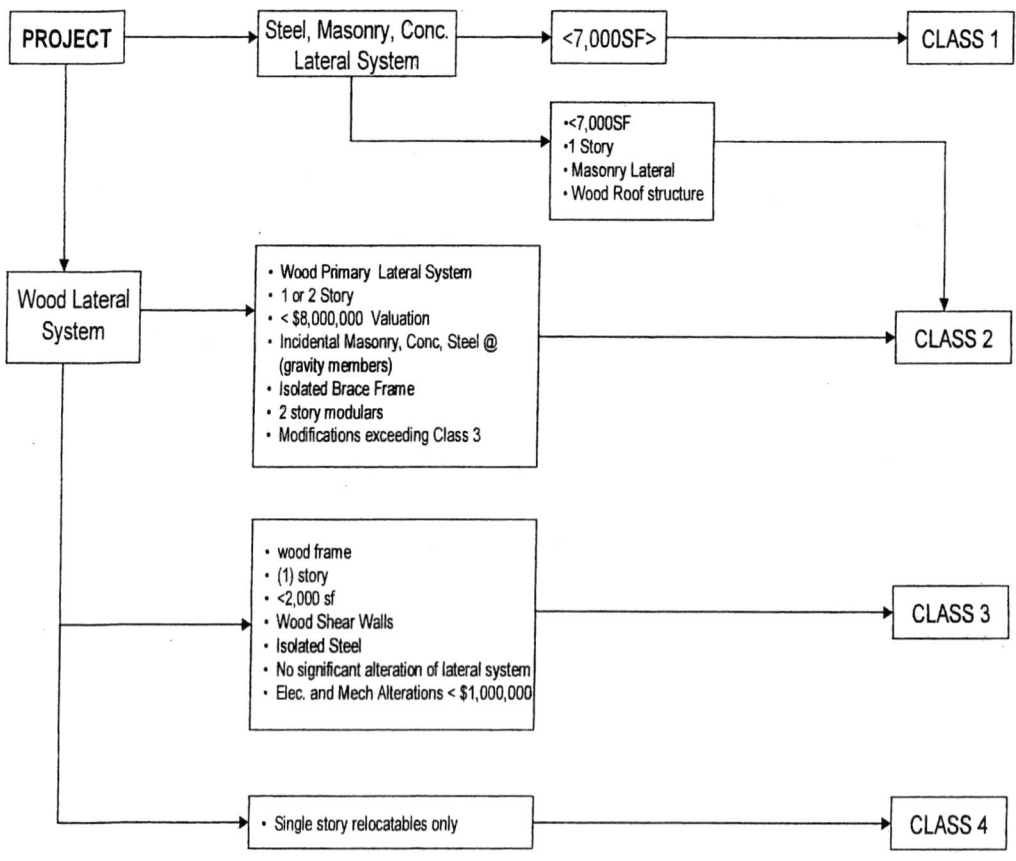

© Professional Study Inc. 2003

Use the experience record forms provided in the application package (Appendix 1), and the matrix provided below to describe your experience, they are the most important part of your exam application. Print out this matrix and highlight the months that you have accounted for in your experience record.

Follow the instructions on the application and submit your application as soon as possible.

Expect a 4 to 6 week delay from when you submit your application to when you get your test date.

Experience Record Matrix

Year	Jan.	Feb.	Mar.	April	May	June	July	Aug.	Sept.	Oct.	Nov.	Dec.
1980												
1981												
1982												
1983												
1984												
1985												
1986												
1987												
1988												
1989												
1990												
1991												
1992												
1993												
1994												
1995												
1996												
1997												
1998												
1999												
2000												
2001												
2002												
2003												
2004												

© Professional Study Inc. 2003

Chapter 2: This Guide and How It Works

As you already know the intention of this course is to help you obtain the basic information and skills necessary to pass the DSA certification examinations and help you get started as a DSA Inspector. The following is an overview of this course and how we suggest that you use it.

Recommended Books and Materials

We recommend that for the purpose of taking this course and for taking any of the DSA Certification exams you purchase the following publications

1. **Title 24, Part 1, Administrative Code** (published by ICC)
2. **Title 24, Part 2, Volume 1** (published by ICC)
3. **Title 24, Part 2, Volume 2** (published by ICC)
4. **Standard 17, Grading Rules for West Coast Lumber** (West Coast Lumber Inspections Bureau)
5. **UBC Code Book Tabs** (ICC)
6. **IR Manual** (published by DSA)

DSA Inspectors are expected to own and be responsible for Parts 1-5 of Title 24, however for the purpose of taking the exam we do not feel that it is absolutely necessary to have all of these publications. If and when you do become a certified DSA inspector we highly recommend that your purchase Parts 1-5 of Title 24.

All of these publications are available at the retail bookstore on our website at:

InspectorAcademy.com

© Professioal Study Inc.2003

Tabbing Your Books

In order to use your code books efficiently you need to be able to turn to the appropriate part of the book quickly, that is why it is important to have an efficient and clear set of Tabs for your books. ICC provides a very clean and professional set of tabs that they have made for the UBC. Use the UBC tabs on your California Building Code (Part 2, Volume 1, and Volume 2) chapters. This will give you an overall organization to work with.

Guidebook Structure

Chapters 1-13 (35) Lessons
(Code Knowledge)

This guide book is divided into 13 chapters containing 35 separate lessons. These materials are those that are relevant to the DSA Certification Exams and also to the practice of Project Inspectors.

The lessons are intended to highlight and identify the necessary materials. It will be up to study the materials. There are three basic types of lesson. Background lessons are intended to give you and overview or a material and methods of construction. Highlighting lists are intended to give you specific excerpts from the applicable codes that we recommend that you highlight for easy reference. And finally the commentary gives you an abbreviated explanation of the code materials in lemans terms.

Recommended Study Sequence

We recommend that you follow the steps below in order to obtain the greatest benefit from this guide book:

1. Purchase the recommended Books and Materials

2. Read and understand any background lessons.

3. Highlight your code books according to the "Highlighting Lists" that are part of this book.

4. Review the "Commentary"

5. Go back through your code books and familiarize yourself with the materials on the Study Guide.

6. Purchase our online study course at **www. InspectorAcademy**.com and use the timed testing resources.

© Professioal Study Inc.2003

Chapter (Sections and Lessons)

All the various lessons will have one or more of the following elements:

1. An outline of the Section lessons and the materials that will be covered in that section.//
2. A narrative introduction which will give you an overall perspective on the section materials and what to look for.
3. The **Background lesson** will often be information on the section material that is helpful to establish your overall understanding of the subject matter but that does not relate specifically to the DSA exams.
4. The **"Highlighting Lists"** are excerpts from the actual code along with commentary intended to clarify or summarize the code language.
5. There may be a lesson on another special publication that we have included in the recommended study materials.

Highlighting Lists

The **"Highlighting Lists"** are the main body of the code knowledge part of the course. Each list is a word for word version of excerpts from the code on the left and commentary on the right side.

Use the code on the left as a template for highlighting your code books in yellow highlighter. We have reduced the highlight material to only that which is relevant to the inspector.

The **"Commentary"** on the right is broken down into four categories and they are as follows:

1. **TEST QUESTION (Highlight in Red)**
   - (Indicates that this material is very likely to be specifically referenced on the DSA exams)

2. **REMEMBER (Highlight in Yellow)**
   - (Indicates that you should know this material and that it is relevant to your work as an inspector)

3. **BEWARE (Highlight in Yellow)**
   - (Indicates that there is something that may not be apparent at first but that the inspector will have to deal with)

4. **SEE ALSO (Highlight in Yellow)**
   - (Indicates that there is another code section that affects this information)

Remember that you don't want to over highlight. Too many different colors, references, and tabs will confuse you in the exam. You need to keep it simple and down to the essentials. As it is there will be a lot of material to highlight.

Chapter 3
Building Codes and How They Work

Building codes are documents that are usually prepared by an entity or organization (The UBC is published by the International Code Council or ICC) that has particular expertise in an aspect of construction and then prepares a set of rules that govern that particular construction activity. The building code regulates buildings in general (Building code) and references a number of other publications (adopted standards, recognized standards) that have more specific information about the materials and processes that are to be regulated.

Model Codes: The model code is a code that is used as a basis for the codes in a geographic location or region. In the case of California the state publishes the California Building Code (CBC) which is modeled on the Uniform Building Code (UBC). The city of Los Angeles publishes the Los Angeles Building Code (LABC) which is also modeled on the (UBC). Each jurisdiction adopts the uniform code and then adds or deletes provisions in order to suit their needs. There are also other model codes such as the National Electric Code, the Uniform Fire Code, the Uniform Plumbing and Mechanical Codes etc. These are all the basis for the codes that are adopted throughout the western part of the U.S.

Standards: Within the uniform code there is also reference to other publications that are known as Standards. These are documents either prepared by ICC or another entity. For example when you are seeking specific information about the precise chemical and quality standards of Portland cement the code refers you to ASTM standard C150. ASTM or the American Society of Testing Materials is an entity that writes standards and construction materials. There are also UBC standards among others. This method provides a way for code writers to concentrate on what they know best and use the knowledge of others.

The 2001 California Building Code which is the current DSA code is based on the 1997 Uniform Building Code.

For the purpose of this lesson you should understand that the building code is only part of the set of regulations that govern school construction in California.

Title 24 and the Field Act

The field act is a law that was passed by the California Legislature after the Long Beach earthquake of the 1930's. This law empowered the government to establish a governmental agency to regulate the construction of school buildings and Essential Services buildings. These buildings all require that a project inspector be present to verify the quality of construction.

© Professioal Study Inc.2003

Title 24 is the legal vehicle or overall code that the state uses to carry out the regulation that was mandated in the field act. It is a set of regulations that has been passed by the California Legislature that regulates school construction in the state.

Title 24 is broken up into parts and some of those parts are broken up further. See the figure below.

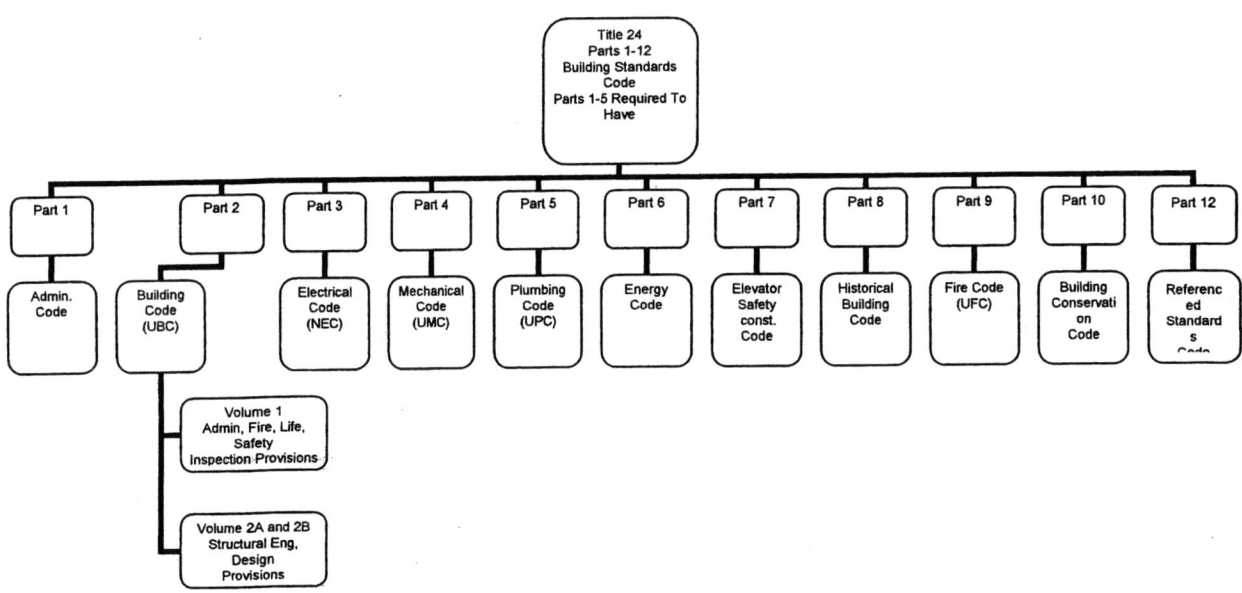

TITLE 24 DESCRIPTION PARTS 1-5

Of the 12 parts that make up the Title 24 Building Standards Code there we as DSA inspectors are asked to be familiar with only portions of Parts 1-5 though Part 6 is said to be gaining in importance.

Part 1: Administrative Code:

This is the part of the code which lays out the rules for the various players in the construction of a public school facility. It sets forth the role of all of the players which are principally the **School District, the Architect / Structural Engineer, the Project Inspector, and the Contractor**. It points out what must be done and by whom in order to have the project certified by DSA. It also lays out what the hiring, and certification requirements are for project inspectors as well as the responsibilities of the project inspector.

Part 2: Building Code:

This part of the 2001 code is made up of Two different volumes.

Volume 1:
Administrative, Fire-and Life-Safety, and Field Inspection Provisions.

The following are the Volume 1 Chapters that will be covered by this course:

Chapter 3: Occupancy:

Regulates the type of use that can take place in a particular space and how it will be treated in the design process. The occupancies of most interest to the DSA inspector are A (assembly), B (business), E (education), and S (storage). There are subdivisions within those designations that will be discussed later.

Chapter 5: General Building Limitations:

This establishes minimum heights and distances with regard to the building parts. The most significant parts of this is Sec. 509-Guardrails and Table-5A which establishes the construction type for various parts of the building.

Chapter 6: Types of Construction:

There are five major construction 'Types'. These are distinguished by the fire resistance of the materials and assemblies that are used. Type I is the most resistive and Type V is the least resistive.
Chapters 3 and 6 work very closely together since the type of occupancy often determines the fire resistive nature of the building housing that occupancy.
Within the construction types there are also subdivisions, these will be discussed at a later point in the course.

Chapter 7: Fire Resistant Materials and Construction:

The most significant part of this chapter to the inspector is the regulation of building parts and materials with respect to fire resistance.
Among the most important are Section 708 fire blocking and draft stops, 709 Walls and Partitions, 710 Floors and Ceilings, and 713 Assemblies for Protection of Openings.

© Professioal Study Inc.2003

Chapter 8: Interior Finishes:

The DSA inspector needs to know the concept of 'flame spread'. All materials used on the interior of a building will have a flame spread rating. This rating is determined through testing. The rating is significant to the inspector because certain materials that have a higher flame spread are not useable in certain occupancies. In addition Chapter 8 also regulates sanitation requirements for the interior finishes in bathrooms.

Chapter 9: Fire-Protection Systems:

This chapter establishes the requirements for automatic fire suppression and detection systems in buildings. Most of the issues addressed in this chapter are long settled before the inspector comes on the job site, however there are certain minimum requirements that the inspector will have to be familiar with.

Chapter 10: Means of Egress:

This chapter is very important. As in other chapters of Volume 1 the standards will already be defined prior to the inspector's involvement. However, you should pay particular attention to penetrations into exit corridors, panic hardware, numbers of exits, etc.

Chapter 11: Accessibility:

Often referred to as handicap accessibility this chapter regulates issues related to accessing different parts of the building. In terms of this course we have treated this chapter in a unique way for the following reasons:
Virtually all of the provisions of this chapter are determined prior to the inspector's involvement. However there are a significant number of questions on this information on the DSA exams. Therefore we have not included a highlighting list for this chapter but rather very extensive checklist for quick reference. The exams may contain any one of hundreds possible questions about particular measurements. As a result it is inefficient to highlight each measurement etc. therefore we will cover the checklist and provide diagrams that are very adequate in addressing any one of the possible questions.

Chapter 14A: Exterior Wall Coverings:

This chapter is most significant to the DSA inspector due to the provisions in Section 1403A Veneer. DSA pays close attention to this chapter since many schools have masonry veneers incorporated in the design. For the purpose of this course chapter 14 is considered part of the masonry materials.

© Professioal Study Inc.2003

Volume 2:
Structural Engineering, Design provisions.

This book contains provisions which regulate the actual design and construction. It is broken down by material and specific design requirements.
Also notice that the chapters are designated as a number with an 'A' next to it. This is to distinguish them from the Uniform Building Code chapters which don't contain the provisions specific to DSA work. Be careful to make the distinction between these texts since they are side by side in the published code books.

The following are the Volume 2 Chapters that will be covered by this course:

Chapter 16A: Seismic Design

This chapter regulates the exceptional design provisions that must be adhered to in areas were seismic activity is anticipated. Virtually all of California is designated a Zone 3 or 4 seismic zone, therefore as a DSA inspector you should be familiar with these provisions. Pay particular attention to Table 16A-O.

Chapter 17A: Special Inspection and Testing

Though this is a very short chapter it is extremely significant to the DSA Inspector. This chapter establishes the rules for special inspection of various aspects of the construction process. It also determines much of the testing as well. Special inspectors are an integral part of the building inspection process and the DSA Inspector must be well versed on the requirements of chapter 17A.

Chapter 18A: Foundations:

This chapter very closely related to chapter 19A (Concrete) for obvious reasons. The difference is that chapter 18A contains provisions that refer to foundations with the exception of the material requirements. This is another short but important chapter.

Chapter 19A: Concrete:

This chapter contains the provisions regulating concrete materials and concrete work. This is perhaps the single most important chapter to the DSA Inspector. A number of the DSA exam questions will come directly from this chapter.

© Professioal Study Inc.2003

Chapter 21A: Masonry

This is another significant chapter. However masonry is not as heavily covered on the Class 2, and 3 DSA exams as it is on the Class 1. The Class 1 inspector should be very familiar with this chapter and the class 2 also study it's provisions.

Chapter 22A: Steel

The steel chapter is significant especially to the Class 1 and 2 exam candidate because it spells out the rules for material identification, and standards. Steel is a unique material since it is more difficult to work and since most if not all of the quality control is done in the manufacturing process. There are two very significant references to adopted codes that are important in chapter 22A.

1. Structural welding and the associated procedures etc. are regulated by the American Welding Societies publication "D1.1" (red and white soft cover), structural welding of reinforcing steel is regulated by the AWS's "D1.4" (red and white soft cover) publication.

2. Structural Steel fabrication standards with regard to tolerances, sizes, strength and bolting are all spelled out by the American Institute of Steel Construction's publication "Manual of Steel Construction" (green hard cover).

Chapter 23A: Wood

Wood, next to concrete, is probably the most frequently used material in construction. In addition most of the above ground portions of school structural systems are made up of wood and wood based composite materials. The DSA exams, especially the Class 3 are very heavily weighted toward wood structural issues.
One particularly significant adopted code standard is "Standard No. 17" published by the West Coast Lumber Inspection Bureau. This publication sets out specific standards for the grading of various species of lumber for the purpose of structural quality control. This course dedicates a whole lesson to this publication since it is well represented in the exams.

Part 3: Electrical Code

The California Electrical Code (CEC) is based on the National Electrical Code (NEC). These codes are virtually identical with some exceptions. For the purposes of this course and the DSA exams you will have to be familiar with some aspects of these codes but not a great deal.

Inspections of electrical work are supposed to be carried out by special inspectors or by the engineer themselves, however in the real world that does not always happen.

Part 4: Plumbing Code

The California Plumbing Code (CPC) is based on the Uniform Plumbing Code (UPC). The situation is much the same for plumbing as it is for electrical, though there is no provision for a special plumbing inspector. The DSA exam covers plumbing in a very general and Life-Safety biased way. There is simply not enough room on the exams to include a significant plumbing part.

Part 5: Mechanical Code

The California Mechanical Code (CMC) is based on the Uniform Mechanical Code. Like the electrical code this aspect of code compliance is supposed to involve an engineer and/or a special inspector. However the work often falls to the DSA inspector. Mechanical is covered in a very general way on the DSA exams.

Conclusion:

As you can see there is a large volume of material that effects school construction. In fact it is practically impossible to study all of the material that DSA has said the inspector should know. The twelve parts of Title 24 alone measure 2 of 3 feet wide. It is for this reason that we have attempted to isolate only that information that is relevant to the DSA inspector and the DSA examinations. We recommend that you purchase the following publications for the purposes of studying for the DSA Exams.

1. Title 24: Part 1: Administrative Standards
2. Title 24: Part 2: Volume 1: Fire-Life Safety Provisions
3. Title 24: Part 2: Volume 2: Structural Design Provisions
4. Standard no. 17: West Coast Lumber Grading Standard
5. Manual of Steel Construction
6. ASTM Concrete Standards

Once you have obtained your DSA Class certification we recommend that you purchase Parts 3-5 of Title 24.

The building code is a conglomeration of a number of different publications that have their own area of emphasis. As a DSA inspector you are not required to know all of the code from memory, however you are required to know where to find that information. Knowing how the code books fit together makes finding the necessary information much easier.

© Professioal Study Inc.2003

Chapter 4
Administrative Code
(Title 24, Part 1)

Now that you have read IR A-8 you can use the following excerpts as a guide for highlighting your code book. Part 1 of Title 24 spells out how a DSA "Project Inspector" is certified, selected, and what will be expected of them. In addition it defines the role of the Architect, Engineer, School District, and Contractor. Study the following pages and pay close attention to the "Test Question" comments.

Highlighting List
Administrative Code
(Title 24, Part 1)

Take out your code book and highlight the code sections as they appear on this list in either red or yellow.

The "**Commentary**" on the right is broken down into four categories and they are as follows:

1. **TEST QUESTION (Highlight in Red)**
   - (Indicates that this material is very likely to be specifically referenced on the DSA exams)

2. **REMEMBER (Highlight in Yellow)**
   - (Indicates that you should know this material and that it is relevant to your work as an inspector)

3. **BEWARE (Highlight in Yellow)**
   - (Indicates that there is something that may not be apparent at first but that the inspector will have to deal with)

4. **SEE ALSO (Highlight in Yellow)**
   - (Indicates that there is another code section that affects this information)

© Professional Study Inc. 2003

Highlighting List
(T-24, Part 1, Administrative Code)

CHAPTER 4. ADMINISTRATIVE REGULATIONS FOR THE DIVISION OF THE STATE ARCHITECT.STRUCTURAL SAFETY (DSA/SS)

4-302. Scope............ school buildings shall comply with the regulations adopted by the Division of the State Architect/Access Compliance (DSA/AC) and the Office of the California State Fire Marshal for the particular occupancies concerned. (See Title 24, C.C.R.)

(b) **Short Term Temporary Buildings.................** [Comment: REMEMBER — Generally applies to relocatable buildings]

(1) .Temporary Certification. is for 24 months.

(7) All construction, except for the building superstructure, is to be inspected by a DSA-certified project inspector for conformance with the drawings provided by the architect. The inspector will submit a completed checklist for each campus and will submit said checklist with the final verified report.

(8) The architect or structural engineer in general responsible charge shall prepare site plans.

4-304. Alternate Materials and Methods of Construction and Modifications. The provisions of these regulations are not intended to prevent the use of any material or method of construction not specifically prescribed by these regulations, provided any alternate has been approved and its use authorized by DSA.

4-306. Approval of New School Buildings, Rehabilitation of School Buildings, and Additions to School Buildings.

Shall be submitted to DSA for approval in accordance with Section 4-315.

4-308. Reconstruction or Alterations Projects Not in Excess of $25,000 in Cost. [Comment: REMEMBER — Any work over $25,000 requires DSA approval]

projects with an estimated cost below $25,000 as described in this section, the school board assumes responsibility for employing an architect or a registered engineer to prepare the plans and specifications and for adequate inspection of the materials and work of construction

© Professional Study Inc. 2003

4-309. Reconstruction or Alteration Projects in Excess of $25,000 in Cost.

(a) **General.** Plans and specifications for any reconstruction or alteration project exceeding $25,000 in cost shall be submitted to DSA for approval in accordance with Section 4-315, except as provided within this section. When the estimated cost of a reconstruction or alteration project exceeds $25,000 but does not exceed $100,000, and a licensed structural engineer determines that the project does not include any work of a structural nature, approval of the project plans and specifications by DSA is not required, provided the following three items are completed:

> **Comment: REMEMBER**
> No DSA approval if less than $100,000 and not part of the structural system

3. Within 10 days of the completion of the project, a DSA-certified project inspector shall sign and submit a verified report to DSA, indicating that the project was completed in conformance with the plans and specifications. (See Section 4-336, Verified Reports.)

(b) **Existing Noncomplying, Nonstructural Elements.** Existing noncomplying, nonstructural elements discovered during the design or construction of a reconstruction, alteration or addition to an existing complying school building and directly affected by the work of construction shall be corrected to comply with the bracing and anchorage requirements of currently effective regulations.

Article 2. Definitions

4-314. Definitions...........

Inspector. shall mean any inspector duly approved by DSA for a particular project. The project inspector shall be responsible for inspecting all work included in the project, except inspection performed by a special inspector.

> **Comment: REMEMBER**
> Project Inspector is responsible for all the work not just the structural.

.Relocatable Building. is any building with an integral floor structure which is capable of being readily moved.

> **Comment: REMEMBER**
> Definition of Relocatable Building

Relocatable buildings that are to be placed on substandard foundations not complying with the requirements of Part 2, Title 24, C.C.R., require a statement from the school district stating that the durability requirements for those foundations may be waived and acknowledging the temporary nature of the foundations.

© Professional Study Inc. 2003

Article 3. Approval of Drawings and Specifications

4-315. Application for Approval of Drawings and Specifications.

(a) **General.** Before awarding a contract or commencing with construction of a school building project the school board shall submit an application to the Division of the State Architect and obtain written approval of the plans and specifications for any of the following:

2. The reconstruction or alteration of an existing school building if the estimated cost exceeds $25,000. (See Section 4-308 and 4-309.)

4-316. Designation of Responsibilities.

(e) **Evidence of Responsibility.** The stamp and signature of the architect or registered engineer on a plan, specification, or other document shall be deemed evidence that full responsibility is assumed by the signatory for the work shown thereon,

> **Comment: REMEMBER**
> This requires stamp of Architect or Structural Engineer plans.

(g) **Deferred Approvals.** Only where a portion of the construction cannot be adequately detailed on the approved plans because of variations in product design and/or manufacturer, the approval of plans for such portion, when specifically accepted by DSA, may be deferred until the material suppliers are selected provided the following conditions are met:

> **Comment: REMEMBER**
> Deferred approvals are often granted for Fire Sprinkle Skylights, Elevators, and other major equipment

1. The project plans clearly indicate that a deferred approval

2. The project plans and specifications adequately describe

> **Comment: REMEMBER**
> Deferred approval is usually indicated on the Title She the plans.

3. An architect or registered engineer stamps and signs the plans and specifications for the deferred approval item

4. Fabrication of deferred approval items shall not begin without first obtaining the approval of plans and specifications by DSA.

> **Comment: REMEMBER**
> This is often not followed.

(h) **Signatures Required.** All original tracings for plans, except those plans for deferred approval items and the original cover sheet for the specifications submitted for approval shall bear the stamp and signature of the architect or professional engineer in general responsible charge of design of the project.

the original cover sheet for the specifications covering that portion of the design shall also bear the signature and stamp of the responsible professional engineer or architect

© Professional Study Inc. 2003

4-318. Procedure for Approval of Application and Voidance of Application.

Changes in plans and specifications, other than changes necessary for correction, made after submission for approval, shall be brought to the attention of DSA in writing or by submission of revised plans identifying those changes clearly at the time of backchecking. Failure to give such notice may result in the voidance any subsequent approval given to the plans and specifications.

(c) **Voidance of Application.** Any change, erasure, alteration or modification of any plans or specification bearing the stamp of DSA may result in voidance of the approval of the application. However, the .written approval of plans. may be extended by DSA to include revised plans and specifications after documents are submitted for review and approved.

> **Comment: TEST QUESTION**
> All changes to the plans must be in the form of addenda or change orders.

Article 5. Certification of Construction

4-330. Time of Beginning Construction and Partial Construction.

Construction work, whether for a new school building, reconstruction, rehabilitation, alteration, or addition, shall not be commenced, and no contract shall be let until the school board has applied for and obtained from DSA **written approval of plans and** specifications. **Construction shall be commenced within one year** after the approval of the application,

> **Comment: TEST QUESTION**
> No construction without approval from DSA

Renewal shall not be granted after a period of four years beyond the initial date of the application approval.

4-331. Notice of Start of Construction.

As soon as a contract has been let, the architect or registered engineer shall furnish to DSA on Form DSA-102 the name and address of the contractor, the contract price, the date on which the contract was let and the date of starting construction (see Section 4-352).

> **Comment: BEWARE**
> The project inspector must also notify DSA of the start of construction though not in writing

4-332. Notice of Suspension of Construction.

(a) When construction is suspended for more than two weeks, the project inspector shall notify DSA [see Section 4-336 (c) 4].

> **Comment: TEST QUESTION**
> Notify DSA if construction stops more than two weeks.

(b) If all construction is suspended or abandoned for any reason for a continuous period of one year following its commencement,

© Professional Study Inc. 2003

4-333. Observation and Inspection of Construction.

(b) **Inspection by Project Inspector.** The school board must provide for and require competent, adequate and continuous inspection by an inspector satisfactory to the architect or registered engineer in general responsible charge of observation of the work of construction, to any architect or registered engineer delegated responsibility for a portion of the work, and to DSA.

> **Comment:** REMEMBER
> The school board hires the Project Inspector

> **Comment:** TEST QUESTION
> The Project Inspector is selected by the School Board and approved by The Architect/Engineer, and DSA on a project basis.

For every project there shall be a project inspector who shall have personal knowledge as defined in Sections 17309 and 81141 of the Education Code of all work done on the project or its parts as defined in Section 4-316. No work shall be carried on except under the inspection of a project inspector approved by DSA.

> **Comment:** REMEMBER
> Every job must be inspected and no work should be done without inspection.

A project inspector shall, under the direction of the architect and/or engineer, be responsible for monitoring the work of the special inspectors and testing laboratories to ensure that the testing program is satisfactorily completed.

> **Comment:** REMEMBER
> Project Inspector is responsible for the Testing and Inspection program

The project inspector and any assistant inspector must be approved by DSA for each individual project.

> **Comment:** TEST QUESTION
> Approval is done through Form DSA 5 (Project Inspector) Form DSA 5A (Assistant Project Inspector)

(c) **Special Inspection.** Special inspection by inspector's specially approved by DSA may be required on masonry construction, glued-laminated lumber fabrication, wood framing using timber connectors, manufactured trusses, epoxy repair of wood or concrete, concrete batching, shot-crete application, prestressed concrete member fabrication or post-tensioning operations, structural steel fabrication, high-strength steel bolt installations, shop and field welding, pile driving, electrical, and mechanical work.

A special inspector may be required to be approved by DSA for an individual project. Application for approval of a special inspector shall be made on an Inspectors Qualification Form (Form DSA-5)

> **Comment:** TEST QUESTION
> Special inspectors also fill out a Form DSA 5

The project inspector may perform special inspections if the project inspector has been specially approved by DSA for such purpose and has the time available

The detailed inspection of all work covered by this section is the responsibility of the project inspector when special inspection is not provided (see Section 4-342).

Where responsibility for observation of construction for mechanical work and electrical work is not delegated to professional engineers registered in these particular branches of engineering [see Section 4-316 (b)], special mechanical and electrical inspecttion shall be provided issue a stop work order.

> **Comment:** REMEMBER
> This is rarely done but a special Electrical Inspector and Mechanical Inspector should be provided.

Construction work that the special inspector finds not to be in compliance with the approved plans and specifications, and which is not immediately corrected upon notifying the contractor, shall be **reported immediately to the project inspector, DSA, the architect and the structural engineer.**

> **Comment:** TEST QUESTION
> This report should be in writing always and provided to the following:
> - Project Inspector
> - Architect
> - DSA

4-335. Tests.

(a) **General**..........
Where job conditions warrant, the architect or registered engineer may waive certain tests with the approval of DSA.

A copy of the list of structural tests and inspections prepared by the responsible architect or structural engineer and acceptable to DSA shall be provided to the designated testing agency and the project inspector prior to the start of construction.

> **Comment:** TEST QUESTION
> This is known as the T & I sheet and the DSA field engineer will want to see it on his first visit to your job.

(b) **Performance of Tests**..........

A letter of acceptance by DSA shall be issued to the testing agency and shall state that the testing agency has demonstrated that it has met the criteria established by DSA for performance of the inspection of work and testing of materials.
Test samples or specimens of material for testing shall be taken by the architect or registered engineer, his or her representative, the inspector or a representative of the testing agency. In no case shall the contractor or vendor select the sample or specimens.

> **Comment:** REMEMBER
> Samples must be taken & Selected by the P.I. or by the test lab, never the contractor

(c) **Payments**..........
When in the opinion of the architect or registered engineer, additional tests are required because of the manner in which the contractor executes his or her work, such tests shall be paid for by the school board, but if so specified the amount paid may be collected from the contractor by the school board.

> **Comment:** BEWARE
> This is a grey area so get approval before ordering new testing.

(d) **Test Reports.** One copy of all test reports shall be forwarded to **DSA, the architect, the structural engineer and the project inspector by the testing agency within 14 days** of the date of the test..........
All reports of test results shall also definitely state whether or not the material or materials tested comply with requirements of the plans and specifications. Reports of test results of materials not found to be in compliance with the requirements of the plans and specifications shall be forwarded immediately to DSA, the architect, the structural engineer and the project inspector.

> **Comment:** TEST QUESTION
> Reports should be received within (2) weeks
> Copies to:
> - DSA
> - Architect / Engineer
> - Project Inspector
> * Notice: The School Board is not included in the mandatory notification list

(e) **Verification of Test Reports.** Each testing agency shall

© Professional Study Inc. 2003

submit to DSA at the completion of the testing program or when required by DSA a verified report covering all of the tests and inspections that were required to be made by that agency. Such report shall be furnished any time that work on the project is suspended, or services of the testing lab are terminated, covering the tests up to that time.

4-336. Verified Reports.

(a) **General**..........

the project inspector, approved special inspectors, and the contractor shall each make and sign under penalty of perjury, a duly verified report to DSA upon a prescribed form or forms, showing that of his or her own personal knowledge the work during the period covered by the report has been performed and materials have been used and installed in every material respect in compliance with the duly approved plans and specifications, and setting forth such detailed statements of fact as shall be required.

> **Comment:** TEST QUESTION
> Verified Report may be a DSA Form 6 or a letter stating what is required.

The term .personal knowledge. as applied to an inspector means the actual personal knowledge that is obtained from the inspecter's personal continuous inspection of the work in all stages of its progress

(b) **Report Form.** Verified reports shall be made on Form DSA-6 by inspectors and contractors and Form DSA-6A/E by architects and engineers.

> **Comment:** REMEMBER
> Verified Reports are required for many different parties but Form DSA-6 and DSA-6A/E are for Inspectors and Architects/Engineers respectively.

(c) **Required Filing.** Verified reports shall be made as follows:
1. By each contractor having a contract with the owner, at the completion of the contract.
2. By the architect, registered engineers, project inspector and approved special inspectors at the completion of the school building.
3. By the architect, registered engineers, project inspector and contractor at the suspension of all work for a period of more than one month.
4. By the architect, registered engineer, project inspector, approved special inspector, or contractor whose services in connection with the project have been terminated for any reason.
5. At any time a verified report is requested by DSA.

> **Comment:** TEST QUESTION
> 1. Contractor at the completion of work.
> 2. Architect / Engineer, Project Inspector at completion o
> 3. Architect / Engineer, Project Inspector at suspension of work for more than one month.
> 4. At Termination
> 5. Any time DSA requests one.

4-337. Semimonthly Reports. In addition to the verified reports (Section 4-336) the project inspector shall make semimonthly reports of the progress of construction to the architect or registered engineer in general responsible charge and the structural engineer if delegated to observe the structural portion of the construction. A copy of each such report shall be sent directly to the school board and directly to DSA.

Semimonthly reports shall state the name of the building, the school and the school district, and give the file and application number. The reports shall include a list of official visitors to the project and whom they represent, a brief statement of the work done, instructions received from the architect or registered engineer during the period covered by the report and pertinent infor-

> **Comment:** REMEMBER
> Semi-Monthly reports due on the first and fifteenth of each month.
> They are addressed to the Architect but DSA is mostly the interested party.

mation regarding any unusual conditions or questions that may have arisen at the job. The semimonthly report shall include problems or non complying conditions which have occurred on the project and how they were resolved or brought into compliance. to comply with this section, in a timely manner **(seven days after reporting period),**

> **Comment:** TEST QUESTION
> The Project Inspector has Seven Days to file a Semi-montly report.

4-338. Addenda and Change Orders.

(b) **Addenda.** Changes or alterations of the approved plans or specifications prior to letting a construction contract

> **Comment:** TEST QUESTION
> Addenda: are changes to the plans and specifications that are made prior to letting the contract.

shall be submitted to and approved by DSA prior to distribution to contractors.

Original copies of addenda shall be stamped and signed by the architect or engineer in general responsible charge of preparation of the plans and specifications and by the architect or registered engineer

(c) **Change Orders.** Changes or alterations of the approved plans or specifications after a contract for the work has been let...

> **Comment:** TEST QUESTION
> Change Orders: are changes made to the plans or specs after the contract has been let.

approved by DSA prior to commencement of the work shown thereon. All change orders and supplementary drawings shall be stamped and signed by the architect or engineer in general responsible charge of observation of the work of construction of the project and by the architect or registered engineer

> **Comment:** REMEMBER
> Any chang to the plans or specs should be approved by DSA regardless of the cost impact.

approval of the school board and shall indicate the associated change in the project cost, if any.

(d) **Preliminary Change Orders.** In order to expedite construction, preliminary change orders may be submitted to DSA. board and directly to DSA.

> **Comment:** TEST QUESTION
> Preliminary Change Order doesn't require Board approval but does signature from architect of engineer.

Preliminary change orders shall meet all the requirements necessary for a change order, with the exception of the approval of the school board and the associated change, if any, in costs. The preliminary change order does not require the stamp or seal, but does require the signature of the architect or engineers. Work may proceed in accordance with the approved preliminary change order.

© Professional Study Inc. 2003

Article 6. Duties under the Act

4-341. Duties of the Architect, Structural Engineer, or Professional Engineer.

(b) General Responsible Charge............

The responsible architect or engineer shall perform general observation of the work of construction, interpret the approved drawings and specifications and **shall provide the project inspector and testing agency with a complete set of stamped plans**, specifications, addenda and change orders prior to the start of construction.

> **Comment:** TEST QUESTION
> Architect must provide a set of stamped plans specs, adde and CO's. If they are not stamped they are to be returned the architect.

(c) Delegated Responsibility................

The architect or registered engineer shall observe the work of construction of his or her portion of the project and shall consult with the design professional in general responsible charge in the interpretation of the approved drawings and specifications.

(d) Approval of Inspectors. The architect or registered engineer in general responsible charge shall submit to DSA the name of the person proposed as project inspector of the work, together with an outline of his or her experience and pertinent qualifications on Form DSA-5, **10 days prior to the time of starting construction work.**

> **Comment:** REMEMBER
> The Architect is responsible for approval of the inspector

In view of the architect or registered engineer's responsibilities for directing the activities of the inspector, such architect or registered engineer shall review and evaluate the inspector's qualifications before recommending the approval of the inspector to DSA.

(f) Verified Reports.

The architect or registered engineer in general responsible charge shall also require that the inspector's, the contractor's and the other architects and engineers verified reports are submitted as required.

> **Comment:** REMEMBER
> The Architect is responsible for coordinating the Verified reports not the Project Inspector.

(g) Testing Program. The architect or registered engineer in general responsible charge shall establish the extent of the testing of materials consistent with the needs of the particular project (see Section 4-335) and shall issue specific instructions to the testing agency prior to start of construction. He or she shall also notify DSA as to the disposition of materials noted on laboratory reports as not conforming to the approved specifications.

> **Comment:** REMEMBER
> The Arch/Engineer determines the testing program and the implements it.

4-342. Duties of the Project Inspector.

(a) General. The project inspector shall act under the direction of the architect or registered engineer. The project inspector is also subject to supervision by a representative of DSA.

1. **Continuous Inspection Requirement.** The project inspector must have actual personal knowledge, obtained by personal and continuous inspection of the work of construction in all stages of its progress, that the requirements of the approved plans and specifications are being completely executed.

> **Comment: TEST QUESTION**
> **Continuous:** means personal knowledge but not every second
> **Constant:** Means that you witness every moment of the work in question.

Continuous inspection means complete inspection of every part of the work. Work, such as concrete work or masonry work which can be inspected only as it is placed, shall require the constant presence of the inspector. Other types of work which can be completely inspected after the work is installed may be carried on while the inspector is not present. In any case, the inspector must personally inspect every part of the work. In no case shall the inspector have or assume any duties that will prevent the inspector from giving continuous inspection. DSA may require verification from the project inspector of time spent at the construction site during all phases of the work.

The project inspector may obtain personal knowledge of the work of construction, either on-site or off-site, performed under the inspection of a special inspector or assistant inspector

2. **Relations with Architect or Engineer.** In no case shall the instruction of the architect or registered engineer be construed to cause work to be done which is not in conformity with the approved contract documents.

3. **Job File.** The project inspector shall keep a file of approved plans and specifications (including all approved addenda or change orders) on the job at all times. The inspector, as a condition of employment, shall have and maintain on the job at all times, the edition of Title 24, **Parts 1, 2, 3, 4 and 5 referred** to in the plans and specifications.

> **Comment: REMEMBER**
> T-24 Parts 1-5 are Admin, Building, Elect., Mech., and Plumbing Codes.

4. **Project Inspectors Semimonthly Reports.** The project inspector shall keep the architect or registered engineer thoroughly informed as to the progress of the work by making semimonthly reports in writing as required in Section 4-337.

> **Comment: BEWARE**
> Keep copies of Semi-monthlies and DSA Field trip notes also.

5. **Notifications to DSA.** The project inspectors shall notify DSA at the following times:
   A. When construction work on the project is started, or restarted if previously suspended per Item D below.
   B. At least 48 hours in advance of the time when foundation trenches will be complete, ready for footing forms.
   C. At least 48 hours in advance of the first placement of

> **Comment: TEST QUESTION**
> Notification can be in the form of FAX, Telephone, or in writing.

© Professional Study Inc. 2003

foundation concrete and 24 hours in advance of any subsequent and significant concrete placement.
D. When all work on the project is suspended for a period of more than two weeks.

6. **Construction Procedure Records.** The project inspector shall keep a record of certain phases of construction procedure including, but not limited to, the following:

   A. **Concrete placing operations.** The record shall show the time and date of placing concrete and the time and date of removal of forms in each portion of the structure.

   > **Comment:** TEST QUESTION
   > Notification and Records are very important to DSA and therefore likely be on the Exams.

   B. **Welding operations.** The record shall include identification marks of welders, lists of defective welds, manner of correction of defects, etc.

   C. **Penetration** under the last 10 blows for each pile when piles are driven for foundations.

7. **Deviations.** The project inspector shall notify the contractor, in writing, of any deviations from the approved plans and specifications which are not immediately corrected by the contractor when brought to the contractor's attention. Copies of such notice shall be forwarded immediately to the architect or registered engineer, and to DSA.

8. **Verified Report.** The project inspector shall make and submit directly to DSA verified reports

> **Comment:** TEST QUESTION
> Verified Reports from special inspectors can be their daily report. However their final report must reflect the status of work overall.

4-343. Duties of the Contractor.

(b) Performance of the Work............

All inconsistencies or items which appear to be in error in the plans and specifications shall be promptly called to the attention of the architect or registered engineer, through the inspector, for interpretation or correction.

> **Comment:** BEWARE
> The contractor is responsible for problems in the plans if they are not reported to the architect through the inspector.

The contractor must notify the project inspector, in advance, of the commencement of construction of each and every aspect of the work.

> **Comment:** BEWARE
> This puts the onus of approval for previous work on the contractor.

(c) Verified Reports. The contractor shall make and submit to DSA from time to time, verified reports as required in Section 4-336.

© Professional Study Inc. 2003

Chapter 5
Lesson 5.1: Occupancy
(Title 24, Part 2, Volume 1, Chapter 3)

Occupancy is a very important concept in the building code. The basic concept is that the different activities that take place in buildings should be treated differently with respect to Fire Life-Safety. Therefore these activities are categorized into what we refer to as "occupancy" types. Different occupancies have different requirements depending on various factors.

For the DSA inspector the most important thing to remember is that one must understand what the occupancy designations mean e. For the most part the DSA inspector does not deal with the concept of occupancy since that is worked out well in advance of the inspector's involvement. Therefore for the purposes of this course we have provided a "Highlighting List" that covers only the occupancies that the DSA inspector will need to know about. These are the following:

1. "A"   Assembly Occupancies (Multi-purpose rooms, Gyms, Auditoriums)
2. "B"   Business Occupancies (Administrative Offices)
3. "E"   Educational (Classrooms)
4. "S"   Storage (Storage Rooms)

Read the directions and study the following materials.

Highlighting List
Occupancy
(Title 24, Part 2, Volume 1, Chapter 3)

Take out your code book and highlight the code sections as they appear on this list in either red or yellow.

The "**Commentary**" on the right is broken down into four categories and they are as follows:

1. **TEST QUESTION (Highlight in Red)**
   - (Indicates that this material is very likely to be specifically referenced on the DSA exams)

2. **REMEMBER (Highlight in Yellow)**
   - (Indicates that you should know this material and that it is relevant to your work as an inspector)

3. **BEWARE (Highlight in Yellow)**
   - (Indicates that there is something that may not be apparent at first but that the inspector will have to deal with)

4. **SEE ALSO (Highlight in Yellow)**
   - (Indicates that there is another code section that affects this information)

© Professional Study Inc. 2003

Highlighting List (T-24, Part 2,)
Chapter 3
USE OR OCCUPANCY

SECTION 301. OCCUPANCY CLASSIFIED

Group A. Assembly (see Section 303.1.1)

Group B. Business (see Section 304.1)

Group E. Educational (see Section 305.1)

Group S. Storage (see Section 311.1)

> **Comment:** BEWARE
> There Are many other occupancies, but these are the ones used for school buildings.

SECTION 302. MIXED USE OR OCCUPANCY

302.3 Types of Occupancy Separations.

1. A four-hour fire-resistive occupancy separation shall have no openings therein and shall not be of less than four-hour fire-resistive construction.

2. **A three-hour fire-resistive occupancy separation** shall not be of less than three-hour fire-resistive construction. **All openings in walls** forming such separation shall be protected by a fire assembly having a **three-hour** fire-protection rating. The total width of all openings..........:

> **Comment:** REMEMBER
> These are rarely used in school buildings, but if you see them pay close attention to the requirements.

shall not exceed 25 percent of the length of the wall............

shall have an area greater than 120 square feet (11 m2).

All openings in floors forming a **three-hour** fire-resistive occupancy separation shall be protected by shaft, stairway, ramp or escalator enclosures extending above and below such openings.

The **walls** of such enclosures shall not be of less than **two-hour** fire-resistive construction and **all openings** therein shall be protected by a fire assembly having a **one- and one-half-hour** fire-protection rating.

3. **A two-hour fire-resistive occupancy separation** shall not be of less than two-hour fire-resistive construction. All **openings** in such separation shall be protected by a fire assembly having a **one- and one-half-hour** fire-protection rating.

> **Comment:** TEST QUESTION
> Two hour separations should have a (1 ½) hour rating at openings.

4. **A one-hour fire-resistive occupancy separation** shall not be of less than one-hour fire-resistive construction. **All openings** in such separation shall be protected by a fire assembly having a **one-hour** fire-protection rating.

> **Comment:** TEST QUESTION
> One hour separations should have a (1) hour rating at openings.

© Professional Study Inc. 2003

302.4 Fire Ratings for Occupancy Separations.

Table 3-B.

TABLE 3-B—REQUIRED SEPARATION IN BUILDINGS OF MIXED OCCUPANCY[1] (HOURS)

	A-1	A-2	A-2.1	A-3	A-4	B	E	F-1	F-2	H-2	H-3	H-4,5	H-6,7[2]	H-1	I	M	R-1	R-3	S-1	S-2	S-3	S-5	U-1[3]
A-1	N	N	N	N	3	N	3	3	4	4	4	4	3	3	3	1	1	3	3	4	3	1	
A-2		N	N	N	1	N	1	1	4	4	4	4	2	3	1	1	1	1	1	3	1	1	
A-2.1			N	N	1	N	1	1	4	4	4	4	2	3	1	1	1	1	1	3	1	1	
A-3				N	N	N	N	N	4	4	4	3	1	2	N	1	1	N	N	3	1	1	
A-4					1	N	1	1	4	4	4	4	1	3	1	1	1	1	1	3	1	1	
B						1	N[5]	N	2	1	1	1	1	2	N	1	1	N	N	1	1	1	
E							1	1	4	4	4	3	2	1	1	1	1	1	1	3	1	1	
F-1								1	2	1	1	1	1	3	N[5]	1	1	N	N	1	1	1	
F-2									2	1	1	1	1	2	1	1	1	N	N	1	1	1	
H-1	NOT PERMITTED IN MIXED OCCUPANCIES. SEE SECTION 307.2.8
H-2										1	1	2	2	4	2	4	4	2	2	2	2	1	
H-3											1	1	1	4	1	3	3	1	1	1	1	1	
H-4,5												1	1	4	1	3	3	1	1	1	1	1	
H-6,7[2]													1	4	1	4	4	1	1	1	1	3	
I														2		2	1	1	2	2	4	3	1
M														1			1	1	1[4]	1[4]	1	1	1
R-1														4				N	3	1	3	1	1
R-3														4					1	1	1	1	1
S-1														1						1	1	1	1
S-2														1							1	1	N
S-3														1								1	1
S-4	OPEN PARKING GARAGES ARE EXCLUDED EXCEPT AS PROVIDED IN SECTION 311.2
S-5														1									N

N—No requirements for fire resistance.

[1] For detailed requirements and exceptions, see Section 302.4.
[2] For special provisions on highly toxic materials, see the Fire Code.
[3] For agricultural buildings, see also Appendix Chapter 3.
[4] See Section 309.2.2 for exception.
[5] For Group F, Division 1 woodworking establishments with more than 2,500 square feet (232.3 m^2), the occupancy separation shall be one hour.

302.5 Heating Equipment Room Occupancy Separation.

Groups A; B;E; F; I;M;R, Division 1; and S Occupancies, rooms containing a boiler, central heating plant or hot-water supply boiler shall be separated from the rest of the building by not less than a one-hour occupancy separation.

> **Comment:** BEWARE
> Boilers exceeding 400K BTU must have a (1)1 separation.

> **EXCEPTIONS:** 1. In Groups A, B, E, F, M and S Occupancies, boilers, central heating plants or hot-water supply boilers where the largest piece of fuel equipment **does not exceed 400,000 Btu per hour** (117.2 kW) input.

In Group E Occupancies, when the opening for a heater or equipment room is protected by a pair of fire doors, the inactive leaf shall be normally secured in the closed position and shall be openable only by the use of a tool. An astragal shall be provided and the active leaf shall be self-closing.

> **Comment:** REMEMBER
> This applies only when the equipment is protec by fire doors.

SECTION 303 . REQUIREMENTS FOR GROUP A OCCUPANCIES

303.1.1 Group A Occupancies defined.

© Professional Study Inc. 2003

Division 2. A building or portion of a building having an assembly room with an occupant load of less than 1,000 and a legitimate stage.

> **Comment:** REMEMBER
> The 'A' signifies assembly auditoriums, MPR's, large dining rooms. Look for stricter egress and fire prevention provisions in this type of occupancy.

Division 2.1. A building or portion of a building having an assembly room with an occupant load of 300 or more without a legitimate stage, including such buildings used for educational purposes and not classed as Group B or E Occupancies.

> **Comment:** REMEMBER
> This is the most common 'A' occupancy used in educational buildings.

SECTION 304. REQUIREMENTS FOR GROUP B OCCUPANCIES

304.1 Group B Occupancies Defined.

7. Civic administration.

> **Comment:** REMEMBER
> The 'B' signifies business. Usually the administrative parts of the school are 'B' occupancies.

304.2.2 Special provisions.

304.2.2.1 Laboratories and vocational shops. Laboratories and vocational shops in buildings used for educational purposes, and similar areas containing hazardous materials, shall be separated from each other and other portions of the building by not less than a one-hour fire-resistive occupancy separation.

> **Comment:** TEST QUESTION
> Labs and vocational shops often require a one hour separation. Look for dampers, fire caulking and unprotected penetrations.

SECTION 305. REQUIREMENTS FOR GROUP E OCCUPANCIES

305.1 Group E Occupancies Defined. Group E Occupancies shall be:
Division 1. Any building used for educational purposes through the 12th grade by 50 or more persons for more than 12 hours per week or four hours in any one day.
Division 2. Any building used for educational purposes through the 12th grade by less than 50 persons for more than 12 hours per week or four hours in any one day.

> **Comment:** REMEMBER
> The 'E' signifies education. All classrooms and most libraries will be 'E' occupancies with the mentioned criteria.

305.9 Fire Alarm Systems...........

In Group E Occupancies provided with an automatic sprinkler or detection system, the operation of such system shall automatically activate the school fire alarm system, which shall include an alarm mounted on the exterior of the building.

> **Comment:** BEWARE
> This applies to schools.

305.9.2 [For SFM]

In buildings containing Group E Occupancies provided with an automatic extinguishing system or detection system, the operation of such system shall automatically activate the building alarm system.

> **Comment:** BEWARE
> This applies to schools

SECTION 311. REQUIREMENTS FOR GROUP S OCCUPANCIES

311.1 Group S Occupancies Defined. Group S Occupancies shall include the use of a building or structure, or a portion thereof, for storage not classified as a hazardous occupancy.

> **Comment:** REMEMBER
> The 'S' signifies storage. Some larger storage areas will be 'S' occupancies. Watch for what is stored in these areas.

Division 2. Low-hazard storage occupancies

Division 3. Division 3 Occupancies shall include repair garages where work is limited to exchange of parts and maintenance requiring no open flame or welding, motor vehicle fuel-dispensing stations, and parking garages not classed as Group S, Division 4 open parking garages or Group U private garages

TABLE 3-A—DESCRIPTION OF OCCUPANCIES BY GROUP AND DIVISION[1]

GROUP AND DIVISION	SECTION	DESCRIPTION OF OCCUPANCY	
A-1		A building or portion of a building having an assembly room with an occupant load of 1,000 or more and a legitimate stage.	
A-2		A building or portion of a building having an assembly room with an occupant load of less than 1,000 and a legitimate stage.	
A-2.1	303.1.1	A building or portion of a building having an assembly room with an occupant load of 300 or more without a legitimate stage, including such buildings used for educational purposes and not classed as a Group E or Group B Occupancy.	
A-3		Any building or portion of a building having an assembly room with an occupant load of less than 300 without a legitimate stage, including such buildings used for educational purposes and not classed as a Group E or Group B Occupancy.	
A-4		Stadiums, reviewing stands and amusement park structures not included within other Group A Occupancies.	
B	304.1	A building or structure, or a portion thereof, for office, professional or service-type transactions, including storage of records and accounts; eating and drinking establishments with an occupant load of less than 50.	
E-1		Any building used for educational purposes through the 12th grade by 50 or more persons for more than 12 hours per week or four hours in any one day.	
E-2	305.1	Any building used for educational purposes through the 12th grade by less than 50 persons for more than 12 hours per week or four hours in any one day.	
E-3		Any building or portion thereof used for day-care purposes for more than six persons.	
F-1	306.1	Moderate-hazard factory and industrial occupancies include factory and industrial uses not classified as Group F, Division 2 Occupancies.	
F-2		Low-hazard factory and industrial occupancies include facilities producing noncombustible or nonexplosive materials that during finishing, packing or processing do not involve a significant fire hazard.	
H-1		Occupancies with a quantity of material in the building in excess of those listed in Table 3-D that present a high explosion hazard as listed in Section 307.1.1.	
H-2		Occupancies with a quantity of material in the building in excess of those listed in Table 3-D that present a moderate explosion hazard or a hazard from accelerated burning as listed in Section 307.1.1.	
H-3	307.1	Occupancies with a quantity of material in the building in excess of those listed in Table 3-D that present a high fire or physical hazard as listed in Section 307.1.1.	
H-4		Repair garages not classified as Group S, Division 3 Occupancies.	
H-5		Aircraft repair hangars not classified as Group S, Division 5 Occupancies and heliports.	
H-6	307.1 and 307.11	Semiconductor fabrication facilities and comparable research and development areas when the facilities in which hazardous production materials are used, and the aggregate quantity of material is in excess of those listed in Table 3-D or 3-E.	
H-7	307.1	Occupancies having quantities of materials in excess of those listed in Table 3-E that are health hazards as listed in Section 307.1.1.	
I-1.1		Nurseries for the full-time care of children under the age of six (each accommodating more than five children), hospitals, sanitariums, nursing homes with nonambulatory patients and similar buildings (each accommodating more than five patients [for SFM] six patients or children).	CL AL
I-1.2	308.1	Health-care centers for ambulatory patients receiving outpatient medical care which may render the patient incapable of unassisted self-preservation (each tenant space accommodating more than five such patients).	
I-2		Nursing homes for ambulatory patients, homes for children six years of age or over (each accommodating more than five persons [for SFM] six patients or children).	CL AL
I-3		Mental hospitals, mental sanitariums, jails, prisons, reformatories and buildings where personal liberties of inmates are similarly restrained.	
M	309.1	A building or structure, or a portion thereof, for the display and sale of merchandise, and involving stocks of goods, wares or merchandise, incidental to such purposes and accessible to the public.	
R-1		Hotels and apartment houses, congregate residences (each accommodating more than 10 persons).	
R-2.1		*Residential care facilities for the elderly (each accommodating more than six nonambulatory clients).*	C A
R-2.2		*Residential care facilities for the elderly (each accommodating more than six ambulatory clients).*	C A
R-2.1.1	310.1	*Residential care facilities for the elderly (each accommodating six or less nonambulatory clients).*	C A
R-2.2.1		*Residential care facilities for the elderly (each accommodating six or less ambulatory clients).*	C A
R-2.3		*Residential-based licensed facilities providing hospice care throughout, accommodating more than six bedridden clients.*	C A
R-2.3.1		*Residential-based facilities providing hospice care throughout, accommodating six or less bedridden clients.*	C A
R-3		Dwellings, lodging houses, congregate residences (each accommodating 10 or fewer persons).	
S-1		Moderate hazard storage occupancies including buildings or portions of buildings used for storage of combustible materials not classified as Group S, Division 2 or Group H Occupancies.	
S-2		Low-hazard storage occupancies including buildings or portions of buildings used for storage of noncombustible materials.	
S-3	311.1	Repair garages where work is limited to exchange of parts and maintenance not requiring open flame or welding, and parking garages not classified as Group S, Division 4 Occupancies.	
S-4		Open parking garages.	
S-5		Aircraft hangars and helistops.	
U-1	312.1	Private garages, carports, sheds and agricultural buildings.	
U-2		Fences over 6 feet (1829 mm) high, tanks and towers.	

[1] For detailed descriptions, see the occupancy definitions in the noted sections.

© Professional Study Inc. 2003

Chapter 5
Lesson 5.2: General Building Limitations
(Title 24, Part 2, Volume 1, Chapter 5)

This chapter is one which has few provisions that are relevant to the DSA inspector. General Building Limitations refers mainly to design limitations that are flushed out long before the Project Inspector is brought into the picture. However there are some important provisions of which you should be aware.

Pay attention to the limitations and minimums for guardrails. These are obviously important when you are dealing with public places, see Section 509. The highlight list below has the important excerpts from this section. Also pay particular attention to Table 5A. This table explains the types of materials and assemblies required for parts of buildings. This is important because structural members often have higher fire resistive requirements than non-structural elements. Familiarize yourself with the provisions covering A, B, and E group occupancies.

1. "A" Assembly Occupancies (Multi-purpose rooms, Gyms, Auditoriums)
2. "B" Business Occupancies (Administrative Offices)
3. "E" Educational (Classrooms)
4. "S" Storage (Storage Rooms)

Read the directions and study the following materials.

Highlighting List
Occupancy
(Title 24, Part 2, Volume 1, Chapter 5)

Take out your code book and highlight the code sections as they appear on this list in either red or yellow.

The "**Commentary**" on the right is broken down into four categories and they are as follows:

1. **TEST QUESTION (Highlight in Red)**
   - (Indicates that this material is very likely to be specifically referenced on the DSA exams)

2. **REMEMBER (Highlight in Yellow)**
   - (Indicates that you should know this material and that it is relevant to your work as an inspector)

3. **BEWARE (Highlight in Yellow)**
   - (Indicates that there is something that may not be apparent at first but that the inspector will have to deal with)

4. **SEE ALSO (Highlight in Yellow)**
   - (Indicates that there is another code section that affects this information)

© Professional Study Inc. 2003

Chapter 5
GENERAL BUILDING LIMITATIONS

SECTION 509. GUARDRAILS

509.1 Where Required. Unenclosed floor and roof openings, open and glazed sides of stairways, aisles, landings and ramps, balconies or porches, which are more than 30 inches (762 mm) above grade or floor below, and roofs used for other than service of the building shall be protected by a guardrail.

> **Comment:** TEST QUESTION
> If drop is 30" or greater a guardrail is required.

509.2 Height. The top of guardrails shall not be less than 42 inches (1067 mm) in height.

> **Comment:** TEST QUESTION
> Minimum height for guardrail is 42".

Where an elevation change of 30 inches (762 mm) or less occurs

between an aisle parallel to the seats (cross aisle) and the adjacent floor or grade below, guardrails not less than 26 inches (660 mm) above the aisle floor shall be provided.

> **Comment:** BEWARE
> This may occur in assembly or bleacher areas.

509.3 Openings. Open guardrails shall have intermediate rails or an ornamental pattern such that a sphere 4 inches (102 mm) in diameter cannot pass through.

> **Comment:** TEST QUESTION
> Max space between any part of a rail is 4".

© Professional Study Inc. 2003

TABLE 5-A—EXTERIOR WALL AND OPENING PROTECTION BASED ON LOCATION ON PROPERTY FOR ALL CONSTRUCTION TYPES[1,2,3]

For exceptions, see Section 503.4.

OCCUPANCY GROUP[4]	CONSTRUCTION TYPE	EXTERIOR WALLS — Bearing	EXTERIOR WALLS — Nonbearing	OPENINGS[5]
		Distances are measured to property lines (see Section 503).		
		× 304.8 for mm		
A-1	I-F.R. II-F.R.	Four-hour N/C	Four-hour N/C less than 5 feet Two-hour N/C less than 20 feet One-hour N/C less than 40 feet NR, N/C elsewhere	Not permitted less than 5 feet Protected less than 20 feet
A-1	II One-hour II-N III One-hour III-N IV-H.T. V One-hour V-N	Group A, Division 1 Occupancies are not allowed in these construction types.		
A-2 A-2.1 A-3 A-4	I-F.R. II-F.R. III One-hour IV-H.T.	Four-hour N/C	Four-hour N/C less than 5 feet Two-hour N/C less than 20 feet One-hour N/C less than 40 feet NR, N/C elsewhere	Not permitted less than 5 feet Protected less than 20 feet
A-2 A-2.1[2]	II One-hour	Two-hour N/C less than 10 feet One-hour N/C elsewhere	Same as bearing except NR, N/C 40 feet or greater	Not permitted less than 5 feet Protected less than 10 feet
A-2 A-2.1[2]	II-N III-N V-N	Group A, Divisions 2 and 2.1 Occupancies are not allowed in these construction types.		
	V One-hour	Two-hour less than 10 feet One-hour elsewhere	Same as bearing	Not permitted less than 5 feet Protected less than 10 feet
A-3	II One-hour	Two-hour N/C less than 5 feet One-hour N/C elsewhere	Same as bearing except NR, N/C 40 feet or greater	Not permitted less than 5 feet Protected less than 10 feet
A-3	II-N	Two-hour N/C less than 5 feet One-hour N/C less than 20 feet NR, N/C elsewhere	Same as bearing	Not permitted less than 5 feet Protected less than 10 feet
A-3	III-N	Four-hour N/C	Four-hour N/C less than 5 feet Two-hour N/C less than 20 feet One-hour N/C less than 40 feet NR, N/C elsewhere	Not permitted less than 5 feet Protected less than 20 feet
A-3	V One-hour	Two-hour less than 5 feet One-hour elsewhere	Same as bearing	Not permitted less than 5 feet Protected less than 10 feet
A-3	V-N	Two-hour less than 5 feet One-hour less than 20 feet NR elsewhere	Same as bearing	Not permitted less than 5 feet Protected less than 10 feet
A-4	II One-hour	One-hour N/C	Same as bearing except NR, N/C 40 feet or greater	Protected less than 10 feet
A-4	II-N	One-hour N/C less than 10 feet NR, N/C elsewhere	Same as bearing	Protected less than 10 feet
A-4	III-N	Four-hour N/C	Four-hour N/C less than 5 feet Two-hour N/C less than 20 feet One-hour N/C less than 40 feet NR, N/C elsewhere	Not permitted less than 5 feet Protected less than 10 feet
A-4	V One-hour	One-hour	Same as bearing	Protected less than 10 feet
A-4	V-N	One-hour less than 10 feet NR elsewhere	Same as bearing	Protected less than 10 feet
B, F-1, M, S-1, S-3	I-F.R. II-F.R. III One-hour III-N IV-H.T.	Four-hour N/C less than 5 feet Two-hour N/C elsewhere	Four-hour N/C less than 5 feet Two-hour N/C less than 20 feet One-hour N/C less than 40 feet NR, N/C elsewhere	Not permitted less than 5 feet Protected less than 20 feet
B F-1 M S-1, S-3	II One-hour	One-hour N/C	Same as bearing except NR, N/C 40 feet or greater	Not permitted less than 5 feet Protected less than 10 feet
B F-1 M S-1, S-3	II-N[3]	One-hour N/C less than 20 feet NR, N/C elsewhere	Same as bearing	Not permitted less than 5 feet Protected less than 10 feet
B F-1 M S-1, S-3	V One-hour	One-hour	Same as bearing	Not permitted less than 5 feet Protected less than 10 feet
B F-1 M S-1, S-3	V-N	One-hour less than 20 feet NR elsewhere	Same as bearing	Not permitted less than 5 feet Protected less than 10 feet

Chapter 5
Lesson 5.3: Types of Construction
(Title 24, Part 2, Volume 1, Chapter 6)

This chapter is important because it contains provisions that regulate the fire resistance of the building as a whole. The Type of construction dictates, within limits, the resistance of all of the structural materials for that building. The provisions of this chapter are not often used by the DSA Inspector since most of these things are done before the inspector's involvement.

You should be familiar with the construction types and what they mean.

1. **Type I**   :   The most fire resistive (Steel, Iron, Masonry, or Concrete)

2. **Type II:**   Second most fire resistive (Steel, Iron, Masonry, or Concrete structural elements)

3. **Type III:**

    a. **Type III:**   Third most fire resistive (Any material)

    b. **Type III-1hr:**   Shall be of one hour resistive materials throughout

4. **Type IV:**   Fourth most fire resistive (May be of any material)

5. **Type V:**

    a. **Type V-N:**   The least fire resistive of all of the building types (Any material)

    b. **Type V-1hr:** All the structural elements must be One hour

Read the directions and study the following materials.

Highlighting List
Types of Construction
(Title 24, Part 2, Volume 1, Chapter 6)

Take out your code book and highlight the code sections as they appear on this list in either red or yellow.

The "**Commentary**" on the right is broken down into four categories and they are as follows:

1. **TEST QUESTION (Highlight in Red)**
    - (Indicates that this material is very likely to be specifically referenced on the DSA exams)

2. **REMEMBER (Highlight in Yellow)**
    - (Indicates that you should know this material and that it is relevant to your work as an inspector)

3. **BEWARE (Highlight in Yellow)**
    - (Indicates that there is something that may not be apparent at first but that the inspector will have to deal with)

4. **SEE ALSO (Highlight in Yellow)**
    - (Indicates that there is another code section that affects this information)

© Professional Study Inc. 2003

Chapter 6
TYPES OF CONSTRUCTION

SECTION 601. CLASSIFICATION OF ALL BUILDINGS BY TYPES OF CONSTRUCTION AND

GENERAL REQUIREMENTS

601.5.5 Trim.

Foam plastic trim covering not more than 10 percent of the wall or ceiling area may be used, provided such trim (1) has a density of no less than 20 pounds per cubic foot (320.4 kg/m3), (2) has a maximum thickness of 1/2 inch (12.7 mm) and a maximum width of 4 inches (102 mm), and (3) has a flame-spread rating no greater than 75.

SECTION 602. TYPE I FIRE-RESISTIVE BUILDINGS

602.1 Definition. The structural elements in Type I fire-resistive buildings shall be of steel, iron, concrete or masonry.

> **Comment:** REMEMBER
> These are generally steel concrete or masonry buildings.

602.2 Structural Framework. Structural framework shall be of structural steel or iron as specified in Chapter 22, reinforced concrete as specified in Chapter 19,

SECTION 603. TYPE II BUILDINGS

603.1 Definition. The structural elements in Type II-F.R. buildings shall be of steel, iron, concrete or masonry.

> **Comment:** REMEMBER
> Very similar to type I buildings with a few exceptions.

SECTION 604. TYPE III BUILDINGS

604.1 Definition. Structural elements in Type III buildings may be of any materials permitted by this code.
Type III One-hour buildings shall be of one-hour fire-resistive construction throughout.

> **Comment:** REMEMBER
> Can be made of wood, though it will not be.

SECTION 605. TYPE IV BUILDINGS

605.1 Definition. Structural elements of Type IV buildings may be of any materials permitted by this code.

> **Comment:** REMEMBER
> The structure is resistant, but other elements do not need to be as resistant.

605.2 Structural Framework. Structural framework shall be of steel or iron as specified in Chapter 22, concrete as specified in Chapter 19, masonry as specified in Chapter 21, or wood as specified in Chapter 23 and this chapter.

SECTION 606. TYPE V BUILDINGS

606.1 Definition. Type V buildings may be of any materials allowed by this code.

Type V One-hour buildings shall be of one-hour fire-resistive construction throughout.

Materials of construction and fire-resistive requirements shall be as specified in Section 601.

> **Comment:** REMEMBER
> This is the type used in class 2 and 3 projects. Generally wood frame can be
> Type V-N (Non-rated) or
> Type V-1 (One Hour)

Chapter 5
Lesson 5.4: Fire Resistive Materials and Construction
(Title 24, Part 2, Volume 1, Chapter 7)

This chapter has to do with the materials and systems that are designed to prevent the spread of fire within and to a building or structure.

In other words, the most important aspects of this chapter with regard to the inspector are the following:

1. Insulation materials
2. Fire blocking and draft stops
3. Penetrations through walls and floors
4. Shaft enclosures
5. Protection of Openings (doors, windows, glazing, fire doors etc.)
6. Ducting (smoke and fire dampers)

Read the highlighting list items and be familiar with these provisions.

© Professional Study Inc. 2003

Highlighting List
Fire Resistive Materials and Construction
(Title 24, Part 2, Volume 1, Chapter 7)

Take out your code book and highlight the code sections as they appear on this list in either red or yellow.

The "**Commentary**" on the right is broken down into four categories and they are as follows:

1. **TEST QUESTION (Highlight in Red)**
   - (Indicates that this material is very likely to be specifically referenced on the DSA exams)

2. **REMEMBER (Highlight in Yellow)**
   - (Indicates that you should know this material and that it is relevant to your work as an inspector)

3. **BEWARE (Highlight in Yellow)**
   - (Indicates that there is something that may not be apparent at first but that the inspector will have to deal with)

4. **SEE ALSO (Highlight in Yellow)**
   - (Indicates that there is another code section that affects this information)

© Professional Study Inc. 2003

Chapter 7
FIRE-RESISTANT MATERIALS AND CONSTRUCTION

SECTION 704. PROTECTION OF STRUCTURAL MEMBERS

704.3.2 Reinforcing. Thickness of protection for concrete or masonry reinforcement shall be measured to the outside of the reinforcement except that stirrups and spiral reinforcement ties may project not more than 1/2 inch (12.7 mm) into the protection.

> **Comment:** SEE ALSO
> Sec 1907A.7.1 for concrete coverage on rebar.

SECTION 707. INSULATION

707.2 Insulation and Covering on Pipe and Tubing. Insulation and covering on pipe and tubing shall have a flame-spread rating not to exceed 25 and a smoke density not to exceed 450 when tested in accordance with UBC Standard 8-1

> **Comment:** SEE ALSO
> Table 8-A
> Flame spread classification.

707.3 Insulation.............
roof-ceiling assemblies, walls, crawl spaces or attics, shall have a flame-spread rating not to exceed 25 and a smoke density not to exceed 450 when tested in accordance with UBC Standard 8-1.

SECTION 708. FIRE BLOCKS AND DRAFT STOPS

708.2 Fire Blocks........................

708.2.1 Where required......................

1. In concealed spaces of stud walls and partitions, including furred spaces, at the ceiling and floor levels and at 10-foot (3048 mm) intervals both vertical and horizontal. See also Section 803, Item 1.

> **Comment:** REMEMBER
> Look for fire blocking in walls.

708.3 Draft Stops...................

708.3.1.1 Floor-ceiling assemblies.

708.3.1.1.3 Other uses. Draft stops shall be installed in floor-ceiling assemblies of buildings or portions of buildings used for other than dwelling or hotel occupancies so that the area of the concealed space does not exceed 1,000 square feet (93 m2) and so that the horizontal dimension between stops does not exceed 60 feet (18 288 mm).

> **Comment:** REMEMBER
> Floors/ceilings
> Draft stops at 1000sf or 60 ft without sprinklers and at 3000sf or 100ft with sprinklers.

> **EXCEPTION:** Where approved automatic sprinklers are installed within the concealed space, the area between draft stops may be 3,000 square feet (279 m2) and the horizontal dimension may be 100 feet (30 480 mm).

© Professional Study Inc. 2003

708.3.1.2 Attics.

708.3.1.2.2 Other uses. Draft stops shall be installed in attics, mansards, overhangs, false fronts set out from walls and similar concealed spaces of buildings having uses other than dwellings or hotels so that the area between draft stops does not exceed 3,000 square feet (279 m2) and the greatest horizontal dimension does not exceed 60 feet (18 288 mm).

> **Comment:** REMEMBER Draft stops at 3000sf or 60ft without sprinklers or at 9000 100ft with sprinklers.

> EXCEPTION: Where approved automatic sprinklers are installed, the area between draft stops 1may be 9,000 square feet (836m2) and the greatest horizontal dimension may be 100 feet (30 480 mm).

708.3.1.3 Draft stop construction. Draftstopping materials shall not be less than 1/2-inch (12.7 mm) gypsum board, 3/8-inch (9.5 mm) wood structural panel, 3/8-inch (9.5 mm) Type 2-Mpar-......

> **Comment:** REMEMBER Draft stop nmaterial ½" Gyp board or 3/8" plywood or particle board.

709.4 Parapets.

709.4.2 Construction. Parapets shall have the same degree of fire resistance required for the wall upon which they are erected.....

> **Comment:** REMEMBER Parapets minimum 30".

.........faces for the uppermost 18 inches (457 mm), including counterflashing and coping materials. The height of the parapet shall not be less than 30 inches (762 mm) above the point where the roof surface and the wall intersect.

709.6 Through Penetrations.

709.6.1 General. Through penetrations of walls *where openings are required to be protected* shall comply with Section 709.6.2 or 709.6.3.

> **Comment:** REMEMBER This is the standard for fire caulking etc.

> 1. In concrete or masonry walls where the penetrating items are a maximum 6-inch (152 mm)

> 2. The material used to fill the annular space shall prevent the passage of flame and hot gases sufficient to ignite cotton waste when subjected to UBC Standard 7-1 time-temperature fire conditions under a

> minimum positive pressure differential of 0.01 inch of water column (2.5 Pa) at the location of the penetration for the time period equivalent to the fire rating of the construction penetrated.

709.7 Membrane Penetrations................

> EXCEPTIONS: 1. Steel electrical boxes.........Outlet boxes on opposite sides of the wall shall be separated by a horizontal distance of not less than 24 inches (610 mm).

> **Comment:** REMEMBER This refers to penetrations in walls mostly.

> 2. The annular space created by the penetration of a fire sprinkler shall be permitted to be unprotected, provided such space is covered by a metal escutcheon plate.

SECTION 710. FLOOR CEILINGS OR ROOF CEILINGS

710.2 Through Penetrations.

710.2.1 General..............

EXCEPTIONS:............................

2. Penetrations in a single concrete floor by steel, ferrous or copper conduits, pipes, tubes and vents with a maximum 6-inch (152 mm) nominal diameter provided concrete, grout or mortar is installed the full thickness of the floor or the thickness required to maintain the fire-resistive rating. The penetrating items with a maximum 6-inch (152 mm) nominal diameter shall not be limited to the penetration of a single concrete floor, provided that the area of the penetration does not exceed 144 square inches (92 903 mm2).

> **Comment:** REMEMBER
> Penetrations in floors maximum 6" in diameter and 144sq inches

SECTION 713. FIRE-RESISTIVE ASSEMBLIES FOR PROTECTION OF OPENINGS

713.6 Hardware.......................

2. Fire assemblies required to have a one- and one-half-hour, one-hour or three-fourths-hour fire-protection rating shall be either automatic- or self-closing fire assemblies.

713.7 Glazed Openings in Fire Doors.
Glazed openings in fire doors shall not be permitted in a fire assembly required to have a three-hour fire-resistive rating.

> **Comment:** REMEMBER
> No glazing in (3) hour doors.

The area of glazed openings in a fire door required to have one- and one-half-hour or one-hour fire-resistive rating shall be limited to 100 square inches (64 500 mm2) with a minimum dimension of 4 inches (102 mm). When both leaves of a pair of doors have observation panels, the total area of the glazed openings shall not exceed 100 square inches (64 500 mm2) for each leaf.

> **Comment:** TEST QUESTION
> Maximum area of glass in (1 ½) hour door is 100sq inches each leaf.

713.8 Fire Window Size.
Fire windows required to have a three-fourths-hour fire-protection rating for protection of openings in exterior walls shall have an area not greater than 84 square feet (7.8 m2) with neither width nor height exceeding 12 feet

713.10 Smoke Dampers.

1. Penetrations of area or occupancy separation walls.

2. Penetrations of the fire-resistive construction of horizontal exit walls or corridors serving as a means of egress.

> **EXCEPTION:** Openings for steel ducts penetrating the required fire-resistive construction of corridors are not required to have smoke dampers when such ducts are of not less than 0.019-inch (0.48 mm) thickness (No. 26 galvanized sheet steel gage) and have no openings serving the corridor.

> **Comment:** BEWARE
> This applies to ducts running through an area, but not opening into it.

3. Penetrations of shaft enclosures.

> **EXCEPTION:** Exhaust-only openings serving continuously operating fans and protected using the provisions of Chapter 9.

Comment: TEST QUESTION
These criteria will be on the test.

4. Penetrations of smoke barriers.

5. Penetrations of elevator lobbies required by Section 403.7 or 1004.3.4.5.

6. Penetrations of areas of refuge.

> **EXCEPTION:** Ventilation systems specifically designed and protected to supply outside air to these areas during an emergency.

713.10.2 Methods of activation.

1. Where a damper is installed within a duct, a smoke detector shall be installed in the duct within 5 feet (1524 mm) of the damper with no air outlets or inlets between the detector and the damper.

Comment: TEST QUESTION
Detector maximum 5' from damper downstream.

713.11 Fire Dampers...........

shall be installed and be accessible for inspection and servicing in the following ducted and unducted air openings at:

Comment: REMEMBER
You will not be expected to determine the need for dampers etc. but you should know where to expect to find them.

1. Penetrations through *[ForSFM]* smoke barriers of Group 1, Division 1.1 Occupancies, area separation walls or occupancy separations.

2. Penetrations of the fire-resistive construction of horizontal exit walls or corridors serving as a means of egress.

> **EXCEPTION:** Openings for steel ducts penetrating the required fire-resistive construction of corridors are not required to have dampers when such ducts are of not less than 0.019-inch (0.48mm) thickness (No. 26 galvanized sheet steel gage) and have no openings serving the corridor.

3. Penetrations of shaft enclosures.

> **EXCEPTIONS:** 1. Duct penetrations by steel exhaust air subducts extending vertically upward at least 22 inches (559 mm) above the top of the opening in a vented shaft where the airflow is upward.
> 2. Penetrations of a fire-resistive floor forming the base of a shaft enclosure may be protected by fire dampers listed for installation in the horizontal position.

4. Penetrations of the ceiling of fire-resistive floor-ceiling or roof-ceiling assemblies.

5. Penetrations of an atrium enclosure element.

6. Penetrations of the building exterior required to have protected openings by Section 503.

7. Penetrations of areas of refuge.

Chapter 5
Lesson 5.5: Interior Finishes
(Title 24, Part 2, Volume 1, Chapter 8)

This regulates the fire resistive characteristics of interior finishes in buildings. There are two major issues of interest to the inspector in this chapter, "Flame Spread", and Sanitation.

Flame Spread refers to the characteristics of a particular material with respect to the speed at which it burns. The higher the "Flame Spread" index of a material the faster it burns. All materials that are to be used as surface finishes in a building should have a flame-spread rating on the packaging.

Interior finishes restricted by a combination of the occupancy of the space in which they are to be applied and their flame spread index. The flame spread index is divided into 3 classes I, II, and III. Table 8-A tells what Class a particular Flame-spread index falls into, and Table 8-B tells you what Class can go in what part of a building or occupancy.

Read the highlighting list items and be familiar with these provisions.

Highlighting List
Interior Finishes
(Title 24, Part 2, Volume 1, Chapter 8)

Take out your code book and highlight the code sections as they appear on this list in either red or yellow.

The "Commentary" on the right is broken down into four categories and they are as follows:

1. **TEST QUESTION (Highlight in Red)**
   - (Indicates that this material is very likely to be specifically referenced on the DSA exams)

2. **REMEMBER (Highlight in Yellow)**
   - (Indicates that you should know this material and that it is relevant to your work as an inspector)

3. **BEWARE (Highlight in Yellow)**
   - (Indicates that there is something that may not be apparent at first but that the inspector will have to deal with)

4. **SEE ALSO (Highlight in Yellow)**
   - (Indicates that there is another code section that affects this information)

Chapter 8
INTERIOR FINISHES

SECTION 804. MAXIMUM ALLOWABLE FLAME SPREAD

804.1 General. The maximum flame-spread class of finish materials used on interior walls and ceilings shall not exceed that set forth in Table 8-B.

> **EXCEPTIONS:** 1. Except in Group I Occupancies and in enclosed vertical exits, Class III may be used in other means of egress and rooms as wainscoting extending not more than 48 inches (1219 mm) above the floor and for tack and bulletin boards covering not more than 5 percent of the gross wall area of the room.
>
> 2. When a sprinkler system complying with UBC Standard 9-1 or 9-3 is provided, the flame-spread classification rating may be reduced one classification, but in no case shall materials having a classification greater than Class III be used.
>
> 3. The exposed faces of Type IV-H.T., structural members, and Type IV-H.T., decking and planking, where otherwise permissible under this code, are excluded from flame-spread requirements.

Comment: BEWARE
Tackboard is common in school applications. Ceiling tile should also be checked.

Comment: REMEMBER
Be familiar with the concept of flame spread. All material should have a rating printed on the packaging. Be sure or the specified materials are used.

804.2 Carpeting on Ceilings. When used as interior ceiling finish, carpeting and similar materials having a napped, tufted, looped or similar surface shall have a Class I flame spread.

SECTION 805. TEXTILE WALL COVERINGS

When used as interior wall finish,........... shall comply with the following:

1. Textile wall coverings shall have a Class I flame spread and shall be protected by automatic sprinklers complying with UBC Standard 9-1 or 9-3, or

SECTION 806. INSULATION

Thermal and acoustical insulation installed on walls or ceilings shall comply with Section 707.

SECTION 807. SANITATION

807.1 Floors and Walls in Water Closet Compartment and Showers.

807.1.1 Floors. In other than dwelling units, toilet room floors shall have a smooth, hard nonabsorbent surface such as portland cement, concrete, ceramic tile or other approved material that extends upward onto the walls at least 5 inches (127 mm).

Comment: REMEMBER
Applies to typical baseboards.

807.1.2 Walls. Walls within 2 feet (610 mm) of the front and sides of urinals and water closets shall have a smooth, hard nonabsorbent surface of portland cement, concrete, ceramic tile or other smooth, hard nonabsorbent surface to a height of 4 feet (1219 mm), and except for structural elements, the materials used

Comment: REMEMBER
Green board with paint is not sufficient. Look for a specia wall covering usually in the interior elevations.

807.1.3 Showers. Showers in all occupancies shall be finished as specified in Sections 807.1.1 and 807.1.2 to a height of not less than 70 inches (1778 mm)

> **Comment:** REMEMBER
> Minimum shower tile etc. 70"

TABLE 8-A—FLAME-SPREAD CLASSIFICATION

MATERIAL QUALIFIED BY:	
Class	Flame-spread Index
I	0-25
II	26-75
III	76-200

TABLE 8-B—MAXIMUM FLAME-SPREAD CLASS[1]

OCCUPANCY GROUP	ENCLOSED VERTICAL EXITWAYS	OTHER EXITWAYS[2]	ROOMS OR AREAS
A	I	II	II[3]
B	I	II	III
E	I	II	III
F	II	III	III
H	I	II	III[4]
I-1.1, I-1.2, I-2	I	I[5]	II[6]
I-3	I	I[5]	I[6]
M	I	II	III
R-1	I	II	III
R-3	III	III	III[7]
S-1, S-2	II	II	III
S-3, S-4, S-5	I	II	III
U	NO RESTRICTIONS		

[1] Foam plastics shall comply with the requirements specified in Section 2602. Carpeting on ceilings and textile wall coverings shall comply with the requirements specified in Sections 804.2 and 805, respectively.

[2] Finish classification is not applicable to interior walls and ceilings of exterior exit balconies.

[3] In Group A, Divisions 3 and 4 Occupancies, Class III may be used.

[4] Over two stories shall be of Class II.

[5] In Group I, Divisions 2 and 3 Occupancies, Class II may be used.

[6] Class III may be used in administrative spaces.

[7] Flame-spread provisions are not applicable to kitchens and bathrooms of Group R, Division 3 Occupancies.

© Professional Study Inc.

Chapter 5
Lesson 5.6: Fire Protection Systems
(Title 24, Part 2, Volume 1, Chapter 9)

This chapter is about the installation and design of the various fire and smoke control systems that are part of modern buildings. Fire alarm systems are covered in chapters 3 and 4 of Volume 1.

The DSA Inspector is mostly interested in the provisions of sections 904 for Group A, and E occupancies which refer to the requirements for fire sprinklers.

You will also need to know about the detection and control systems (see sec. 905)

See the following highlighting list sections.

Highlighting List
Fire Protection Systems
(Title 24, Part 2, Volume 1, Chapter 8)

Take out your code book and highlight the code sections as they appear on this list in either red or yellow.

The "Commentary" on the right is broken down into four categories and they are as follows:

1. **TEST QUESTION (Highlight in Red)**
   - (Indicates that this material is very likely to be specifically referenced on the DSA exams)

2. **REMEMBER (Highlight in Yellow)**
   - (Indicates that you should know this material and that it is relevant to your work as an inspector)

3. **BEWARE (Highlight in Yellow)**
   - (Indicates that there is something that may not be apparent at first but that the inspector will have to deal with)

4. **SEE ALSO (Highlight in Yellow)**
   - (Indicates that there is another code section that affects this information)

Chapter 9
FIRE-PROTECTION SYSTEMS

SECTION 903. DEFINITIONS

STANDPIPE SYSTEM is a wet or dry system of piping, valves, outlets and related equipment designed to provide water at specified pressures and installed exclusively for the fighting of fires, including the following:

> **Comment:** REMEMBER
> This will be determined long before you are brought onto a job, but you should be familiar with the terms.

[For SFM, SL] **Class I** is a *dry* standpipe system *without a directly connected water supply* and equipped with **2 1/2-inch** (63.5 mm) outlets *for use by the fire department or trained personnel.*

[For SFM, SL] **Class II** is a *wet* standpipe system directly connected to a water supply and equipped with **1 1/2-inch (38.1 mm) outlets** and hose *intended for use by the building occupants.*

[For SFM, SL] **Class III** is a *combination* standpipe system directly connected to a water supply and **equipped with both 1 1/2-inch (38.1 mm) outlets for use by the building occupants and** 2 1/2-inch (63.5 mm) outlets *for use by the fire department or trained personnel,* **or 2 1/2-inch (63.5 mm) and 1 1/2-inch (38.1 mm) outlets when a 1 1/2-inch (38.1 mm) hose is required.** Hose connections for Class III systems may be made through 2 1/2-inch (63.5 mm) hose valves with easily removable 2 1/2-inch by 1 1/2-inch (63.5 mm by 38.1 mm) reducers.

> **EXCEPTION:** Outlets for use by the fire authorities shall be of the size determined by the fire authority having jurisdiction.

SECTION 904. FIRE-EXTINGUISHING SYSTEMS

904.2.3 Group A Occupancies.

904.2.3.7 Stages. All stages shall be provided with an automatic sprinkler system. Such sprinklers shall be provided throughout the stage and in dressing rooms, workshops, storerooms and other accessory spaces contiguous to such stages.

> **EXCEPTIONS:** 1. Sprinklers are not required for stages 1,000 square feet (92.9 m2) or less in area and 50 feet (15 240 mm) or less in height where curtains, scenery or other combustible hangings are not retractable vertically. Combustible hangings shall be limited to a single main curtain, borders, legs and a single backdrop.
> 2. Under stage areas less than 4 feet (1219 mm) in clear height used exclusively for chair or table storage and lined on the inside with 5/8-inch (16 mm) Type X gypsum wallboard or an approved equal.

> **Comment:** REMEMBER
> Stages with chair storage below are very common in schools. Watch these areas carefully.

© Professional Study Inc. 2003

904.2.4 Group E Occupancies.

904.2.4.1 General. An automatic fire sprinkler system shall be installed throughout all buildings containing a Group E, Division 1 Occupancy.

> **EXCEPTIONS:** 1. When each room used for instruction has at least one exterior exit door at ground level and when rooms used for assembly purposes have at least one half of the required exits directly to the exterior ground level, a sprinkler system need not be provided.
>
> 2. When area separation walls, or occupancy separations having a fire-resistive rating of not less than two hours subdivide the building into separate compartments such that each compartment contains an aggregate floor area not greater than 20,000 square feet (1858 m2), an automatic sprinkler system need not be provided.

Comment: BEWARE
Watch for the appropriate assemblies in any area separations, especially in administration areas.

SECTION 905 . SMOKE CONTROL

905.9 Detection and Control Systems.

905.9.2 Wiring. In addition to meeting requirements of the Electrical Code, all wiring, regardless of voltage, shall be fully enclosed within continuous raceways.

Comment: REMEMBER
All fire alarms should be in conduit.

905.11 Marking and Identification. The detection and control systems shall be clearly marked at all junctions, accesses and terminations.

905.14 Response Time. Smoke-control system activation shall be initiated immediately after receipt of an appropriate automatic or manual activation command..........

1. Control air isolation valves	Immediately
2. Smoke damper closing	15 seconds
3. Smoke damper opening	15 seconds maximum
4. Fan starting (energizing)	15 seconds maximum
5. Fan stopping (de-energizing)	Immediately
6. Fan volume modulation	30 seconds maximum
7. Pressure control modulation	15 seconds maximum
8. Temperature control safety override	Immediately
9. Positive indication of status	15 seconds maximum

Comment: TEST QUESTION
These times may be asked to make sure you know where to find them. These things should be checked by the air balancing subcontractor.

905.15 Acceptance Testing.

905.15.4 Dampers. Dampers shall be tested for function in their installed condition.

TABLE 9-A—STANDPIPE REQUIREMENTS

OCCUPANCY	NONSPRINKLERED BUILDING[1]		SPRINKLERED BUILDING[2,3]	
× 304.8 for mm × 0.0929 for m²	Standpipe Class	Hose Requirement	Standpipe Class	Hose Requirement
1. Occupancies exceeding 150 feet in height and more than one story	III	Yes	I	No
2. Occupancies four stories or more but less than 150 feet in height, except Group R, Division 3[6]	[I and II[4]] (or III)	[5] Yes	I	No
3. Group A Occupancies with occupant load exceeding 1,000[7]	II	Yes	No requirement	No
4. Group A, Division 2.1 Occupancies over 5,000 square feet in area used for exhibition	II	Yes	II	Yes
5. Groups I; H; B; S; M; F, Division 1 Occupancies less than four stories in height but greater than 20,000 square feet per floor[6]	II[4]	Yes	No requirement	No
6. Stages more than 1,000 square feet in area	II	No	III	No

[1] Except as otherwise specified in Item 4 of this table, Class II standpipes need not be provided in basements having an automatic fire-extinguishing system throughout.

[2] The standpipe system may be combined with the automatic sprinkler system.

[3] Portions of otherwise sprinklered buildings that are not protected by automatic sprinklers shall have Class II standpipes installed as required for the unsprinklered portions.

[4] In open structures where Class II standpipes may be damaged by freezing, the building official may authorize the use of Class I standpipes that are located as required for Class II standpipes.

[5] Hose is required for Class II standpipes only.

[6] For the purposes of this table, occupied roofs of parking structures shall be considered an additional story. In parking structures, a tier is a story.

[7] Class II standpipes need not be provided in assembly areas used solely for worship.

© Professional Study Inc. 2003

Chapter 5
Lesson 5.7: Means of Egress
(Title 24, Part 2, Volume 1, Chapter 10)

Chapter 10 is one of the most important chapters in Volume 1 with respect to the DSA Inspector. Of the questions on the certification exams that are taken from Chapters 3-10 a large portion of them will be from this chapter. Means of egress is obviously an important topic when one is discussing building safety.

There are three main concepts which the chapter tries to address:

1. Exit Access (mainly distance, means of access to the exit path including signage etc.)
2. The Exit (size and usability of the exit path, also the protection of the exit)
3. Exit Discharge (where the exit leads sizes etc.)

See the following highlighting list sections.

Highlighting List
Means of Egress
(Title 24, Part 2, Volume 1, Chapter 10)

Take out your code book and highlight the code sections as they appear on this list in either red or yellow.

The "**Commentary**" on the right is broken down into four categories and they are as follows:

1. **TEST QUESTION (Highlight in Red)**
   - (Indicates that this material is very likely to be specifically referenced on the DSA exams)

2. **REMEMBER (Highlight in Yellow)**
   - (Indicates that you should know this material and that it is relevant to your work as an inspector)

3. **BEWARE (Highlight in Yellow)**
   - (Indicates that there is something that may not be apparent at first but that the inspector will have to deal with)

4. **SEE ALSO (Highlight in Yellow)**
   - (Indicates that there is another code section that affects this information)

© Professional Study Inc.

Chapter 10
MEANS OF EGRESS
NOTE: This chapter has been revised in its entirety.

1003.3.3.8 Alternative stairways.

1003.3.3.13 Stairway identification .... The sign shall be located approximately 5 feet (1524 mm) above the landing floor in a position that is readily visible when the door is in either the open or closed position. Signs shall comply with requirements of UBC Standard 10-2.

> **Comment:** REMEMBER
> Be familiar with these requirements.

SECTION 1004. THE EXIT ACCESS

1004.2.5 Travel distance.

1004.2.5.2.1 Nonsprinklered buildings. In buildings not equipped with an automatic sprinkler system throughout, the travel distance shall not exceed 200 feet (60 960 mm).

> **Comment:** REMEMBER
> Be familiar with these requirements.

1004.2.5.2.2 Sprinklered buildings. In buildings equipped with an automatic sprinkler system throughout, the travel distance shall not exceed 250 feet (76 200 mm).

1004.3.4 Corridors.

1004.3.4.2 Width. The width of corridors shall be determined as specified in Section 1003.2.3, but such width shall not be less than 44 inches (1118 mm), except as specified herein. Corridors serving an occupant load of less than 50 shall not be less than 36 inches (914 mm) in width.

The required width of corridors shall be unobstructed.

> EXCEPTION: Doors, when fully opened, and handrails shall not reduce the required width by more than 7 inches (178 mm). Doors in any position shall not reduce the required width by more than one half.
> Other nonstructural projections such as trim and similar decorative features may project into the required width 1 1/2 inches (38 mm) from each side.

> **Comment:** BEWARE
> Watch projections of handrails, drinking fountains etc. into paths of travel.

1004.3.4.3 Construction. Corridors *of Groups C; I and R, Division 2 Occupancies having an occupant load of seven or more in Group E* shall be fully enclosed by walls, a floor, a ceiling and permitted protected openings. The walls and ceilings of corridors shall be constructed of fire-resistive materials as specified in Section 1004.3.4.3.1.

> 7. *[For SFM] Group E Occupancies, when each room used for instruction has at least one exit door directly to the exterior at ground lev-*

el, and when rooms used for assembly purposes have at least one half
of the required .access to exits. that exit directly to the exterior at ground level.

1004.3.4.3.1 Fire-resistive materials.

For wall and ceiling finish requirements, see Table 8-B.

1004.3.4.3.2 Openings. Openings in corridors shall be protected in accordance with the requirements of this section.

1004.3.4.3.2.1 Doors. All exit-access doorways and doorways from unoccupied areas to a corridor shall be protected by tight fitting smoke- and draft-control assemblies having a fire-protection rating of not less than 20 minutes when tested in accordance with UBC Standard 7-2, Part II. Such doors shall not have louvers ,mail lots or similar openings. The door and frame shall bear an approved label or other identification showing the rating there of, followed by the letter .S,. the name of the manufacturer and the identification of the service conducting the inspection of materials

> **Comment:** TEST QUESTION
> 20 minute door and assembly from an unoccupied area to a corridor.

1004.3.4.3.2.2 Windows. Windows in corridor walls shall be protected by fixed glazing listed and labeled or marked for a fire-protection rating of at least three-fourths hour and complying with Sections 713.8 and 713.9. The total area of windows in a corridor shall not exceed 25 percent of the area of a common wall with any room.

> **Comment:** TEST QUESTION
> Maximum 25% of wall area may be window to corridor ¾ hour protection required.

1004.3.4.3.2.3 Duct openings. For duct openings in corridors, see Sections 713.10 and 713.11. Where both smoke dampers and
fire dampers are required by Sections 713.10 and 713.11, combination fire/smoke dampers shall be used.

SECTION 1005 . THE EXIT

1005.3.4.2 Width. The width of exit passageways shall be determined as specified in Section 1003.2.3, but such width shall not be less than 44 inches (1118 mm), except as specified herein. Exit
passageways serving an occupant load of less than 50 shall not be
less than 36 inches (914 mm) in width.

> **Comment:** TEST QUESTION
> Exits are never less then 36" wide and are usually 44" wide for more then 50.

1005.3.4.3 Construction. Exit passageways less than 400 feet (121 920 mm) in length shall have walls, floors and ceilings of not
less than one-hour fire-resistive construction. Exit passageways
400 feet (121 920 mm) or more in length shall have walls, floors and ceilings of not less than two-hour fire-resistive construction. Exit passageways in buildings of Type I or II construction shall be of noncombustible construction exceptwhere combustible materials are permitted in applicable building elements by other provisions of this code. Exit passageways in buildings of Type III, IV or V construction may be of combustible or noncombustible construction.

> **Comment:** REMEMBER
> Exit passages means corridors, stairways etc. Minimum (1) hour construction less then 400L.F. and (2) hour construction more then 400 L.F.

1005.3.4.4 Openings and penetrations.

All interior exit doors in an exit passageway shall be protected by a fire assembly having a fire-protection rating of not less than one hour where one-hour exit passageway construction is permitted in Section 1005.3.4.3 and not less than one and one-half hourswhere two-hour exit passageway construction is required by
Section 1005.3.4.3.

Comment: BEWARE
All interior exit doors to be (1) hour for (1) hour construction and (1 ½) hour for (2) hour construction

1005.3.4.6 Dead ends.........

sageway to a separate exit door, except for dead ends not exceeding 20 feet (6096 mm) in length.

Comment: REMEMBER
No dead ends longer then 20'

1005.3.5 Horizontal exits.

1005.3.5.3 Openings and penetrations.
Openings in a horizontal exit shall be protected by a fire assembly having a fire-protection rating of not less than one and one-half hours.

SECTION 1007. MEANS OF EGRESS REQUIREMENTS BASED ON OCCUPANCY

1007.2 Group A Occupancies.

1007.2.5 Panic hardware.
Exit and exit-access doors serving Group A Occupancies shall not be provided with a latch or lock unless it is panic hardware.

Comment: REMEMBER
Panic hardware is required at higher use occupancies.

1007.2.6 Posting of room capacity.
Any room that is used for an assembly, *[for SFM] dining, drinking or similar* purpose where fixed seats are not installed shall have the capacity of the room posted in a conspicuous place on an approved sign near the main
exit or exit-access doorway from the room.

Comment: BEWARE
Look for these signs in the assembly areas at punchlist time

1007.3 Group E Occupancies.

1007.3.2 Separate means of egress systems required.
Every room with an occupant load of 300 or more shall have one of its exits or exit-access doorways lead directly into a separate means
of egress system. Not more than two required exits or exit-access
doorways shall enter into the same means of egress system.

Comment: BEWARE
The means of egress can be a hallway etc. This should be caught by the planchecker.

1007.3.3 Travel distance.

1007.3.3.1 In rooms.
The travel distance from any point in a room shall not exceed 75 feet (22 860 mm) to a corridor or an exit.

EXCEPTIONS: 1. In buildings not more than two stories in height

Comment: BEWARE
This issue may come up during a change order situation.

© Professional Study Inc.

throughout, the travel distance may be increased to 110 feet (33 528 mm).

1007.3.8 Laboratories. Laboratories having a floor area of 200 square feet (18.6m2) or more shall have access to not less than two separate exits or exit-access doorways. All portions of such laboratories shall be within 75 feet (22 860 mm) of an exit or exit-access door.

Chapter 6
Lesson 6.1; Structural Design Requirements
(Title 24, Part 2, Volume 2, Chapter 16A)

The purpose of this chapter is to regulate the design of buildings and their parts. With respect to the DSA Inspector the most relevant aspects have to do with the bracing of equipment and objects inside of the buildings. Structural design is normally thoroughly worked out in the plan check process, however bracing of equipment, furniture etc is not always detailed in advance. This is why the DSA inspector must know what the requirements are in order to catch these things out in the field.

Section 1632A is related to lateral forces effecting non-structural elements of a building. Pay particular attention to Sec. 1632A.6 related to ductwork, piping, plumbing etc. Also important is Table 16A-O which sets out the rules for equipment, pipes etc. Be sure that you study the footnotes carefully as they have a lot of information that will be tested on the exams.

See the highlighting list for more information

Highlighting List
Structural Design Requirements
(Title 24, Part 2, Volume 2, Chapter 16)

Take out your code book and highlight the code sections as they appear on this list in either red or yellow.

The "**Commentary**" on the right is broken down into four categories and they are as follows:

1. **TEST QUESTION (Highlight in Red)**
    - (Indicates that this material is very likely to be specifically referenced on the DSA exams)

2. **REMEMBER (Highlight in Yellow)**
    - (Indicates that you should know this material and that it is relevant to your work as an inspector)

3. **BEWARE (Highlight in Yellow)**
    - (Indicates that there is something that may not be apparent at first but that the inspector will have to deal with)

4. **SEE ALSO (Highlight in Yellow)**
    - (Indicates that there is another code section that affects this information)

Highlighting List (T-24, Part 2, Vol. 2, Ch. 16A)
Chapter 16A *[For DSA/SS, OSHPD 1 & 4]*
STRUCTURAL DESIGN REQUIREMENTS

SECTION 1605A . DESIGN

EXCEPTION: Unless otherwise required by the building official,
buildings or portions thereof that are constructed in accordance with
the conventional light-framing requirements specified in Chapter 23A
of this code shall be deemed to meet the requirements of this section.

1605A.5 Construction Procedures. *Where unusual erection or*
construction procedures are considered essential by the project
architect or structural engineer in order to accomplish the intent
of the design or influence the design, such procedures shall be in-
dicated on the plans or in the specifications and shall have the
prior approval of the enforcement agency.

1607A.3.5 Live loads posted. *The live loads used in the design*
of floor and other areas listed in Category 8, 9, 10, 11, 17, 18, 19 or
20 of Table 16A-A, or for other special-purpose areas shall be
conspicuously posted in that part of each story in which they apply
using durable metal signs. The sign shall be in letters not less than
1 inch (25 mm) high on contrasting background

> **Comment:** REMEMBER
> Look for these in assembly areas and libraries

1607A.3.5.1 [For DSA-SS]. *The owner or school board shall be*
responsible for keeping the actual load below the allowable limits.

1629A.4.1 Seismic zone............

© Professional Study Inc. 2003

Seismic Zone 4 shall include all of the area within the boundaries of the state of California except for those areas designated as being in Seismic Zone 3.

> **Comment:** REMEMBER
> Almost all of California is Zone 4 unless you know otherwise

1632A.6 HVAC Ductwork, Plumbing/Piping and Conduit Systems.

All pipes, ducts and conduit shall be braced to resist the forces prescribed in Section 1630A.2.

Seismic restraints may be omitted for the following conditions, where flexible connections are provided between components and the associated ductwork, piping and conduit:
1. *Fuel piping less than 1 inch (25 mm) inside diameter.*
2. *All other piping less than 2.5 inches (64 mm) diameter, except medical gas including vacuum piping, or*
All piping suspended by individual hangers 12 inches (305 mm) or less in length from the top of the pipe to the bottom of the structural support for the hanger, or
All electrical conduit less than 2.5 inches (64 mm) trade size.
3. *All rectangular air-handling ducts less than 6 square feet (0.56 m2) in cross-sectional area, or*
All round air-handling ducts less than 28 inches (711 mm) in diameter, or
All ducts suspended by hangers 12 inches (305 mm) or less in length from the top of the duct to the bottom of the structural support for the hanger, where the hangers are detailed to avoid bending of the hangers and their connections.

> **Comment:** TEST QUESTION
> This material is often on the exams, though the combinations change. Be sure you understand what is being described in the question.

Where lateral restraints are omitted, the piping, ducts or conduit shall be installed such that lateral motion of the piping or duct will not cause damaging impact with other systems or structural members, or loss of vertical support.

1632A.6.1 *All trapeze assemblies supporting pipes, ducts and conduit shall be braced to resist the forces of Section 1632A.2, considering the total weight of the elements on the trapeze.*

Pipes, ducts and conduit supported by a trapeze where none of those elements would individually be braced need not be braced if connections to the pipe/conduit/ductwork or directional changes do not restrict the movement of the trapeze.

SECTION 1633A. DETAILED SYSTEMS DESIGN REQUIREMENTS

1633A.2.8 Anchorage of concrete or masonry walls.

In addition, in Seismic Zones 3 and 4, diaphragm to wall anchorage using embedded straps shall have the straps attached to or hooked around the reinforcing steel or otherwise terminated to effectively transfer forces to the reinforcing steel.

> **Comment:** REMEMBER
> This is relevant to the masonry sections and to veneers. Hooks go around rebar.

SECTION 1637A. SITE DATA FOR STATE-OWNED OR STATE-LEASED ESSENTIAL SERVICES BUILDINGS

1637A.2.1 Geotechnical report.

*1637A.1.1 Geologic and earthquake engineering reports shall be
required for all proposed construction.
report shall include, but shall not be limited to, site-specific evalu-*

> ***EXCEPTIONS:** 1. Reports are not required for one-story, wood-
> frame and light-steel-frame buildings of Type II or Type V construction
> and 4,000 square feet (371m2) or less in floor area; nonstructural,*

TABLE 16A-A—UNIFORM AND CONCENTRATED LOADS

USE OR OCCUPANCY		UNIFORM LOAD[1] (psf) × 0.0479 for kN/m²	CONCENTRATED LOAD (pounds) × 0.00448 for kN
Category	Description		
1. Access floor systems	Office use	50	2,000[2]
	Computer use	100	2,000[2]
2. Armories		150	0
3. Assembly areas[3] and auditoriums and balconies therewith	Fixed seating areas	50	0
	Movable seating and other areas	100	0
	Stage areas and enclosed platforms	125	0
4. Cornices and marquees		60[4]	0
5. Exit facilities[5]		100	0[6]
6. Garages	General storage and/or repair	100	[7]
	Private or pleasure-type motor vehicle storage	50	[7]
7. Hospitals	Wards and rooms	40	1,000[2]
8. Libraries[12]	Reading rooms	60	1,000[2]
	Stack rooms	125	1,500[2]
9. Manufacturing[12]	Light	75	2,000[2]
	Heavy	125	3,000[2]
10. Offices[12]		50	2,000[2]
11. Printing plants[12]	Press rooms	150	2,500[2]
	Composing and linotype rooms	100	2,000[2]
12. Residential[8]	Basic floor area	40	0[6]
	Exterior balconies	60[4]	0
	Decks	40[4]	0
	Storage	40	0
13. Restrooms[9]			
14. Reviewing stands, grandstands, bleachers, and folding and telescoping seating		100	0
15. Roof decks	Same as area served or for the type of occupancy accommodated		
16. Schools	Classrooms	50	1,000[2]
17. Sidewalks, pedestrian bridges and driveways[12]	Limited access	100	[7]
	Public access	250	[7]
18. Storage[12]	Light	125	
	Heavy	250	
19. Stores[12]	Retail	75	2,000[2]
	Wholesale	100	3,000[2]
20. Pedestrian bridges and walkways		100	
21. Press box floor and roof with railing	TV cameras and equipment	100	1,000[2]
22. Dining areas	Not used for assembly areas	100	1,000[2]
23. Kitchens and serving areas		50	1,000[2]
24. Mechanical and electrical equipment areas[10]	Open areas around equipment	50	[11]
25. Shops[12]	Light	75	2,000[2]
	Heavy	125	3,000[2]

[1] See Section 1607A for live load reductions.
[2] See Section 1607A.3.3, first paragraph, for area of load application.
[3] Assembly areas include such occupancies as dance halls, drill rooms, gymnasiums, playgrounds, plazas, terraces and similar occupancies that are generally accessible to the public.
[4] When snow loads occur that are in excess of the design conditions, the structure shall be designed to support the loads due to the increased loads caused by drift buildup or a greater snow design as determined by the *enforcement agency*. See Section 1614A. For special-purpose roofs, see Section 1607A.4.4.
[5] Exit facilities shall include such uses as corridors serving an occupant load of 10 or more persons, exterior exit balconies, stairways, fire escapes and similar uses.
[6] Individual stair treads shall be designed to support a 300-pound (1.33 kN) concentrated load placed in a position that would cause maximum stress. Stair stringers may be designed for the uniform load set forth in the table.
[7] See Section 1607A.3.3, second paragraph, for concentrated loads. See Table 16A-B for vehicle barriers.
[8] Residential occupancies include private dwellings, apartments and hotel guest rooms *and dormitories*.
[9] Restroom loads shall not be less than the load for the occupancy with which they are associated, but need not exceed 50 pounds per square foot (2.4 kN/m²).
[10] See Part 7, Title 24, for elevator machine room *floor loads and equipment loads*.
[11] See Table 16A-B for equipment design loads.
[12] See Section 1607A.3.5 for posting requirements.

TABLE 16A-O—HORIZONTAL FORCE FACTORS, a_p AND R_p

ELEMENTS OF STRUCTURES AND NONSTRUCTURAL COMPONENTS AND EQUIPMENT[1]	a_p	R_p	FOOTNOTE
1. Elements of Structures			
A. Walls including the following:			
(1) Unbraced (cantilevered) parapets.	2.5	3.0	
(2) Exterior walls at or above the ground floor and parapets braced above their centers of gravity.	1.0	3.0	2
(3) All interior-bearing and nonbearing walls.	1.0	3.0	2, 8
B. Penthouse (except when framed by an extension of the structural frame).	2.5	4.0	
C. Connections for prefabricated structural elements other than walls. See also Section 1632A.2.	1.0	3.0	3, 20
2. Nonstructural Components			
A. Exterior and interior ornamentations and appendages.	2.5	3.0	20
B. Chimneys, stacks and trussed towers supported on or projecting above the roof:			
(1) Laterally braced or anchored to the structural frame at a point below their centers of mass.	2.5	3.0	
(2) Laterally braced or anchored to the structural frame at or above their centers of mass.	1.0	3.0	
C. Signs and billboards.	2.5	3.0	
D. Storage racks (include contents) *with upper storage level more than 5 feet (1524 mm) in height*	2.5	4.0	4, 23
E. Permanent floor-supported cabinets and book stacks more than 6 feet (1829 mm) in height (include contents).	1.0	3.0	5, 20, 23, 24
F. Anchorage and lateral bracing for suspended ceilings and light fixtures.	1.0	3.0	3, 6, 7, 8
G. Access floor systems.	1.0	3.0	9, 20
H. Masonry or concrete fences over 6 feet (1829 mm) high.	1.0	3.0	
I. Partitions.	1.0	3.0	8
J. *Wall hung cabinets and storage shelving (plus contents)*	*1.0*	*3.0*	
3. Equipment			20
A. Tanks and vessels (include contents), including support systems.	1.0	3.0	
B. Electrical, mechanical and plumbing equipment and associated conduit and ductwork and piping, *and machinery. In essential services buildings, this includes all piping, electrical conduits, cable trays and air-handling ducting necessary to the continuing operation of the facility.*	1.0	3.0	5, 10, 11, 12, 13, 14, 15, 16, 20
C. Any flexible equipment laterally braced or anchored to the structural frame at a point below their center of mass.	2.5	3.0	5, 10, 14, 15, 16, 20
D. Anchorage of emergency power supply systems and essential communications equipment. Anchorage and support systems for battery racks and fuel tanks necessary for operation of emergency equipment. See also Section 1632A.2.	1.3	3.0	17, 18, 20, 21
E. Temporary containers with flammable or hazardous materials.	1.0	3.0	19
F. *Power cable-driven elevators or hydraulic elevators with lifts over 5 feet (1524 mm):*			25
(1) Hoistway structural framing providing the support for guide rail brackets			
(2) Guide rails and guide rail brackets			
(3) Car and counterweight auxiliary guiding members or retainer plates			
(4) Driving machinery, pump unit tanks operating devices and control equipment cabinets			
4. Other Components			
A. Rigid components with ductile material and attachments.	1.0	3.0	1, 20
B. Rigid components with nonductile material or attachments.	1.0	1.5	1, 20
C. Flexible components with ductile material and attachments.	2.5	3.0	1, 20
D. Flexible components with nonductile material or attachments.	2.5	1.5	1, 20

Notes for Table 16A-O

1 See Section 1627A for definitions of flexible components and rigid components. See Section 1632A for formula using ap. Horizontal forces are to be applied in any horizontal direction. The value of ap shall not be reduced for all walls. Welded, bolted or other intermittent connections such as inserts for anchorage of nonstructural components shall not be allowed the one-third increase in allowable stress permitted in Section 1612A.3.2.

2 See Sections 1633A.2.4 and 1633A.2.8 for concrete and masonry walls and Section 1632A.2 for connections for panel connectors for panels.

3 Applies to Seismic Zones 2, 3 and 4 only.

4 Ground supported steel storage racksmay be designed using the provisions of Section 1634A. Chapter 22A, DivisionVI, may be used for design, provided seismic design forces are equal to or greater than those specified in Section 1632A.5 or 1634A.5, as appropriate.

5 Only attachments, anchorage or restraints need be designed.

6 Ceiling weight shall include all light fixtures and other equipment or partitions that are laterally supported by the ceiling. For purposes of determining the seismic force, a ceiling weight of not less than 4 psf (0.19 kN/m2) shall be used.

7 Ceilings constructed of lath and plaster or gypsum board screw or nail attached to suspendedmembers that support a ceiling at one level extending from wall to wall need not be analyzed, provided the walls are not over 50 feet (15 240 mm) apart.

8 Light fixtures andmechanical services installed inmetal suspension systems for acoustical tile and lay-in panel ceilings shall be independently supported fromthe structure above as specified in UBC Standard 25-2, Part III. See also Section 1611A.5 for minimum load and deflection criteria for interior partitions.
(Continued)

> **Comment:** TEST QUESTION Refers to lights in T-Bar ceilings.

© Professional Study Inc. 2003

9 Wp for access floor systems shall be the dead load of the access floor system plus 25 percent of the floor live load plus a 10-psf (0.48 kN/m2) partition load allowance.

10 Equipment includes, but is not limited to, boilers, chillers, heat exchangers, pumps, air-handling units, cooling towers, control panels, motors, switchgear, transformers and life-safety equipment. It shall include major conduit, ducting and piping, which services such machinery and equipment and fire sprinkler systems.
See Section 1632A.2 for additional requirements for determining ap for nonrigid or flexibly mounted equipment.

> **Comment:** REMEMBER
> Flexible connections at equipment

11 Deleted.

12 Seismic restraints may be omitted from electrical raceways, such as cable trays, conduit and bus ducts, if all the following conditions are satisfied:
    12.1 Lateral motion of the raceway will not cause damaging impact with other systems.
    12.2 Lateral motion of the raceway does not cause loss of system vertical support.
    12.3 Rod-hung supports of less than 12 inches (305 mm) in length have top connections that cannot develop moments.
    12.4 Support members cantilevered up from the floor are checked for stability.

> **Comment:** REMEMBER
> Supports longer than 12" must be braced.

13 Piping, ducts and electrical raceways, which must be functional following an earthquake, spanning between different buildings or structural systems shall be sufficiently flexible to withstand relative motion of support points assuming out-of-phase motions.

> **Comment:** REMEMBER
> Flexible connections at expansion joints and between buildings.

14 Vibration isolators supporting equipment shall be designed for lateral loads or restrained from displacing laterally by other means. Restraint shall also be provided, which limits vertical displacement, such that lateral restraints do not become disengaged. ap and Rp for equipment supported on vibration isolators shall be taken as 2.5 and 1.5, respectively, except that if the isolation mounting frame is supported by shallow or expansion anchors, the design forces for the anchors calculated

> **Comment:** REMEMBER
> These connections must be designed and on approved plans.

by Formula (32A-1), (32A-2) or (32A-3) shall be additionally multiplied by a factor of 1.3.

15 Equipment anchorage shall not be designed such that lateral loads are resisted by gravity friction (e.g., friction clips).

16 Expansion anchors, which are required to resist seismic loads in tension, shall not be used where operational vibrating loads are present.

17 Movement of components within electrical cabinets, rack- and skid-mounted equipment and portions of skid-mounted electromechanical equipment that may cause damage to other components by displacing, shall be restricted by attachment to anchored equipment or support frames.

18 Batteries on racks shall be restrained against movement in all directions due to earthquake forces.

19 Seismic restraints may include straps, chains, bolts, barriers or other mechanisms that prevent sliding, falling and breach of containment of flammable and toxic materials. Friction forces may not be used to resist lateral loads in these restraints unless positive uplift restraint is provided which ensures that the friction forces act continuously.

20 The component anchorage shall be designed for the horizontal force, Fp, acting simultaneously with a vertical seismic force equal to one third of the horizontal force, Fp.

21 Emergency equipment should be located where there is the least likelihood of damage due to earthquake. Such equipment should be located at ground level, and where it can be easily maintained to assure its operation during an emergency.

22 Not used.

23 Floor-supported storage racks, cabinets or book stacks not more than 5 feet (1524 mm) in height need not be

Comment: TEST QUESTION
Racks and cabinets taller than 5'-0" must be anchored

anchored if the width of the supporting base or width between the exterior legs is equal to or greater than two thirds the height. In addition to gravity loads, storage racks or cabinets shall be designed and constructed to resist the horizontal force, Fp, with the base assumed to be anchored.

24 Mobile storage racks or cabinets mounted on wheels and not restrained by fixed tracks are not subject to approval by the enforcement agency when the rack or cabinet is not more than 5 feet (1524 mm) in height and the width of the supporting base or width between the exterior legs/wheels is equal to or greater than two thirds the height. All such racks or cabinets shall be restrained to prevent movement when not in use. Movable storage racks or cabinets mounted on wheels or glides restrained by fixed tracks shall be designed and constructed to resist the horizontal force, Fp, with the base of the rack or cabinet assumed to be anchored.
Provisions shall be made to resist translation perpendicular to the track and overturning both perpendicular and parallel to the track.

25 Suspension systems for light fixtures which have passed shaking table tests approved by the enforcement agency, or which, as installed, are free to swing a minimum of 45 degrees from the vertical in all directions without contacting obstructions, shall be assumed to comply with the lateral-force requirements of Section 1632A.2. Unless the cable-type, free-swinging suspension systems shall have a safety wire or cable attached to the fixture and structure at each support capable of supporting four times the supported load.

> **Comment:** REMEMBER
> This applies to pendant lights, fans, etc.

26 For suspended and surface-mounted light fixtures, the product of I ap need not exceed 1.5 for any value of I.
27 See Section 1633A.2.13.

Chapter 6
LESSON 6.2: Structural Tests and Inspections
(Title 24, Part 2, Volume 2, Chapter 17A)

This chapter is of particular importance to the DSA Inspector. Although Chapter 17A is short it lays out the requirements for Special Inspections. Since you as the Project Inspector are in charge of the inspection and testing program of the project, it is your responsibility to make sure that the Special Inspection process is adhered to and that nothing slips through the cracks.

Normally special inspectors are provided by the laboratory of record, however as the project inspector you are ultimately responsible for their work.

DSA requires special inspectors for the following: (partial list)

1. Structural Concrete
2. Structural Masonry
3. Structural Welding (including reinforcement welding)
4. Pre-stress
5. High Strength Bolting

See the highlighting list for a complete list.

Concrete: The most important thing that you as a project inspector need to know is who you need and when. Unless specifically required you do not need to hire a special inspector for structural concrete. However this is assuming that you as the project inspector are providing "constant" inspection during any structural placement operations.

Masonry: For structural masonry, or adhered veneer work you must have a "DSA approved" structural masonry inspector providing constant inspection. This means that you must provide a DSA Form 5 (Inspector Qualification Form) to DSA through the architect and that must be accepted by DSA. The inspector must be a DSA Certified Masonry Inspector which is a special DSA certification separate from the Project Inspector Certifications.

Structural Welding: A Structural welding special inspector is required when there is any field or shop welding of structural materials. DSA requires that a welding inspector be an AWS CWI (American Welding Society Certified Welding Inspector).

© Professional Study Inc. 2003

Pre-Stress: DSA requires that you have a DSA approved special inspector for this work. This means that you must submit a Form DSA 5 with the inspector's qualifications outlined and that these qualifications be accepted by DSA.

High Strength Bolting: This is another grey area of the DSA rules but formally you are required to submit a DSA Form 5 in order to obtain approval. Many times your structural steel special inspector will also do this type of inspection. However be aware that AWS CWI is only a welding certification. Therefore if the inspector is not versed in high-strength bolting you may be in for a surprise. ICC (ICBO) certified welding inspectors are tested in both welding and high-strength bolting. I would suggest that you make sure that any inspector doing HSB work on your site have the appropriate skills.

See the highlighting list for more information.

Highlighting List
Structural Tests and Inspections
(Title 24, Part 2, Volume 2, Chapter 17A)

Take out your code book and highlight the code sections as they appear on this list in either red or yellow.

The "**Commentary**" on the right is broken down into four categories and they are as follows:

1. **TEST QUESTION (Highlight in Red)**
   - (Indicates that this material is very likely to be specifically referenced on the DSA exams)

2. **REMEMBER (Highlight in Yellow)**
   - (Indicates that you should know this material and that it is relevant to your work as an inspector)

3. **BEWARE (Highlight in Yellow)**
   - (Indicates that there is something that may not be apparent at first but that the inspector will have to deal with)

4. **SEE ALSO (Highlight in Yellow)**
   - (Indicates that there is another code section that affects this information)

© Professional Study Inc. 2003

Chapter 17A [For DSA/SS, OSHPD 1 & 4]
STRUCTURAL TESTS AND INSPECTIONS

SECTION 1701A. SPECIAL INSPECTIONS

1701A.2 *Project and* Special Inspector.

1701A.2.1 [For DSA/SS] The *project inspectors and all* special inspectors shall be qualified persons who shall demonstrate competence, to the satisfaction of the *enforcement agency,* for inspection of the particular type of construction or operation requiring special inspection *in accordance with Title 24, Part 1, Section 4-333.*

> **Comment:** TEST QUESTION
> This requires that you file a form DSA-5

1701A.3 Duties and Responsibilities of the *Project and* Special Inspectors.

1701A.3.1 [For DSA/SS] The *project and* special inspectors shall observe the work assigned for conformance to the approved design drawings and specifications.

> **Comment:** REMEMBER
> This makes you responsible for the Special Inspector

The *project inspector and* special inspectors shall *submit* inspection reports to the *enforcement agency* and other designated persons *as required by Title 24, Part 1, Sections 4-336 and 4-342.* All discrepancies shall be brought to the immediate attention of the contractor for correction *in accordance with Title 24, Part 1, Section 4-342.*

> **Comment:** TEST QUESTION
> Special inspectors are required to file a DSA-Form 6 "Verified Report"

The *project inspector and* special inspectors shall submit reports *as required by Title 24, Part 1, Section 4-336 and 4-342* stating that they have personal knowledge that *the work has been performed and that the materials used and installed are in compliance with* the approved plans and specifications and the applicable workmanship provisions of this code.

1701A.5 Types of Work *Requiring Constant Presence of the Project or Special Inspector.*

constant presence and inspection

1. **Concrete.** During the taking of test specimens and placing of reinforced concrete.

> **Comment:** REMEMBER
> Usually the Project Inspector

2. **Bolts installed in concrete.** Prior to and during the placement of concrete around bolts.

> **Comment:** REMEMBER
> Usually the Project Inspector

3. **Special moment-resisting concrete frame........**
the *proect or* special inspector . . . shall provide *constant* inspection of the placement of the reinforcement and concrete.

5. **Structural welding.** *Special inspector required.*

   5.1 General. During the welding of any member or connection that is designed to resist loads and forces required by this code.

> **Comment:** REMEMBER
> AWS-CWI: Certified Welding inspector. You are required to file a Form DSA-5 for the Special Inspector

   EXCEPTION: The special inspector need not be *constantly* present during welding of the following items, provided the materials, qualifications of welding procedures and welders are verified prior to the start of work

   1. Floor and roof deck welding.
   2. Welded studs when used for structural diaphragm or composite

systems.

3. Welded sheet steel for cold-formed steel framing members such as studs and joists *which are not part of a lateral-force-resisting system.*

4. Welding of stairs and railing systems.

5.3 **Welding of reinforcing steel.** During the welding of reinforcing steel. *See Chapter 19A, Division IX, Section 1929A for additional requirements.*
ments.

6. **High-strength bolting.** *Special inspector required.* The inspection of high-strength A 325 and A 490 bolts shall be in accordance with *the standards adopted as part of this code,* approved nationally recognized standards and the requirements of this section.

   the special inspector shall determine that the requirements for bolts, nuts, washers and paint; bolted parts; and installation and tightening in such standards are met. . . . The special inspector shall observe the calibration procedures when such procedures are required by the plans or specifications and shall monitor the installation of bolts to determine that all plies of connected materials have been drawn together and that the selected procedure is properly used to tighten all bolts.

   > **Comment:** REMEMBER
   > Not all CWI's are qualified to do High Strength Bo
   > Verify qualifications.

7. **Structural masonry.** *Special inspector required.*

   7.1 For masonry, . . . during preparation and taking of any required prisms or test specimens, placing of all masonry units, placement of reinforcement, inspection of grout space, immediately prior to closing of cleanouts, and during all grouting operations. *See Section 2105A for additional requirements*

   > **Comment:** TEST QUESTION
   > Must be DSA Certified Masonry Inspector and perl
   > constant inspection

12. **Shotcrete.** *Special inspector required.* A

14. **Smoke-control system.**

    14.1 During erection of ductwork and prior to concealment for the purposes of leakage testing and recording of device location.

    14.2 Prior to occupancy and after sufficient completion for the purposes of pressure difference testing, flow measurements, and detection and control verification.

15. **Special cases.**

16. **Manufactured trusses.**

17. **Glued-laminated Timber.**

    > **Comment:** TEST QUESTION
    > DSA Certified Inspectors are required in the plant.
    > "Verified Report" must accompany the materials to site.

18. **Post Installed Anchors.** The installation of drilled-in expansion or chemical-type anchors in concrete or masonry shall be continuously inspected by a qualified inspector approved by the enforcement agency.

    > **Comment:** TEST QUESTION
    > DSA Certified Inspectors are required in the plant.
    > "Verified Report" must accompany the materials to site.

SECTION 1702A. OBSERVATION OF THE CONSTRUCTION

1702A.1 [For DSA/SS] Observation of the construction shall be provided *by the architect or engineer in general responsible charge as set forth in Title 24, Part 1, Sections 4-333 and 4-341.*

> **Comment:** REMEMBER
> Usually done by the Project Inspector.

© Professional Study Inc. 2003

Chapter 7
Lesson 7.1: CONCRETE CONSTRUCTION

Concrete has been divided into four major lessons.

1. Background and General Information
2. Code Book highlighting Ch 19A Concrete Sections 1903A – 1906A
3. Code Book highlighting Ch 19A Concrete Sections 1906A – 1929A
4. Code Study Guide.

Each code Lesson has a quiz at the end. Read the lesson information and then answer the quiz questions prior to moving on the next lesson.

Use the code summary Study guide to help answer the questions on the quizzes.

Lesson #1 is background information to familiarize you with concrete work. The information in this lesson will not likely be on the DSA exam though any DSA inspector should have a good working knowledge of concrete.

CONCRETE BACKGROUND INFORMATION

More than 2000 years ago, in some ancient province, a Roman citizen mixed slaked lime with pozzolan (volcanic ash), added stone and water, and thus created the world's first concrete. The development was very likely an accident, and the material was - by today's standards - relatively unsophisticated. However, the discovery of concrete changed the shape of the ancient world, and after 20 centuries, it continues to influence the appearance of our world today.

The Romans developed an admiration for concrete for many of the same reasons that we continue to regard it so highly. First of all, it is a material that can be used almost anywhere, since the basic ingredients are virtually universal. Secondly, it requires a minimum of highly skilled labor to prepare and place. Finally, concrete is as strong as natural stone, it is durable and resistant to exposure, and the design of its final shape is unusually flexible, limited only by imagination and a worker's ability to construct the required formwork. The hundreds of monumental Roman structures that survive today confirm the durability and ancient popularity of this remarkable material.

After the fall of the Roman Empire, the knowledge of concrete construction was either lost or more likely abandoned by subsequent civilizations, which had neither the manpower nor inclination to build in the Roman fashion. The technology of the Industrial Revolution, however, changed that outlook. In 1824, portland cement became a manufactured product; and the result was readily available cement that was cheap, strong, and uniform. Within 50 years there was a variety of European experiments with "ferro concrete", in which iron was used to reinforce the concrete mass; and by the year 1900, reinforced concrete came into widespread use nearly everywhere. Concrete remains today one of the most important materials in the world of construction.

COMPOSITION OF CONCRETE

Cement is the term applied to any adhesive substance which is capable of uniting non-adhesive materials. In concrete construction, the adhesive substance is portland cement, since that is the most widely used cement in existence.

Portland cement is manufactured from lime, silica, iron oxide and alumina, with gypsum to control the setting time. Properly proportioned ingredients are ground and burned to form clinkers; the clinkers are then pulverized to produce cement. This final step is strictly controlled, since the fineness of grinding has a direct bearing on the strength of the cement. Portland cement hardens by reacting to water. The two materials first form a paste which loses its plasticity as it begins to set. The initial set occurs within an hour, and the final set takes about ten hours. The cement continues to harden, however, over a long period of time. Cement paste is the chemically active ingredient in concrete, and is referred to as the matrix.

The table on the following page summarizes the various types of portland cement used in building construction.

Aggregates are the chemically inert ingredients which are combined with

INTRODUCTION

Concrete is a man-made construction material which is the result of mixing fine aggregate (sand), coarse aggregate (gravel or crushed rock), cement, and water together in the proper proportions. The product is not concrete unless all four of these ingredients are present. A mixture of sand, cement, and water - without coarse aggregate - is not concrete at all; it is mortar or grout. And while on the subject of nomenclature, there is no such thing as a "cement" wall or "cement" paving; it is always concrete.

The aggregates in concrete are the inert ingredients, while cement and water are the active ingredients. The inert ingredients, usually sand and gravel, are first mixed thoroughly with the cement. As water is added,
a chemical reaction takes place between the water and cement. This reaction, referred to as hydration, creates heat and causes the concrete to harden.

Thus, it is not - as some may believe - the drying out of the mix that causes hardening of the concrete. In fact, during the curing process, concrete must be kept moist for satisfactory hydration of the cement. Confirmation of this chemical process is the fact that concrete will harden just as well under water as it will in the air.

The use of concrete as a building material has greatly increased in recent years to a point where all types of structures from simple bus shelters to multistory buildings are constructed from essentially this one material. Concrete is used for foundations, floors, columns, walls, beams, and roofs, for precast panels in floors and walls, in thin-shell structures, in rigid frames, in decorative cast shapes, and for bricks and blocks that are used in concrete masonry construction. Concrete, it would appear, is a material for all purposes and all times.

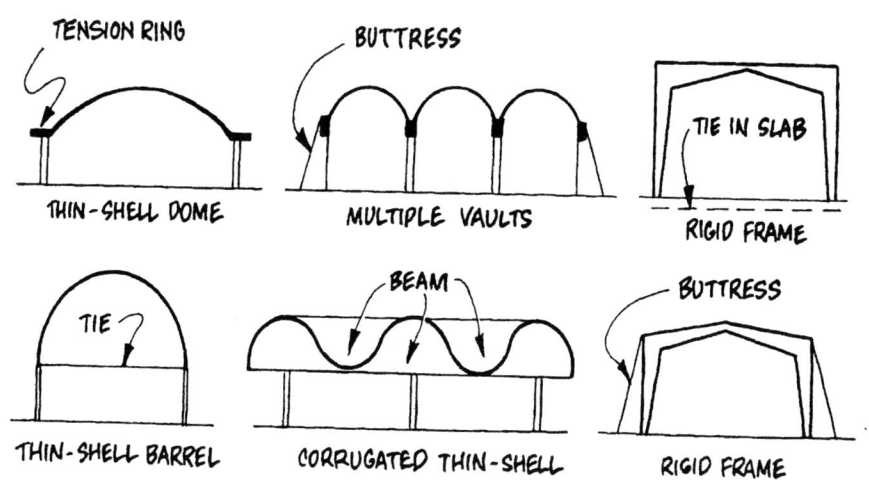

TYPES OF THIN-SHELL AND RIGID FRAME CONCRETE FORMS

Portland Cement	Type of Concrete	Primary Use
Type I	Standard	For general all-purpose use
Type II	Modified	For slow setting and less heat
Type III	High Early Strength	For quick setting and early strength
Type IV	Low Heat	For very slow setting (little heat)
Type V	Sulphate Resisting	For alkaline water and soils

cement and water to make concrete. Aggregates serve several important purposes in the concrete mix: first, they affect the quality of the concrete; secondly, they reduce shrinkage of the concrete; and finally, they serve as a filler, for economy.

Aggregates are classified by size: fine aggregate (usually sand) is material 3/16 inches or less in diameter, while coarse aggregate (gravel or crushed stone) varies in size from 1/4 to 1-1/2 inches in diameter. For economy, concrete used in massive structures, such as dams, may contain natural stones or rocks ranging up to six inches in size.

© Professional Study Inc. 2003

The general requirement for natural aggregates is that they should be hard, durable, clean, and free from any harmful matter which would adversely affect the concrete mix. Bank-run gravel aggregates consist of completely rounded shapes that vary in strength, whereas crushed rock aggregates consist of irregular and angular shapes, the strength of which is consistent with the type of rock that is crushed. Irregular or angular-shaped particles are preferred for maximum strength, as water-rounded pebbles may preclude a proper bond with the cement paste. Rounded particles, on the other hand, require less cement paste and improve workability. Most importantly, the grading of aggregates (the distribution of particle sizes) is critical to a proper mix.

A concrete mix is basically composed of large, coarse aggregate particles between which smaller and finer particles are fitted until all the voids in the mixture are as solidly filled as possible. This requires predetermined percentages of particle sizes, implemented by various sieve

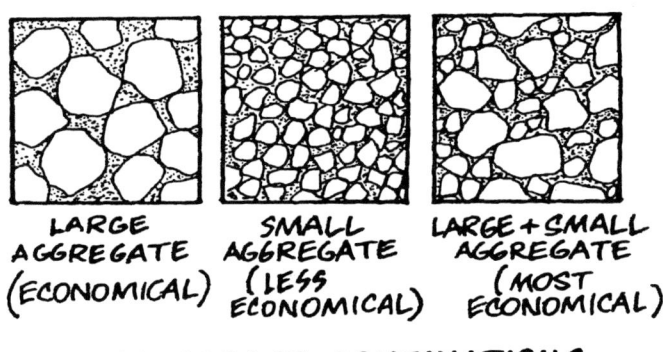

AGGREGATE COMBINATIONS

tests. Ultimately, when the cement paste is added to a well-graded aggregate mixture, each particle is coated with the paste and forever bonded to the adjacent particles.

The aggregate size is generally no greater than 1/4 the thickness of the concrete slab. In reinforced concrete, the aggregate size should not exceed 3/4 of the space between reinforcing bars.

Admixtures are prepared substances which are added to concrete mixes to alter certain characteristics or to achieve some special qualities. Some common admixtures are listed in the table below. In addition to the substances listed, there are also surface applications or finishes for concrete, which include hardeners, pigments, special aggregates, sealers, abrasives, and fillers for patching. (See later discussion on finishes.) The various types of portland cement are normally manufactured with admixtures as part of the cement. The admixtures used are air-entraining agents, accelerators, and retarders.

CONCRETE MIX DESIGN

The proportioning of the ingredients which comprise concrete is referred to as the mix. Since the mix of the concrete must develop sufficient strength (in pounds per square inch) to meet the structural requirements of a building, it is common practice to specify the psi requirements, as for example, 2500 psi for pumped concrete, 3000 psi for controlled concrete, etc. To satisfy these requirements several mixes are prepared and tested which meet the strength requirements and which are durable, workable, and economical.

The unit of measurement for concrete is the cubic foot, and ordinary concrete weighs about 150 pounds per cubic foot. A standard sack of portland cement contains one cubic foot of material which weighs 94 pounds.

Aggregates are measured by either weight or volume (dry sand and gravel weigh about 100 pounds per cubic foot), and water is measured by the gallon, which weighs about 8 pounds.

For small concrete work, the mix is generally expressed by volume. For example, a 1:3:5 mix consists of one part cement, three parts of fine aggregate (sand), and five parts of coarse aggregate (crushed rock or bank-run gravel).

Concrete mix design is governed by the strength and durability required, as well as the workability and economy desired. In this regard, the grading and proportioning of aggregates (discussed earlier) is significant, but perhaps more important is the amount of mixing water used.

The water-cement ratio, which is expressed as the number of gallons of water for each sack of cement, is the major factor controlling concrete strength, and to a large extent, its durability. Maximum strength is obtained by using the minimum amount of water required to complete hydration of the cement, but a mix of this type is too dry and relatively unworkable. Thus, a plastic or workable mix always contains more water than the amount needed to attain maximum strength. In other words, concrete strength decreases as the extra water required for workability increases.

The optimum water-cement ratio provides the minimum amount of cement paste that coats each aggregate particle and fills all voids, while at the same time allows for maximum concrete strength and adequate workability. Incidentally, excess water not only, reduces the concrete's strength and durability, but it also may produce laitance, which is a chalky surface deposit of low strength. If laitance does appear, it must be removed before any new concrete is poured, in order that the new bonds to the old.

Concrete mixes develop a wide range of compressive strength values, depending on their water-cement ratios. For example, a mix using about 72 gallons of water for each sack of cement will develop a compressive strength of about 2000 psi after 28 days. High early strength concrete mixes develop a compressive strength in about 7 days equal to that developed by normal portland cement mixes in 28 days.

TYPE OF ADMIXTURE	INGREDIENTS	PRINCIPAL USE
Accelerators	Calcium chloride	Speed up setting time
Air-entraining agents	Resins, fats, and oils	Resist freezing action
Pigments	Chemical oxides	For permanent coloring
Retarders	Starches, sugars, & acids	Slow down setting time
Waterproofing	Stearate compounds	Decrease water absorption
Workability agents	Powdered silicas & lime	Improve workability

MIXING

Concrete can be mixed by hand, that is, in a batch mixer at the site, but this method is slow, relatively imprecise, and generally not recommended for quantities in excess of a few cubic yards. More commonly, concrete is mixed in a plant and transported to the building site in a special truck designed for that purpose.

Ready mixed concrete is prepared at a central mixing plant and transported to the building site in an agitator truck with a revolving chamber. Ordinarily this type of concrete must be placed within one and a half hours after water is added to the mix. Therefore, jobs using ready mixed concrete are limited to those within a specific radius of the mixing plant.

Transit mixed concrete involves trucks that perform as traveling concrete mixers. The dry materials are mixed at a central plant and placed in a mixer truck that carries a water tank. The mixer continues to revolve the dry mix while en-route to the site; after arrival, water is added, mixed, and the concrete is deposited.

© Professional Study Inc. 2003

FORMWORK

Forms are the molds into which the concrete is placed and held in shape until it has hardened and developed sufficient strength to support its own weight. Formwork may be job constructed or prefabricated units of standard lumber, plywood, metal, fiberboard, paper pulp, or a variety of reinforced synthetics.

STEEL FORMS FOR
WAFFLE PATTERN CEILING

The most important requirement for all formwork is that it be strong enough to support the lateral forces of wet concrete, which, at a weight of 150 pounds per cubic foot, can be considerable. Forms must also be tight so that there will be no significant loss of cement paste. Finally, since the plastic concrete will take on the shape, texture, and peculiarities of the forming material, the choice of formwork should be carefully considered from the stand point of aesthetics.

Form ties are metal devices used to prevent concrete forms from spreading. The location of form ties is an important design factor in wall surface appearance, as shown in the illustrations.

Forms, or parts of forms, are often omitted where there is a firm earth surface capable of supporting or molding the concrete. In most footings, for example, the bottom of the footing is cast directly against the earth (undisturbed earth, not fill or modified soil), and only the sides are molded in forms.

Before concrete is placed, the forms are usually coated with a suitable oil or other material which will prevent water absorption or bond between the form and the concrete. Excessive oiling should be avoided, however, as it may permanently stain the concrete or otherwise interfere with the final concrete finish. It is important
that the oil or other coating material is applied to the forms before setting the steel reinforcement in order to avoid accidental coating of the steel, as this will prevent bonding between the concrete and steel.

© Professional Study Inc. 2003

All formwork is expensive, often representing the major cost of concrete work. For this reason, forms should be designed and constructed so that they are practical to erect, simple to strip, and capable of being reused. In many areas the formwork for large buildings is designed by a structural engineer.

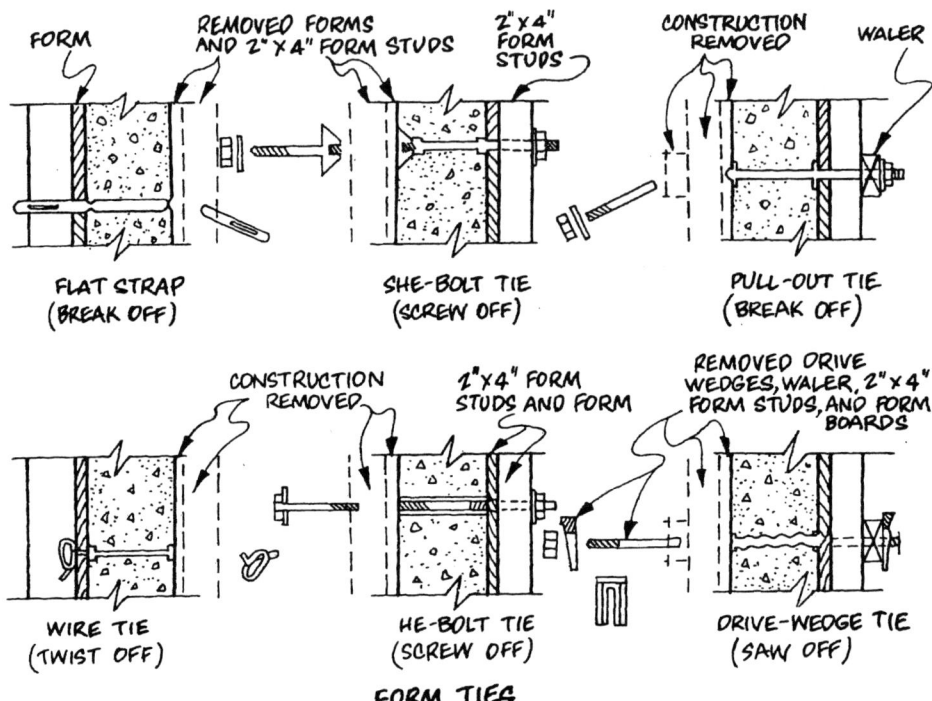

FORM TIES

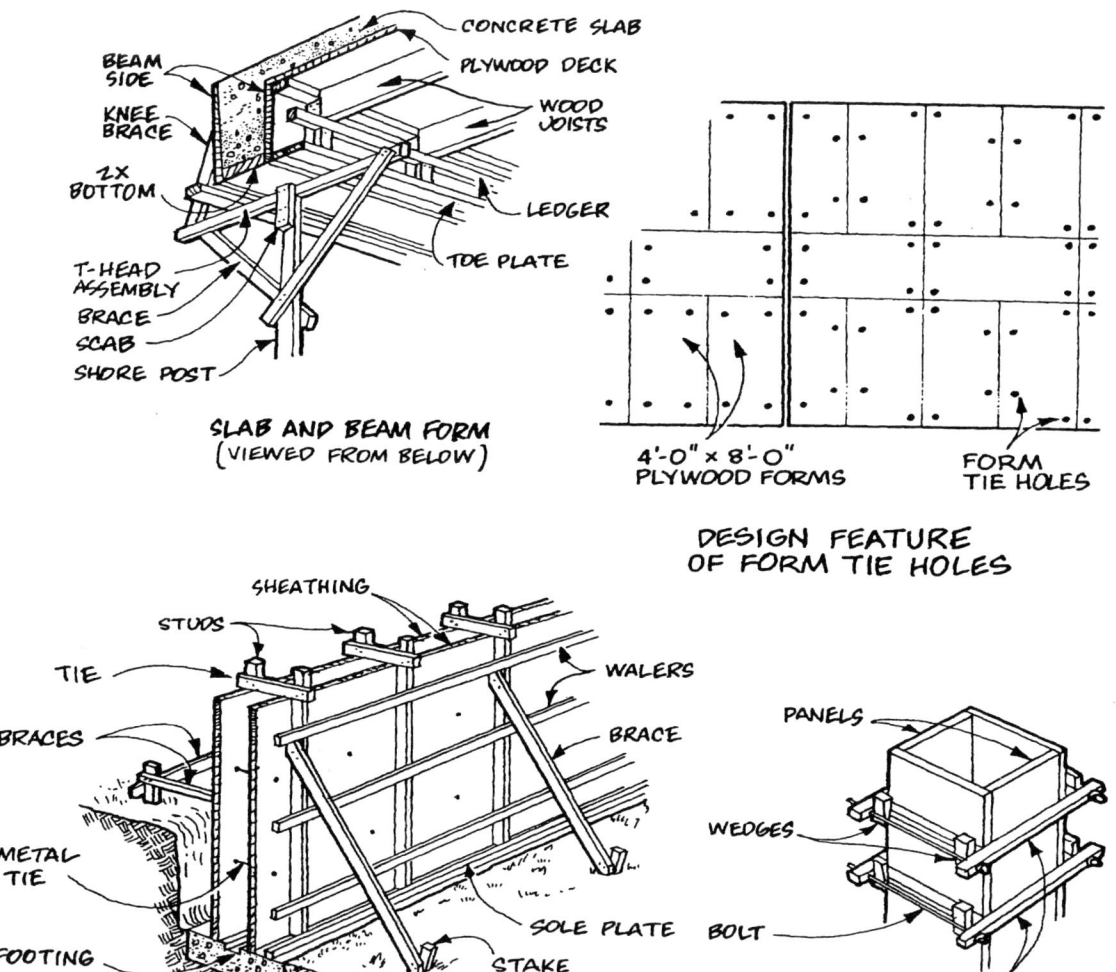

REINFORCED CONCRETE

Concrete is strong in compression, but relatively weak in tension; the reverse is true for the slender steel bars used to reinforce concrete. Thus, when the two materials are used together, one makes up for the deficiency of the other. Reinforced concrete, therefore, is steel embedded in concrete in a manner which exploits the greatest strength of each material.

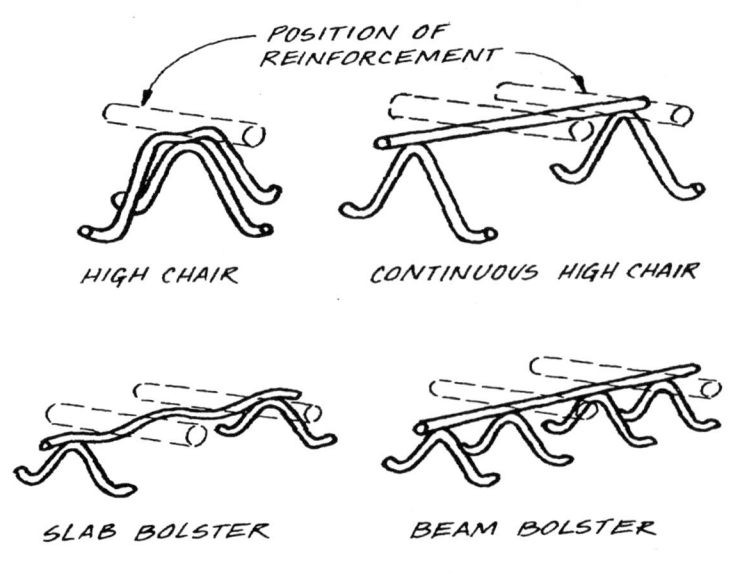

HIGH CHAIR   CONTINUOUS HIGH CHAIR

SLAB BOLSTER   BEAM BOLSTER

REBAR SUPPORT DEVICES

Most reinforcing steel for concrete is in the form of bars or wire mesh. Reinforcing bars are deformed, which means they have regular deformations, or projections, which greatly increases their bond with the concrete. Reinforcing bars are numbered in eighths of an inch, from #3 through #11, #14, and #18. For example, a #5 bar is 5/8" in diameter.

Steel fabric, or wire mesh, is manufactured from cold-drawn steel wires which usually intersect at right angles. This type of reinforcement may be used for floors, walls, roofs, or other large expanses of concrete slab. There are several different types of wire reinforcement; the welded wire mesh, however, is by far the most commonly used.

Reinforcing mesh is designated as follows: WWF6 x 12 - W16 x W26, for example, which indicates woven wire fabric with size 16 longitudinal wires 6" o.c. and size 26 transverse wires 12 o.c.

Wire rope or cable is used extensively in prestressed concrete and is designated as 6x7, for example, which indicates that the rope consists of 6 strands of wire with each strand containing 7 wires each. It is generally zinc-coated for resistance to corrosion. Wire rope is also used for elevators, suspension bridges, and a variety of cable-supported structures.

Steel reinforcement is designed to perform in harmony with the concrete. In this regard, it must be clean, accurately placed, and have a sufficient protective covering of concrete. Before placement, reinforcing steel should be cleaned of all loose rust, oil, mud, paint, or any other foreign matter that might reduce the bond between the bars and the concrete.
Reinforcement may be bent, lapped, spliced, tied, welded, or in many cases, pre-assembled. Column reinforcement, for example, is often completely assembled before being placed within the formwork. The proper placement of reinforcement is usually shown on the structural drawings.

When concrete is poured over a network of steel reinforcement, the pressures may dislodge the complex steel arrangement. Therefore, reinforcement must be held rigidly in place, with sufficient supports and ties, so that the steel will end up in precisely the right location. For this purpose there are a number of devices, such as ties, chairs, and supports, that are used to hold reinforcing steel in its exact location.

Once embedded in the concrete, steel reinforcement must be adequately protected from any harmful substances which might penetrate the concrete and corrode the steel. Thus, footings should have at least three inches of concrete between the steel and the ground; retaining walls require 2 inches of protection; beams and columns, 1/ inches; and slabs, 3/4 inch.

LIGHTWEIGHT CONCRETE

Lightweight concrete is commonly a mixture in which the normal heavy aggregates are replaced with lightweight aggregates. There are, however, two other types of lightweight concrete: aerated concrete and no-fines concrete. The aerated mixture is formed by introducing air or gas into a matrix of cement, while the no-fines mixture is made by omitting the fine aggregate, which creates voids in the concrete.

All lightweight concretes have superior thermal insulation and fire resistive properties. In addition, they are easier to handle, require less complex supporting structures, and are easier to cut and nail into. On the other hand, lightweight concrete lacks the compressive strength of normal concrete. It is well suited, however, to situations where strength is of secondary concern.

The strength and weight of lightweight concrete varies with the type of aggregate used. Some common aggregates used are expanded shale, expanded slag, expanded clay, pumice, vermiculite, and perlite.

The major use of lightweight concrete is on floors and roofs for acoustic and thermal control, on roofs to slope water to roof drains, and for precast concrete planks where loads are moderate.

PLACEMENT OF CONCRETE

Prior to placing concrete, trenches and formwork should be thoroughly cleaned out, reinforcement should be checked for position, and the forms should be wetted, if that is required. Concrete may be placed by spouts or chutes, it may be pumped, it may be placed pneumatically (gunite), or it may even be deposited under water with the use of a tremie.

In any event, the material must be placed evenly, continuously, and - most essentially - in a manner that avoids segregation of the aggregates.

Concrete should be placed as close as possible to its final location. A load of concrete should not be dumped at one point and permitted to flow over long distances, as this will lead of concrete results in greater density, homogeneity, durability, and a more complete contact with the reinforcing. Vibration also allows the use of stiffer mixes with a reduced cement content. It does not, however, make the concrete stronger.

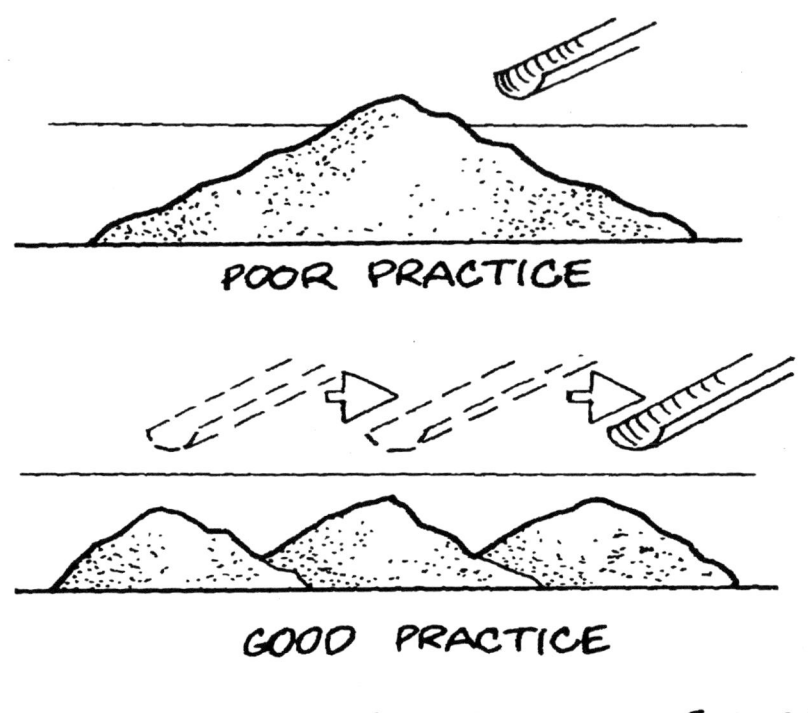

PLACING CONCRETE IN FORMS

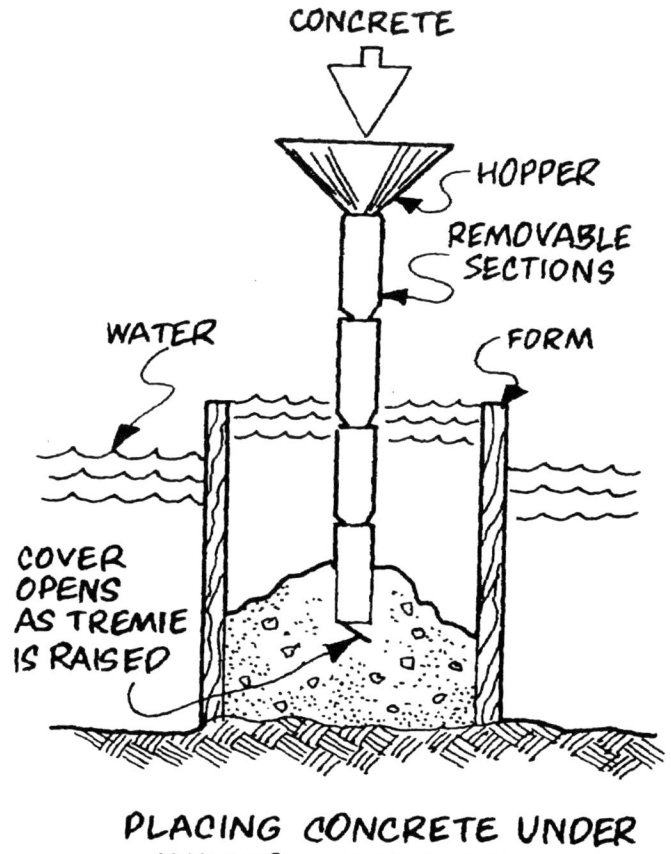

PLACING CONCRETE UNDER WATER WITH A TREMIE

to the segregation of water and fine particles from the rest of the mass.

Dropping the mixture from excessive heights will also cause it to separate. Vertical drops should generally be limited to four feet.

When concrete is placed, air bubbles are frequently trapped in the body of the mixture. If allowed to remain, these air bubbles will produce a honeycomb effect which can cause a substantial reduction in concrete strength, as well as an unsightly finish. To eliminate this condition, concrete is compacted, or consolidated by hand tools or by use of mechanical vibrators. The formwork can be vibrated externally, or vibrators can be immersed in the mix itself. Vibration of concrete results in greater density, homogeneity, durability, and a more complete contact with the reinforcing. Vibration also allows the use of stiffer mixes with a reduced cement content. It does not, however, make the concrete stronger.

Concrete may be placed during almost any weather condition, but special methods and procedures are required during both extremes of hot and cold weather. Concrete must not be allowed to dry out too rapidly or to freeze.

TESTING

In order to be certain that a particular concrete mix is everything it is supposed to be, there are several tests that may be performed on mixed concrete. Among the most common of these are the slump test and the cylinder test.

The slump test measures the consistency and workability of the mix and is usually performed in the field.

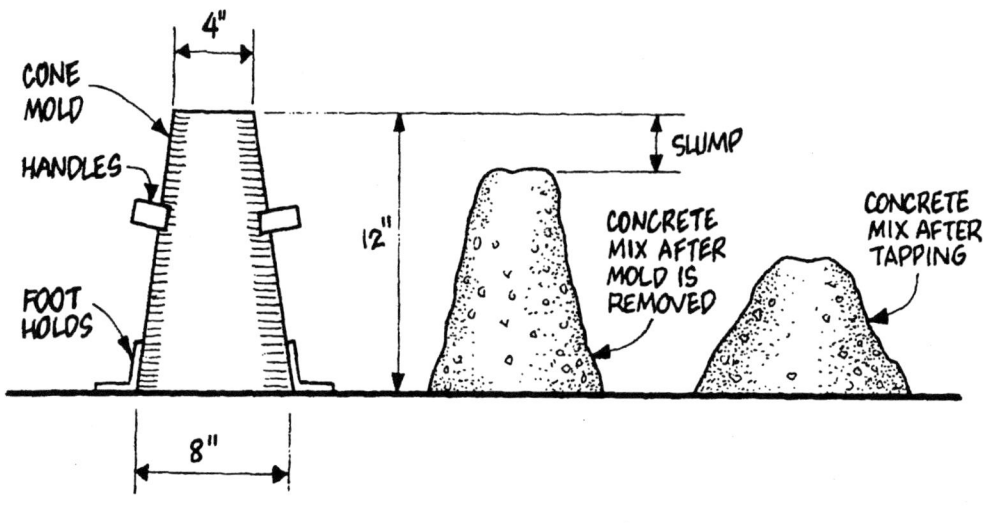

PROCEDURE FOR SLUMP TEST

The test employs a standard slump cone mold which is set on a level surface and filled with 4-inch layers of concrete taken directly from the mixer. Each layer in the mold is rodded and finally leveled, at which point the mold is carefully lifted and the wet concrete is permitted to slump. The mold is then placed alongside the slumped concrete and the difference in height measured directly. Three to four inches of slump is generally acceptable, one inch of slump indicates a stiff, impractical mixture, and a slump of six inches or more represents a loose, too wet mixture.

After the measurement is completed, the side of the concrete is tapped gently to determine the workability or placeability of the mix. A well proportioned mix will merely slump lower, while a mix of an improper amount of sand will segregate or crumble.

The cylinder test measures the compressive strength of concrete and utilizes test cylinders 6 inches in diameter and 12 inches long. From

each batch of concrete, at least two cylinders are cast, laboratory-cured for 7 and 28 days, and tested in a crushing machine. If the cylinders fail to attain the specified strength, cores may be cut from the actual job and tested for compression.

The air-entraining test is another investigation that measures the air content of a concrete mix using a special testing instrument.

CURING

Hydration is the chemical reaction that takes place as concrete hardens. It continues for a long period and results in a gradual increase in the strength of concrete. Hydration requires the presence of moisture, and the process called curing is designed to prevent surface evaporation of water for the first five to seven days after the concrete is poured.

Concrete may be cured in the following ways:

1. By supplying additional moisture (occasional spraying)
2. By covering with sand, burlap or straw which is kept moist
3. By covering with a membrane or curing compound that prevents evaporation.

The most favorable temperature for curing concrete is between 50 and 70 degrees F. The chemical reaction of hydration generates internal heat in the concrete, and this must always be considered. Extremes of cold or heat may produce expansion or shrinkage cracking, unless precautions are taken during the curing process. During periods of very cold weather, an entire poured building section can be enclosed with plastic sheets, heated, and kept moist until cured.

Forms that are left in place will aid in the curing of the concrete: however, if the formwork is to be re-used, it must be stripped as soon as possible after the concrete is capable of supporting its own weight.

CONCRETE JOINTS

Construction joints are the horizontal or vertical lines formed between two successive concrete pours. These lines exist whenever concreting is interrupted, or when new concrete is placed against old. Joints should be straight, and their form and position should be designed carefully.

To insure the maximum bond between old and new pours, the old surface should be roughened, cleaned and wetted before placing the new concrete. In many cases reinforcing rods are used to help connect the new and previously poured concrete. Construction joints always remain planes of weakness, and therefore, they should be located at sections of minimum shear.

Expansion joints are designed to allow free movement of adjacent parts due to expansion or contraction of the concrete. This movement may be caused by shrinkage or changes in temperature. Expansion joints are planes of complete separation that extend through a structure, from the top of the footings to the roof. They are waterproof, weather tight, and generally filled with an elastic joint filler. The placement and size of joints is a function of the size of the building and the maximum expected temperature differential.

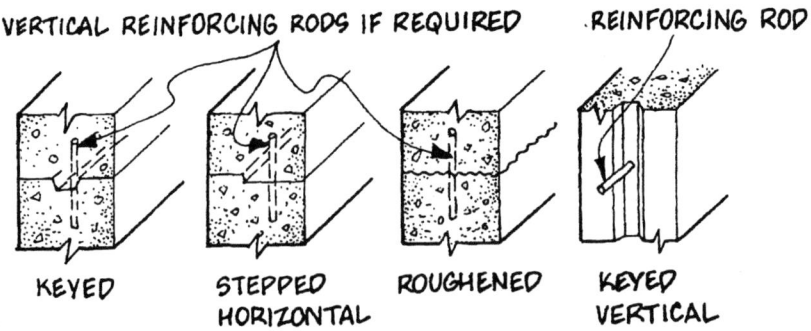

CONCRETE CONSTRUCTION JOINTS

Expansion joints are required in buildings over 200 feet long, at joints of building wings, and at additions to existing buildings.

Control joints are tooled, sawed, or pre-molded joints installed to allow for the shrinkage of large concrete areas. Control joints create a weakened section that induces cracking to occur along the joint, rather than in a random fashion.

Isolation joints provide a separation of one concrete section from another so that each can move independently. Isolation joints are commonly used in floors at columns, footings, and at junctions between floors and walls.

CONCLUSION:

The above information will not be asked on the DSA Certification exams, however as an inspector you will be expected to have a working knowledge of concrete, and it's uses. Therefore we suggest that you study the material.

Chapter 7: Concrete
LESSON 7.2: Foundations and Retaining Walls
(Title 24, Part 2, Volume 2, Chapter 18A)

This chapter is very closely related to Chapter 19A which is the main chapter on concrete. The most important thing to remember about this material are the different types of foundations that are used and what the issues are.

Pay particular attention to the following:

1. Sec. 1806A.4 Stepped Foundations,
2. 1806A.6 Foundation Plates or Sills,
3. 1806A.11 Pipes and Trenches,
4. 1809A.6 and 1809A.7 Piles and Caissons respectively.

These are the most critical parts of this chapter for the DSA inspector.

The most important thing to know is that DSA is very strict on structural issues and as a consequence these same issues will be represented on the certification exams.

Read through the following highlighting list and study these materials.

© Professional Study Inc. 2003

**Highlighting List
Foundations and Retaining Walls**
(Title 24, Part 2, Volume 2, Chapter 18A)

Take out your code book and highlight the code sections as they appear on this list in either red or yellow.

The "**Commentary**" on the right is broken down into four categories and they are as follows:

1. **TEST QUESTION (Highlight in Red)**
   - (Indicates that this material is very likely to be specifically referenced on the DSA exams)

2. **REMEMBER (Highlight in Yellow)**
   - (Indicates that you should know this material and that it is relevant to your work as an inspector)

3. **BEWARE (Highlight in Yellow)**
   - (Indicates that there is something that may not be apparent at first but that the inspector will have to deal with)

4. **SEE ALSO (Highlight in Yellow)**
   - (Indicates that there is another code section that affects this information)

Chapter 18A *[For DSA/SS]*
FOUNDATIONS AND RETAINING WALLS
Division I. GENERAL

SECTION 1806A. FOOTINGS

1806A.1 General............

The horizontal dimensions of unformed concrete footings shall be increased 1 inch (25 mm) at every vertical surface at which concrete is placed directly against the soil.

> **Comment:** TEST QUESTION
> This means that all trenches for footings should be 2" wider than the plans call for to make up for unevenness of the dirt.

1806A.3 Bearing Walls............

Where a design is not provided, the minimum foundation requirements for stud bearing walls shall be as set forth in Table 18A-I-C.

1806A.4 Stepped Foundations. Foundations for all buildings where the surface of the ground slopes more than 1 unit vertical in 10 units **horizontal (10% slope)** shall be level or shall be stepped so that both top and bottom of such foundation are level.

> **Comment:** TEST QUESTION
> Step footings when they exceed 10% slope.

1806A.5.5 Foundation elevation. On graded sites, the top of any exterior foundation shall extend above the elevation of the street gutter at point of discharge or the inlet of an approved drainage device a minimum of 12 inches (305 mm) plus 2 percent. The building official may approve alternate elevations, provided it can be demonstrated that required drainage to the point of discharge and away from the structure is provided at all locations on the site.

1806A.6 Foundation Plates or Sills.

1806A.6.1 [For DSA/SS] Sills under bearing or shear walls shall be bolted as required by Section 2320A.6. Wood plates or sills shall be bolted to the foundation or foundation wall. Steel bolts with a minimum nominal diameter of 1/2 inch (12.7 mm) shall be used in Seismic Zones 0 through 3. Steel bolts with a minimum nominal diameter of 5/8 inch (16 mm) shall be used in Seismic Zone 4.

> **Comment:** TEST QUESTION
> No ½" Sill plate bolts
> Minimume 5/8" diameter bolts in Zone 4 for bearing walls.

Bolts shall be embedded at least 7 inches (178 mm) into the concrete or masonry and shall be spaced not more than 4 feet (1829 mm) apart. There shall be a minimum of two bolts per piece with one bolt located not more than 9 inches from ends

> **Comment:** TEST QUESTION
> ANCHOR BOLT REQUIREMENTS:
>   Min. 7" Embedment
>   Max. 4'-0" apart
>   Max. 9" from ends of a piece of sill plate
>   Minimum (2) bolts per piece

1806A.7.1 Foundations with stemwalls. Foundations with stemwalls shall be provided with a minimum of one No. 4 bar at the top of the wall and one No. 4 bar at the bottom of the footing

> **Comment:** TEST QUESTION
> *Minimum #4 rebar Top and Bottom in any footing.

1806A.7.2 Slabs-on-ground with turned-down footings. Slabs-on-ground with turned-down footings shall have a minimum of one No. 4 bar at the top and bottom.

> **EXCEPTION:** For slabs-on-ground cast monolithically with a footing, one No. 5 bar may be located at either the top or bottom.

1806A.8.3 Backfill.

1. Backfill shall be of concrete with an ultimate strength of 2,000 pounds per square inch (13.79 MPa) at 28 days. The hole shall not be less than 4 inches (102 mm) larger than the diameter of the column at its bottom or 4 inches (102 mm) larger than the diagonal dimension of a square or rectangular column.

2. Backfill shall be of clean sand......... in layers not more than 8 inches (203 mm) in depth.

> **Comment:** REMEMBER
> No rocks in backfill

1806A.11 Pipes and Trenches. Unless otherwise recommended by the soils report, open or backfilled trenches parallel with a footing shall not be below a plane having a downward slope of 1 unit vertical to 2 units horizontal (50% slope) from a line 9 inches (229 mm) above the bottom edge of the footing, and not closer than 18 inches (457 mm) from the face of such footing.
Where pipes cross under footings, the footings shall be specially designed. Pipe sleeves shall be provided where pipes cross through footings or footing walls and sleeve clearances shall provide for possible footing settlement, but not less than 1 inch (25 mm) all around pipe.

> **Comment:** TEST QUESTION
> See Figure 7.2.1

Figure 7.2.1

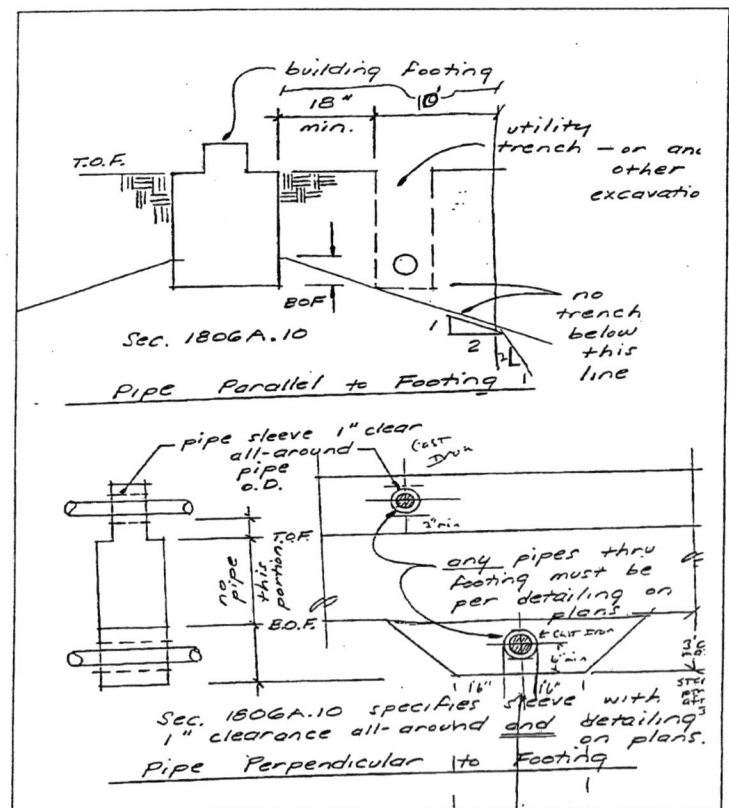

1807A.2 Interconnection. Individual pile caps and caissons of every structure subjected to seismic forces shall be interconnected by ties

> **Comment:** REMEMBER
> Refers to grade beams.

SECTION 1808A. SPECIFIC PILE REQUIREMENTS

1808A.2 Uncased Cast-in-place Concrete Piles.

1808A.2.1 Material.

The length of such pile shall be limited to not more than 30 times the average diameter.

> **Comment:** REMEMBER
> Caissons & Piles are limited to 30 times the diameter

EXCEPTION: The length of pile may exceed 30 times the diameter provided the design and installation of the pile foundation is in accordance with an approved investigation report.

TABLE 18A-I-C—FOUNDATIONS FOR STUD BEARING WALLS—MINIMUM REQUIREMENTS[1, 2, 3, 4]

NUMBER OF FLOORS SUPPORTED BY THE FOUNDATION[4]	THICKNESS OF FOUNDATION WALL (inches) × 25.4 for mm		WIDTH OF FOOTING (inches)	THICKNESS OF FOOTING (inches)	DEPTH BELOW UNDISTURBED GROUND SURFACE (inches)
	Concrete	Unit Masonry	× 25.4 for mm		
1	6	6	12	6	12
2	8	8	15	7	18
3	10	10	18	8	24

[1] Where unusual conditions or frost conditions are found, footings and foundations shall be as required in Section 1806A.1.
[2] The ground under the floor may be excavated to the elevation of the top of the footing.
[3] Not adopted by the State of California.
[4] Foundations may support a roof in addition to the stipulated number of floors. Foundations supporting roofs only shall be as required for supporting one floor.

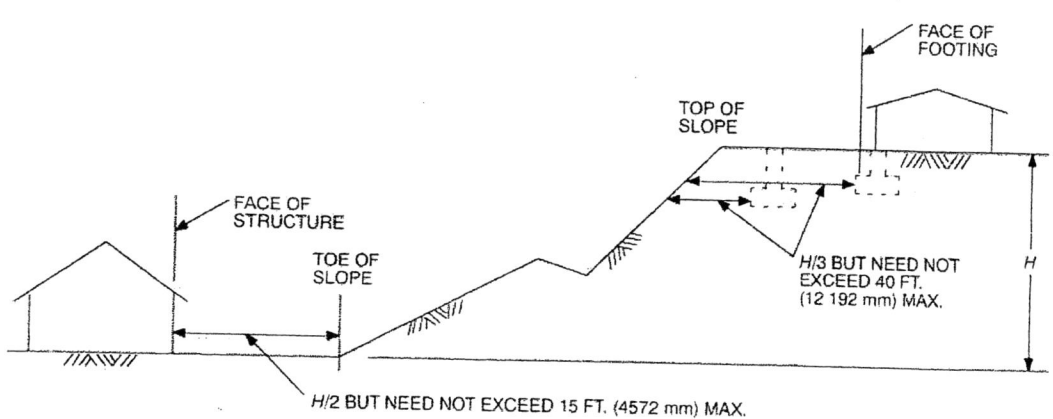

FIGURE 18A-I-1—SETBACK DIMENSIONS

Chapter 7
LESSON 7.3: Concrete
(Title 24, Part 2, Volume 2, Chapter 19A)
(Sections 1901A – 1906A)

This chapter is perhaps the most important with respect to the DSA inspector. Many questions on the certification exams will be drawn from the concrete chapter. The following in is a brief synopsis of the important sections of this chapter and the information covered:

Section 1903A: Specifications for Tests and Materials
- Covers aggregate size, reinforcement standards and testing, and admixtures

Section 1904A: Durability Requirements
- Covers exposure in extreme conditions and what should be done (freezing etc.)

Section 1905A: Concrete Quality, Mixing and Placing
- Pay attention to 1905A.6.1 Frequency of testing. This will be on the exam.
- Also covered are Standards for placing and quality control of concrete. This is very important to the inspector since you are the quality control on the job.

Section 1906: Formwork Embedded Pipes and Construction Joints
- Pay attention to the standards for removal of forms, spacing and sizing of pipes embedded in concrete, and the location (approval of location) for control joints.

Read through the following highlighting list and study these materials.
The next lesson will contain the remaining sections of the concrete chapter.

© Professional Study Inc. 2003

Highlighting List
Foundations and Retaining Walls
(Title 24, Part 2, Volume 2, Chapter 18A)

Take out your code book and highlight the code sections as they appear on this list in either red or yellow.

The "**Commentary**" on the right is broken down into four categories and they are as follows:

1. **TEST QUESTION (Highlight in Red)**
   - (Indicates that this material is very likely to be specifically referenced on the DSA exams)

2. **REMEMBER (Highlight in Yellow)**
   - (Indicates that you should know this material and that it is relevant to your work as an inspector)

3. **BEWARE (Highlight in Yellow)**
   - (Indicates that there is something that may not be apparent at first but that the inspector will have to deal with)

4. **SEE ALSO (Highlight in Yellow)**
   - (Indicates that there is another code section that affects this information)

© Professional Study Inc. 2003

Highlight List (T-24, Part 2, Ch.19A)
Chapter 19A [For DSA/SS & OSHPD 1 & 4]
CONCRETE

SECTION 1903A. SPECIFICATIONS FOR TESTS AND MATERIALS

1903A.1 Tests of Materials.

1903A.1.1 The *enforcement agency* may require the testing of any materials used in concrete construction to determine if materials are of quality specified.

1903A.3.2.1 [For DSA/SS] The nominal maximum size of coarse aggregate shall not be larger than:
1. One fifth the narrowest dimension between sides of forms, or
2. One third the depth of slabs, or
3. Three fourths the minimum clear spacing between individual reinforcing bars or wires, bundles of bars, or pre-stressing tendons or ducts.

> **Comment: TEST QUESTION**
> Limits on the size of aggregate, are triggered by any of these conditions

These limitations may be waived if, in the judgment of the *structural engineer and the enforcement agency,*

Section 1912A.13.2.
Reinforcement shall be deformed reinforcement, except that plain reinforcement may be used for spirals or tendons, and reinforcement consisting of structural steel,

If mill test reports are not available, chemical analysis shall be made of bars representative of the bars to be welded. Bars with a carbon equivalent (C.E.) above 0.75 shall not be welded. Welding shall not be done on or within two bar diameters of any bent portion of a bar that has been bent cold. Welding of crossing bars shall not be permitted for assembly of reinforcement unless authorized by the structural engineer and approved by the enforcement agency per approved procedures.

> **Comment: REMEMBER**
> Weldable rebar is A706 rebar and must be marked as such. Look for the 'W' that indicates A706

> **Comment: SEE ALSO**
> SECTION 1929A.12

1903A.6 Admixtures.

1903A.6.1 Admixtures to be used in concrete shall be subject to prior approval by the *enforcement agency.*

> **Comment: REMEMBER**
> All admixtures should be approved by DSA which is done through the approval of a Mix Design

1903A.6.3 Calcium chloride or admixtures containing chloride from other than impurities from admixture ingredients shall not be used in pre-stressed concrete, in concrete containing embedded aluminum, or in concrete cast against stay-in-place galvanized steel forms. See Sections 1904A.3.2 and 1904A.4.1.

> **Comment: BEWARE**
> Calcium Chloride often referred to as 'CC' is a red flag and should be avoided. It is sometimes requested by the finishers to make their job easier. This material must be pre-approved for use in concrete.

1903A.6.6 Fly ash or other pozzolan can be used as a partial substitute for ASTM 150 portland cement, as follows:

> *2. More than 15 percent by weight of fly ash or other pozzolans shall be permitted to be substituted for ASTM C 150 portland cement if the mix design is proportioned by Method B or C. See Section 1904A for durability requirements.*

> **Comment: REMEMBER**
> 15% Maximum Flyash. This will generally be caught in the Mix Design approval process but may be overlooked by the design professional.

1904A.2 Freezing and Thawing Exposures.

© Professional Study Inc. 2003

1904A.2.1 Normal-weight and lightweight concrete exposed to freezing and thawing or deicing chemicals shall be air entrained with air content indicated in Table 19A-A-1.

1904A.2.2 Concrete that will be subjected to the exposures given in Table 19A-A-2 s

1904A.3.2 Calcium chloride as an admixture shall not be used in concrete to be exposed to severe or very severe sulfate-containing solutions, as defined in Table 19A-A-4.

SECTION 1905A. CONCRETE QUALITY, MIXING AND PLACING

1905A.2.3 Concrete specified by compressive strength shall be proportioned by one of the following methods:

> Comment: REMEMBER
> No 3/8" Pea Gravel Mixes are allow for structural work without DSA approval.
> Maximum 0.62 Gal/Lbs Water/Cer ratio for 3000psi concrete. This ma useful when contemplating adding in the middle of a batched concrete

1905A.6.1 Frequency of testing.

1905A.6.1.1 Samples for strength tests of each class of concrete placed each day shall be taken not less than once a day, or not less than once for each *50 cubic yards (345*m3) of concrete, or not less than once for each *2,000* square feet *(186* m2) of surface area for slabs or walls. *Additional samples for seven-day compressive strength tests shall be taken for each class of concrete at the beginning of the concrete work or whenever the mix or aggregate is changed.*

> Comment: TEST QUESTION
> (1) 1 Set of 2 sample cylinders per cyds delivered or 2000SF of Slab o Wall.
> (2) 1 Extra cylinder for a 7 day tes the first day of any mix design

1905A.6.1.2 On a given project, if the total volume of concrete is such that the frequency of testing required by Section 1905A.6.1.1 would provide less than five strength tests for a given class of concrete, tests shall be made from at least five randomly selected batches or from each batch if fewer than five batches are used.

> Comment: REMEMBER
> This is an obscure code requiremen is rarely adhered to and would only to a small job. However, it may be necessary to take samples from eve truck delivered according to this se

1905A.6.1.4 A strength test shall be the average of the strengths of two cylinders made from the same sample of concrete and tested at 28 days or at test age designated for determination of f_c.

> Comment: REMEMBER
> Definition of a Strength Test, (2) sa cylinders

1905A.6.2.3 Strength level of an individual class of concrete shall be considered satisfactory if both the following requirements are met

1. Average *of all sets* of any three consecutive strength tests equals or exceeds f_c.
2. No individual strength test (average of two cylinders) falls below f_c by more than 500 psi (3.45 MPa).

> Comment: TEST QUESTION
> f_c Is the designation for the des strength of concrete.

1905A.6.4 Investigation of low-strength test results.

1905A.6.4.4 Concrete in an area represented by core tests shall be considered structurally adequate if the *average* of three cores is equal to at least 85 percent of f_c and if no single core is less than 75 percent of f_c.

> Comment: TEST QUESTION
> This may be asked in several differe ways but has been on the test in the

1905A.7.1 Preparation before concrete placement shall include the following:

1. All equipment for mixing and transporting concrete shall be clean.

> Comment: REMEMBER
> All of these criteria are important ar should be familiar with them in case is a question related to any one of th

2. All debris and ice shall be removed from spaces to be occupied by concrete
3. Forms shall be properly coated.
4. Masonry filler units that will be in contact with concrete shall be well drenched.
5. Reinforcement shall be thoroughly clean of ice or other deleterious coatings.
6. Water shall be removed from place of deposit before concrete is placed unless a tremie is to be used or unless otherwise permitted by the *enforcement agency*.
7. All laitance and other unsound material shall be removed before additional concrete is placed against hardened concrete.
8. Concrete shall not be placed until the forms and reinforcement have been inspected, all preparations for the placement have been completed, and the preparations have been checked by the project inspector, all subject to the observation of the structural engineer or architect.

1905A.8 Mixing.

5. A detailed record shall be kept to identify:
5.1 Number of batches produced;
5.2 Proportions of materials used;
5.3 Approximate location of final deposit in structure;
5.4 Time and date of mixing and placing.

1905A.10.4 Retempered concrete or concrete that has been re-mixed after initial set shall not be used unless approved by the *enforcement official*

1905A.10.5 After concreting is started, it shall be carried on as a continuous operation until placing of a panel or section, as defined by its boundaries or predetermined joints, is completed,

1905A.10.9 In depositing concrete in columns, walls or thin sections of considerable height, openings in forms, elephant trunks, tremies or other approved devices shall be used that will permit the concrete to be placed in a manner that will prevent segregation and accumulations of hardened concrete on the forms or metal reinforcement above the level of the concrete. Unless otherwise approved by the enforcement agency, the unconfined vertical drop of concrete from the end of such devices to the placement surface shall not be greater than 6 feet (1829 mm).

1906A.1.2 Forms shall be substantial and sufficiently tight to prevent leakage of mortar.

1906A.2.1 Removal of forms. Forms shall be removed in such a manner as not to impair safety and serviceability of the structure. Concrete to be exposed by form removal shall have sufficient strength not to be damaged by removal operation. *No portion of the forming and shoring system may be removed less than 12 hours after placing.* When stripping time is less than the specified curing time, measures shall be taken to provide adequate curing and thermal protection of the stripped concrete.

1906A.2.2.1 Before starting construction, the contractor shall develop a procedure and schedule for removal of shores and installation of reshores and for calculating the loads transferred to the structure during the process.

> **Comment:** TEST QUESTION
> You should be aware of the concrete placement records that are required to be kept by the project inspector
> SEE ALSO
> Part 1, Administrative Code 4-342 / 6

> **Comment:** BEWARE
> Retempered concrete in structural applications is a big no no and is very unlikely to be approved.
> Puddling and Stacking of concrete are also prohibited.

> **Comment:** REMEMBER
> Construction Joints must be pre-approved and on the plans, therefore if the contractor wants to cut the work off at a certain location it must be on the plans.

> **Comment:** TEST QUESTION
> 6' Max drop for concrete otherwise the contractor must use a tremie.

> **Comment:** TEST QUESTION
> This section applies to all forms though sometimes some forms are removed in order to finish the work properly. When in doubt go with this requirement.

> **Comment:** BEWARE
> Shoring and reshoring may be required to be designed by an engineer

3. Sufficient strength shall be demonstrated by structural analysis considering proposed loads, strength of forming and shoring system and concrete strength data. Concrete strength data may be based on tests of field-cured cylinders or, when approved by the *enforcement agency*, on other procedures to evaluate concrete strength.

Comment: REMEMBER
When concrete samples are taken b that enough are made so that at leas broken at 28 days and others are us determine the strength for removal forms.
The Design professional must deter the strength at which removal of fo may by undertaken.

1906A.3 Conduits and Pipes Embedded in Concrete.

1906A.3.1 Conduits, pipes and sleeves of any material not harmful to concrete and within limitations of this subsection **may be embedded in concrete with approval of the** *enforcement agency*, provided they are not considered to replace structurally the displaced concrete.

Comment: REMEMBER
Embedment of pipes must be detail the contract documents.
Sleeves must be provided generally around.

1906A.3.5.1 They shall not be larger in outside dimension than one third the overall thickness of slab, wall or beam in which they are embedded.

Comment: TEST QUESTION
Maximum pipe diameter 1/3 thickn slab or wall.

1906A.3.5.2 They shall be spaced not closer than three diameters or widths on center.

Comment: TEST QUESTION
Minimum spacing of pipes 3 diame center to center.

1906A.3.6.2 They are of uncoated or galvanized iron or steel not thinner than standard **Schedule 40 steel pipe.**

1906A.3.10 Concrete cover for pipes, conduit and fittings shall not be less than 1 1/2 inches (38 mm) for concrete exposed to earth or weather, or less than 3/4 inch (19 mm) for concrete not exposed to weather or in contact with ground.

Comment: TEST QUESTION
Miniumum cover exposed to weath 1/2" and ¾" not exposed to weather

1906A.3.13 Openings larger than 12 inches (305 mm) in any dimension shall be detailed on the structural plans. Nothing in this section shall be construed to permit work in violation of fire and panic or other safety standards.

Comment: TEST QUESTION
Openings larger that 12" in concrete be detailed on the plans.

1906A.4.3 Construction joints shall be so made and located as not to impair the strength of the structure *as determined by the structural engineer and shall conform to the typical details. Typical details and proposed locations of construction joints shall be indicated on the plans.*

Comment: TEST QUESTION
Construction Joint locations must al on the plans

1906A.4.7 The surface of all horizontal construction joints shall be cleaned and roughened by removing the entire surface and exposing clean aggregate solidly embedded in mortar **matrix.** *¼" exposed*

Comment: TEST QUESTION
Minimum ¼" Matrix at construction joints in concrete to concrete conne

Chapter 7: CONCRETE
LESSON 7.4

Concrete
(Title 24, Part 2, Volume 2, Chapter 19A)
(Sections 1907A – 1929A)

This part of chapter 19A is the most important for you to know in the code book. The following is a brief synopsis of each important section and what you should pay particular attention to:

Section 1907A: Details of Reinforcement
- This section will tell you what the tolerances are for the placement of steel reinforcement, the amount of concrete cover in any particular situation, and some other details that relate to the placement of the reinforcement.

Section 1911A: Look at Section 1911A.7.9 regarding meeting existing concrete w/ new.

Section 1912A: Development and Splices of Reinforcement
- This information will often be on the plans, however it is important for the inspector to know what limitations there are on splices. Most of this section is for engineers, but there are some things from it that are very important to the inspector. See the highlighting list that follows.

Section 1914A: Walls
- Covers conditions that at unique to walls. Pay particular attention to the minimums on reinforcing.

Section 1921A: Reinforced Concrete Structures Resisting Forces Induced by Earthquake Motions
- Pay attention to the requirements for seismic hooks and ties. Know what the difference is between standard and seismic hooks.

Section 1923A: Anchorage to Concrete
- This section covers both expansion anchors and epoxy (chemical anchors). Pay attention to the standards for testing of each type of anchor and the percentages that are required.

Section 1929A: Testing and Inspection
- This is obviously a very important section to the inspector. Be sure you are well versed in the regulations surrounding batch plant inspection and the

waiving of it, cement testing, placing record, and welded rebar. Get a good understanding of all of the different materials / procedures and how they are to be tested etc.

Read through the following highlighting list and study these materials.
The next lesson will contain the remaining sections of the concrete chapter.

Highlighting List
Concrete
(Title 24, Part 2, Volume 2, Chapter 19A)
(Sections 1907A – 1929A)

Take out your code book and highlight the code sections as they appear on this list in either red or yellow.

The "**Commentary**" on the right is broken down into four categories and they are as follows:

1. **TEST QUESTION (Highlight in Red)**
   - (Indicates that this material is very likely to be specifically referenced on the DSA exams)

2. **REMEMBER (Highlight in Yellow)**
   - (Indicates that you should know this material and that it is relevant to your work as an inspector)

3. **BEWARE (Highlight in Yellow)**
   - (Indicates that there is something that may not be apparent at first but that the inspector will have to deal with)

4. **SEE ALSO (Highlight in Yellow)**
   - (Indicates that there is another code section that affects this information)

CONCRETE LESSON 7.4

1907A Reinforcement in Concrete

1907A.1 Standard Hooks. ...Standard hook.. as used in this code is one of the following:

1907A.1.1 One-hundred-eighty-degree bend plus $4d_b$ extension, but not less than 2 1/2 inches (64 mm) at free end of bar.

1907A.1.3 For stirrup and tie hooks:
   1. No. 5 bar and smaller, 90-degree bend plus $6d_b$ extension at free end of bar, or
   2. No. 6, No. 7 and No. 8 bar, 90-degree bend, plus $12d_b$ extension at free end of bar, or
   3. No. 8 bar and smaller, 135-degree bend plus $6d_b$ extension at free end of bar.
   4. For stirrups and tie hooks in Seismic Zones 3 and 4, refer to the hoop and crosstie provisions of Section 1921A.1.

> **Comment:** BEWARE
> In Seismic Zones 3 and 4 refer to 1921A.1 Seismic Hooks (135 degree w/ min 3" extensions or 6 db.
> This applies to practically all work in California.

1907A.2 Minimum Bend Diameters.

1907A.2.1 Diameter of bend measured on the inside of the bar No. 3 through No. 5, shall not be less than the values in Table 19A-B.

1907A.2.2 Inside diameter of bends for stirrups and ties shall not be less than $4d_b$ for No. 5 bar and smaller. For bars larger than No. 5, diameter of bend shall be in accordance with Table 19A-B.

> **Comment:** TEST QUESTION
> SEE REBAR BENDING DIAGRAM

1907A.3 Bending.

1907A.3.1 All reinforcement shall be bent cold, unless otherwise permitted by the *enforcement agency*.

> **Comment:** TEST QUESTION
> Absolutely no heating of rebar for bending

1907A.3.2 Reinforcement partially embedded in concrete shall **not be field bent, except as shown on the design drawings** or permitted by the *enforcement agency*.

> **Comment:** TEST QUESTION
> No field bending unless authorized on plans or specs of approved by DSA

1907A.4 Surface Conditions of Reinforcement.

1907A.4.1 At the time concrete is placed, reinforcement shall be free from mud, oil or other nonmetallic coatings that decrease bond. Epoxy coatings of bars in accordance with Section 1903A.5.3.7 shall be permitted.

> **Comment:** TEST QUESTION
> It's ok to have light rust on rebar. No flaking.

1907A.5 Placing Reinforcement.

1907A.5.2 Unless otherwise *approved by the enforcement agency*, reinforcement, prestressing tendons and prestressing ducts shall be placed within the following tolerances:

© Professional Study Inc. 2003

	TOLERANCE ON d	TOLERANCE ON MINIMUM CONCRETE COVER
$d \leq 8$ in. (203 mm)	$\pm \, ^3/_8$ in. (9.5 mm)	$- \, ^3/_8$ in. (9.5 mm)
$d > 8$ in. (203 mm)	$\pm \, ^1/_2$ in. (12.7 mm)	$- \, ^1/_2$ in. (12.7 mm)

1907A.5.2.2 Tolerance for longitudinal location of bends and ends of reinforcement shall be ± 2 inches (± 51 mm) except at discontinuous ends of members where tolerance shall be ± 1/2 inch (± 12.7 mm).

1907A.6.1 The minimum clear spacing between parallel bars in a layer shall be d_b but not less than 1 inch (25 mm). See also Section 1903A.3.2.

> **Comment:** TEST QUESTION
> Min. Spacing of 1 d_b between bars but never less than 1"

1907A.6.2 Where parallel reinforcement is placed in two or more layers, bars in the upper layers shall be placed directly above bars in the bottom layer with clear distance between layers not less than 1 inch (25 mm).

> **Comment:** TEST QUESTION
> Min. space between layers also 1"

1907A.6.3 In spirally reinforced or tied reinforced compression members, clear distance between longitudinal bars shall not be less than $1.5d_b$ or less than 1 1/2 inches (38 mm). See also Section 1903A.3.2.

> **Comment:** REMEMBER
> This refers to columns with spiral reinforcing between the main rebar.

1907A.6.4 Clear distance limitation between bars shall apply also to the clear distance between a contact lap splice and adjacent splices or bars.

> **Comment:** REMEMBER
> Min 1" Spacing applies to splices also

1907A.6.5 In walls and slabs other than concrete joist construction, primary flexural reinforcement shall not be spaced farther apart than three times the wall or slab thickness, or 18 inches (457 mm).

> **Comment:** TEST QUESTION
> Maximum Spacing of reinforcement in slabs of walls is 18" or 3 times the wall slab thickness.

1907A.6.6 Bundled bars.

1907A.6.6.1 Groups of parallel reinforcing bars bundled in contact to act as a unit shall be limited to four bars in one bundle.

> **Comment:** REMEMBER
> Max number of bars in a bundle is 4

1907A.6.6.2 Bundled bars shall be enclosed within stirrups or ties.

> **Comment:** REMEMBER
> Bundled bars always enclosed in stirrups ties

1907A.6.6.3 Bars larger than No. 11 shall not be bundled in beams.

> **Comment:** REMEMBER
> No. 11 bars are maximum size in bundle

1907A.6.6.4 Individual bars within a bundle terminated within the span of flexural members shall terminate at different points with at least $40d_b$ stagger

> **Comment:** REMEMBER
> Stagger Splices 40 db

1907A.7 Concrete Protection for Reinforcement.

1907A.7.1 Cast-in-place concrete (nonprestressed). The following minimum concrete cover shall be provided for reinforcement:

1. Concrete cast against and permanently exposed to earth 3 (76)
2. Concrete exposed to earth or weather:
   No. 6 through No. 18 bar 2 (51)
   No. 5 bar, W31 or D31 wire, and smaller 1 1/2 (38)
3. Concrete not exposed to weather or in contact with ground:
   Slabs, walls, joists:
   No. 14 and No. 18 bar 1 1/2 (38)
   No. 11 bar and smaller 3/4 (19)
   Beams, columns:
   Primary reinforcement, ties, stirrups, spirals 1 1/2 (38)
   Shells, folded plate members:
   No. 6 bar and larger 3/4 (19)
   No. 5 bar, W31 or D31 wire, and smaller 1/2 (12.7)
4. Concrete tilt-up panels cast against a rigid horizontal surface, such as a concrete slab, exposed to the weather:
   No. 8 and smaller 1 (25)
   No. 9 through No. 18 .... 2 (51)

> **Comment:** TEST QUESTIONS
> Be ready for test questions from this part of the code.
> Concrete cover questions are a favorite on the exam.
> Make sure that you know what any question is asking and what the conditions of the exposure will be before you answer.

1907A.8.1.1 Slope of inclined portion of an offset bar with axis of column shall not exceed 1 in 6

> **Comment:** TEST QUESTION
> Often used for dowels from footings into masonry walls

1907A.8.1.3 Horizontal support at offset bends shall be provided by lateral ties, spirals or parts of the floor construction............ Lateral ties or spirals, if used, shall be placed not more than 6 inches (152 mm) from points of bend.

> **Comment:** REMEMBER
> These connections should be detailed on the plans.

1907A.10 Lateral Reinforcement for Compression Members.

> **Comment:** REMEMBER
> Refers to columns, caissons, piles Etc.

1907A.10.3 It shall be permitted to waive the lateral reinforcement requirements of Sections 1907A.10, 1910A.16 and 1918A.11 where tests and structural analyses show adequate strength and feasibility of construction.

1907A.10.4.2 For cast-in-place construction, size of spirals shall not be less than 3/8-inch (9.5 mm) diameter.

> **Comment:** REMEMBER
> Min. #3 rebar for spirals

1907A.10.4.3 Clear spacing between spirals shall not exceed 3 inches (76 mm) or be less than 1 inch (25 mm). See also Section 1903A.3.2.

> **Comment:** TEST QUESTION
> Minimum Spacing 1"
> Maximum Spacing 3"

1907A.10.4.5 Splices in spiral reinforcement shall be lap splices of $48d_b$, but not less than 12 inches (305 mm) or welded.

> **Comment:** TEST QUESTION
> Spiral Splices Minimum 48 db or 12" min.

© Professional Study Inc. 2003

1907A.10.5 Ties.

1907A.10.5.1 All nonprestressed bars shall be enclosed by lateral ties, at least No. 3 in size for longitudinal bars No. 10 or smaller, and at least No. 4 in size for Nos. 11, 14 and 18 and bundled longitudinal bars. Deformed wire or welded wire fabric of equivalent area shall be permitted.

> **Comment:** TEST QUESTION
> Ties Minimum #3 bars for #10 & #4 No. 11 and larger

1907A.10.5.2 Vertical spacing of ties shall not exceed 16 longitudinal bar diameters, 48 tie bar or wire diameters, or least dimension of the compression member.

> **Comment:** TEST QUESTION
> Max Tie Spacing Main Bar bd, 48 db diameters, or the least dimension of tl member

1907A.10.5.4 Ties shall be located vertically not more than one half a tie spacing above the top of footing or slab in any story and shall be spaced as provided herein to not more than one half a tie spacing below the lowest horizontal reinforcement *in members supported above.*

> **Comment:** REMEMBER
> 1/2 a tie dimension for the top and fro bottom

1907A.10.5.5 Where beams or brackets frame from four directions into a column, termination of ties not more than 3 inches (76 mm) below reinforcement in shallowest of such beams or brackets shall be permitted.

1907A.10.5.6 Column ties shall have hooks as specified in Sections 1907A.1.3,

1907A.11 Lateral Reinforcement for Flexural Members.

> **Comment:** REMEMBER
> Flexural Members are beams, grade be etc.

1907A.11.1 Compression reinforcement in beams shall be enclosed by ties or stirrups satisfying the size and spacing limitations in Section 1907A.10.5

1907A.11.2 Lateral reinforcement for flexural framing members subject to stress reversals or to torsion at supports shall consist of closed ties, closed stirrups, or spirals extending around the flexural reinforcement.

1907A.12.2.2 Shrinkage and temperature reinforcement shall be spaced not farther apart than five times the slab thickness, or 18 inches (457 mm).

> **Comment:** BEWARE
> Temperature Steel has max spacing of times slab or wall thickness but reinforcement has a 3 times maximum spacing.
> Refer to 1907A6.5

1911A.7.9……….. when concrete is placed against previously hardened concrete, the interface for shear transfer shall be clean and free of laitance. If μ is assumed equal to 1.0ë, interface shall be roughened to a full amplitude **of approximately 1/4 inch (6.4 mm).**

> **Comment:** SEE ALSO
> Section 1906A4.7
> Masonry requires 1/16"

1912A.14 Splices of Reinforcement.

1912A.14.1 Splices of reinforcement shall be made only as required or permitted on design drawings or in specifications, or as authorized by the *enforcement agency.*
ing requirements are met:

> **Comment:** REMEMBER
> Splice Lengths need to be on the plans.
> Usually in the structural general notes.

1912A.14.2.2 Lap splices of bars in a bundle .... Individual bar splices within a bundle shall not overlap. Entire bundles shall not be lap spliced.

1912A.15.4.1 Splices shall be staggered at least 24 inches (610

> **Comment:** TEST QUESTION
> Minimum 24" stagger on lap splices

1912A.14.2.3 Bars spliced by noncontact lap splices in flexural members shall not be spaced transversely farther apart than one fifth the required lap splice length, or 6 inches (152 mm).

> **Comment:** REMEMBER
> Non-contact lap splices are 2" to 6" apart and are usually in shotcrete or gunite work where clearance is very important.

1912A.15.1 Minimum length of lap for tension lap splices shall be as required for Class A or B splice, but not less than 12 inches (305 mm), where:

Class A splice .... $1.0 l_d$

Class B splice .... $1.3 l_d$

> **Comment:** REMEMBER
> The class of lap probably won't be important to the inspector however it is worth knowing what is being talked about.

SECTION 1914A . WALLS

1914A.3.5 Vertical and horizontal reinforcement shall not be spaced farther apart than three times the wall thickness, nor 18 inches (457 mm).......... *horizontal reinforcement shall be placed within one half of the specified spacing at the top and bottom of the wall.*

> **Comment:** BEWARE
> Related to 1907A12.2.2 and 1907A6.5

1914A.3.7 In addition to the minimum reinforcement required by Section 1914A.3.1, not less than two No. 5 bars shall be provided around all window and door openings. Such bars shall be extended to develop the bar beyond the corners of the openings but not less than 24 inches (610 mm).

> **Comment:** SEE ALSO
> Masonry
> Extend (2) #5 bars past the edge of an opening 24" minimum

1914A.10 Foundation Walls............... Where concrete foundation walls or curbs extend above the floor line and support wood-frame or light-steel exterior, bearing or shear walls, they shall be doweled to the foundation wall below with a minimum of No. 3 bars at 24 inches (610 mm) on center. Where the height of the wall above the floor line exceeds 18 inches (457 mm), the wall above and below the floor line shall meet the requirements of Section 1914A.3. See Section 1633A.2.12 for additional requirements.

> **Comment:** REMEMBER
> This usually applies to stem walls at the tops of footings. Look for dowels tying into the footings.

SECTION 1921A . REINFORCED CONCRETE STRUCTURES RESISTING FORCES INDUCED BY EARTHQUAKE MOTIONS

SEISMIC HOOK is a hook on a stirrup, hoop or crosstie having a bend not less than 135 degrees with a six-bar-diameter [but not less than 3 inches (76 mm)], extension that engages the longitudinal reinforcement and projects into the interior of the stirrup or hoop.

> **Comment:** SEE ALSO
> Seismic Hooks 1907A.1

1921A.4.4.8 Ties at anchor bolts. Anchor bolts which are set in the top of a column shall be provided with ties which enclose at least four vertical column bars. Such ties shall be in accordance with Section 1907A.1.3, Item 3, shall be within 5 inches (127 mm) of the top of the column, and shall consist of at least two No. 4 or three No. 3 bars. the joint.

© Professional Study Inc. 2003

SECTION 1923A . ANCHORAGE TO CONCRETE

1923A.1 Service Load Design.
All bolts shall be accurately and securely set prior to placement of concrete, except as indicated in Section 1916A.4.2.

1923A.3.4 Combined tension and shear.
When tension and shear act simultaneously, all of the following shall be met:

1923A.3.5 Drilled-in expansion bolts or chemical-type anchors in concrete.
When drilled-in expansion-type anchors are used in lieu of cast-in place bolts, the allowable shear and tension values and test loads shall be acceptable to the enforcement agency. When expansion-type anchors are listed for sill plate bolting applications, 10 percent of the anchors shall be tension tested. When expansion-type anchors are used for other structural applications, all such expansion anchors shall be tension tested. Expansion-type anchors shall not be used as hold-down bolts. When expansion-type anchors are used for nonstructural applications such as equipment anchorage, 50 percent or alternate bolts in a group, including at least one-half the anchors in each group, shall be tension tested. The tension testing of the expansion anchors shall be done in the presence of the project inspector and a report of the test results shall be submitted to the enforcement agency. If any anchors fail the tension-testing requirements, the additional testing requirements shall be acceptable to the enforcement agency. The above requirements shall also apply to bolts or anchors set in concrete with chemical if the long-term durability and stability of the chemical material and its resistance to loss of strength and chemical change at elevated temperatures are established to the satisfaction of the enforcement agency.

> **Comment:** TEST QUESTION
> 1. Expansion Anchors and Epoxy anc @ sill plates Test 10%
> 2. Other Structural Applications. Tes 100%
> 3. No use as Hold Downs
> 4. Any anchors used to anchor equipn Test 50% per group of   anchors

SECTION 1929A . TESTING AND INSPECTION

1929A.1 Cementitious Material Test.

If such information is not available, one grab sample of cementitious material used on the project shall be taken for each days pour and shall be tested as directed by the structural engineer, architect or enforcement agency. See Section 1929A.6 for waiver of tests.

> **Comment:** REMEMBER
> Grab samples of cement are usually on record with the laboratory therefore it i needed on every job. This is an expens test to do therefore be sure before you s demanding this testing.

1929A.2 Tests of Reinforcing Bars.
Where samples are taken from bundles as delivered from the mill, with the bundles identified as to heat number and provided the mill analyses accompany the report, one tensile test and one bend test shall be made from a specimen from each 10 tons (9080 kg) or fraction thereof of each size of reinforcing steel.
Where positive identification of the heat number cannot be made or where random samples are to be taken, one series of tests shall be made from each 2 1/2 tons (2270 kg) or fraction thereof of each size of reinforcing steel. See Section 1929A.6 for waiver of tests.

> **Comment:** TEST QUESTION
> Identified Reinforcement
>   Heat # and Mill certs have been prov and match material
>   (1) Test per 10 tons
>
> Unidentified Reinforcement
>   (1) Test per 2-1/2 tons
>
> Test Consists of
>   (2) pieces of each rebar size
>   1 bending test, and 1 tension test

1929A.5 Waiver of Batch Plant Inspection.
Batch plant inspection may be waived under either of the following conditions:

> **Comment:** TEST QUESTION
> Waiver of batch plant inspection is in tl interest of the school district but not in interest of the contractor.
>
> Remember: To be exempt it has to be approved by DSA regardless of the oth factors

© Professional Study Inc. 2003

1. The concrete plant complies fully with the requirements of ASTM C 94, Sections 8 and 9, and has a current certificate from the National Ready Mixed Concrete Association or another agency acceptable to the enforcement agency. The certification shall indicate that the plant has automatic batching and recording capabilities.

2. For one-story wood-frame or one-story light-steel buildings and isolated mat-type foundations supporting equipment only, where the specified compressive strength f_c of the concrete delivered to the jobsite is 3,500 psi (24.13 MPa) and where the f_c used in design is not greater than 2,500 psi (17.24 MPa). When batch plant inspection is waived, the following requirements shall apply and shall be described in the contract specifications:

Approved inspector of the testing laboratory shall check the first batching at the start of work and furnish mix proportions to the licensed weigh-master.

Licensed weigh-master to positively identify materials as to quantity and certify to each load by a ticket.

Tickets shall be transmitted to the project inspector by a truck driver with load identified thereon. Inspector will not accept the load without a load ticket identifying the mix and will keep a daily record of placements, identifying each truck, its load and time of receipt, and approximate location of deposit in the structure will transmit a copy of the daily record to the enforcement agency.
At the end of the project, the weigh-master shall furnish an affidavit to the enforcement agency on form SSS 411-8 certifying that all concrete furnished conforms in every particular to proportions established by mix designs.

Comment: BEWARE
When Batch Plant inspection is waived for a project you must pay attention to all of these other requirements.

1929A.6 Waiver of Material Testing. Tests of cement and reinforcing bars may be waived by the architect or structural engineer with the approval of the enforcement agency for one-story buildings where the specified compressive strength of the concrete f_c delivered to the jobsite is 3,500 psi (24.13 MPa) and where the f_c used in design is 2,500 psi (17.24 MPa).

Comment: REMEMBER
Waivers must be approved by DSA

1929A.7 Placing Record. A record shall be kept on the site of the time and date of placing the concrete in each portion of the structure. Such record shall be kept until the completion of the structure and shall be open to the inspection of the enforcement agency.

1929A.8 Composite Construction Cores. Cores of the completed composite concrete construction shall be taken to demonstrate the shear strength along the contact surfaces. The cores shall be tested when the cast-in-place concrete is approximately 28 days old and shall be tested by a shear loading parallel to the joint between the precast concrete and the cast-in-place concrete. Theminimum unit shear strength of the contact surface area of the core shall not be less than 100 psi (689 kPa).
At least one core shall be taken from each building for each 5,000 square feet (465m2) of area of composite concrete construction and not less than three cores shall be taken from each project. The architect or structural engineer in responsible charge of the project or his or her representative shall designate the location for sampling.

1929A.9 Inspection of Prestressed Concrete.

1929A.9.1 In addition to the general inspection required for concrete work, all plant fabrication of prestressed concrete members or tensioning of posttensioned members constructed at the site shall be continuously inspected by an inspector specially approved for this purpose by the enforcement agency.

1929A.9.2 To be eligible for approval, the inspector shall be examined as to his or her knowledge and experience in prestressed concrete construction.

1929A.9.3 The prestressed concrete plant fabrication inspector shall check the materials, equipment, tensioning procedure and construction of the prestressed members. The inspector shall

1929A.10 Inspection of Pneumatically Placed Concrete Work (Shotcrete). All shotcrete work shall be continuously inspected during placing by an inspector specially approved for that purpose by the enforcement agency. The special shotcrete inspector shall check the materials, placing equipment, details of construction and construction procedure. The inspector shall furnish a verified report that of his or her own personal knowledge the work covered by the report has been performed and materials used and installed in every material respect in compliance with the duly approved plans and specifications.

> **Comment:** REMEMBER Shotcrete must be installed with a DSA approved special inspector present. SEE ALSO Chapter 17A for further in

> **Comment:** REMEMBER A Verified Report is a DSA Form 6

1929A.12 Inspection of Welded Reinforcing Bars. Inspection of all shop and field structural welding operations shall be made by a qualified welding inspector approved by the enforcement agency. Such inspector shall be trained and thoroughly experienced in inspecting reinforcing bar welding operations. The inspectors ability to distinguish between sound and unsound welding shall be reliably established.

> **Comment:** SEE ALSO Section 1701A, and 4-342.6

> **Comment:** REMEMBER The welding inspector must be an AWS CWI (American Welding Society-Certified Welding Inspector), and you submit a DSA Form 5.

The welding inspector shall make a systematic record of all welds. This record shall include:

1. Identification marks of welders.
2. List of defective welds.
3. Manner of correction of defects.

The welding inspector shall check the material, equipment, details of construction, and procedures as well as the welds. The inspector shall also check the ability of the welder. The welding inspector shall furnish the architect, structural engineer and the enforcement agency with a verified report that the welding which is required to be inspected is proper and has been done in conformity with the approved plans and specifications. The welding inspector shall use all means necessary to determine the quality of the weld. The inspector may use gamma ray, magnaflux, trepanning, sonics or any other aid to visual inspection which the inspector may deem necessary to assure the adequacy of the welding.

> **Comment:** REMEMBER This includes a Welding Procedure Specification for all welds, even pre-qualified welds.

				MINIMUM CONCRETE STRENGTH (psi)							
				× 0.00689 for MPa							
				$f'_c = 2,000$			$f'_c = 3,000$			$f'_c = 4,000$		
BOLT DIAMETER (inches)	MINIMUM[4] EMBEDMENT (inches)	EDGE DISTANCE (inches)	SPACING (inches)	Tension	Shear Loaded Toward an Edge[9]	Shear— Other Cases[8]	Tension	Shear Loaded Toward an Edge[9]	Shear— Other Cases[8]	Tension	Shear Loaded Toward an Edge[9]	Shear— Other Cases[8]
× 25.4 for mm				× 4.5 for newtons							
1/4	2 1/2	1 1/2	3	400	90	400	400	110	500	400	120	500
3/8	3	2 1/4	4 1/2	1,000	200	800	1,000	250	1,100	1,000	280	1,100
1/2	4	3	6	1,900	350	1,250	1,900	400	1,250	1,900	500	1,250
	4	5	6	2,800	950	1,550	3,000	1,200	1,650	3,100	1,400	1,750
5/8	4 1/2	3 3/4	7 1/2	3,000	550	2,750	3,000	650	2,750	3,000	800	2,750
	4 1/2	6 1/4	7 1/2	4,100	1,500	2,900	4,400	1,850	3,000	4,800	2,150	3,050
3/4	5	4 1/2	9	4,500	800	2,940	4,500	950	3,560	4,500	1,100	3,560
	5	7 1/2	9	5,400	2,200	4,250	5,900	2,700	4,300	6,400	3,100	4,400
7/8	6	5 1/4	10 1/2	4,500	1,050	3,350	4,500	1,300	4,050	4,500	1500	4,050
1	7	6	12	5,700	1,400	3,750	6,400	1,700	4,500	6,400	2100	5,300
1 1/8	8	6 3/4	13 1/2	6,400	1,800	4,750	6,400	2,200	4,750	6,400	2500	4,750
1 1/4	9	7 1/2	15	6,400	2,200	5,800	6,400	2,700	5,800	6,400	3100	5,800

1 Values are *for* natural stone aggregate concrete and bolts of A 307 quality. Bolts shall have a standard head or an equal deformity in the embedded portion. *L or J bolts shall not be used to resist seismic forces. Bolts, except holddowns, anchoring light frame sills and having a minimum edge or end distance equal to or greater than 5 diameters, may use L or J bolts.*

4 *The minimum depth of embedment shall be 12 diameters*

8 *Values shown are for bolts loaded away from an edge or end or parallel to an edge, or a bolt loaded toward an edge with an edge distance equal to or greater than 12 diameters.*

9 *Values shown are for bolts loaded toward an edge or end with the tabular edge distance. For bolts loaded toward an edge or end with an edge or end distance between 6 and 12 diameters, use linear interpolation between the values for Shear Loaded Toward an Edge and Shear.Other Cases.*

Comment: TEST QUESTION
This note effectively prohibits any L or J bolts in any shear walls.

Chapter 8: Masonry

LESSON 8.0 : Background

Masonry construction refers to building with individual units that are joined together with mortar. Small masonry units are either solid or hollow and include brick, structural clay tile, concrete block, gypsum block, and glass block. Larger units include terra cotta, ceramic veneer, pre-cast concrete, and various types of stone.

HISTORY

Masonry construction began when a prehistoric person first piled up rocks to create the earliest protection from wind, rain, and wild animals. Where stone was not available, mud from nearby river beds was fashioned into convenient building units. These primitive bricks were at first sun dried and later burned by fire to make them hard and more durable. As civilization progressed, builders learned how to span great distances using small shaped units, first by corbelling, then by using the arch, the vault, and the dome.

Every civilization that has existed employed some form of masonry construction. Through centuries of exposure, in all types of climate, magnificent masonry monuments remain for us to see today, from the ancient Egyptian pyramids to the glorious Gothic cathedrals.

Masonry construction continues to be a popular building method today. Despite our technical advances, there remains an admiration for this ancient craft, which no doubt results from masonry's ageless character, distinctive texture, and human scale.

BRICK

A brick is a rectangular unit of construction, formed from various clay and shale mixtures, which has been hardened by heat or chemical action. The physical and chemical characteristics of the ingredients vary considerably, and this, along with the temperatures at which they are fired, account for the variations in color and hardness. The differences among finished bricks are also dependent on the method of molding used in their manufacture.

The soft mud process uses molds into which the wet clay is pressed by hand or machine.

The stiff mud process forces the mixture through a die, extruding a clay ribbon which is cut to shape by tightly stretched wires (wire-cut brick).

The dry-press process uses a relatively dry mixture that is pressed into gang molds by plungers under high pressure. This process produces the most accurately formed brick.

Bricks are produced in solid, cored, and hollow units, although cored brick is classified as solid if at least 75% of its total cross-sectional area is solid. In hollow brick, at least 60% of the total cross-sectional area is solid. Most natural brick colors are in the red or buff ranges, while the commonly available surface textures are smooth, water- and sandstruck, scored, wire-cut, combed, and roughened. Brick can also be finished with a fire-bonded ceramic glaze in either a satin or gloss finish.

Building brick, sometimes referred to as common brick, is the type most widely used in construction. It is made from clay which is fired at about 1850 degrees F., it is usually red in color, and it is available in standard and modular sizes.

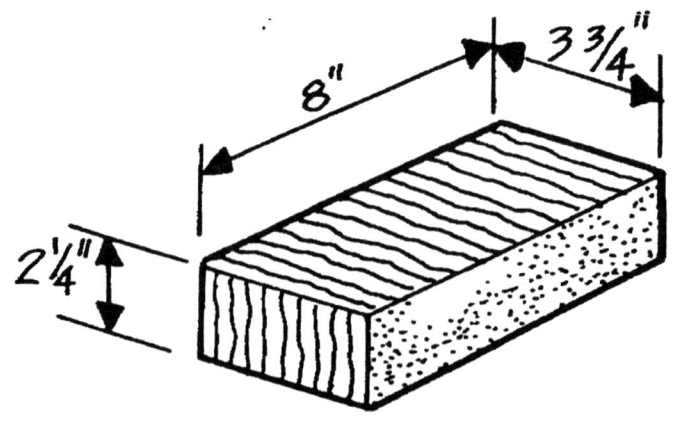

STANDARD BUILDING BRICK

Building brick is classified in accordance with the probable weather conditions to which it will be exposed, as follows:

GRADE SW (Severe weathering.) Used in areas of heavy rain and below freezing temperatures.

GRADE MW (Moderate weathering) Used in areas of moderate rain and freezing temperatures.

GRADE NW (Negligible weathering) Used in areas of minimum rain and above freezing temperatures.

Face brick is made from controlled mixtures of clay or shale and carefully manufactured to produce high quality units in specific sizes, textures, and colors. Face brick, too, is rated for durability to exposure, and is available in SW and MW grades. In addition, it is classified according to factors affecting its appearance, as follows:

GRADE FBX - High degree of mechanical perfection and narrow color range.

GRADE FBS - Variations in mechanical perfection and wide color range.

GRADE FBA - Non-uniform in size, color, and texture of units.

Hollow brick is classified SW or MW, as well as by those factors affecting its appearance, as follows:

GRADE HBX - High degree of mechanical perfection, minimum size variations, and narrow color range.

GRADE HBS - Greater size variations and wide color range.

GRADE HBA - Non-uniform in size, color, and texture.

Other types of brick, besides building and face brick, include the following:

Back-up brick: Inferior units used behind face brick.

Paving brick: Very hard and dense facing units used on floor surfaces.

Fire brick: Great resistance to high temperatures, as in a fireplace.

Sewer brick: Low absorption for use in sewerage and storm drains.

Adobe brick: Made from a mixture of natural clay and straw, then placed in molds and dried in the sun. Require protection from rain and sub-surface moisture.

Nail-on brick: Flat units generally used on interiors where solid masonry cannot be structurally supported.

Hollow brick tile: Masonry units cored in excess of 25% of the gross cross-sectional area, used where building brick is used.

Most bricks are manufactured in standard sizes, but among manufacturers there exist minor dimensional variations. To a large degree this variation is caused by the differences in clays used and the amount of shrinkage that occurs when they are fired.

Standard building and face bricks are usually 2-1/4 inches deep, 3-3/4 inches wide, and 8 inches long.

Modular bricks were developed to regulate coursing dimensions. For example, an Economy-8 modular brick $3^{1}2$" x $7^{1}2$" x 32" in size, laid with 2" joints will produce regular courses exactly 4" in height and 8" in length. Other modular bricks are: Roman, 12" high; Standard, 2-2/3" high; Economy-8 and Economy-12, both 32" high.

Brick nomenclature is a virtual language used to identify, classify, and describe brick shapes, surfaces, and placement within a wall. For example, the six surfaces of a brick are called the face, the side, the cull, the end, and the beds, as shown in the illustration below. Frequently, the mason must cut bricks into various shapes in order to fill in the spaces at corners and other places where a full brick will not fit. The more common cut shapes are shown in the next illustration

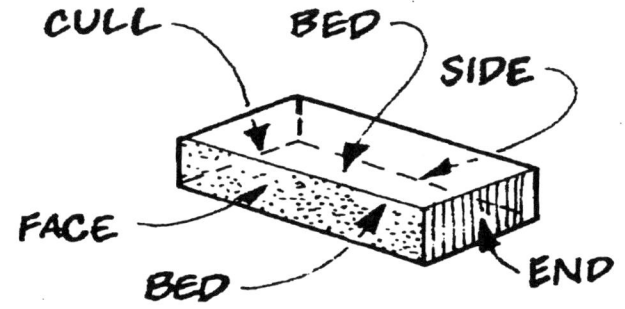

SURFACES OF A BRICK

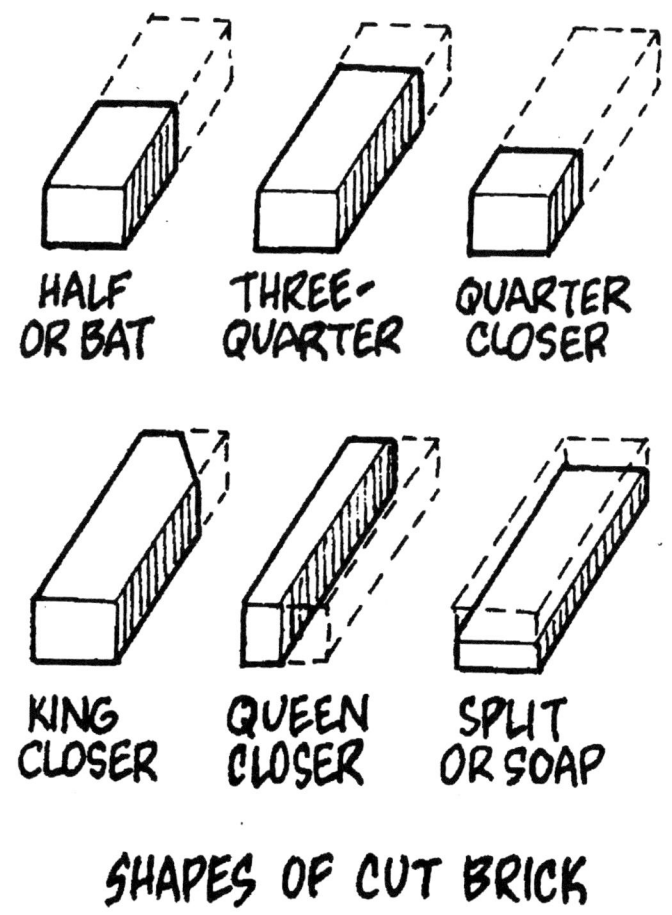

SHAPES OF CUT BRICK

Bricks may also be identified by their particular placement within a wall. For example, if they are laid with the end or cull (short sides) exposed, they are called headers; but if they are laid with the face (long side) exposed they are called stretchers. Various other positions are illustrated on the following page.

<u>Bricklaying</u> has always been a manual, rather than a mechanical, process. Therefore, successful brickwork depends to a large extent on individual workmanship. In this regard, there are several standard practices of the trade with which one should be familiar. For example, bricks should be laid when the temperature is between 40 and 90 degrees F., for the best results.

In addition, bricks should be wetted prior to setting in order to minimize absorption of water from the mortar. Loss of water will cause the mortar

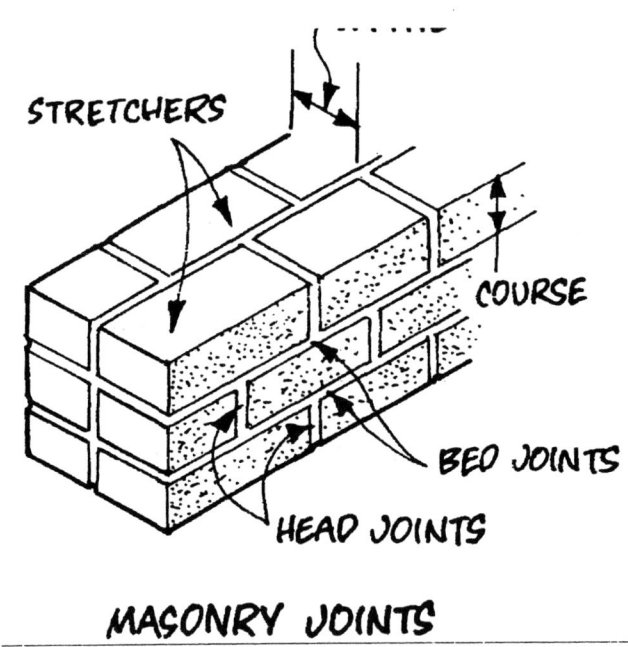

MASONRY JOINTS

to set too soon, and the bond between brick and mortar will be weak. Wetting bricks will also wash dust from the brick surface, resulting in better bond. Tests have indicated that the absorption rate of wetted brick should not exceed 0.7 ounces of water per minute. If the absorption rate exceeds this amount, the bricks should be rewetted until the desired value is achieved.

Bricks should always be set in a full bed of mortar with mortar solidly filling all vertical head joints. Standard joint thicknesses vary, although the most common range between ¼ to ½ inch. As a rule of thumb, 3 bricks plus 3 joints equals 8 inches in height. Few brick walls today are laid solid. Most walls are the cavity type in which two tiers, or wythes, of masonry are separated by two or three inches of air space. Rigid foam insulation, applied to the inside wythe, occupies about half this space, thus increasing the R value of the wall. In reinforced masonry work, steel reinforcing is placed in this air space and solidly grouted with a mixture of cement, sand, water, and - quite often - pea gravel.

Brick bonding is used primarily to strengthen a solid wall by interlocking individual bricks, so that the entire assembly acts as a single structural unit. By bonding brick, various design patterns are created, of which the more common are shown.

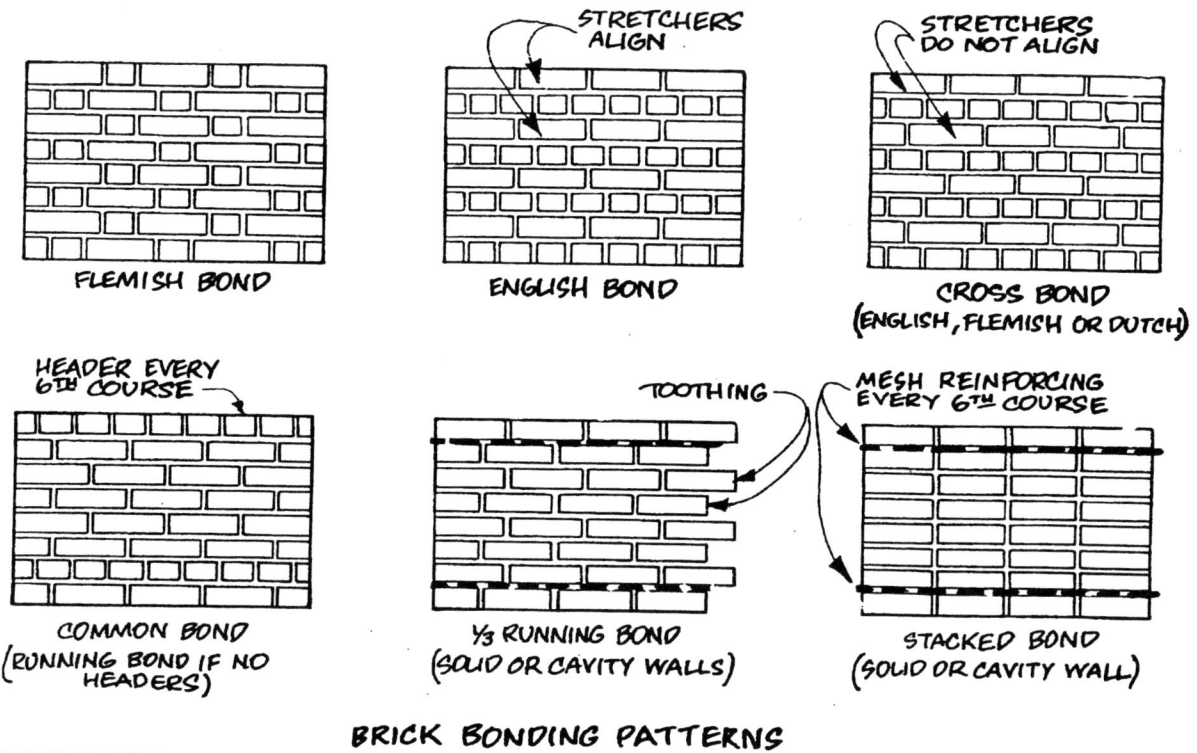

BRICK BONDING PATTERNS

At about every sixth course, a brick header course should be used to bind the tiers together. Walls laid in Flemish or English bond will have full brick header courses by virtue of their arrangement. In other patterns, bonding may also be achieved by the use of metal wall ties.

<u>Veneering</u> is the term applied to exposed masonry which is attached, but not structurally bonded to the backing. The veneer units are held in place by wires, metal clips, or patented wire lath.

<u>Efflorescence</u> is a white, powdery deposit on the masonry surface caused by soluble salts in the units or in the mortar. These salts are leached out by water that penetrates the masonry and results in unsightly patches of discoloration.

Efflorescence can be prevented, or at least minimized, by selecting materials free of harmful salts and by preventing water from penetrating the masonry. The latter is accomplished by the use of solid and tight mortar joints, capped walls, effective flashing, and adequate weather protection of the masonry during the course of construction.

When efflorescence appears, it is removed by washing with high pressure water, by light sandblasting, or most commonly—by washing with a 5% solution of muriatic acid in water.

Expansion joints are required in all masonry structures over 200 feet in length, or where there are two or more wings in a building. Temperature changes cause expansion or contraction, but in masonry walls much of the movement is assimilated by the wall itself because of the flexibility in the many mortar joints. Nevertheless, to avoid harmful cracking, joints such as those shown below should be used.

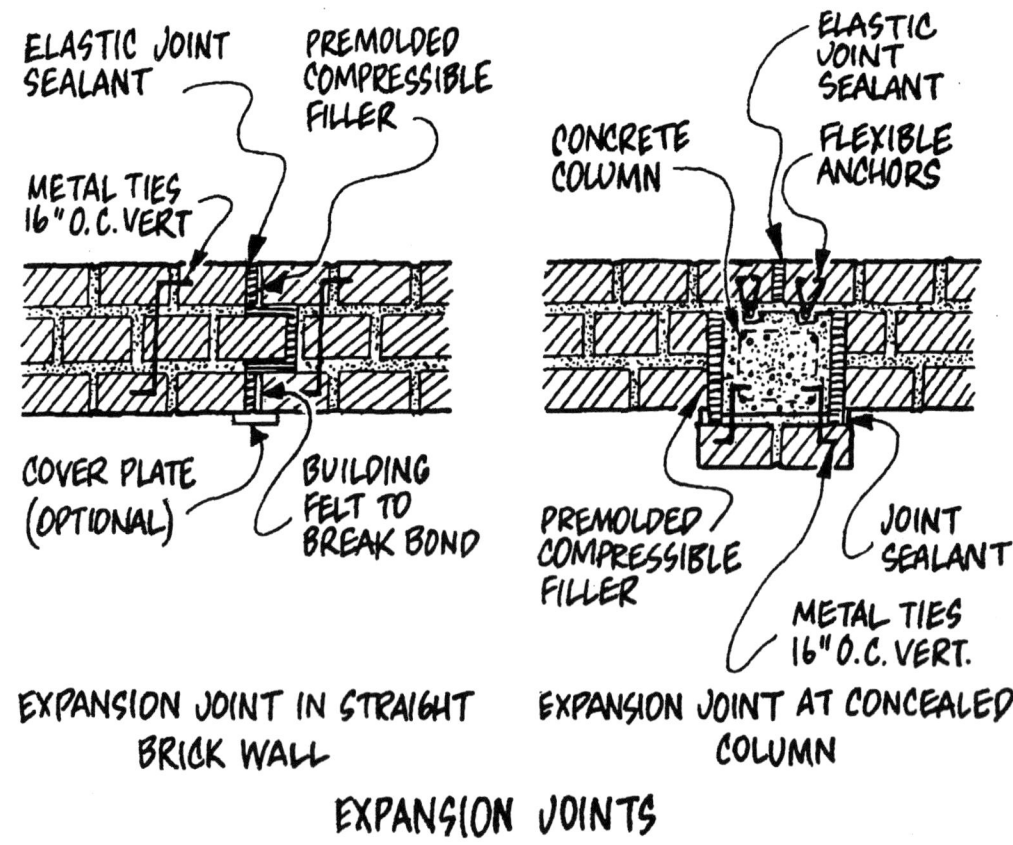

EXPANSION JOINTS

CONCRETE MASONRY

A wide variety of manufactured building products are made from conventional concrete mixes, using either normal or lightweight aggregates. These include concrete bricks, concrete blocks, concrete tile, and cast (concrete) stone. The most widely used of these masonry products is concrete block, which has become increasingly important as a construction material.

Concrete blocks are easy and relatively inexpensive to manufacture; they are light, strong, and have good fire resistance; and they can be used for foundations, partitions, and loadbearing or non-load bearing walls. Concrete blocks are modular, so that a nominal 8x8x16 block actually measures 7-5/8 x 7-5/8 x 15-5/8 inches to allow for 3/8 inch mortar joints, both horizontally and vertically.

Individual blocks are manufactured with 2 or 3 cores and also solid. 2-core concrete block reduces heat conduction about 4%, is about 4 pounds lighter, and has more space for mechanical pipes and conduits.

Load-bearing concrete block is classified in two grades:
1. N for more severe exposures and
2. S for block requiring protection from the weather.

Concrete block walls are normally constructed one block thick and laid with staggered vertical joints. Steel reinforcement is almost always used and placed vertically in the middle of grout-filled cells, as well as horizontally, generally every sixth course. Block walls may be left unfinished, thus displaying the color of the cement used in the manufacturing process, or they may receive a coating of cement plaster, cement paint, or clear waterproof sealer.

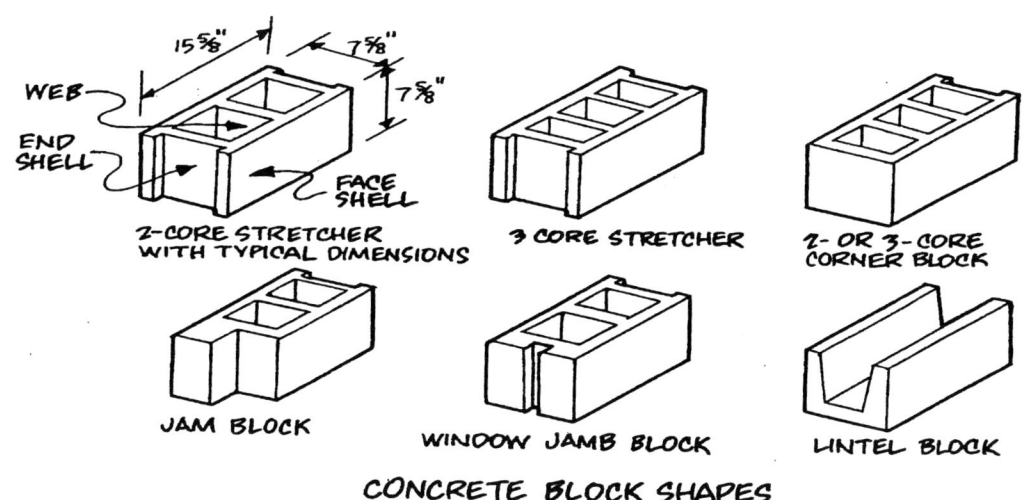

CONCRETE BLOCK SHAPES

STRUCTURAL CLAY TILE

Structural clay tiles are hollow, burned-clay masonry units with parallel cells. They are made from the same clays as brick, and may be loadbearing or non-load-bearing (partition tile). Clay tile are divided into two broad groups according to function: back-up tile and facing tile.

They are available in a variety of textures, in natural colors (usually in the range of brick reds), or in a multitude of glazed finishes. Structural clay tile is used in building construction for interior partitions; or, in combination with other masonry, as back up for exterior walls. Depending on the orientation of the cells, the tile is referred to as a side-construction tile (cells horizontal) or an end-construction tile (cells vertical).

Architectural terra cotta is a clay tile that is available in various colors, textures, and shapes. It is used primarily for multicolored decorative designs.

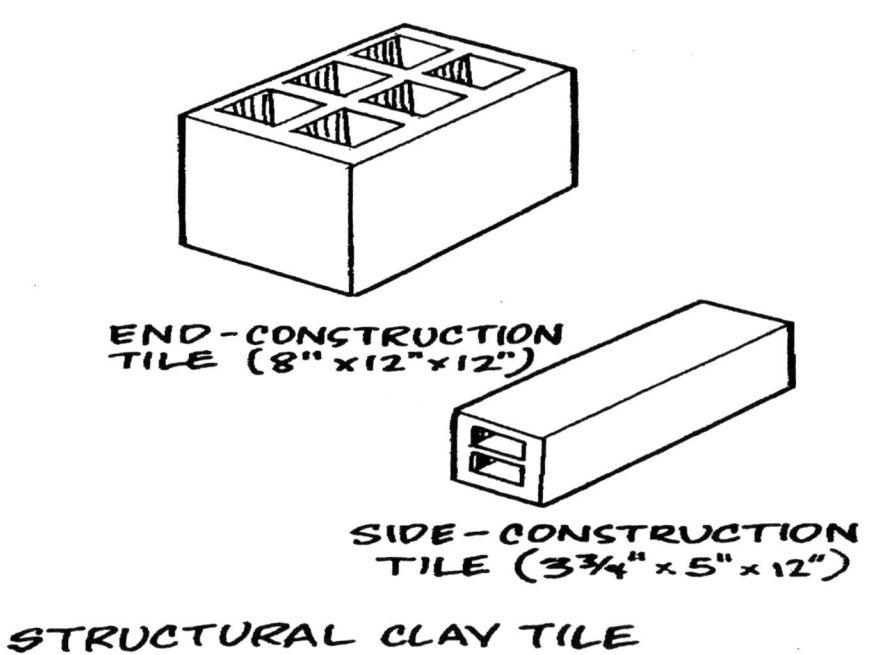

END-CONSTRUCTION TILE (8" x 12" x 12")

SIDE-CONSTRUCTION TILE (3¾" x 5" x 12")

STRUCTURAL CLAY TILE

Ceramic veneer is a terra cotta available in large face dimensions, thin sections, and a variety of natural and glazed finishes. It is applied with a mortar setting bed, or by using a metal anchor and mortar.

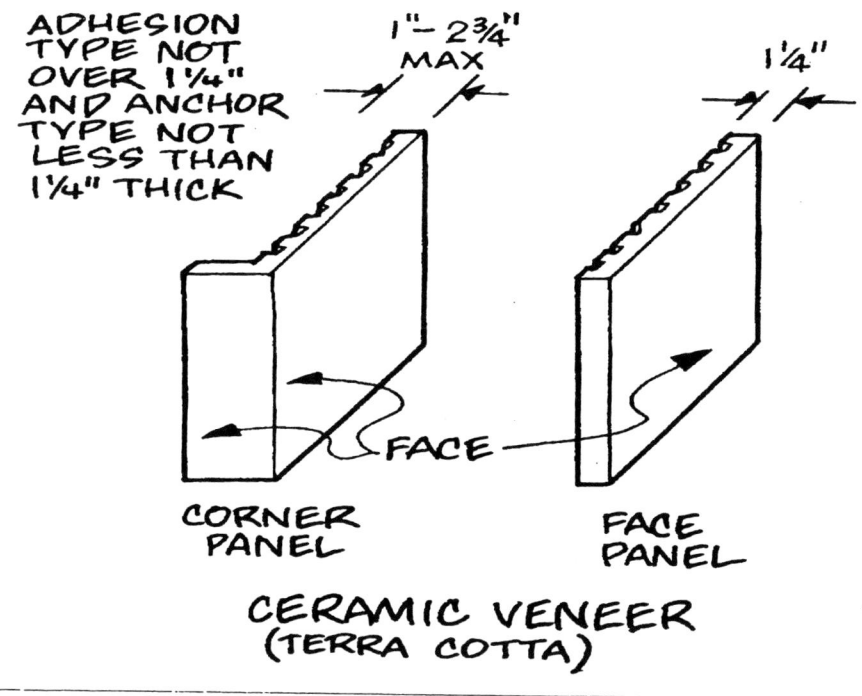

GYPSUM BLOCK

Gypsum blocks, often referred to as gypsum tiles, are solid or cored units manufactured from gypsum plaster. They are available in thicknesses from 2 to 6 inches, and in standard panels 12 x 30 inches in size.

Gypsum block is used for interior, non load-bearing partitions, and, because of its chemical properties, for lightweight, fireproofing protection. For example, two inches of gypsum block has the same fire rating as four inches of concrete block. Gypsum block cannot be used on the exterior or in areas subject to continued dampness. It is always set with gypsum mortar, on top of a base course of water-resistant material. the demand for greater R factors in exterior wall materials.

Walls of glass block are limited in length, height, and area; and they may never be used to support structural loads. The blocks are always set in a stacked bond pattern. When using glass block, one must give special consideration to the mortar mix, because of the poor bond between glass and mortar. In addition, control joints are critical because of the large coefficient of thermal expansion that exists in glass. Also critical are the meeting joints with other materials, which should be filled with resilient expansion joint material. Glass blocks were very popular following their introduction in the 1930's; however, due to overuse and frequent misuse, their popularity waned in the post-war period. In recent years, there has been steadily increasing interest in glass block be appropriate to the stone type and suitable for the function it must perform. Surface finishes range from very rough (quarry face, split face, or sawed finish) to quite smooth (rubbed finish, honed finish, or polished finish). All stone is affected by rapid temperature change, and therefore, it should not be used where fire resistance is important.

STONE

Stone is one of the original natural materials used in construction by prehistoric man. As such, it has served literally as the foundation of all architectural efforts, from prehistory to the turn of the last century. Today stone is used for aggregates or as a surface finish material, including veneers, paving, shingles, counters, and decorative items.

Stone is small or quarried pieces of rock, and rocks are classified into three groups according to the method of their formation. These are listed below together with the principal building stones in each group that are commonly used in construction.

TYPE OF ROCK	NAME OF STONE
Igneous	Granite
Sedimentary	Limestone, Sandstone, Bluestone, Brownstone
Metamorphic	Marble Soapstone Slate

Stone is available in a number of forms and used in construction in a variety of ways. The most commonly used categories are as follows:

Rough stone (field stone) - Natural stone used decoratively.

Rubble stone - Irregular stone with at least one good face used for ashlar veneers, copings, sills, curbs, etc.

Dimension stone - Cut stone, used for surface veneers, toilet partitions, flooring, stair treads, etc.

Flagstone - Thin slabs used for paving, treads, counter tops, etc.

Monumental stone - Used for sculpture, monuments, gravestones, etc.

Crushed stone - Used as aggregate for concrete, asphaltic concrete, terrazzo, built-up roof surfacing, etc.

Stone dust - Used as filler in asphalt flooring, shingles, paints, etc.

©Professional Study Inc.

The properties of natural stone vary considerably, and therefore, one must choose carefully with regard to strength, porosity, absorption, and permeability. It is also important to select a surface finish that will be appropriate to the stone type and suitable for the function it must perform. Surface finishes range from very rough (quarry face, split face, or sawed finish) to quite smooth (rubbed finish, honed finish, or polished finish). All stone is affected by rapid temperature change, and therefore, it should not be used where fire resistance is important.

Stone masonry is classified in two principal groups:

Rubble masonry, in which the stones are left in their natural rough state,

Ashlar masonry, in which the stones are shaped and smoothed (dressed) into rectangular blocks.

Stone masonry is further categorized by the way the stones are arranged in relation to one another. Several stonework patterns are illustrated.

Stone masonry should be set with nonstaining portland cement mortar, and care should be taken to avoid moisture penetration of the stone. This is usually accomplished by dampproofing the backup material. There are many varieties of anchors and ties used to secure stone veneer or stone trim, and several of these are shown.

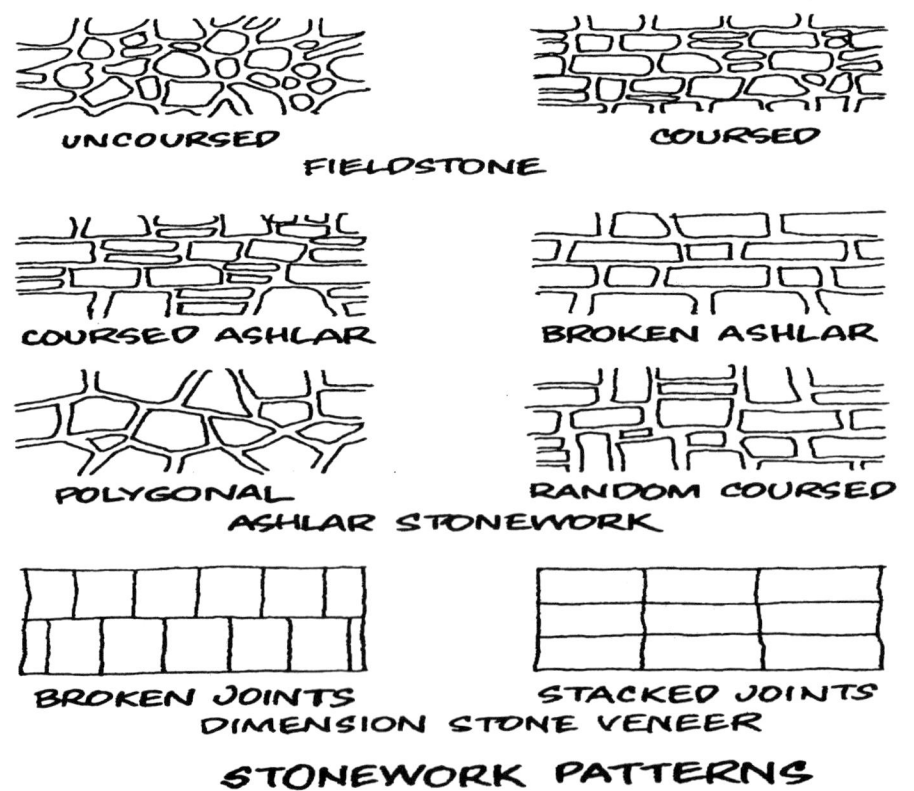

STONEWORK PATTERNS

STONE VENEER ATTACHMENT SYSTEMS

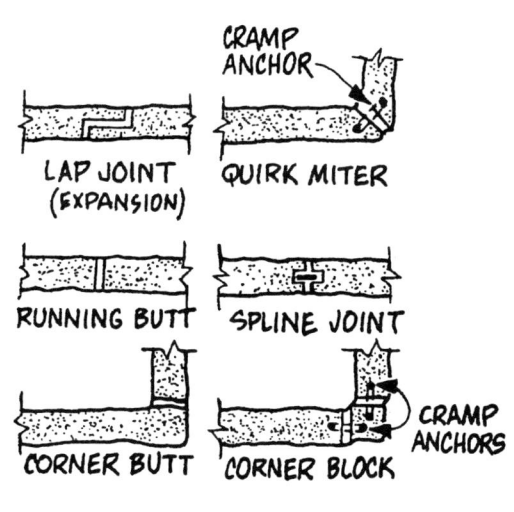

STONE VENEER JOINTS

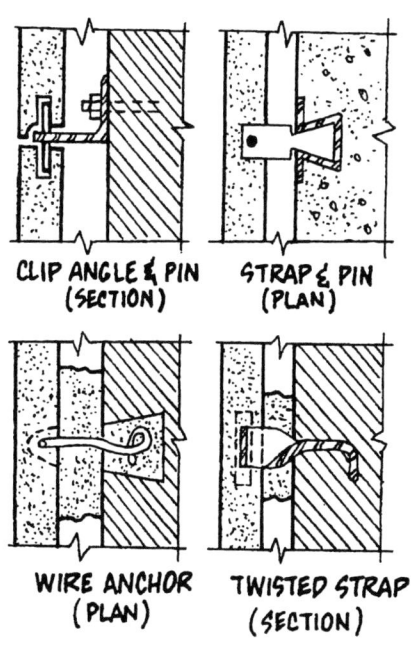

STONE VENEER ANCHORING DETAILS

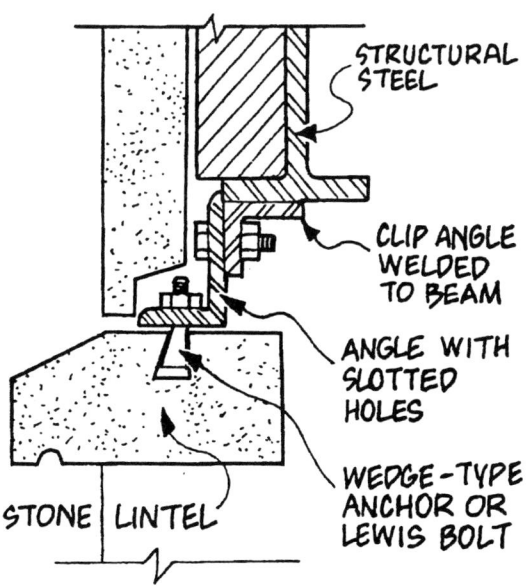

SECTION OF STONE LINTEL

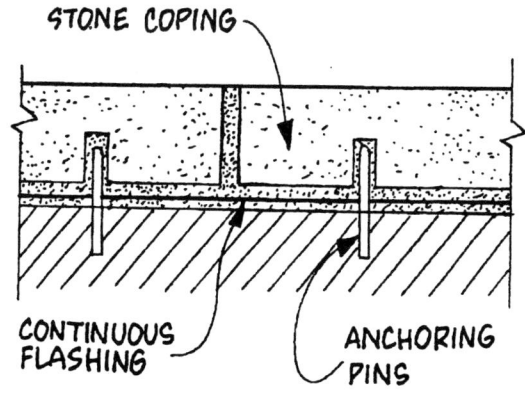

PARALLEL SECTION THROUGH STONE COPING

MORTAR

All masonry units are bonded with mortar, the purpose of which is to join the units to each other, or to their supporting members, while preventing moisture penetration of the joints. Mortar is composed of varying quantities of portland cement, sand, lime, and water. Mortar sand should be free from organic material, and its grading is based on the thickness, of the mortar joint. Lime putty or hydrated lime is added to the mix to improve workability and water retentivity. Admixtures are permitted, but except for powdered coloring agents, they are not recommended where high bond strength is desired.

Mortars may be tested for slump or flow, similar to concrete, in order to insure a proper mix. Mixes that have lost water through evaporation may be retempered (water added); however, mortar should not be used after three hours from the time it is mixed.

Reproduced below is a table of mortar proportions that meet ASTM requirements. For reinforced masonry that is load-bearing and exposed to the weather, types M and S mortars are generally specified. Types N and O mortars are used where a lesser compressive strength is required.
High-strength mortars are used for preassembled masonry units, and as such they have greater compressive strength.

TABLE 21A-A—MORTAR PROPORTIONS FOR UNIT MASONRY

MORTAR	TYPE	Portland Cement or Blended Cement	Masonry Cement[1] M	S	N	Mortar Cement[2] M	S	N	Hydrated Lime or Lime Putty	AGGREGATE MEASURED IN A DAMP, LOOSE CONDITION
Cement-lime	M	1	—	—	—	—	—	—	¼	Not less than 2¼ and not more than 3 times the sum of the separate volumes of cementitious materials.
	S	1	—	—	—	—	—	—	over ¼ to ½	
Mortar cement	M	1	—	—	—	—	—	1	—	
	M	—	—	—	—	1	—	—	—	
	S	½	—	—	—	—	—	1	—	
	S	—	—	—	—	—	1	—	—	
Masonry cement	M	1	—	—	1	—	—	—	—	
	M	—	1	—	—	—	—	—	—	
	S	½	—	—	1	—	—	—	—	
	S	—	—	1	—	—	—	—	—	

[1]Masonry cement conforming to the requirements of UBC Standard 21-11.
[2]Mortar cement conforming to the requirements of UBC Standard 21-14.

MORTAR JOINTS

The exterior surface of mortar joints, the part exposed to the weather, is finished to make the masonry more waterproof and/or to achieve a specific aesthetic appearance. Joints may be made with a trowel, a special jointing tool, or a raking device. In each case, the joint should be entirely filled with mortar to begin with, and the face of the joint should be smooth and dense when the joint is completed. Shown on the page below are several common masonry joints used in construction.

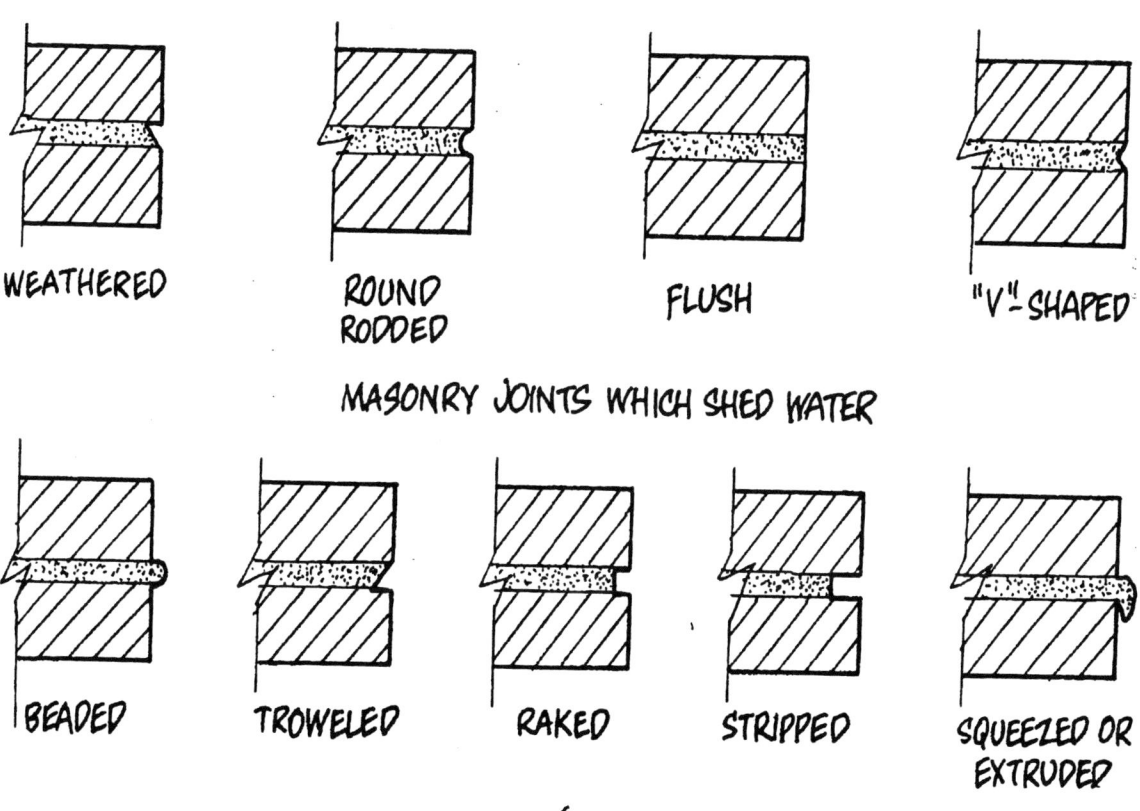

COMMON MORTAR JOINTS

Masonry accessories are readily available for each type of masonry unit; they include anchors, ties, reinforcing, fillers, wire mesh, etc., as well as various accessories for installing masonry ceilings, as shown in the illustration.

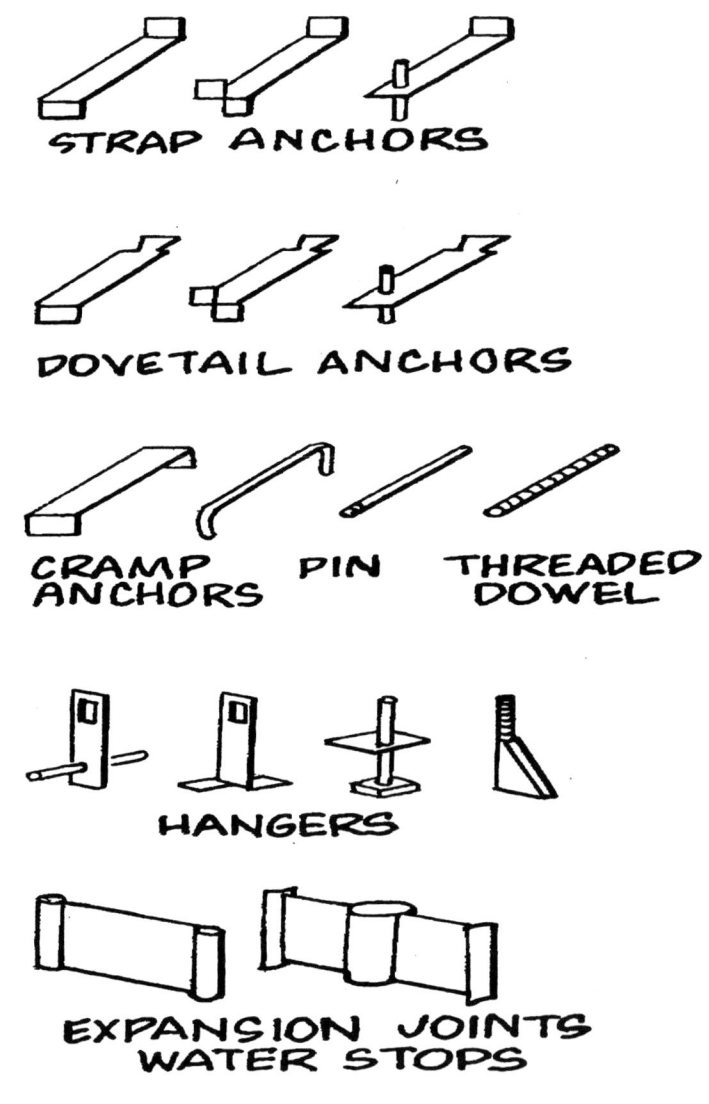

MASONRY ACCESSORIES

CONCLUSION

The use of masonry has been called an anachronism in the modern world of construction. Since most masonry work is performed very much as it has been for centuries, there is no doubt that it is labor intensive, and that means expensive. However, recent technology has produced prefabricated units, preassembled panels, and high bond adhesives, all of which translates to decreased costs and expanded use.

Modern mastonry systems have proven to be a reliable material with respect to earthquake resistance in addition the durability of the material makes it ideal for school construction which is always looking to limit long range costs. For the DSA inspector masonry poses a unique problem since it is a complex structural system that demands a great deal of attention to detail. It is for this reason that special inspectors are so necessary during masonry construction.

Chapter 8: MASONRY
Lesson 8.2
TITLE 24   Part 2 Volume 2
Chapter 21A

SECTION 2102A - MATERIAL STANDARDS

2102A.2 Standards of Quality 2. Cement
2.2 ASTM C 150
Air entrainment not recommended

5. CMU

Masonry units of concrete.
UBC Standard 21-4
Concrete masonry units must be Grade N-1 (moisture controlled).
Testing for strength, absorption and shrinkage is required for masonry units.
Concrete masonry units are to be kept protected from rain/snow.

8. Mortar.

8.2 UBC Standard 21-16
Field Sampling of mortar
UBC Standard 21-16,
2" diameter x 4" cylinder. Mortar is spread on a masonry unit to absorb moisture prior to placing mortar in the cylinder.

9. Grout.
9.1 UBC Standard 21-18
Field sampling or grout
UBC Standard 21-18. Typically, 4" x 4" x 8" height grout samples are taken.
2103A.3.1 General.
Mortar is generally supplied to the jobsite as factory-blended (pre-mixed).
2104A.2 Materials: Handling, Storage and Preparation.

LOW LIFT GROUTED BRICK MASONRY

Clean outs:
no cleanouts needed for 24 in. high lifts or less.
Joints:
Brick shall be laid with full shoved head and bed joints Grout space: min. 2 1/2 in.
Floaters:
used when grout space is larger than 5 in. wide and shall have 1 in. clearance between floater and wythes and 1 bar diameter from steel, 1/2 of the floater is embedded in grout. Wythes: 1 tier of the

wythes can be laid up to 12 in. max. before grouting. The other
shall be grouted in 1 course increments. (1 masonry unit)
If grouting is stopped for more than 1 hour:
constructions joints shall be formed by stopping all tiers at the
same elevation with the grout stopping 1/2 in. below the top of the
last course.
Toothing: is not permitted. Racking should be held to a min.
Wall ties: shall bond all tiers together.

Moisture: 3-5% at the time of laying

BRICK MASONRY

HIGH LIFT GROUTED

Wall ties:
shall bond together all wythes.
Ties hall be not less than 49 gage wire in the form of rectangles 2x4 in.
but less in width than the width of the wall.
Wythes: can be built up not more than 16 in. more than the other wythe.

Ties:
shall be laid out 24 in. o/c horiz. and 16 in. vert. for running bond
24 in. o/c. horiz. and 12 vert. for stack bond.

Grout space: min. 3 1/2 in.
Grout clearance:
between re-bar and masonry is 1 bar diameter.
Vert grout barriers (or dams): shall be built across the entire grout space
the entire height of the wall to control the flow of grout horizontally
Spaced not more than 30 ft. apart.

Admixture: shall be added to grout to prevent shrinkage.
Grouting height: shall be done in lifts not to exceed 4 ft.
Consolidation:
Grout shall be consolidated by mechanical vibration and re-consolidated
before plastisity is lost. With no delay between grouting more than 1 hr.
and grouted entire section in one day.

BLOCK MASONRY

LOW LIFT GROUTED BLOCK MASONRY
Reinforcement bars must be clean of grout spatter, dirt and any other materials other than tight mill scale or light rust.

Clean outs: 48 in. or less no clean outs needed.

BLOCK MASONRY:

HIGH LIFT GROUTING
Reinforcement bars must be clean of grout spatter, dirt and any other
materials other than tight mill scale or light rust.
Can only be done when approved by DSA.

© Professional Study Inc. 2003

Full height of wall between cold joints to be grouted in one day with no delay greater than 1 hour.
Head and bed joints shall be as thick as the block face wall.
Mortar: Type N can not be used
Type m or s. Must be used

Type M:
1 part cement, ¼ Part lime, 2 1/4 - 3 parts sand
Type S:
1 part cement, 1/4-1/2 lime, 2 1/4 - 3 sand.
Bond: running bond shall be used.
Stack bond: steel must be 16 o/c each way

2104A.6.2 GENERAL REQUIREMENTS
Continuous inspection is required for all masonry construction by an inspector specially approved by DSA
(Form 5 required).
The masonry inspector shall successfully complete the DSA masonry exam
Reinforcement bars must be clean of grout spatter, dirt and any other materials other than tight mill scale or light rust.
Reinforcement bars shall be sampled and tested per Section 1928A.2.
Sampling should be done at reinforcement bar fabricator's shop, when bundles are opened.
The lab technician must document the bundle identification (pin bar) and tag the bars to be delivered to the jobsite.

METHODS FOR DESIGN COMPLIANCE

Verify the method to be used in accordance with the approved plans/specifications.
(3) Methods of Design Compliance (one must be used)

Masonry prism testing per Sec. 2105A.3.2 - suggested for high-strength masonry ($f'm$= 2500 psi)

Masonry prism test record per Sec. 2105A.3.3 - never used

Unit strength method per Sec. 2105A.3.4 - commonly used

2105A. Masonry prism testing.
Five shall be built and tested before construction begins.
Three shall be built and tested during construction for each 5,000 sq.ft. of building. 2105A.7 Masonry Inspection.
Masonry prism testing is suggested for high-strength masonry
$f'm = 2500$ psi is the maximum allowed, standard strength

is 1500 psi).
Prism testing has lead time requirement
Since prisms must be built, cured and tested before compliance is determined (and construction can commence).

2105A. The unit strength method f'm =2500 psi
The unit strength method is commonly used on standard strength masonry (1500 psi) projects
The masonry units should be sampled and pallets tagged by the materials test laboratory at the manufacturer's plant.
requires the masonry unit and grout strength of 3750 psi (Table 21A-D, footnotes 2, 4).
The 3750 psi strength can be difficult to attain;
The prism testing must meet the 2500 psi strength, which should not be difficult

2105A.3.3 Masonry prism test record.
Masonry prism test record is rarely, if ever, used.

Testing and Inspections prior to start:
- masonry units
- mortar
- rebar
- concrete
- grout
- admixture

Tests During Work:
Mortar: one test shall be taken on three sucsessive working days.
At least sampled and tested at one week intervals.
Also tests shall be conducted when conditions, mortar type, or material changes
Mortar specimens: 3 per test.
Grout specimens: 3 per test. 3x3x6 in.

PRIOR TO GROUTING:
grout space shall be clean so that all spaces that are to be filled with grout do not contain mortar projections larger than 1/4 in.
Reinforcement bars must be clean of grout spatter, dirt and any other materials other than tight mill scale or light rust.

Wall grouting:
Any one wall section shall be completed in 1 day with no delay greater than 1 hr.

Between grout pours:
A horizontal construction joint shall be formed by stopping all wythes at the same elevation and with the grout stopping 1 1/2 in. below a mortar joint except at the top of wall,

Where bond beams occur the grout pour shall be stopped 1/2 in. below the top of masonry.

Vert grout space:
> Shall be no less than 2x3 in. for low lift and 3x3 for high lift.

Units: at time of laying shall be free from ice, dust and dirt.

Re-bar clearance:
> 1 bar diameter between bar and block.

Re-bar grout coverage:
> Over re-bar is 1 in. (i.e.. top of wall).
>
> Bond beam channel: Shall not be less than 1 1/2 in. x 3 in. from top of the unit.

Clean outs: at the bottom of each cell of grout pour.
> If open ended bond beam units are used clean outs need only be at reinforcing cells)
>
> Clean outs shall be sealed before grouting.
>
> Shall be placed and secured against moving prior to grouting.
>
> Bolts shall be accurately set with templates or approved equivalent means and held in place to prevent dislocation during grouting.

Grout pours: greater than 12 in.high
> shall be mechanically vibrated (consolidated and (reconsolidated).
>
> Grout not mechanically vibrated (less than 12 in.) shall be puddled.

Masonry cores:
> not less than 2 cores having a diameter of 6 in. shall be taken from each project.
>
> Two stores shall be taken from each building for each 5,000 sq.ft. of the greater of the masonry wall area or floor area or fraction there of.
>
> Coring Shall be watched and reported on by IOR

MAXIMUM HIGHT OF GROUT LIFTS

8 in. block----12 ft.
12 in. block---16 ft.
Slump: 9-10 in.

PIPES AND CONDUITS IN MASONRY:
Must be detailed in approved plans.

RE-BAR

Max: 24 x 24 in. spacing.
At top of openings,walks, are roof and floor levels.
12 in. block: shall have two layers of reinforcement.

Openings:
> over 24 in. in either direction shall have 1#5 or 2#4 on all sides and adjacent to opening.
>
> Bars shall extend 48 bar diameters in each direction past opening.

Column Reinforcement Spacing: 2106A.1.12.4 Special provisions for Seismic Zones 3 and 4.
> Column ties not greater than 8 bar diameters (of vert. bars) or
> 24 tie diameters.

Concrete abutting structural masonry: shall be roughened to a full amplitude 1/16 in. exposed aggregate matrix.
Starter wall: minimum 4 in. tall.
Parallel bar clearance: 1 bar diameter of 1 in.

PLACEMENT OF EMBEDDED ANCHOR BOLTS:

Reinforcement and embeded items:
 No "wet-setting" of embedded items (bolts, plates with headed studs, etc.) is allowed;
 All items must be secured in place prior to placement of the grout and
 Must allow access for proper grout placement
 Min Size of Embeded hex head bolts:
  6 in. wall use 1/2 in. bolts
  8 in. wall use 3/4 in. bolts
  10 in. wall use 7/8 in. bolts 12 in. wall use 1 in. bolts
Embedment:
 Shall be min. 8 bolt diameters not less than 4 in.
Spacing: between bolts
 shall be min 8 bolt diameters center to center
 not less than 4 in.
Glass masonry
 shall not be load bearing.

2104A.4 Placing Masonry Units.

MORTAR JOINT SIZE
 Bed joint on starter curb:
  max. 1 in.--- min. 1/4 in.
 Bed joint wall courses:
  max. 5/8 in. --- min. 1/4 in.

Chapter 9: Steel
LESSON 9.1: Background

INTRODUCTION

All metals come from the earth, where most exist in combination with other substances. These compounds are usually mixed with rock or soil to form metallic ores. There are a few metals, however, that are found in a purer state, such as gold, silver, and copper, for example.

The knowledge of metals, as well as their earliest use, dates back to prehistoric times. The Bronze Age, in fact, was named after the metal tools, art objects, and every-day utensils which were developed during that period. Metals were also employed in early construction for a variety of purposes. In addition to purely decorative applications, lead was used for plumbing and bronze was used for concrete reinforcement in ancient Rome. Copper roofing covered Gothic cathedrals, and somewhat later, iron chains were used as tensile ties, as for example, in the base of Michelangelo's dome for St. Peter's in Rome.

It was not until the Industrial Revolution of the mid-18th century, however, that the first metal members intended for construction were produced. Metal as a total structural material, however, was neither easily available nor architecturally acceptable until the beginning of the 19th century. Thus, the use of metal to support building loads is a relatively modern development.

With the manufacture of cast iron girders, beams, and columns, metal bridges began to appear. Later, large halls and factory buildings were framed with these new cast iron sections. Pioneer designers such, as Labrouste with his libraries, Eiffel with his famous tower, and William Jenney with his multistoried structures, paved the way for the acceptance of metal-framed construction.

The development of reinforced concrete was one further advance in the use of metal for construction. Here, the combination of steel with its tensile strength and concrete with its compressive strength led to the development of a modern structural material, which was able to express completely new design concepts.

Today, the skyline of every major city in the world reflects our dependence on the use of metal for tall building construction. In addition, modern architects continue to rely on the vast supply of metal products developed through modern technology for the construction industry.

It is perhaps ironic that metals, which were originally formed when the earth was created, furnish many of the modern building products that are invaluable for today's architecture.

CHARACTERISTICS

Metals are substances which are characterized by their luster, opaqueness, and hardness; their ability to conduct heat and electricity; and by their superior ability to resist deformation.

Extracting a metal from its ore is called smelting, and invariably this involves some sort of heat treatment. Even after it is extracted, the metal still contains small amounts of impurities, which may be further removed by various refining processes. In some cases minor impurities may enhance the metal by forming an alloy that have special properties, such as increased strength, hardness, or corrosion resistance. Since some metals (for example lead, copper, and iron) are very soft in their pure form, metals used in building are frequently alloys, or mixtures, which contain controlled quantities of different minerals.

The physical, chemical, and mechanical properties of metals are so diverse that architects generally know only the most significant data concerning the metals widely used in construction. This data may include strength, toughness, corrosion resistance, appearance, cost, and methods of forming, joining, and handling. As an example, if a dense metal were required, one should know that lead is over four times as dense as aluminum, but, on the other hand, it will melt at half the temperature required to melt aluminum.

Metals are classified as either ferrous or non-ferrous. The ferrous metals are those containing a substantial proportion of iron, such as stainless steel and galvanized iron; while the nonferrous metals are all the others, such as aluminum, copper, and zinc.

DETERIORATION

Almost all metals deteriorate as a result of exposure to air, water, soil, and other chemical agents. Surface discoloration, or tarnish, is merely unsightly; however, internal corrosion - such as the rusting of iron - may lead to physical failure.

Galvanic action, or electrolysis, is

a relatively common type of deterioration that occurs when different metals (or alloys) are in contact. If this contact takes place in the presence of an electrolyte, such as moisture, an electrical current will flow from one metal to another, and in time, one metal will corrode while the other will remain intact. The degree and speed of deterioration depends on the amount of moisture present. Dry air will produce slow action, while an ocean atmosphere will produce intense and swift deterioration. The following list of metals has been arranged in order of galvanic activity. Each metal can be corroded by all that follows it; for example, lead is corroded by brass, and gold is virtually corrosion-proof. In general, metals far apart on the list should not be placed in contact with each other.

1. Aluminum
2. Zinc
3. Iron and Steel 4. Stainless Steel 5. Tin
6. Lead 7. Brass 8. Copper 9. Bronze
10. Gold

In order to prevent galvanic action, different metals should be isolated from one another, or compatible metals should be used instead. For example, if aluminum siding is applied with steel nails, the nails should be insulated from the siding with neoprene washers, or - better yet - aluminum nails should be used in place of steel nails. If uninsulated steel nails are used, the aluminum around the nail will be gradually eaten away, and the siding may eventually fall off.

Other forms of corrosion may be prevented by changing the chemical composition of the metal or by applying a surface treatment. An example of the former is alloying, such as stainless steel; while an example of a surface treatment is using protective coatings, such as galvanizing or anodizing.

FORMING METAL

Forming is the process whereby the extracted metal is transformed into useful products that conform to a particular finished shape. Products may be either cast or wrought.

Cast products are those obtained by pouring molten metal into a mold of the required shape and allowing it to cool.

Wrought products are those obtained by forcibly shaping solid metal to a required form by a variety of methods. These methods include hot or cold rolling (bars, sheets,

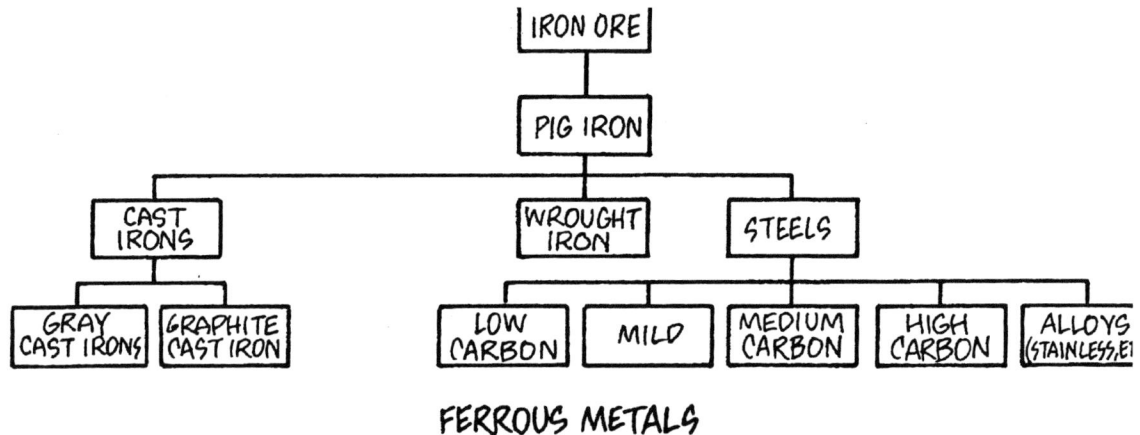

FERROUS METALS

strips, angles, channels, etc.), forging (hammering hot metal), pressing (from sheets), drawing (into wires or tubes), and extruding (forcing a hot mass of metal through an opening which has the shape of the required section, as for example, rods, strips, pipes, and door and window frames). A particular metal or alloy may be more suited to one method of forming than another. In this regard, one should be familiar with the metal's mechanical properties, such as malleability (ease of hammering), ductility (ease of drawing), toughness (resistance to fracture), and hardness (resistance to abrasion).

FERROUS METALS

The principal constituent of all ferrous metals is iron, which is the second most abundant metal and the fourth most abundant element on earth.
All commercial forms of ferrous metals contain some amounts of carbon, and small variations in carbon content have an important influence on their properties. Pure iron, which is difficult to obtain, is tough, malleable, easily magnetized, and fast to oxidize.

Iron is extracted from its ore by smelting, a skill that goes back over 5000 years. Today, blast furnaces are used to reduce the ore to pig iron,
the raw material from which all ferrous metals are made. Pig iron contains about 93% iron, 4% carbon, and small quantities of silicon, phosphorus, and sulfur.

Wrought Iron is almost pure iron with a very low carbon content. It is soft but strong, extremely ductile, easily worked, and relatively resistant to corrosion. It can be forged, bent, or rolled into shape, but it cannot be cast, tempered, or easily welded. Historically, wrought iron was the prime metal used for tension members, such as chains, crane hooks, and anchors. In construction today, however, it is used for ornamental ironwork, grilles, plumbing pipes, and outdoor furniture. Wrought iron is available in pipe, sheet, bar, and bent shapes.

Cast Iron is produced by resmelting pig iron with steel scrap. It has a relatively high carbon content (2% or more) and is available in a variety of types, each with distinct characteristics (white cast iron, grey cast iron, malleable iron, etc.).

Cast iron has a high compressive but low tensile strength. It is easily cast into almost any shape, but it is generally too hard and brittle to be shaped by hammering, rolling, or pressing. Cast iron surfaces are somewhat rough and uneven, but they have good resistance to corrosion.

Historically, cast iron was used for compression members (as in the columns and arches of the Crystal Palace, which was built in 1851). Today, however, the material is used for pipes, certain plumbing fixtures, ornamental iron work, hardware, and a multitude of special castings.

Steel is an alloy of iron that contains no more than 2 percent carbon. The material is produced by the openhearth or Bessemer process in which the impurities are removed from pig iron and the proportions of ingredients
are accurately controlled. The largescale use of steel dates from the latter part of the 19th century, nearly coinciding with the construction of the Eiffel Tower - the last great monument built of wrought iron.

Steel is a hard, strong material that
is also tough and malleable. It is the most widely used structural metal in building construction, because it provides great strength at relatively low cost. Steel can be rolled, drawn, bent, cast, and joined by rivets, bolts, or welds. It is used for structural framing, concrete reinforcing bars, lathing, conduit, pipes, fixtures, miscellaneous and ornamental work, and for all kinds of connectors, such as nails, pins, and bolts.

Listed below are various types of steel together with some of their properties:

Structural steel - Steel used for structural purposes, contains varying amounts of carbon and other elements. Included in this type are also a variety of high strength steels.

Alloy steel - Steel containing other elements which are added to provide special properties. For example, stainless steel, containing chromium and nickel, is strong, hard, and corrosion resistant.

Weathering steel - Steel containing up to 1/2 percent copper which develops an oxide coating when exposed to the weather. It requires no finish. Heat treated steel - Steel that is reheated, or annealed, for improved workability. Case hardened steel - Steel that is reheated and cooled to produce a hard, high carbon surface.

NON-FERROUS METALS

Almost all non-ferrous metals share one desirable characteristic: they resist corrosion. In addition, they generally have superior working properties. On the other hand, the first cost of non-ferrous metals is usually much greater than that of ordinary ferrous metals. As with iron and steel, almost all non-ferrous metals used in construction are alloys.

Aluminum is the most abundant element of the earth's crust. It is obtained from bauxite clay by the electrolytic method, which was developed less than
a hundred years ago. Before that time, aluminum was considered a precious metal.

The important properties of aluminum include its light weight (about one third that of steel), good conductivity to heat and electricity, and high resistance to corrosion (except for galvanic action and some oxidation). It also has high reflective properties, making it useful as a barrier to radiant heat transmission.

Pure aluminum is soft, but as an alloy it can become as hard and strong as mild steel. It is available in nearly all fabricated forms, such as castings, extrusions, sheets, strips, bars, and rods. Aluminum may be joined by riveting, welding, soldering, or adhesive bonding. The material takes a great variety of finishes, including etching, embossing, anodizing, plating, baked enameling, and painting (although never with a lead-based paint).

Each year, aluminum is used more extensively in construction. It is commonly used to frame lightweight structures, ornamentally (such as railings and grilles), for siding and curtain walls, for windows, doors, flashing, insulation, roofing, screening, and hardware.

Copper is a useful metal that is malleable, ductile, and of fairly high mechanical strength. It is remarkably resistant to corrosive agents, particularly sea water, and it has an extremely high electrical and thermal conductivity.

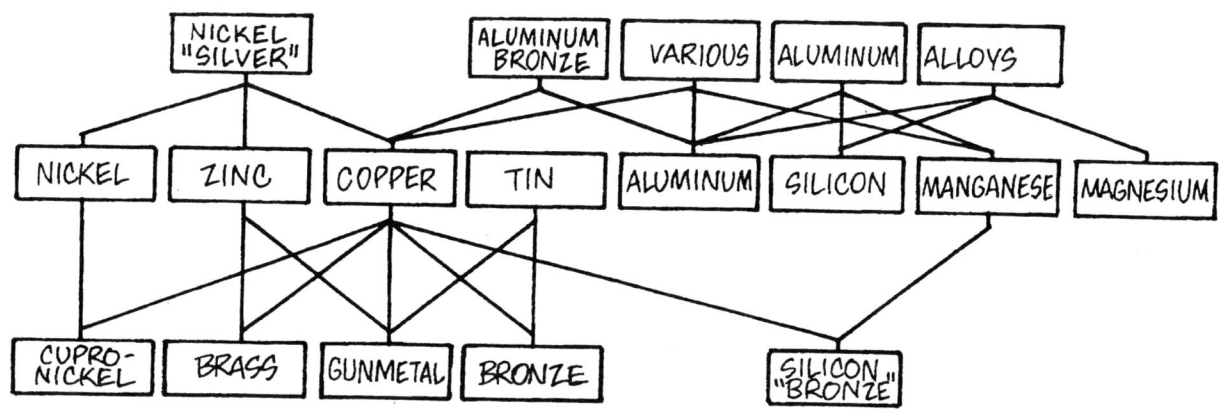

NON-FERROUS METALS AND ALLOYS

Copper is used in construction for electrical work, water distribution lines, roofing and flashings, and for screening mesh. When exposed to the elements, copper develops a distinctive green patina that makes any further finish unnecessary.

Brass is a common alloy of copper and zinc. In general, all brasses resist corrosion and are easily worked. They are used for precise castings, finish hardware, and for plumbing, heating, and air-conditioning components and fittings.

Bronzes are alloys of copper and tin, with small amounts of other metals. Their properties and uses are very similar to brass.

Lead is a heavy, soft, toxic metal of low strength. It is easily worked, corrosion resistant, and relatively impenetrable to radiation. It is used in construction for acid and radiation resistance, for vibration control under foundations and machinery, in rough hardware items, and for roofing and flashing (some examples of which are 2000 years old). However, lead is rarely used these days for plumbing (a term derived from the Latin "plumbum", or lead), due to the danger of lead poisoning.

Zinc is a relatively low strength corrosion resistant metal that is used in building construction for roof covering and flashings and for protective coatings on steel, such as galvanizing.

Monel is a nickel-copper alloy that is strong, bright, ductile, and corrosion resistant. Its uses in construction include roofing, flashing, counter tops, sinks, and other commercial kitchen equipment.

© Professional Study Inc. 2003

METAL FINISHES

Finishes are applied to metals for the sake of appearance or for protection from corrosion. All metals can be mechanically finished by means of grinding, polishing, sandblasting, hammering, or otherwise treating the surface to obtain a special textural effect. In addition, metals may be treated with an applied coating, such as electroplating, enameling, spraying, dipping, or sherardizing (coating with zinc dust).

Most non-ferrous metals, as well as stainless steels, can be (and often are) left to weather with no additional treatment. Ferrous metals, however, require a protective coating to prevent corrosion. One exception, of course, is weathering steel, which acquires a brownish-colored protective oxide coating that deters further rust and corrosion.

Anodizing is a type of metal finish restricted to aluminum, which begins by inserting the material into an electrolyte. When an electric current is applied, a coating is formed on the aluminum surface in a wide choice of colors and hues.

Galvanizing is, by far, the most popular method of protecting iron and steel against corrosion. In this process, a coating of zinc is applied by means of hot dipping, and the amount of coating is expressed in ounces per square foot of sheet. The importance of zinc coating derives from the fact that, if through wear or damage the material becomes exposed, galvanic action causes the zinc to corrode and form compounds that cover and continue to protect the iron or steel for as long as any zinc remains. Because of the effective protection it affords at a relatively low price, this use of zinc represents the largest consumption of the metal in this country.

Galvanized sheet and strip are available in plain flat, corrugated, and special shapes. They are commonly used in construction for roofing, siding, decking, flashing, and cladding, as in kalamein doors (sheet metal-covered wood core doors used for high fire resistance).

Although zinc is considerably more resistant to corrosion than steel, it is not immune to deterioration. Therefore, when zinc-coated products are exposed to corrosive conditions, they require the additional protection of paint. Most paints will not adhere to galvanized metal unless the surface has been completely cleaned and prepared. For this purpose a phosphatizing solution may be used to provide the necessary paint bond. Among the available products, portland cementbased paint is an excellent primer for galvanized surfaces.

THE USE OF METALS IN CONSTRUCTION

The use of metals in construction can be classified into six major categories, as follows:

1. Structural - including structural steel and reinforcing elements for concrete, such as mesh, rods, and wire rope.

2. Hollow metalwork - including doors, bucks, partitions, panels, windows, mullions, curtain walls, and other panel systems which incorporate a variety of materials, such as glass, stone, plastic, etc.

3. Miscellaneous metalwork - including stairs, railings, fencing, gratings, rough hardware, ladders, etc.

4. Ornamental metalwork - including plaques, letters, finish hardware, railings, screens, grilles, expansion joint covers, etc.

5. Flashing - including base and cap flashing, gutters and leaders, spandrel and through-wall flashing, copings, termite shields, etc. This group is further discussed in Lesson 6

6. Miscellaneous - including rough hardware, nuts and bolts, rivets, screws, nails, washers, inserts, hangers, anchors, wire, etc.

STRUCTURAL STEEL CONSTRUCTION

Structural steel construction comprises the fabrication and erection of hot-rolled standard sections which are manufactured from medium carbon grade steel (one-quarter to one-half percent carbon). These sections are available in a vast number of weights and sizes, and they include wideflanged beams and columns (W shape), American standard beams (S shape), channels (C shape), angles (L shape), tees (WT shape - cut from W shape), tubing (TS shape), as well as bars and plates.

© Professional Study Inc. 2003

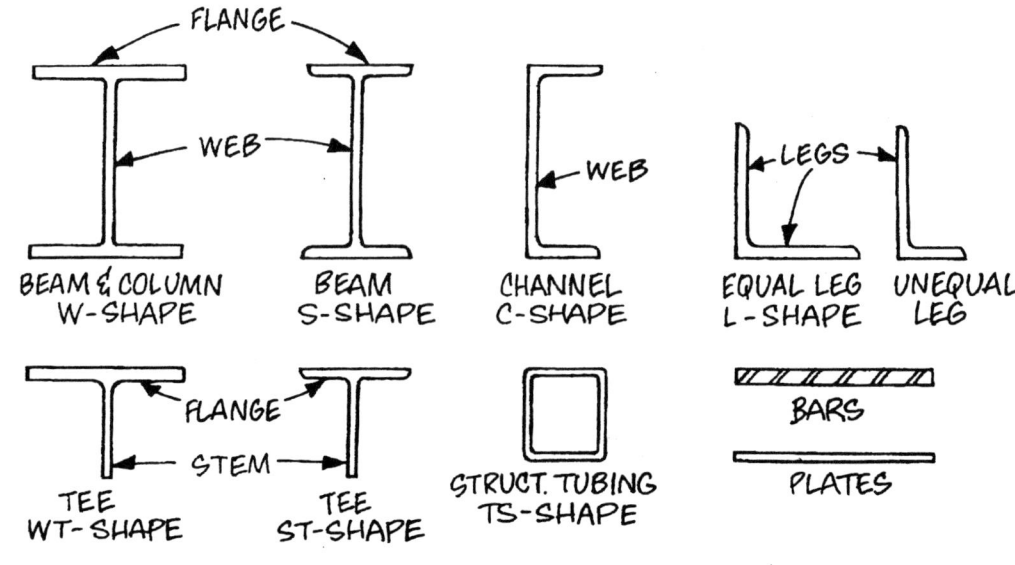

ROLLED STEEL SECTIONS

In addition to the sections above, an infinite number of built-up shapes can be constructed from combinations of standard shapes. The resulting configurations, such as plate girders, built-up columns, truss sections, rigid bents, etc. are employed to solve special structural problems.

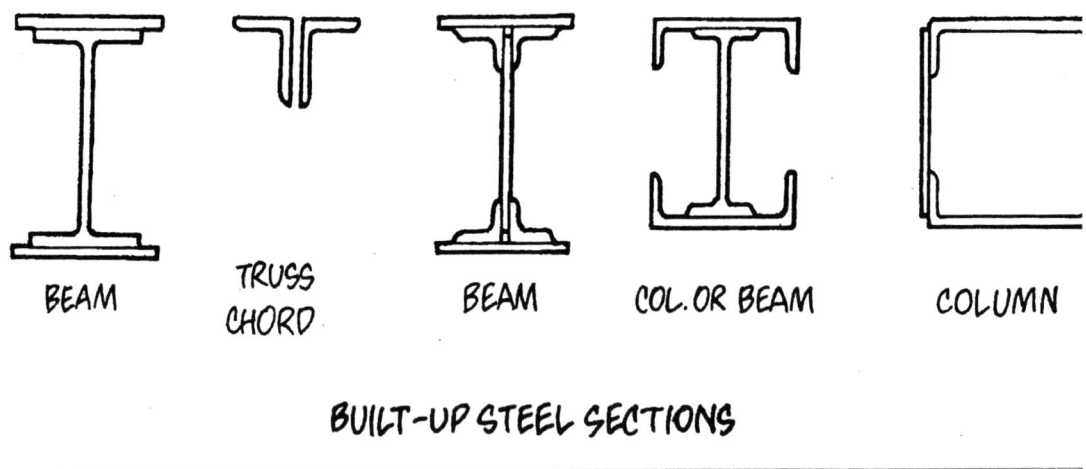

BUILT-UP STEEL SECTIONS

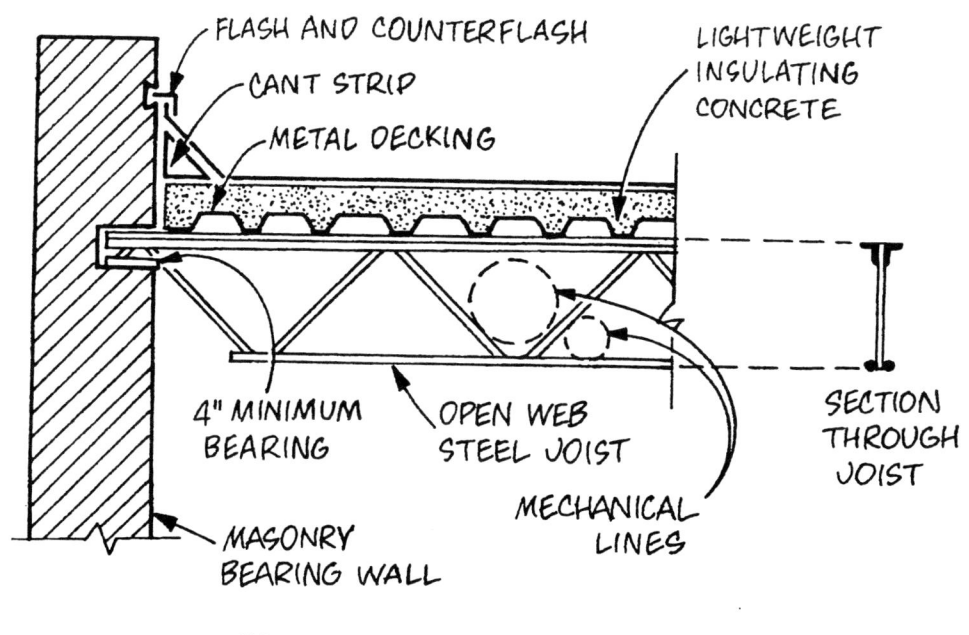

OPEN WEB JOIST CONSTRUCTION

Structural steel is most often used in a post and beam system that results in a skeleton frame, which is often designed to carry relatively heavy loads over long spans. Since steel sections are difficult to work on the site, as much as possible they are cut, shaped and often bolted, or welded in a fabricating shop according to the required specifications. Structural steel construction requires fire-resistant protection, and - where exposed - treatment against corrosion.

METAL DECKING

Metal decking is manufactured from sheet steel in a corrugated, ribbed, or cellular form. The edges overlap or interlock to form a working platform during construction and

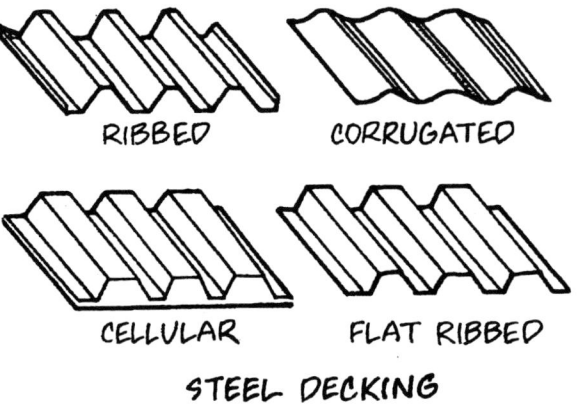

STEEL DECKING

permanent formwork for a concrete floor slab. The material is either plain or galvanized, with long, narrow sections having ribs about 6 inches on center and 1-1/2 to 4 inches or more in depth. Cellular steel decking has the additional advantage of providing mechanical raceways to accommodate electrical lines.

ORNAMENTAL METAL

Non-ferrous metals are used most frequently for ornamental metal work, but in some cases stainless steel is also used. These items are fabricated from rolled shapes, cast shapes, or cold-formed (bent) shapes. Among these are decorative grilles and louvers, mesh and wire cloth, metal treillage, and flagpoles.

Ornamental expanded metal is made by slitting a sheet of soft metal and then expanding it in a direction normal to the slits.

MISCELLANEOUS METAL

The ferrous metals are generally used for the multitude of metal items required for a specific project. Quite often these items employ conventional fabricated shapes, and they may include metal stairs, railings, fire escapes, gratings, and fences. For this type of work, shop drawings are usually furnished, in order to check sizes, details, and methods of anchorage.

The use of metals in contemporary construction has proliferated in direct proportion to technological developments. Today, there are literally thousands of metal items included in every building project, regardless of the framing material used. Thus, even in masonry buildings, lightweight metal door bucks and hollow metal doors are often used.

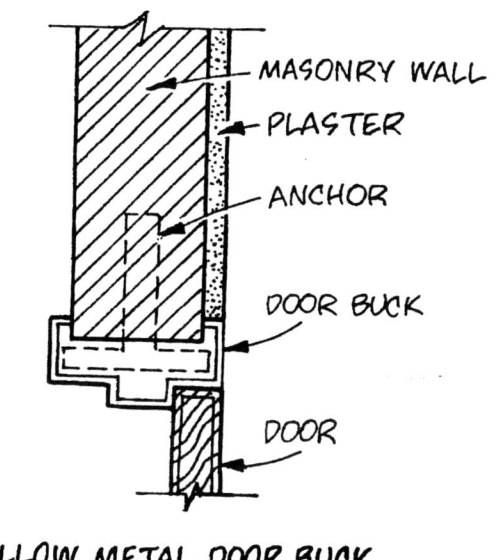

HOLLOW METAL DOOR BUCK

Similarly, in the simplest woodframed structures one can find sheet metal ventilation louvers, aluminum windows, and brass fittings. From curtain walls to flashings to finish hardware, there are metal products used in construction that fulfill the required functions in a way no substitute material is able to do. We can assume, therefore, that metals will enjoy continued popularity in the foreseeable future of the construction industry.

CONCLUSION

For the purpose of the DSA exam you as the inspector candidate should be familiar with the structural uses of steel and the methods for connection. Welding and bolting are the methods used for connection of steel construction shapes. The following lessons will familiarize you with the critical issues dealing with steel construction.

Chapter 9: Steel
LESSON 9.2

STRUCRTURAL STEEL
(Title 24, Part 2, Volume 2, Chapter 22A)

Structural steel is perhaps the most difficult material to deal with in terms of the DSA Inspector. Chapter 22A of the California Building Code establishes the ground rules for inspecting and material identification of for steel and a few other referenced code books do the rest of the work. The following is a short explanation of the books and what it is that they do.

CBC Part 2, Volume 2, Chapter 22A:
- This is the building code structural steel chapter. It establishes the testing and material ID Standards for structural steel, and for high strength bolts.
- See the highlighting list for more information.

AISC ASD (Manual of Steel Construction)
- This is a referenced code.
- It is used to define the physical properties of the various shapes and grades of structural steel. In addition it defines the limits for high strength bolting.
- The Project inspector needs only to know how use this book to verify component dimensions. Beyond this is the realm of the special inspector.

AWS D1.1 (American Welding Society)
- This is a very technical book that defines the standards and procedures for structural welding inspections.
- As a project inspector you should know what this book is and you should have a general understanding of the concept of WPS (Welding Procedure Specifications)

AWS D1.4 (American Welding Society)
- This book is very similar in nature to the D1.1 except that it is written to specifically govern the welding of reinforcing steel.

Read through the following highlighting list and study these materials.

© Professional Study Inc. 2003

Highlighting List
STRUCRTURAL STEEL
(Title 24, Part 2, Volume 2, Chapter 22A)

Take out your code book and highlight the code sections as they appear on this list in either red or yellow.

The "**Commentary**" on the right is broken down into four categories and they are as follows:

1. **TEST QUESTION (Highlight in Red)**
   - (Indicates that this material is very likely to be specifically referenced on the DSA exams)

2. **REMEMBER (Highlight in Yellow)**
   - (Indicates that you should know this material and that it is relevant to your work as an inspector)

3. **BEWARE (Highlight in Yellow)**
   - (Indicates that there is something that may not be apparent at first but that the inspector will have to deal with)

4. **SEE ALSO (Highlight in Yellow)**
   - (Indicates that there is another code section that affects this information)

© Professional Study Inc. 2003

Highlight List (T-24, Part 2, Ch.22A)
Chapter 22A [DSA/SS & OSHPD]
STEEL

Division I. GENERAL

SECTION 2203A. MATERIAL IDENTIFICATION

2203A.1 General. Steel furnished for structural load-carrying purposes shall be properly identified for conformity to the ordered grade in accordance with approved national standards, the provisions of this chapter and the appropriate UBC standards. Steel which is not readily identifiable as to grade from marking and test records shall be tested to determine conformity to such standards.

> **Comment:** REMEMBER
> Material Must be ID'd prior to cutting into smaller pieces

2203A.2 Structural Steel. structural steel shall be identified by the mill in accordance with approved national standards. When

The fabricator shall maintain identity of the material and shall maintain suitable procedures and records attesting that the specified grade has been furnished in conformity with the applicable standard.

When structural steel is furnished to a specified minimum yield point greater than 36,000 psi (248 MPa), the ASTM or other specification designation shall be included near the erection mark on each shipping assembly or important construction component over any shop coat of paint prior to shipment from the fabricator's plant

> **Comment:** REMEMBER
> Important pieces should be ID'd when sent to the site over or through the primer

    Pieces of such steel which are to be cut to smaller sizes shall, before cutting, be legibly marked with the fabricator's identification mark on each of the smaller-sized pieces to provide continuity of identification. When subject to fabrication operations, prior to

> **Comment:** REMEMBER
> Chain of custody (See note above)

assembling into members, which might obliterate paint marking, such as blast cleaning, galvanizing or heating for forming, such pieces of steel shall be marked by steel die stamping or by a substantial tag firmly attached.

2205A.4.1 Steel Deck Diaphragms.

Welding inspection shall conform to Section 2231A, Division XII.

2205A.10 Welding. Welding procedures, welder qualification requirements and welding electrodes shall be in accordance with Division II, III, VI or VII and approved national standards.

2205A.10.2 No welded splices shall be made except those shown on approved plans.

> **Comment:** BEWARE
> No welded Splices unless on plans.

2205A.11 Bolts. The use of high-strength A 325 and A 490 bolts shall be in accordance with the requirements of Divisions II and III.

> **Comment:** REMEMBER
> For High Strength Bolts See ANSC Book (Green)
> Pg. 5-265 to 5-277

Anchor bolts shall be set accurately to the pattern and dimensions called for on the plans. The protrusion of the threaded ends through the connected material shall be sufficient to fully engage the threads of the

nuts, but shall not be greater than the length of threads on the bolts.
Base plate holes for anchor bolts may be oversized as follows:

Bolt Size, inches (mm)	Hole Size, inches (mm)
3/4 (19.1)	5/16 (7.9) oversized
7/8 (22.2)	5/16 (7.9) oversized
1 < 2 (25.4 < 50.8)	1/2 (12.7) oversized
> 2 (> 50.8)	1 (25.4) > bolt diameter

> **Comment:** TEST QUESTION
> Oversizing of Both Holes

Division II. DESIGN STANDARD FOR LOAD AND RESISTANCE FACTOR
DESIGN SPECIFICATION FOR STRUCTURAL STEEL BUILDINGS
American Institute of Steel Construction
(December 1, 1993)
See Section 1602A, *California Building Code*

Division III. DESIGN STANDARD FOR SPECIFICATION FOR STRUCTURAL STEEL BUILDINGS
ALLOWABLE STRESS DESIGN AND PLASTIC DESIGN

SECTION 2209A. AMENDMENTS

Bolts in Combination with Welds. *In new work, A307 bolts or high-strength bolts used in bearing-type connections shall not be considered as sharing the stress in combinations with welds. The welds shall be made before the bolts are tensioned. Welds, if used, shall be provided to carry the entire stress in the connection. High-strength bolts proportioned for slip-critical connections may be considered as sharing the stress with the welds.*

> **Comment:** TEST QUESTION
> Combination welded and bolted connections to be welded first and then tightened (bolted)

Division IV. SEISMIC PROVISIONS FOR STRUCTURAL STEEL BUILDINGS
Based on Seismic Provisions for Structural Steel Buildings
of the American Institute of Steel Construction.
(April 15, 1997)

Division V. SEISMIC PROVISIONS FOR STRUCTURAL STEEL BUILDINGS FOR USE WITH ALLOWABLE STRESS DESIGN

2213A.4 Materials.

2213A.4.1 Quality. Structural steel used in lateral-force-resisting systems shall conform to A 36, A 500, A 501, *A 992*, A 572 (Grades 42 and 50), A913 (Grades 50 and 65) and A588. Structural steel conforming to A283 (Grade D) may be used for base plates and anchor bolts.

> **Comment:** SEE ALSO AISC for further information on these steel types Table 1

> **EXCEPTION:** Other steels permitted in this code may be used for the following:
> 1. One-story buildings.
> 2. Light-framed wall systems in accordance with Division VIII.

Division XII. TESTING AND INSPECTION

SECTION 2231A. GENERAL PROVISIONS

2231A.1 Tests of Structural Steel......................... Any steel not properly identified shall be tested to meet the minimum chemical and mechanical requirements of the ASTM standard appropriate for the steel specified for the structure. **CHAP. 22A, DIV. XII**

> **Comment:** REMEMBER Chemical and Mechanical tests are Required. Chemical Testing is expensive and not often carried out.

> **EXCEPTION:** No mechanical tests are required for unidentified steel when the minimum yield stress required by the design is less than or equal to 25 ksi (172 MPa) and the steel is not part of the designated lateral-force-resisting system.

2231A.2 Tests of High-strength Bolts, Nuts and Washers. High-strength bolts, nuts and washers shall be sampled and tested by an approved independent testing laboratory for conformance with the requirements of Division III.

> **Comment:** REMEMBER High Strength Bolts must also be tested.

2231A.3 Tests of End-welded Studs. End-welded studs shall be sampled, tested and inspected per the requirements of the Structural Welding Code. Steel, 1998 edition, published by the American Welding Society.

2231A.4 Inspection of Shop Fabrication. Inspection of shop fabrication shall be required for significant structural detailed connection and fabrication work as directed by the enforcement agency. This inspection shall be made by a qualified inspector approved by the enforcement agency.

> **Comment:** REMEMBER Shop inspections also required to ID the materials.

2231A.5 Inspection of Welding......................... inspecting welding operations. The inspector's ability to distinguish between sound and unsound welding shall be reliably established. The minimum requirements for a qualified welding inspector shall be as those for an AWS certified welding inspector (CWI), as defined in the provisions of the ANSI/AWS QCI-1-96, Standard for AWS Certification of Welding Inspectors published by the American Welding Society. All welding inspectors shall be as approved by the enforcement agency.

> **Comment:** TEST QUESTION Welding inspector to be AWS CWI and approved by DSA (Form DSA 5)

The welding inspector shall make a systematic record of all welds. This record shall include in addition to other required records:

    1. Identification marks of welders.
    2. List of defective welds.
    3. Manner of correction of defects.

The welding inspector shall check the material, equipment, details of construction and procedure, as well as the welds. The inspector shall also check the ability of the welder. The inspector shall verify that the installation procedure for automatic end-welded stud shear connectors is in accordance with the requirements of AWS D1.1, Structural Welding Code.Steel, 1998

> **EXCEPTION:** *Plant welding inspection of open-web steel joists may be waived with the approval of the enforcement agency where welding inspection is provided at the jobsite.*

2231A.6 Inspection of High-strength Bolt Installations. *Inspection of high-strength bolt installations shall bemade in accordance with Division III by an inspector specially approved for tha purpose by the enforcement agency. The inspector shall check the materials, equipment, details of construction and installation procedure*

> **Comment:** REMEMBER
> High Strength Bolting is different from Welding Inspection sure of your inspector's credentials.

Chapter 9: Steel
LESSON 9.3

STRUCRTURAL STEEL
(AISC ASD)

This publication is a referenced and adopted code that is used to determine the standardized physical characteristics of steel construction elements. In other words it is the book where you would go to find out what size, shape, and configuration some piece or assembly would be.

For example if you have a delivery of what are supposed to be W14x68 beams, how do you verify that they are the size and dimensions that they should be. You can use this book to determine that. Also critical to this book is the specification for tolerances that are outlined here. This will give you the tools to either accept or reject piece of structural steel that has physical imperfections.

Various types of approved structural connections are described here along with the methods for tightening high strength bolts. This is a very complex and strange process that the project inspector does not need to fully understand but that they need to have a working knowledge of.

The following is a brief description of the pertinent sections of the book:

Part 1: 1-1 through 1-158 :   Dimensions and Properties
This part contains a number of tables that detail the exact dimensions of various structural steel shapes. We have included a number of the tables from this part in order for you to become familiar with the process. Use the included tables for practice, however the practice questions and may be from tables not included in the online materials. Therefore you will have to be proficient at using your book.

Parts 2-4: 2-1 through 4-175: Design of Beams, Girders, Columns, and Connections:
These parts of the Steel manual are rarely if ever used by the project inspector. Do not concern yourself with this material.

Part 5: 5-265 through 5-277: ASTM A325 and A490 (High Strength Bolts)
You should read through these pages and have an understanding of what the methods of bolt tightening are and what the terminology means. The excerpts that we have included here should be sufficient.

Study the following excerpts from the AISC Steel Manual and use them to highlight your book as shown and to practice using the various resources.

Part 1: 1-1 through 1-158 : Dimensions and Properties

Comment: TURN TO PAGE 1-8 (AISC ASD) Green Book

TABLE 2
Structural Shape Size Groupings for Tensile Property

Structural Shapes	Group 1	Group 2	Group 3	Group 4
shapes	W 24x55, 62 W 21 x44 to 57 incl. W 18x35 to 71 incl. W 16x26 to 57 incl. W 14x22 to 53 incl. W 12x14 to 58 incl. W 10x12 to 45 incl. W 8x10 to 48 incl. W 6x9 to 25 incl. W 5x16, 19 W 4x13	W 44 x 198, 224 W 40x149 to 268 incl. W 36x135 to 210 incl. W 33x118 to 152 incl. W 30x90 to 211 incl. W 27x84 to 178 incl. W 24x68 to 162 incl. W 21 x62 to 147 incl. W 18x76 to 143 incl. W 16x67 to 100 incl. W 14x61 to 132 incl. W 12x65 to 106 incl. W 10x49 to 112 incl. W 8x58, 67	W44 x 248, 285 W 40x277 to 328 incl. W 36x230 to 300 incl. W 33x201 to 291 incl. W 30x235 to 261 incl. W 27x 194 to 258 incl. W 24x176 to 229 incl. W 21 x166 to 223 incl. W 18x158 to 192 incl. W 14x145 to 211 incl. W 12x120 to 190 incl.	W 40x362 to 655 incl. W 36x328 to 798 incl. W 33x318 to 619 incl. W 30x292 to 581 incl. W 27 x 281 to 539 incl. W 24x250 to 492 incl. W 21 x248 to 402 incl. W 18x211 to 311 incl. W 14x233 to 550 incl. W 12x210 to 336 incl.
M Shapes	to 37.7 lb./ft incl.			
S Shapes	to 35 lb./ft incl.			
HP Shapes		to 102 lb./ft incl.	over 102 lb./ft	
American Standard Channels (C)	to 20.7 lb./ft incl.	over 20.7 lb./ft		
Miscellaneous Channels (MC)	to 28.5 lb./ft incl.	over 28.5 lb./ft		
Angles (L) Structural Bar-size	to $\frac{1}{2}$ in. incl.	over $\frac{1}{2}$ to $\frac{3}{4}$ in. incl.	over $\frac{3}{4}$ in.	

Notes: Structural tees from W, M and S shapes fall into the same group as the structural shape from which *they* are cut.
Group 4 and Group 5 shapes are generally contemplated for application as columns or compression components. When used in other applications (e.g., trusses) and when thermal cutting or welding is required, special material specification and fabrication procedures apply to minimize the possibility of cracking. (See Part 5, Specification Sects. A3.1, J1.7, J1.8, J2.7, and M2.2 and corresponding Commentary sections.)

1-9

DIMENSIONS AND PROPERTIES

W

Shapes
M Shapes
S Shapes
HP Shapes
American Standard Channels (C)
Miscellaneous Channels (MC)
Angles (L)

STRUCTURAL SHAPES
DESIGNATIONS, DIMENSIONS AND PROPERTIES

The hot rolled shapes shown in Part 1 of this Manual are published in ASTM Specification A6/A6M, *Standard Specification for General Requirements for Rolled Steel Plates, Shapes, Sheet Piling, And Bars For Structural Use.*

W shapes have essentially parallel flange surfaces. The profile of a W shape of a given nominal depth and weight available from different producers is essentially the same except for the size of fillets between the web and flange.

HP bearing pile shapes have essentially parallel flange surfaces and equal web and flange thicknesses. The profile of an HP shape of a given nominal depth and weight available from different producers is essentially the same.

American Standard beams (S) and American Standard channels (C) have a slope of approximately 16⅔% (2 in 12 in.) on their inner flange surfaces. The profiles of S and C shapes of a given nominal depth and weight available from different producers are essentially the same.

The letter M designates shapes that cannot be classified as W, HP or S shapes. Similarly, MC designates channels that cannot be classified as C shapes. Because many of the M and MC shapes are only available from a limited number of producers, or are infrequently rolled, their availability should be checked prior to specifying these shapes. They have various slopes on their inner flange surfaces, dimensions for which may be obtained from the respective producing mills.

The flange thickness given in the tables for S, M, C and MC shapes is the *average* flange thickness.

In calculating the theoretical weights, properties and dimensions of the rolled shapes listed in Part 1 of this Manual, fillets and roundings have been included for all shapes except angles. The properties of these rolled shapes are based on the *smallest* theoretical size fillets produced; dimensions for detailing are based on the *largest* theoretical size fillets produced. These properties and dimensions are either exact or slightly conservative for all producers who offer them.

Equal leg and unequal leg angle (L) shapes of the same nominal size available from different producers have profiles which are essentially the same, except for the size of fillet between the legs and the shape of the ends of the legs. The k distance given in the tables for each angle is based on the largest theoretical size fillet available. Availability of certain angles is subject to rolling accumulation and geographical location, and should be checked with material suppliers.

AMERICAN INSTITUTE OF STEEL CONSTRUCTION

W SHAPES
Dimensions

Designation	Area A in.²	Depth d in.	Web Thickness t_w in.	$\frac{t_w}{2}$ in.	Flange Width b_f in.	Flange Thickness t_f in.	Distance T in.	Distance k in.	Distance k_1 in.
W 44×285	83.8	44.02 44	1.024 1	1/2	11.811 11 3/4	1.772 1 3/4	38 5/8	2 11/16	1 3/8
×248	72.8	43.62 43 5/8	0.865 7/8	7/16	11.811 11 3/4	1.575 1 9/16	38 5/8	2 1/2	1 5/16
×224	65.8	43.31 43 1/4	0.787 13/16	7/16	11.811 11 3/4	1.416 1 7/16	38 5/8	2 3/8	1 5/16
×198	58.0	42.91 42 7/8	0.709 11/16	3/8	11.811 11 3/4	1.220 1 1/4	38 5/8	2 1/8	1 1/4
W 40×328	96.4	40.00 40	0.910 15/16	1/2	17.910 17 7/8	1.730 1 3/4	33 3/4	3 1/8	1 11/16
×298	87.6	39.69 39 3/4	0.830 13/16	7/16	17.830 17 7/8	1.575 1 9/16	33 3/4	3	1 5/8
×268	78.8	39.37 39 3/8	0.750 3/4	3/8	17.750 17 3/4	1.415 1 7/16	33 3/4	2 13/16	1 9/16
×244	71.7	39.06 39	0.710 11/16	3/8	17.710 17 3/4	1.260 1 1/4	33 3/4	2 5/8	1 9/16
×221	64.8	38.67 38 5/8	0.710 11/16	3/8	17.710 17 3/4	1.065 1 1/16	33 3/4	2 7/16	1 9/16
×192	56.5	38.20 38 1/4	0.710 11/16	3/8	17.710 17 3/4	0.830 13/16	33 3/4	2 1/4	1 9/16
W 40×655*	192.0	43.62 43 5/8	1.970 2	1	16.870 16 7/8	3.540 3 9/16	33 3/4	4 15/16	2 1/4
×593*	174.0	42.99 43	1.790 1 13/16	15/16	16.690 16 3/4	3.230 3 1/4	33 3/4	4 5/8	2 1/8
×531*	156.0	42.34 42 3/8	1.610 1 5/8	13/16	16.510 16 1/2	2.910 2 15/16	33 3/4	4 5/16	2
×480*	140.0	41.81 41 3/4	1.460 1 7/16	3/4	16.360 16 3/8	2.640 2 5/8	33 3/4	4	2
×436*	128.0	41.34 41 3/8	1.340 1 5/16	11/16	16.240 16 1/4	2.400 2 3/8	33 3/4	3 13/16	1 15/16
×397*	116.0	40.95 41	1.220 1 1/4	5/8	16.120 16 1/8	2.200 2 3/16	33 3/4	3 5/8	1 7/8
×362*	106.0	40.55 40 1/2	1.120 1 1/8	9/16	16.020 16	2.010 2	33 3/4	3 7/16	1 13/16
×324	95.3	40.16 40 1/8	1.000 1	1/2	15.905 15 7/8	1.810 1 13/16	33 3/4	3 1/4	1 3/4
×297	87.4	39.84 39 7/8	0.930 15/16	1/2	15.825 15 7/8	1.650 1 5/8	33 3/4	3 1/16	1 11/16
×277	81.3	39.69 39 5/8	0.830 13/16	7/16	15.830 15 7/8	1.575 1 9/16	33 3/4	3	1 5/8
×249	73.3	39.38 39 3/8	0.750 3/4	3/8	15.750 15 3/4	1.420 1 7/16	33 3/4	2 13/16	1 9/16
×215	63.3	38.98 39	0.650 5/8	5/16	15.750 15 3/4	1.220 1 1/4	33 3/4	2 5/8	1 9/16
×199	58.4	38.67 38 5/8	0.650 5/8	5/16	15.750 15 3/4	1.065 1 1/16	33 3/4	2 7/16	1 9/16
W 40×183[b]	53.7	38.98 39	0.650 5/8	5/16	11.810 11 3/4	1.220 1 1/4	33 3/4	2 5/8	1 9/16
×167	49.1	38.59 38 5/8	0.650 5/8	5/16	11.810 11 3/4	1.025 1	33 3/4	2 7/16	1 9/16
×149	43.8	38.20 38 1/4	0.630 5/8	5/16	11.810 11 3/4	0.830 13/16	33 3/4	2 1/4	1 1/2

*For application refer to Notes in Table 2.
[b]Heavier shapes in this series are available from some producers.
Shapes in shaded rows are not available from domestic producers.

AMERICAN INSTITUTE OF STEEL CONSTRUCTION

Sample Question: *What is the flange thickness of a W44x198?*

Answer: 1.220 in.   1-1/4"

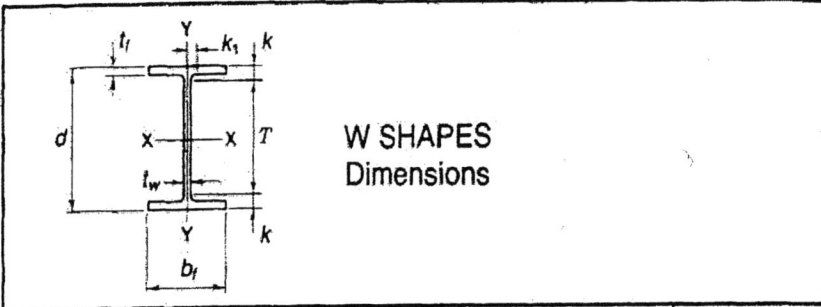

W SHAPES
Dimensions

Desig- nation	Area A	Depth d		Web			Flange			Distance		
				Thickness t_w		$\frac{t_w}{2}$	Width b_f		Thickness t_f		T	k	k_1
	In.²	-	In.	In.		In.	In.		In.		In.	In.	In.
W 14×132	38.8	14.66	14⅝	0.645	⅝	5/16	14.725	14¾	1.030	1	11¼	1 11/16	15/16
×120	35.3	14.48	14½	0.590	9/16	5/16	14.670	14⅝	0.940	15/16	11¼	1⅝	15/16
×109	32.0	14.32	14⅜	0.525	½	¼	14.605	14⅝	0.860	⅞	11¼	1 9/16	⅞
× 99	29.1	14.16	14⅛	0.485	½	¼	14.565	14⅝	0.780	¾	11¼	1 7/16	⅞
× 90	26.5	14.02	14	0.440	7/16	¼	14.520	14½	0.710	11/16	11¼	1⅜	⅞
W 14× 82	24.1	14.31	14¼	0.510	½	¼	10.130	10⅛	0.855	⅞	11	1⅝	1
× 74	21.8	14.17	14⅛	0.450	7/16	¼	10.070	10⅛	0.785	13/16	11	1 9/16	15/16
× 68	20.0	14.04	14	0.415	7/16	¼	10.035	10	0.720	¾	11	1½	15/16
× 61	17.9	13.89	13⅞	0.375	⅜	3/16	9.995	10	0.645	⅝	11	1 7/16	15/16
W 14× 53	15.6	13.92	13⅞	0.370	⅜	3/16	8.060	8	0.660	11/16	11	1 7/16	15/16
× 48	14.1	13.79	13¾	0.340	5/16	3/16	8.030	8	0.595	⅝	11	1⅜	⅞
× 43	12.6	13.66	13⅝	0.305	5/16	3/16	7.995	8	0.530	½	11	1 5/16	⅞
W 14× 38	11.2	14.10	14⅛	0.310	5/16	3/16	6.770	6¾	0.515	½	12	1 1/16	⅝
× 34	10.0	13.98	14	0.285	5/16	3/16	6.745	6¾	0.455	7/16	12	1	⅝
× 30	8.85	13.84	13⅞	0.270	¼	⅛	6.730	6¾	0.385	⅜	12	15/16	⅝
W 14× 26	7.69	13.91	13⅞	0.255	¼	⅛	5.025	5	0.420	7/16	12	15/16	9/16
× 22	6.49	13.74	13¾	0.230	¼	⅛	5.000	5	0.335	5/16	12	⅞	9/16

AMERICAN INSTITUTE OF STEEL CONSTRUCTION

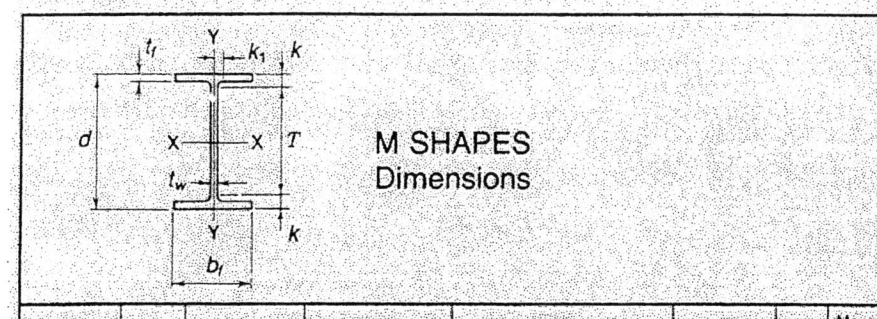

M SHAPES
Dimensions

Desig-nation	Area A	Depth d		Web Thickness t_w		$\frac{t_w}{2}$	Flange Width b_f		Thickness t_f		Distance T	k	Grip	Max. Flge. Fastener
	In.²	In.		In.		In.	In.		In.		In.	In.	In.	In.
M 14×18	5.10	14.00	14	0.215	3/16	1/8	4.000	4	0.270	1/4	12¾	5/8	1/4	3/4
M 12×11.8	3.47	12.00	12	0.177	3/16	1/8	3.065	3⅛	0.225	1/4	10⅞	9/16	1/4	—
M 12×10.8	3.18	11.97	12	0.160	3/16	1/16	3.065	3⅛	0.210	1/4	11	1/2	1/4	1/2
M 12×10	2.94	11.97	12	0.149	3/16	1/16	3.250	3¼	0.180	3/16	11	1/2	3/16	1/2
M 10×9	2.65	10.00	10	0.157	3/16	1/8	2.690	2¾	0.206	3/16	8⅞	9/16	3/16	—
M 10×8	2.35	9.95	10	0.141	3/16	1/16	2.690	2¾	0.182	3/16	9⅛	7/16	3/16	3/8
M 10×7.5	2.21	9.99	10	0.130	1/8	1/16	2.690	2¾	0.173	3/16	9⅛	7/16	3/16	3/8
M 8×6.5	1.92	8.00	8	0.135	1/8	1/16	2.281	2¼	0.189	3/16	7	1/2	3/16	—
M 6×4.4	1.29	6.00	6	0.114	1/8	1/16	1.844	1⅞	0.171	3/16	5⅛	7/16	3/16	—
M 5×18.9	5.55	5.00	5	0.316	5/16	3/16	5.003	5	0.416	7/16	3¼	7/8	7/16	7/8

AMERICAN INSTITUTE OF STEEL CONSTRUCTION

Comment: TURN TO PAGE 1- (AISC ASD) Green Book

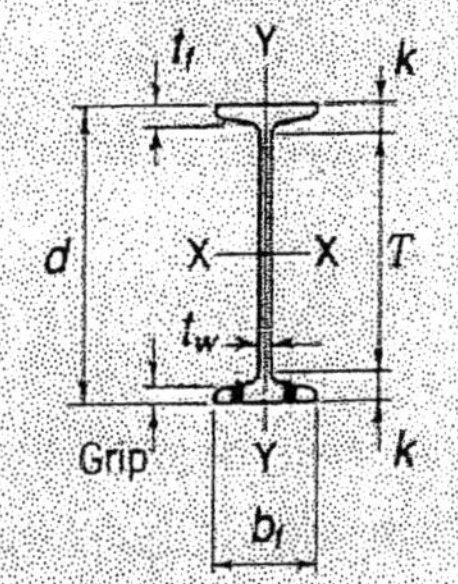

S SHAPES
Dimensions

Designation	Area A	Depth d		Web Thickness t_w		$\frac{t_w}{2}$	Flange Width b_f		Flange Thickness t_f		Distance T	Distance k	Grip	Max. Flge. Fastener
	In.²	In.		In.		In.	In.		In.		In.	In.	In.	In.
S 24×121	35.6	24.50	24½	0.800	13/16	7/16	8.050	8	1.090	1 1/16	20½	2	1⅛	1
×106	31.2	24.50	24½	0.620	⅝	5/16	7.870	7⅞	1.090	1 1/16	20½	2	1⅛	1
S 24×100	29.3	24.00	24	0.745	¾	⅜	7.245	7¼	0.870	⅞	20½	1¾	⅞	1
×90	26.5	24.00	24	0.625	⅝	5/16	7.125	7⅛	0.870	⅞	20½	1¾	⅞	1
×80	23.5	24.00	24	0.500	½	¼	7.000	7	0.870	⅞	20½	1¾	⅞	1
S 20×96	28.2	20.30	20¼	0.800	13/16	7/16	7.200	7¼	0.920	15/16	16¾	1¾	15/16	1
×86	25.3	20.30	20¼	0.660	11/16	⅜	7.060	7	0.920	15/16	16¾	1¾	15/16	1
S 20×75	22.0	20.00	20	0.635	⅝	5/16	6.385	6⅜	0.795	13/16	16¾	1⅝	13/16	⅞
×66	19.4	20.00	20	0.505	½	¼	6.255	6¼	0.795	13/16	16¾	1⅝	13/16	⅞
S 18×70	20.6	18.00	18	0.711	11/16	⅜	6.251	6¼	0.691	11/16	15	1½	11/16	⅞
×54.7	16.1	18.00	18	0.461	7/16	¼	6.001	6	0.691	11/16	15	1½	11/16	⅞
S 15×50	14.7	15.00	15	0.550	9/16	5/16	5.640	5⅝	0.622	⅝	12¼	1⅜	9/16	¾
×42.9	12.6	15.00	15	0.411	7/16	¼	5.501	5½	0.622	⅝	12¼	1⅜	9/16	¾
S 12×50	14.7	12.00	12	0.687	11/16	⅜	5.477	5½	0.659	11/16	9⅛	1 7/16	11/16	¾
×40.8	12.0	12.00	12	0.462	7/16	¼	5.252	5¼	0.659	11/16	9⅛	1 7/16	⅝	¾
S 12×35	10.3	12.00	12	0.428	7/16	¼	5.078	5⅛	0.544	9/16	9⅝	1 3/16	½	¾
×31.8	9.35	12.00	12	0.350	⅜	3/16	5.000	5	0.544	9/16	9⅝	1 3/16	½	¾
S 10×35	10.3	10.00	10	0.594	⅝	5/16	4.944	5	0.491	½	7¾	1⅛	½	¾
×25.4	7.46	10.00	10	0.311	5/16	3/16	4.661	4⅝	0.491	½	7¾	1⅛	½	¾
S 8×23	6.77	8.00	8	0.441	7/16	¼	4.171	4⅛	0.426	7/16	6	1	7/16	¾
×18.4	5.41	8.00	8	0.271	¼	⅛	4.001	4	0.426	7/16	6	1	7/16	¾
S 7×20	5.88	7.00	7	0.450	7/16	¼	3.860	3⅞	0.392	⅜	5⅛	15/16	⅜	⅝
×15.3	4.50	7.00	7	0.252	¼	⅛	3.662	3⅝	0.392	⅜	5⅛	15/16	⅜	⅝
S 6×17.25	5.07	6.00	6	0.465	7/16	¼	3.565	3⅝	0.359	⅜	4¼	⅞	⅜	⅝
×12.5	3.67	6.00	6	0.232	¼	⅛	3.332	3⅜	0.359	⅜	4¼	⅞	⅜	—
S 5×14.75	4.34	5.00	5	0.494	½	¼	3.284	3¼	0.326	5/16	3⅜	13/16	5/16	—
×10	2.94	5.00	5	0.214	3/16	⅛	3.004	3	0.326	5/16	3⅜	13/16	5/16	—
S 4×9.5	2.79	4.00	4	0.326	5/16	3/16	2.796	2¾	0.293	5/16	2½	¾	5/16	—
×7.7	2.26	4.00	4	0.193	3/16	⅛	2.663	2⅝	0.293	5/16	2½	¾	5/16	—
S 3×7.5	2.21	3.00	3	0.349	⅜	3/16	2.509	2½	0.260	¼	1⅝	11/16	¼	—
×5.7	1.67	3.00	3	0.170	3/16	⅛	2.330	2⅜	0.260	¼	1⅝	11/16	¼	—

AMERICAN INSTITUTE OF STEEL CONSTRUCTION

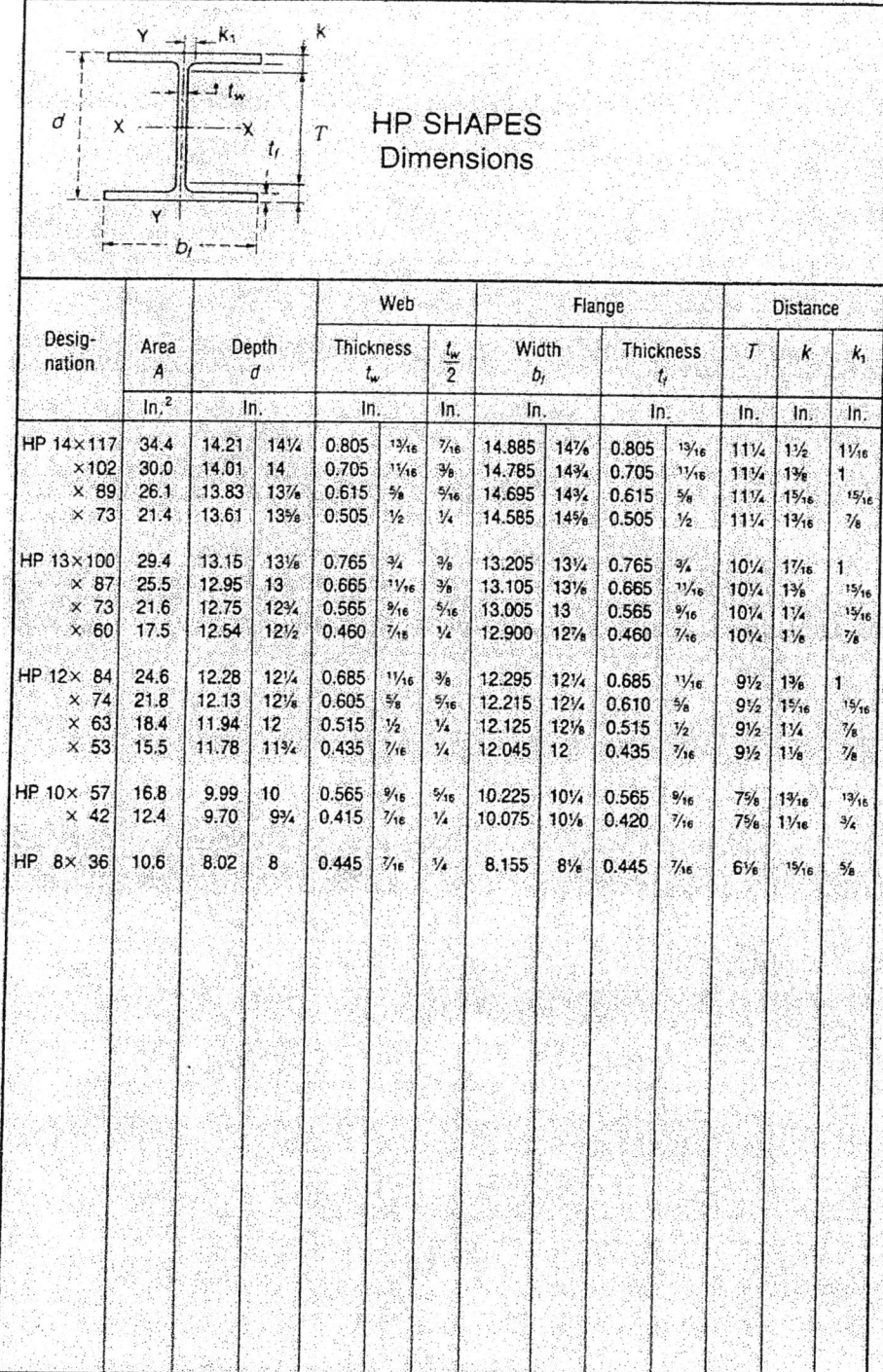

Sample Question: *What is the web thickness for an HP13x87?*
Answer: *.665 inches   11/16 in.*

Comment: TURN TO PAGE 1-
(AISC ASD) Green Book

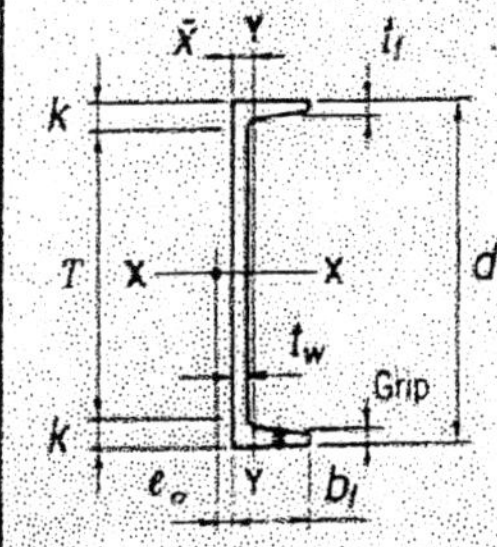

CHANNELS
AMERICAN STANDARD
Dimensions

Designation	Area A	Depth d	Web Thickness t_w		$\frac{t_w}{2}$	Flange Width b_f		Flange Average thickness t_f		Distance T	Distance k	Grip	Max. Flge. Fastener
	In.²	In.	In.		In.	In.		In.		In.	In.	In.	In.
C 15×50	14.7	15.00	0.716	11/16	3/8	3.716	3 3/4	0.650	5/8	12 1/8	1 7/16	5/8	1
×40	11.8	15.00	0.520	1/2	1/4	3.520	3 1/2	0.650	5/8	12 1/8	1 7/16	5/8	1
×33.9	9.96	15.00	0.400	3/8	3/16	3.400	3 3/8	0.650	5/8	12 1/8	1 7/16	5/8	1
C 12×30	8.82	12.00	0.510	1/2	1/4	3.170	3 1/8	0.501	1/2	9 3/4	1 1/8	1/2	7/8
×25	7.35	12.00	0.387	3/8	3/16	3.047	3	0.501	1/2	9 3/4	1 1/8	1/2	7/8
×20.7	6.09	12.00	0.282	5/16	1/8	2.942	3	0.501	1/2	9 3/4	1 1/8	1/2	7/8
C 10×30	8.82	10.00	0.673	11/16	5/16	3.033	3	0.436	7/16	8	1	7/16	3/4
×25	7.35	10.00	0.526	1/2	1/4	2.886	2 7/8	0.436	7/16	8	1	7/16	3/4
×20	5.88	10.00	0.379	3/8	3/16	2.739	2 3/4	0.436	7/16	8	1	7/16	3/4
×15.3	4.49	10.00	0.240	1/4	1/8	2.600	2 5/8	0.436	7/16	8	1	7/16	3/4
C 9×20	5.88	9.00	0.448	7/16	1/4	2.648	2 5/8	0.413	7/16	7 1/8	15/16	7/16	3/4
×15	4.41	9.00	0.285	5/16	1/8	2.485	2 1/2	0.413	7/16	7 1/8	15/16	7/16	3/4
×13.4	3.94	9.00	0.233	1/4	1/8	2.433	2 3/8	0.413	7/16	7 1/8	15/16	7/16	3/4
C 8×18.75	5.51	8.00	0.487	1/2	1/4	2.527	2 1/2	0.390	3/8	6 1/8	15/16	3/8	3/4
×13.75	4.04	8.00	0.303	5/16	1/8	2.343	2 3/8	0.390	3/8	6 1/8	15/16	3/8	3/4
×11.5	3.38	8.00	0.220	1/4	1/8	2.260	2 1/4	0.390	3/8	6 1/8	15/16	3/8	3/4
C 7×14.75	4.33	7.00	0.419	7/16	3/16	2.299	2 1/4	0.366	3/8	5 1/4	7/8	3/8	5/8
×12.25	3.60	7.00	0.314	5/16	3/16	2.194	2 1/4	0.366	3/8	5 1/4	7/8	3/8	5/8
× 9.8	2.87	7.00	0.210	3/16	1/8	2.090	2 1/8	0.366	3/8	5 1/4	7/8	3/8	5/8
C 6×13	3.83	6.00	0.437	7/16	3/16	2.157	2 1/8	0.343	5/16	4 3/8	13/16	5/16	5/8
×10.5	3.09	6.00	0.314	5/16	3/16	2.034	2	0.343	5/16	4 3/8	13/16	3/8	5/8
× 8.2	2.40	6.00	0.200	3/16	1/8	1.920	1 7/8	0.343	5/16	4 3/8	13/16	5/16	5/8
C 5× 9	2.64	5.00	0.325	5/16	3/16	1.885	1 7/8	0.320	5/16	3 1/2	3/4	5/16	5/8
× 6.7	1.97	5.00	0.190	3/16	1/8	1.750	1 3/4	0.320	5/16	3 1/2	3/4	—	—
C 4× 7.25	2.13	4.00	0.321	5/16	3/16	1.721	1 3/4	0.296	5/16	2 5/8	11/16	5/16	5/8
× 5.4	1.59	4.00	0.184	3/16	1/16	1.584	1 5/8	0.296	5/16	2 5/8	11/16	—	—
C 3× 6	1.76	3.00	0.356	3/8	3/16	1.596	1 5/8	0.273	1/4	1 5/8	11/16	—	—
× 5	1.47	3.00	0.258	1/4	1/8	1.498	1 1/2	0.273	1/4	1 5/8	11/16	—	—
× 4.1	1.21	3.00	0.170	3/16	1/16	1.410	1 3/8	0.273	1/4	1 5/8	11/16	—	—

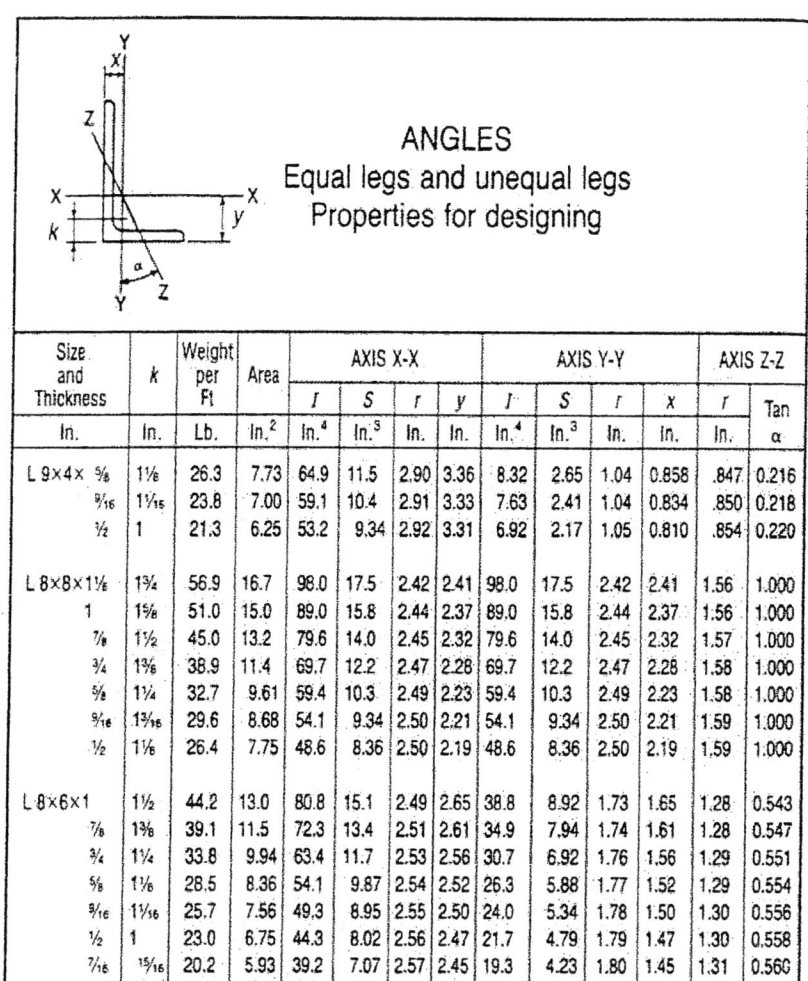

ANGLES
Equal legs and unequal legs
Properties for designing

Size and Thickness	k	Weight per Ft	Area	AXIS X-X				AXIS Y-Y				AXIS Z-Z	
				I	S	r	y	I	S	r	x	r	Tan α
In.	In.	Lb.	In.²	In.⁴	In.³	In.	In.	In.⁴	In.³	In.	In.	In.	
L 9×4× ⅝	1⅛	26.3	7.73	64.9	11.5	2.90	3.36	8.32	2.65	1.04	0.858	.847	0.216
9/16	1 1/16	23.8	7.00	59.1	10.4	2.91	3.33	7.63	2.41	1.04	0.834	.850	0.218
½	1	21.3	6.25	53.2	9.34	2.92	3.31	6.92	2.17	1.05	0.810	.854	0.220
L 8×8×1⅛	1¾	56.9	16.7	98.0	17.5	2.42	2.41	98.0	17.5	2.42	2.41	1.56	1.000
1	1⅝	51.0	15.0	89.0	15.8	2.44	2.37	89.0	15.8	2.44	2.37	1.56	1.000
⅞	1½	45.0	13.2	79.6	14.0	2.45	2.32	79.6	14.0	2.45	2.32	1.57	1.000
¾	1⅜	38.9	11.4	69.7	12.2	2.47	2.28	69.7	12.2	2.47	2.28	1.58	1.000
⅝	1¼	32.7	9.61	59.4	10.3	2.49	2.23	59.4	10.3	2.49	2.23	1.58	1.000
9/16	1 3/16	29.6	8.68	54.1	9.34	2.50	2.21	54.1	9.34	2.50	2.21	1.59	1.000
½	1⅛	26.4	7.75	48.6	8.36	2.50	2.19	48.6	8.36	2.50	2.19	1.59	1.000
L 8×6×1	1½	44.2	13.0	80.8	15.1	2.49	2.65	38.8	8.92	1.73	1.65	1.28	0.543
⅞	1⅜	39.1	11.5	72.3	13.4	2.51	2.61	34.9	7.94	1.74	1.61	1.28	0.547
¾	1¼	33.8	9.94	63.4	11.7	2.53	2.56	30.7	6.92	1.76	1.56	1.29	0.551
⅝	1⅛	28.5	8.36	54.1	9.87	2.54	2.52	26.3	5.88	1.77	1.52	1.29	0.554
9/16	1 1/16	25.7	7.56	49.3	8.95	2.55	2.50	24.0	5.34	1.78	1.50	1.30	0.556
½	1	23.0	6.75	44.3	8.02	2.56	2.47	21.7	4.79	1.79	1.47	1.30	0.558
7/16	15/16	20.2	5.93	39.2	7.07	2.57	2.45	19.3	4.23	1.80	1.45	1.31	0.560
L 8×4×1	1½	37.4	11.0	69.6	14.1	2.52	3.05	11.6	3.94	1.03	1.05	0.846	0.247
¾	1¼	28.7	8.44	54.9	10.9	2.55	2.95	9.36	3.07	1.05	0.953	0.852	0.258
9/16	1 1/16	21.9	6.43	42.8	8.35	2.58	2.88	7.43	2.38	1.07	0.882	0.861	0.265
½	1	19.6	5.75	38.5	7.49	2.59	2.86	6.74	2.15	1.08	0.859	0.865	0.267
L 7×4× ¾	1¼	26.2	7.69	37.8	8.42	2.22	2.51	9.05	3.03	1.09	1.01	0.860	0.324
⅝	1⅛	22.1	6.48	32.4	7.14	2.24	2.46	7.84	2.58	1.10	0.963	0.865	0.329
½	1	17.9	5.25	26.7	5.81	2.25	2.42	6.53	2.12	1.11	0.917	0.872	0.335
⅜	⅞	13.6	3.98	20.6	4.44	2.27	2.37	5.10	1.63	1.13	0.870	0.880	0.340

AMERICAN INSTITUTE OF STEEL CONSTRUCTION

> Comment: TURN TO PAGE 1-1 (AISC ASD) Green Book

1-145

STANDARD MILL PRACTICE
General Information

Rolling structural shapes and plates involves such factors as roll wear, subsequent roll dressing, temperature variations, etc., which cause the finished product to vary from published profiles. Such variations are limited by the provisions of the American Society for Testing and Materials Specification A6. Contained in this section is a summary of these provisions, not a reproduction of the complete specification. In its entirety, A6 covers a group of common requirements, which, unless otherwise specified in the purchase order or in an individual specification, shall apply to rolled steel plates, shapes, sheet piling and bars.

In accordance with Table *1*, *carbon steel* refers to ASTM Designations A36 and A529; *high-strength, low-alloy steel* refers to Designations A242, A572, and A588; *alloy steel* refers to Designation A514; and low-alloy steel refers to A852.

For further information on mill practices, including permissible variations for rolled tees, zees and bulb angles in structural and bar sizes, pipe, tubing, sheets and strip, and for other grades of steel, see ASTM A6, A53, A500, A568 and A618, and the AISI Steel Products Manuals and Producers' Catalogs.

The data on spreading rolls to increase areas and weights, and mill cambering of beams, is not a part of A6.

Additional material on mill practice is included in the descriptive material preceding the "Dimensions and Properties" tables for shapes and plates.

Letter symbols representing dimensions on sketches shown herein are in accordance with ASTM A6, AISI and mill catalogs and *not necessarily as defined by the general nomenclature of this manual.*

Methods of increasing areas and weights by spreading rolls   1-146
Cambering of rolled beams 1-147
Positions for measuring camber and sweep 1-148
W Shapes, permissible variations 1-149
S Shapes, M Shapes, and Channels, permissible variations 1-151
Tees split from **W, M** and S Shapes, permissible variations   1-152
Angles split from Channels, permissible variations 1-152
Angles, structural size, permissible variations 1-153
Angles, bar size, permissible variations 1-154
Steel Pipe and Tubing, permissible variations 1-155
Plates, permissible variations for sheared, length and width   1-156
Plates, permissible variations for universal mill, length 1-156
Plates, permissible variations for universal mill, width 1-156
Plates, permissible variations for camber 1-157
Plates, permissible variations for flatness 1-158

AMERICAN INSTITUTE OF STEEL CONSTRUCTION

Study the following pages. The figures and descriptions set out the rules acceptable tolerances for steel structural shapes. Study the sample questions and use your book as a reference.

STANDARD MILL PRACTICE
Methods of increasing areas and weights by spreading rolls

W SHAPES

To vary the area and weight within a given nominal size, the flange width, the flange thickness and the web thickness are changed, as shown in Fig. 1.

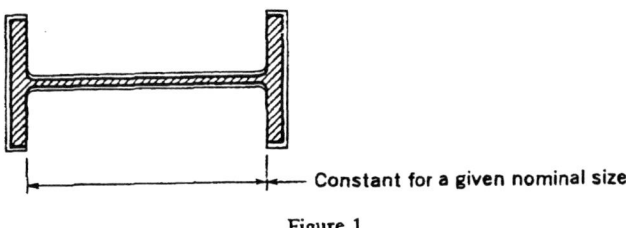

Figure 1

S SHAPES AND AMERICAN STANDARD CHANNELS

To vary the area and weight within a given nominal size, the web thickness and the flange width are changed by an equal amount, as shown in Figs. 2 and 3.

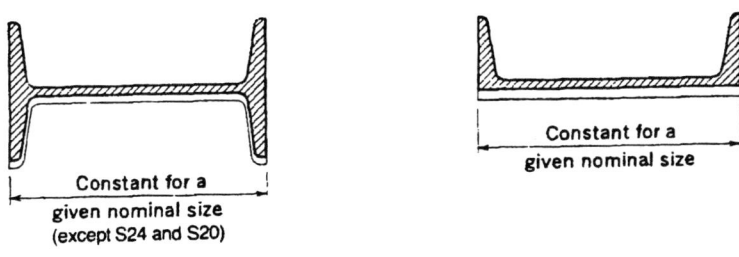

Figure 2   Figure 3

ANGLES

To vary area and weight for a given leg length, the thickness of each leg is changed. Note that leg length is changed slightly by this method (Fig. 4).

Figure 4

AMERICAN INSTITUTE OF STEEL CONSTRUCTION

STANDARD MILL PRACTICE

W Shapes
HP Shapes

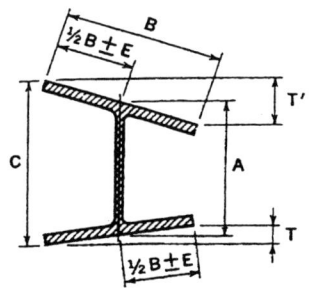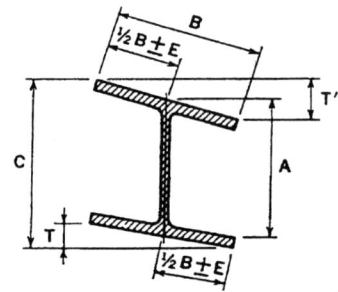

PERMISSIBLE VARIATIONS IN CROSS SECTION

Section Nominal Size, In.	A, Depth, In.		B, Flg. Width, In.		T + T′, Flanges, Out of Square, Max, In.	E,[a] Web off Center, Max, In.	C, Max, Depth at any Cross-Section over Theoretical Depth, In.
	Over Theoretical	Under Theoretical	Over Theoretical	Under Theoretical			
To 12, incl.	1/8	1/8	1/4	3/16	1/4	3/16	1/4
Over 12	1/8	1/8	1/4	3/16	5/16	3/16	1/4

[a] Variation of 5/16-in. max. for sections over 426 lb./ft.

PERMISSIBLE VARIATIONS IN LENGTH

W Shapes	Variations from Specified Length for Lengths Given, In.			
	30 ft and Under		Over 30 ft	
	Over	Under	Over	Under
Beams 24 in. and under in nominal depth	3/8	3/8	3/8 plus 1/16 for each additional 5 ft or fraction thereof	3/8
Beams over 24 in. nom. depth; all columns	1/2	1/2	1/2 plus 1/16 for each additional 5 ft or fraction thereof	1/2

AMERICAN INSTITUTE OF STEEL CONSTRUCTION

STANDARD MILL PRACTICE
S shapes, M shapes and channels

PERMISSIBLE VARIATIONS IN CROSS-SECTION

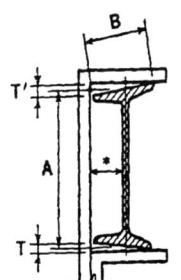
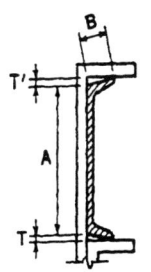

Section	Nominal Size, in.	A, Depth, In.[a]		B, Flange Width, In.		T + T', Out of Square per Inch of B, In.
		Over Theoretical	Under Theoretical	Over Theoretical	Under Theoretical	
S shapes and M shapes	3 to 7, incl.	3/32	1/16	1/8	1/8	1/32
	Over 7 to 14, incl.	1/8	3/32	5/32	5/32	1/32
	Over 14 to 24, incl.	3/16	1/8	3/16	3/16	1/32
Channels	3 to 7, incl	3/32	1/16	1/8	1/8	1/32
	Over 7 to 14, incl.	1/8	3/32	1/8	5/32	1/32
	Over 14	3/16	1/8	1/8	3/16	1/32

[a] A is measured at centerline of web for beams; and at back of web for channels.
[b] T + T applies when flanges of channels are tied in or out.

PERMISSIBLE VARIATIONS IN LENGTH

Section	Variations from Specified Length for Lengths Given, In.									
	To 30 Ft, incl.		Over 30 to 40 Ft, incl.		Over 40 to 50 Ft, incl.		Over 50 to 65 Ft, incl.		Over 65 Ft	
	Over	Under	Over	Under	Over	Under	Over	Under	Over	Under
S shapes, M shapes and Channels	1/2	1/4	3/4	1/4	1	1/4	1 1/8	1/4	1 1/4	1/4

OTHER PERMISSIBLE VARIATIONS

Area and Weight Variation: ±2.5% theoretical or specified amount.
Ends Out-of-Square: S shapes and channels 1/64 in. per in. of depth.

Camber: 1/8 in. × $\dfrac{\text{total length, ft}}{5}$

AMERICAN INSTITUTE OF STEEL CONSTRUCTION

ALLOWABLE STRESS DESIGN

> Comment: TURN TO PAGE 5-
> (AISC ASD) Green Book

Specification for Structural Joints Using ASTM A325 or A490 Bolts

Approved by Research Council on Structural Connections of the
Engineering Foundation, November 13, 1985.
Endorsed by American Institute of Steel Construction
Endorsed by Industrial Fasteners Institute

1. Scope

This Specification relates to the allowable stress design for strength and slip resist-ance of structural joints using ASTM A325 high-strength bolts, ASTM A490 heat treated high-strength bolts or equivalent fasteners, and for the installation of such bolts in connections of structural steel members. The Specification relates only to those aspects of the connected materials that bear upon the performance of the fasteners. Construction shall conform to an applicable code or specification for structures of carbon, high strength low alloy steel or quenched and tempered structural steel.

The attached Commentary provides background information in order that the user may better understand the provisions of the Specification.

2. Bolts, Nuts, Washers and Paint

(a) Bolt Specifications. Bolts shall conform to the requirements of the cur-rent edition of the Specifications of the American Society for Testing and Materials for High-strength Bolts for Structural Steel Joints, ASTM A325, or Heat Treated Steel Structural Bolts, 150 ksi Minimum Tensile Strength, ASTM A490, except as provided in paragraph (d) of this section. The designer shall specify the type of bolts to be used.

(b) Bolt Geometry. Bolt dimensions shall conform to the current requirements of the American National Standards Institute for Heavy Hex Structural Bolts, ANSI Standard B 18.2. 1, except as provided in paragraph (d) of this section. The length of bolts shall be such that the end of the bolt will be flush with or outside the face of the nut when properly installed.

AMERICAN INSTITUTE OF STEEL CONSTRUCTIO

(c) **Nut Specifications.** Nuts shall conform to the current chemical and mechanical requirements of the American Society for Testing and Materials Standard Specification for Carbon and Alloy Steel Nuts, ASTM A563 or Standard Specification for Carbon and Alloy Steel Nuts for Bolts for High Pressure and High Temperatures Service, ASTM A194. The grade and surface finish of nuts for each type shall be as follows:

A325 Bolt Type	Nut Specification, Grade and Finish
1 and 2, plain (uncoated) and 2H; plain	A563 C, C3. D, DH. and D3 or A 194 2
1 and 2, galvanized	A563 DH or A 194 2H; galvanized
3 plain	A563 C3 and DH3

A490 Bolt Type	Nut Specification, Grade and Finish
1 and 2, plain	A563 DH and DH3 or A 194 2H; plain
3 plain	A563 DH3

Nut dimensions shall conform to the current requirements of the American National Standards Institute for Heavy Hex Nuts, ANSI Standard BI 8.2.2.. except as provided in paragraph (d) of this section.

(d) **Alternate Fastener Designs.** Other fasteners or fastener assemblies which meet the materials, manufacturing and chemical composition requirements of ASTM Specification A325 or A490 and which meet the mechanical property requirements of the same specifications in full-size tests, and which have a body diameter and bearing areas under the head and nut not less than those provided by a bolt and nut of the same nominal dimensions prescribed by paragraphs 2(b) and 2(c), may be used subject to the approval of the responsible Engineer. Such alternate fasteners may differ in other dimensions from those of the specified bolts and nuts. Their installation procedure and inspection may differ from procedures specified for regular high-strength bolts in Sections 8 and 9. When a different installation procedure or inspection is used, it shall be detailed in a supplemental specification applying to the alternate fastener and that specification must be approved by the engineer responsible for the design of the structure.

(e) **Washers.** Flat circular washers and square or rectangular beveled washers shall conform to the current requirements of the American Society for Testing and Materials Standard Specification for Hardened Steel Washers. ASTM F436.

(1) **Load Indicating Devices.** Load indicating devices may be used in conjunction with bolts, nuts and washers specified in 2(a) through 2(e) provided they satisfy the requirements of 8(d)(4). Their installation procedure and inspection shall be detailed in supplemental specifications provided by the manufacturer and subject to the approval of the engineer responsible for the design of the structure.

(g) Faying Surface Coatings. Paint, if used on faying surfaces of connections which are not specified to be slip critical, may be of any formulation. Paint, used on the faying surfaces of connections specified to be slip critical, shall be qualified by test in accordance with *Test Method to Determine the Slip Coefficient for Coatings Used in Bolted Joints* as adopted by the Research Council on Structural Connections, see Appendix A. Manufacturer's certification shall include a certified copy of the test report.

3. Bolted Parts

(a) Connected Material. All material within the grip of the bolt shall be steel. There shall be no compressible material such as gaskets or insulation within the grip. Bolted steel parts shall fit solidly together after the bolts are tightened, and may be coated or noncoated. The slope of the surfaces of parts in contact with the bolt head or nut shall not exceed 1:20 with respect to a plane normal to the bolt axis.

(b) Surface Conditions. When assembled, all joint surfaces, including surfaces adjacent to the bolt head and nut, shall be free of scale, except tight mill scale, and shall be free of dirt or other foreign material. Burrs that would prevent solid seating of the connected parts in the snug tight condition shall be removed. Paint is permitted on the faying surfaces unconditionally in connections except in slip critical connections as defined in Section 5(a). The faying surfaces of slip critical connections shall meet the requirements of the following paragraphs, as applicable.

> **Comment:** REMEMBER No paint on faying surfaces of Slip Critical Connections

(1) In noncoated joints, paint, including any inadvertent overspray, shall be excluded from areas closer than one bolt diameter but not less than one inch from the edge of any hole and all areas within bolt pattern.

(2) Joints specified to have painted faying surfaces shall be blast cleaned and coated with a paint which has been qualified as class A or B in accordance with the requirements of paragraph 2(g), except as provided in 3(b)(3).

(3) Subject to the approval of the Engineer, coatings providing a slip coefficient less than 0.33 may be used provided the mean slip coefficient is established by test in accordance with the requirements of paragraph 2(g), and the allowable slip load per unit area established. The allowable slip load per unit area shall be taken as equal to the allowable slip load per unit area from Table 3 for Class A coatings as appropriate for the hole type and bolt type times the slip coefficient determined by test divided by 0.33.

(4) Coated joints shall not be assembled before the coatings have cured for the minimum time used in the qualifying test.

(5) Galvanized faying surfaces shall be hot dip galvanized in accordance with ASTM Specification A 123 and shall be roughened by means of hand wire brushing. Power wire brushing is not permitted.

AMERICAN INSTITUTE OF STEEL CONSTRUCTION

(c) Hole Types. Hole types recognized under this specification are standard holes, oversize holes, short slotted holes and long slotted holes. The nominal dimensions for each type hole shall be not greater than those shown in Table 1. Holes not more than 1/32 inch larger in diameter than the true decimal equivalent of the nominal diameter that may result from a drill or reamer of the nominal diameter are considered acceptable. The slightly conical hole that naturally results from punching operations is considered acceptable. The width of slotted holes which are produced by flame cutting or a combination of drilling or punching and flame cutting shall generally be not more than 1/32 inch greater than the nominal width except that gouges not more than 1/16 inch deep shall be permitted. For statically loaded connections, the flame cut surface need not be ground. For dynamically loaded connections, the flame cut surface shall be ground smooth.

Table 1. Nominal Hole Dimensions

Bolt Dia.	Standard (Dia.)	Oversize (Dia.)	Short Slot (Width x Length)	Long Slot (Width x Length)
1/2	9/16	5/8	9/16 x 11/16	9/16 x 1 1/4
5/8	11/16	13/16	11/15 x 7/8	11/16 x 1 9/16
3/4	13/16	15/16	13/16 x 1	13/16 x 1 7/8
7/8	15/16	1 1/16	15/16 x 1 1/8	15/16 x 2 3/16
1	1 1/16	1 1/4	1 1/16 x 1 5/16	1 1/16 x 2 1/2
$\geq$ 1 1/8	$d + 1/16$	$d + 5/16$	$(d + 1/16) \times (d + 3/8)$	$(d + 1/16) \times (2.5 \times d)$

4. Design for Strength of Bolted Connections

(a) Allowable Strength. The allowable working stress in shear and bearing, independent of the method of tightening, for *A325* and *A490* bolts is given in Table 2. Also given in Table 2 is the allowable working stress in axial tension for *A325* and *A490* bolts which are tightened to the minimum fastener tension specified in Table 4. The allowable working stresses in Table 2 are to be used in conjunction with the cross sectional area of the bolt corresponding to the nominal diameter.

(b) Bearing Force. The computed bearing force shall be assumed to be distributed over an area equal to the nominal bolt diameter times the thickness of the connected part. A value of allowable bearing pressure on the connected material at a bolt greater than permitted by Table 2 can be justified provided deformation around the bolt hole is not a design consideration and adequate pitch and end distance L is provided according to:

$$F_\sim = LF_a/2d < 1.5F_a$$

AMERICAN INSTITUTE OF STEEL CONSTRUCTION

5. Design Check for Slip Resistance

(a) Slip-Critical Joints. Slip-critical joints are defined as joints in which slip would be detrimental to the serviceability of the structure. They include:

(1) Joints subject to fatigue loading.
(2) Joints with bolts installed in oversized holes.
(3) Except where the Engineer intends otherwise and so indicates in the contract documents, joints with bolts installed in slotted holes where the force on the joint is in a direction other than normal (between approximately 80 and 100 degrees) to the axis of the slot.
(4) Joints subject to significant load reversal.
(5) Joints in which welds and bolts share in transmitting load at a common faying surface. See Commentary.
(6) Joints in which, in the judgement of the Engineer, any slip would be critical to the performance of the joint or the structure and so designated on the contract plans and specifications.

> **Comment:** TEST QUESTION Know where to find these definition "Slip Critical"

(b) Allowable Slip Load. In addition to the requirements of Section 4, the force on a slip-critical joint shall not exceed the allowable resistance (P_s) of the connection (See Commentary) according to:

$$P_s = F_s A_b N_b N_s$$

Where
F_s = allowable slip load per unit area of bolt from Table 3
A_b = area corresponding to the nominal body area of the bolt
N_b = number of bolts in the joint
N_s = number of slip planes

Class A, B or C surface conditions of the bolted parts as defined in Table 3 shall be used in joints designated as slip-critical except as permitted in 3(b)(3).

6. Increase in Allowable Stresses

When the applicable code or specification for design of connected members per-mits an increase in working stress for loads in combination with wind or seismic forces, the permitted increases in working stresses may be applied with wind or seismic forces, the permitted increases in working stresses may be applied to the allowable stresses in Sections 4 and 5. When the effect of loads in combination with wind or seismic forces are accounted for by reduction in the load factors, the allowable stresses in Sections 4 and 5 may not be increased.

7. Design Details of Bolted Connections

(a) Standard Holes. In the absence of approval by the engineer for use of other hole types, standard holes shall be used in high strength bolted connections.

Table 3. Allowable Load for Slip-critical Connections
(Slip Load per Unit of Bolt Area, ksi)

Contact Surface of Bolted Parts	Hole Type and Direction of Load Application							
	Any Direction				Transverse		Parallel	
	Standard		Oversize & Short Slot		Long Slots		Long Slots	
	A325	A490	A325	A490	A325	A490	A325	A490
Class A (Slip Coefficient 0.33) Clean mill scale and blast-cleaned surfaces with Class A coatings[a]	17	21	15	18	12	15	10	13
Class B (Slip Coefficient 0.50) Blast-cleaned surfaces and blast-cleaned surfaces with Class B coatings[a]	28	34	24	29	20	24	17	20
Class C (Slip Coefficient 0.40) Hot dip Galvanized and roughened surfaces	22	27	19	23	16	19	14	16

[a]Coatings classified as Class A or Class B includes those coatings which provide a mean slip coefficient not less than 0.33 or 0.50, respectively, as determined by Testing Method to Determine the Slip Coefficient for Coatings Used in Bolted Joints, see Appendix A.

(b) Oversize and Slotted Holes. When approved by the Engineer, oversize, short slotted holes or long slotted holes may be used subject to the following joint detail requirements:

(1) Oversize holes may be used in all plies of connections in which the allowable slip resistance of the connection is greater than the applied load.

(2) Short slotted holes may be used in any or all plies of connections designed on the basis of allowable stress on the fasteners in Table 2 provided the load is applied approximately normal (between 80 and 100 degrees) to the axis of the slot. Short slotted holes may be used without regard for the direction of applied load in any or all plies of connections in which the allowable slip resistance is greater than the applied force.

(3) Long slotted holes may be used in one of the connected parts at any individual faying surface in connections designed on the basis of allowable stress on the fasteners in Table 2 provided the load is applied approximately normal (between 80 and 100 degrees) to the axis of the slot. Long slotted holes may be used in one of the connected parts at any individual faying sur-face without regard for the direction of applied load on connections in which the allowable slip resistance is greater than the applied force.

(4) Fully inserted finger shims between the faying surfaces of load transmitting elements of connections are not to be considered a long slot element of a connection.

AMERICAN INSTITUTE OF STEEL CONSTRUCTION

(c) Washer Requirements. Design details shall provide for washers in high strength bolted connections as follows:

(1) Where the outer face of the bolted parts has a slope greater than 1:20 with respect to a plane normal to the bolt axis, a hardened beveled washer shall be used to compensate for the lack of parallelism.

(2) Hardened washers are not required for connections using A325 and A490 bolts except as required in paragraphs 7(c)(3) through 7(c)(7) for slip-critical connections and connections subject to direct tension or as required by paragraph 8(c) for shear/bearing connections.

(3) Hardened washers shall be used under the element turned in tightening when the tightening is to be performed by calibrated wrench method.

(4) Irrespective of the tightening method, hardened washers shall be used under both the head and the nut when A490 bolts are to be installed and tightened to the tension specified in Table 4 in material having a specified yield point less than 40 ksi.

(5) Where A325 bolts of any diameter or A490 bolts equal to or less than I inch in diameter are to be installed and tightened in an oversize or short slotted hole in an outer ply, a hardened washer conforming to ASTM F436 shall be used.

(6) When A490 bolts over 1 inch in diameter are to be installed and tightened in an oversize or short slotted hole in an outer ply, hardened washers conforming to ASTM F436 except with $^5/_{16}$ inch minimum thickness shall be used under both the head and the nut in lieu of standard thickness hardened washers. Multiple hardened washers with combined thickness equal to or greater than $^5/_{16}$ inch do not satisfy this requirement.

(7) Where A325 bolts of any diameter or A490 bolts equal to or less than I inch in diameter are to be installed and tightened in a long slotted hole in an outer ply, a plate washer or continuous bar of at least $^5/_{16}$ inch thickness with standard holes shall be provided. These washers or bars shall have a size sufficient to completely cover the slot after installation and shall be of structural grade material, but need not be hardened except as follows. When A490 bolts over 1 inch in diameter are to be used in long slotted holes in external plies, a single hardened washer conforming to ASTM F436 but with $^5/_{16}$ inch minimum thickness shall be used in lieu of washers or bars of structural grade material. Multiple hardened washers with combined thickness equal to or greater than $^5/_{16}$ inch do not satisfy this requirement.

(8) Alternate design fasteners meeting the requirements of 2(d) with a geometry which provides a bearing circle on the head or nut with a diameter equal to or greater than the diameter of hardened washers meeting the requirements ASTM F436 satisfy the requirements for washers specified in paragraphs 7(c)(4) and 7(c)(5).

8. Installation and Tightening

(a) Handling and Storage of Fasteners. Fasteners shall be protected from dirt and moisture at the job site. Only as many fasteners as are anticipated to be installed and tightened during a work shift shall be taken from protected storage. Fasteners not used shall be returned to protected storage at the end

AMERICAN INSTITUTE OF STEEL CONSTRUCTION

of the shift. Fasteners shall not be cleaned of lubricant that is present in as-delivered condition. Fasteners for slip critical connections which must be cleaned of accumulated rust or dirt resulting from job site conditions, shall be cleaned and relubricated prior to installation.

(b) Tension Calibrator. A tension measuring device shall be required at all job sites where bolts in slip-critical joints or connections subject to direct tension are being installed and tightened. The tension measuring device shall be used to confirm: (1) the suitability to satisfy the requirements of Table 4 of the complete fastener assembly, including lubrication if required to be used in the work, (2) calibration of wrenches, if applicable, and (3) the understanding and proper use by the bolting crew of the method to be used. The frequency of confirmation testing, the number of tests to be performed and the test procedure shall be as specified in 8(d), as applicable. The accu-racy of the tension measuring device shall be confirmed through calibration by an approved testing agency at least annually.

> **Comment:** REMEMBER
> This method determines the amount of torque that is required on a given bolt to establish a particular amount of tension. When done properly this is probably the most precise method of bolt tightening.

(c) Joint Assembly and Tightening of Shear/Bearing Connections. Bolts in connections not within the slip-critical category as defined in Section 5(a) nor subject to tension loads nor required to be fully tensioned bearing-type connections shall be installed in properly aligned holes, but need only be tightened to the snug tight condition. The snug tight condition is defined as the tightness that exists when all plies in a joint are in firm contact. This may be attained by a few impacts of an impact wrench or the full effort of a man using an ordinary spud wrench. See Commentary. If a slotted hole occurs in an outer ply, a flat hardened washer or common plate washer shall be installed over the slot. Bolts which may be tightened only to a snug tight condition shall be clearly identified on the drawings.

> **Comment:** REMEMBER
> Definition of "Snug Tight"

(d) Joint Assembly and Tightening of Connections Requiring Full Pre-tensioning. In slip-critical connections, connections subject to direct tension, and fully pre-tensioned bearing connections, fasteners, together with washers of size and quality specified, located as required by Section 7(c), shall be installed in properly aligned holes and tightened by one of the methods described in Subsections 8(d)(1) through 8(d)(4) to at least the minimum tension specified in Table 4 when all the fasteners are tight. Tightening may be done by turning the bolt while the nut is prevented from rotating when it is impractical to turn the nut. Impact wrenches, if used, shall be of adequate capacity and sufficiently supplied with air to perform the required tightening of each bolt in approximately 10 seconds.

(1) Turn-of-nut Tightening. When turn-of-nut tightening is used, hardened washers re not required except as may be specified in 7(c). A representative sample of not less than three bolts and nuts of each diameter, length and grade to be used in the work shall be checked at the start of work in a device capable of indicating bolt tension. The test shall demonstrate that the method of estimating the snug-tight condition and controlling turns from snug tight to be used by the bolting crews develops a tension not less than five percent greater than the tension required by Table 4. Bolts shall be installed in all holes of the connection and brought to a snug-tight condition. Snug tight is defined as the tightness that exist when the plies of the joint are in firm contact. This may be attained by a few

Table 4. Fastener Tension Required for Slip-critical Connections and Connections Subject to Direct Tension

Nominal Bolt Size, Inches	Minimum Tension[a] in 1000's of Pounds (kips)	
	A325 Bolts	A490 Bolts
½	12	15
⅝	19	24
¾	28	35
⅞	39	49
1	51	64
1⅛	56	80
1¼	71	102
1⅜	85	121
1½	103	148

[a]Equal to 70 percent of specified minimum tensile strengths of bolts (as specified in ASTM Specifications for tests of full size A325 and A490 bolts with UNC threads loaded in axial tension) rounded to the nearest kip

impacts of an impact wrench or the full effort of a man using an ordina spud wrench. Snug tightening shall progress systematically from the me rigid part of the connection to the free edges, and then the bolts of the co nection shall be retightened in a similar systematic manner as neccessa until all bolts are simultaneously snug tight and the connection is fully cor pacted. Following this initial operation all bolts in the connection shall I tightened further by the applicable amount of rotation specified in Table During the tightening operation there shall be no rotation of the part n turned by the wrench. Tightening shall progress systematically from tl most rigid part of the joint to its free edges.

(2) Calibrated Wrench Tightening. Calibrated wrench tightening m- be used only when installation procedures are calibrated on a daily bas and when a hardened washer is used under the element turned in tightenin See the Commentary to this Section. This specification does not recogni2 standard torques determined from tables or from formulas which ai assumed to relate torque to tension.

When calibrated wrenches are used for installation, they shall be set provide a tension not less than 5 percent in excess of the minimum tensic specified in Table 4. The installation procedures shall be calibrated at lea once each working day for each bolt diameter, length and grade using fa tener assemblies that are being installed in the work. Calibration shall 1 accomplished in a device capable of indicating actual bolt tension by tigh ening three typical bolts of each diameter, length and grade from the bolt being installed and with a hardened washer from the washers being used i the work under the element turned in tightening. Wrenches shall be recal brated when significant difference is noted in the surface condition of th bolts threads, nuts or washers. It shall be verified during actual installatio in the assembled steelwork that the wrench adjustment selected by the cal: bration does not produce a nut or bolt head rotation from snug tight greate than that permitted in Table 5. If manual torque wrenches are used, nut shall be turned in the tightening direction when torque is measured.

AMERICAN INSTITUTE OF STEEL CONSTRUCTION

Table 5. Nut Rotation from Snug Tight Condition[a,b]

Bolt length (Under side of head to end of bolt)	Disposition of Outer Face of Bolted Parts		
	Both faces normal to bolt axis	One face normal to bolt axis and other sloped not more than 1:20 (beveled washer not used)	Both faces sloped not more than 1:20 from normal to the bolt axis (beveled washer not used)
Up to and including 4 diameters	1/3 turn	1/2 turn	2/3 turn
Over 4 diameters but not exceeding 8 dia.	1/2 turn	2/3 turn	5/6 turn
Over 8 diameters but not exceeding 12 dia.[c]	2/3 turn	5/6 turn	1 turn

[a] Nut rotation is relative to bolt regardless of the element (nut or bolt) being turned. For bolts installed by 1/2 turn and less, the tolerance should be plus or minus 30 degrees; for bolts installed by 2/3 turn and more, the tolerance should be plus or minus 45 degrees.

[b] Applicable only to connections in which all material within the grip of the bolt is steel.

[c] No research has been performed by the Council to establish the turn-of-nut procedure for bolt lengths exceeding 12 diameters. Therefore, the required rotation must be determined by actual test in a suitable tension measuring device which simulates conditions of solidly fitted steel.

When calibrated wrenches are used to install and tension bolts in a connection, bolts shall be installed with hardened washers under the element turned in tightening bolts in all holes of the connection and brought to a snug tight condition. Following this initial tightening operation, the connection shall be tightened using the calibrated wrench. Tightening shall progress systematically from the most rigid part of the joint to its free edges. The wrench shall be returned to "touch up" previously tightened bolts which may have been relaxed as a result of the subsequent tightening of adjacent bolts until all bolts are tightened to the prescribed amount.

(3) Installation of Alternate Design Bolts. When fasteners which incorporate a design feature intended to indirectly indicate the bolt tension or to automatically provide the tension required by Table 4 and which have been qualified under Section 2(d) are to be installed, a representative sample of not less than three bolts of each diameter, length and grade shall be checked at the job site in a device capable of indicating bolt tension. The test assembly shall include flat hardened washers, if required in the actual connection, arranged as in the actual connections to be tensioned. The calibration test shall demonstrate that each bolt develops a tension not less than five percent greater than the tension required by Table 4. Manufacturer's installation procedure as required by Section 2(d) shall be followed for installation of bolts in the calibration device and in all connections.

When alternate design features of the fasteners involve an irreversible mechanism such as yield or twist-off of an element, bolts shall be installed

AMERICAN INSTITUTE OF STEEL CONSTRUCTION

- 276 • RCSC Specification for Structural Joints (11/13/85)

in all holes of the connection and initially brought to a snug tight condition. All fasteners shall then be tightened, progressing systematically from the most rigid part of the connection to the free edges in a manner that will min-imize relaxation of previously tightened fasteners prior to final twist-off or yielding of the control or indicator element of the individual fasteners. In some cases, proper tensioning of the bolts may require more than a single cycle of systematic tightening.

(4) Direct Tension Indicator Tightening. Tightening of bolts using direct tension indicator devices is permitted provided the suitability of the device can be demonstrated by testing a representative sample of not less than three devices for each diameter and grade of fastener in a calibration device capable of indicating bolt tension. The test assembly shall include flat hardened washers, if required in the actual connection, arranged as those in the actual connections to be tensioned. The calibration test shall demonstrate that the device indicates a tension not less than five percent greater than that required by Table 4. Manufacturer's installation proce-dure as required by Section 2(d) shall be followed for installation of bolts in the calibration device and in all connections. Special attention shall be given to proper installation of flat hardened washers when load indicating devices are used with bolts installed in oversize or slotted holes and when the load indicating devices are used under the turned element.

When the direct tension indicator involves an irreversible mechanism such as yielding or fracture of an element, bolts shall be installed in all holes of the connection and brought to snug tight condition. All fasteners shall then be tightened, progressing systematically from the most rigid part of the connection to the free edges in a manner that will minimize relaxation of previously tightened fasteners prior to final twist-off or yielding of the con-trol or indicator element of the individual devices. In some cases, proper tensioning of the bolts may require more than a single cycle of systematic tightening.

(e) Reuse of Bolts. A490 bolts and galvanized A325 bolts shall not be reused. Other A325 bolts may be reused if approved by the Engineer responsible. Touching up or retightening previously tightened bolts which may have been loosened by the tightening of adjacent bolts shall not be considered as reuse provided the snugging up continues from the initial position and does not require greater rotation, including the tolerance, than that required by Table 5.

9. Inspection

(a) Inspector Responsibility. While the work is in progress, the Inspector shall determine that the requirements of Sections 2, 3 and 8 of this Specifi-cation are met in the work. The Inspector shall observe the calibration pro-cedures when such procedures are required by contract documents and shall monitor the installation of bolts to determine that all plies of connected material have been drawn together and that the selected procedure is prop-erly used to tighten all bolts.

In addition to the requirement of the foregoing paragraph, for all con-nections specified to be slip critical or subject to axial tension, the Inspector shall assure that the specified procedure was followed to achieve the preten-sion specified in Table 4. Bolts installed by procedures in Section 8(d) may

> **Comment:** REMEMBER
> These are the responsibilities of the Special Inspector. The Project inspector needs to verify that this has been done

AMERICAN INSTITUTE OF STEEL CONSTRUCTION

reach tensions substantially greater than values given in Table 4, but this shall not be cause for rejection. ==Bolts in connections identified as not being slip-critical nor subject to direct tension need not be inspected for bolt tension other than to ensure that the plies of the connected elements have been brought into snug contact.==

(b) Arbitration Inspection. When high strength bolts in slip-critical connec-tions and connections subject to direct tension have been installed by any of the tightening methods in Section 8(d) and inspected in accordance with Section 9(a) and a disagreement exists as to the minimum tension of the installed bolts, the following arbitration procedure may be used. Other methods for arbitration inspection may be used if approved by the engineer.

(1) The Inspector shall use a manual torque wrench which indicates torque by means of a dial or which may be adjusted to give an indication that the job inspecting torque has been reached.

(2) This Specifcation does not recognize standard torques determined from tables or from formulas which are assumed to relate torque to tension. Testing using such standard torques shall not be considered valid.

(3) A representative sample of five bolts from the diameter, length and grade of the bolts used in the work shall be tightened in the tension measuring device by any convenient means to an initial condition equal to approximately 15 percent of the required fastener tension and then to the minimum tension specified in Table 4. Tightening beyond the initial condition must not produce greater nut rotation than 1 1/2 times that permitted in Table 5. The job inspecting torque shall be taken as the average of three values thus determined after rejecting the high and low values. The inspecting wrench shall then be applied to the tightened bolts in the work and the torque neces-sary to turn the nut or head 5 degrees (approximately 1 inch at 12 inch radius) in the tightening direction shall be determined.

(4) Bolts represented by the sample in the foregoing paragraph which have been tightened in the structure shall be inspected by applying, in the tightening direction, the inspecting wrench and its job torque to 10 percent of the bolts, but not less than 2 bolts, selected at random in each connection in question. If no nut or bolt head is turned by application of the job inspect-ing torque, the connection shall be accepted as properly tightened. If any nut or bolt is turned by the application of the job inspecting torque, all bolts in the connection shall be tested, and all bolts whose nut or head is turned by the job inspecting torque shall be tightened and reinspected. Alternatively, the fabricator or erector, at his option, may retighten all of the bolts in the connection and then resubmit the connection for the specified inspection.

(c) Delayed Verification Inspection. The procedure specified in Sections 9(a) and (b) are intended for inspection of bolted connections and verifica-tion of pretension at the time of tensioning the joint. If verification of bolt tension is required after a passage of a period of time and exposure of the completed joints, the procedures of Section 9(b) will provide indication of bolt tension which is of questionable accuracy. Procedures appropriate to the specific situation should be used for verification of bolt tension. This might involve use of the arbitration inspection procedure contained herein, or might require the development and use of alternate procedures.

See Commentary.

Chapter 10: Wood
LESSON 10.1

INTRODUCTION

Wood is a building material, that is in a class by itself; it is the only major construction material that grows, rather than being manufactured. Each year a new layer of wood develops on a tree with little or no human help. Therefore, with intelligent planning and use of this resource, the supply of wood should remain available forever.

Since wood grows, it does not have the precise properties of a manufactured product. On the contrary, wood has numerous and varied imperfections, such as checks, knots, pitch pockets, and shakes. To control the end product, there has been continuous research in the modification of wood, such as laminating, impregnating, and bonding, in order to create a more precisely engineered product.

Historically, wood, mud, and stone comprise the first natural building materials used by prehistoric people. As civilizations advanced, trees were cut and the logs used for protective walls, lintels, and roofs. Some form of wood architecture was developed by every civilization that had access to forests. Often, these historic structures displayed great imagination and beauty, as in the Norwegian stave churches of the 12th Century.

In the New World, the westward movement and development would have been impossible without the virgin forests, which provided the material for log cabins, farm buildings, and eventually, whole towns.

In the past two centuries, wood construction has developed from the relatively crude use of logs, poles, and heavy timbers to a sophisticated structural system employing engineered timber products never dreamed of by the early pioneers. Wood and wood products today constitute an important industry that continues to be valued by architects and builders in much the same way that it was esteemed by their predecessors.

TERMINOLOGY AND CLASSIFICATION

The terms wood, lumber, and timber are often used interchangeably, but each term has a distinct meaning.

Wood is the hard fibrous substance lying beneath the bark of trees. Regardless of its use, it is a basic material, just as steel and concrete are basic materials.

Lumber: is wood that has been sawn into construction members.

Timber: is lumber that is 5 inches or larger in its least sectional dimension.

Wood is classified as soft or hard, and is obtained from two classes of trees:

- needle-leaved conifers (cone bearing trees), which are evergreen;
- broad-leaved trees which are generally deciduous (those shedding their leaves each year).

Softwoods, such as pine, fir, and spruce, come from the evergreens.

Hardwoods, such as maple, oak, and sycamore, come from deciduous trees.

These terms are botanical, not structural, and they do not always indicate the relative hardness or strength of a particular wood. Thus, Douglas Fir, a softwood, is much harder and stronger

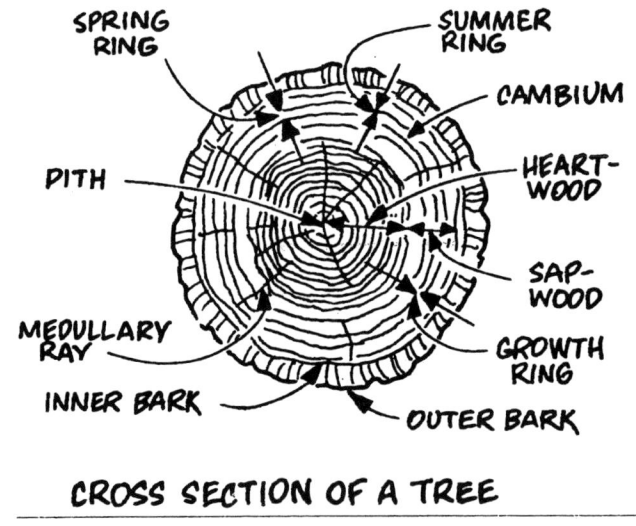

CROSS SECTION OF A TREE

than Basswood, which is classified as a hardwood. And Balsa, one of the most spongy and lightweight woods that exists, is also classified as a hardwood. Softwoods are used structurally in general construction for framing, sheathing, bracing, etc.; while hardwoods are mainly used for flooring, paneling, interior trim, and for furniture.

CHARACTERISTICS

Wood is the handiest and most accommodating of all construction materials. It is available almost everywhere, it is readily transported, and it is easily worked with simple carpenter's tools. Wood framed structures are strong, durable, and usually lower in cost than comparable concrete, masonry, or steel structures.

Wood framing, especially heavy timber construction, can often withstand fire better than unprotected steel construction. In addition, wood construction has great popular appeal, since light wood framing requires relatively little technical knowledge, and it may be worked with simple tools that are owned by almost everyone. In fact, the home woodworking shop continues to enjoy popularity year after year. Wood also has a beauty and warmth to sight and touch that is unique among construction materials; it is considered to be one of the more "humane" materials.

The chemical composition of wood comprises approximately 70% cellulose, which is used as a base for paper products, plastics, and textiles; 28% lignin, which is the adhesive giving strength to the wood; and 2% minerals and extractives, which give wood the properties of color, odor, and resistance to decay.

STRENGTH OF WOOD

The strength of wood varies with the direction of its grain. For example, compressive forces are resisted very effectively when loads are applied parallel to the grain. In some cases, as a matter of fact, wood has a compressive strength greater than steel in relation to their respective weights. Tensile forces, too, can be resisted most efficiently when applied parallel to the grain, although wood is generally stronger in compression than it is in tension.

The resistance of wood members to compressive and tensile forces applied perpendicular to the grain is less than in the direction parallel to the grain. In general, a piece of wood can resist less than half the compressive force perpendicular to the grain than it can parallel to the grain. For tensile forces, the difference is even more pronounced; the strength of wood in tension perpendicular to the grain is very low, and this type of stress can easily cause the wood to split. In the case of shear, wood is stronger across the grain than parallel to the grain, and therefore, it is usually unnecessary to compute the strength of beams in vertical (cross-grain) shear.

When specifying lumber for construction, it is necessary to stipulate the precise strength of wood that will resist the anticipated compressive, tensile, and shear forces.

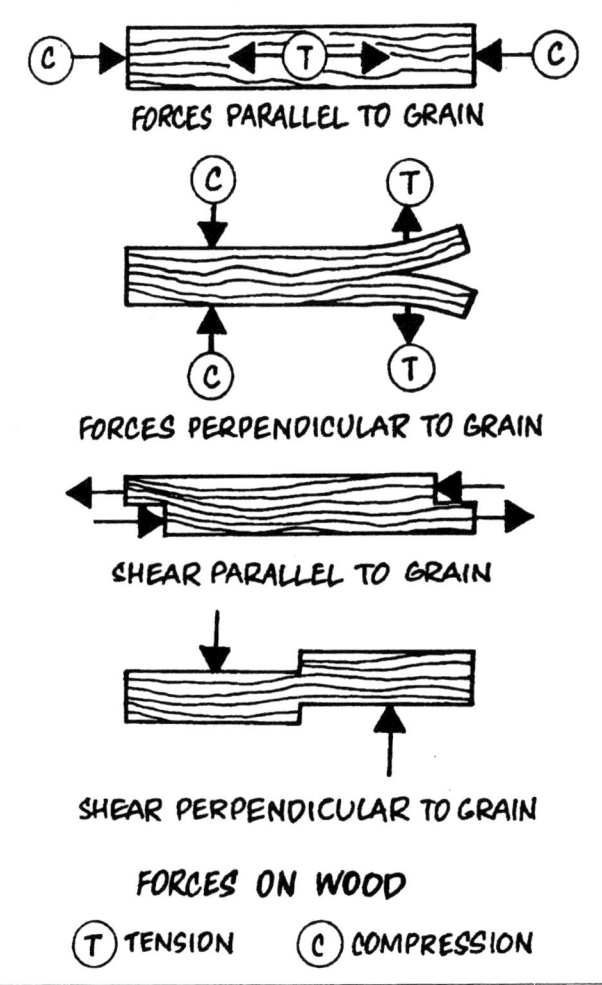

FORCES ON WOOD
(T) TENSION   (C) COMPRESSION

SEASONING WOOD

Making wood suitable for construction requires more than simply cutting down a tree and "shaking out the squirrels", as they say; it requires a curing process. All lumber, when it is first cut from trees, is "green", which means that it has a high moisture content. The maximum amount of moisture which can be held in wood cells is know as the fiber saturation point, and for most species it is about 30 percent of the dry weight of the wood.

The moisture content of lumber varies not only with the species, but also with the climate prevailing where a structure is built. This can be critical for interior elements such as flooring, paneling, and built-ins.

Before it can be used, wood should be seasoned either by air-drying, which is the lengthy process of allowing a log to age, or kiln-drying. Seasoning lumber reduces its weight and its susceptibility to shrinkage and warping; it improves its resistance to fungi, decay, and insects; ao:fi it increases its strength, nail-holding power, and ability to hold paint. Air-drying takes several months and leaves 10 to 20 percent moisture in the wood, while kiln-drying takes only a few days and leaves less than 10 percent moisture. Framing lumber is considered "dry" if the moisture content is 19 percent or less.

It is impossible to seal a piece of wood completely to prevent changes in moisture content. When the relative humidity is high, wood will absorb moisture and swell; when it is low, wood will lose moisture and shrink. This change in shape must always be taken into account when detailing and constructing wood connections.

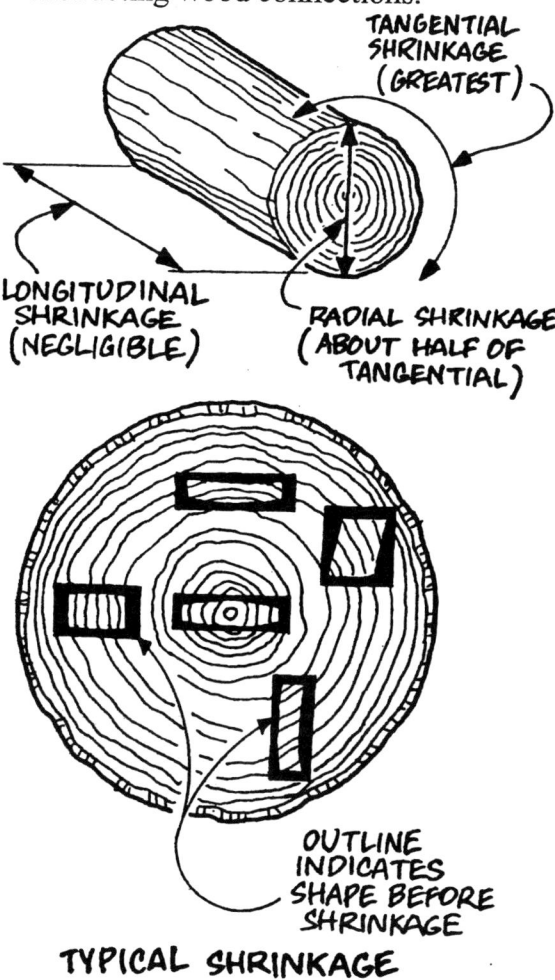

TYPICAL SHRINKAGE

CUTTING AND SAWING LUMBER

Shrinkage, distortion, and warpage of lumber are a function of the location of the annual growth rings of a tree. Therefore, how lumber is cut from a tree is extremely important. Wood shrinks most in the direction of the annual rings (across the grain or tangentially), less across the annual rings (radially), and very little parallel to the grain.

The way in which lumber is cut from a tree also affects its strength and appearance. In general, boards are either plainsawed or quartersawed.

Plainsawed lumber has the following characteristics:

1. Noticeable grain pattern (slash grained)

2. May twist, cup, and wear unevenly.

3. Tends to have raised grain.

4. Shrinks and swells more in width, less in thickness.

Quartersawed lumber has the following characteristics:

1. Relatively even grain pattern.

2. Wears evenly with less warpage.

3. Shrinks and swells more in thickness, less in width.

4. More waste in cutting and therefore, more costly.

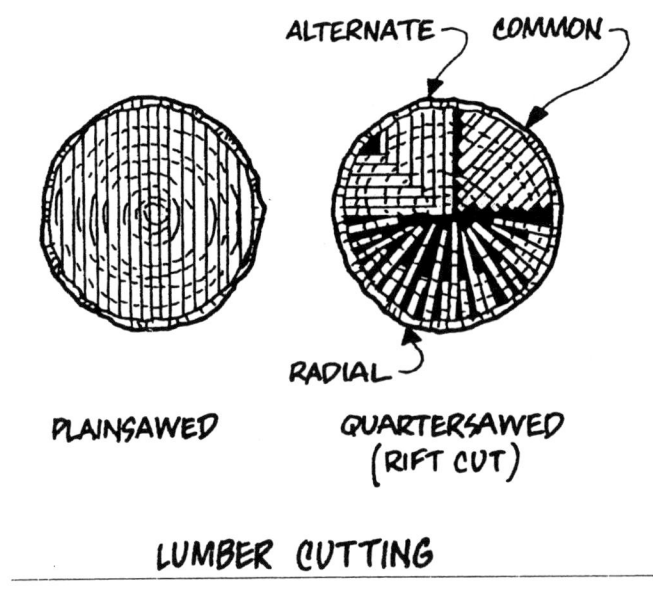

LUMBER CUTTING

WOOD DEFECTS

There are a variety of defects in wood that affect the strength, appearance, use, and grading of lumber. Defects include natural characteristics, such as knots and shakes, as well as manufacturing imperfections, such as splits and checks. In addition to these defects, wood can be damaged by insects, decayed by fungus, and of course, destroyed by fire.

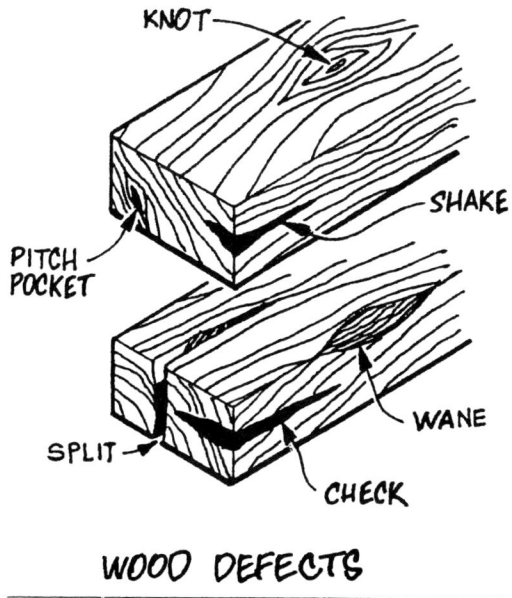

WOOD DEFECTS

Natural defects are deviations in the wood resulting from natural causes. Some of these are listed below.

    Knot - Part of a branch embedded in a growing tree.

    Peck - Pitted area sometimes found in cedar and cypress.

    Pitch pocket - Deposit of resin between growth rings.

    Shake - Lengthwise grain separation in a standing tree.

Manufacturing defects are those imposed on wood at some stage in its seasoning or processing. Some of these are listed below.

    Check - Lengthwise grain separation caused by nonuniform seasoning.

    Split - Lengthwise separation of wood extending from one face to another. Wane - Edge or corner defect that lacks sufficient wood.

    Warp - Shrinkage distortion of a plane surface; includes bow, crook, cup, and twist.

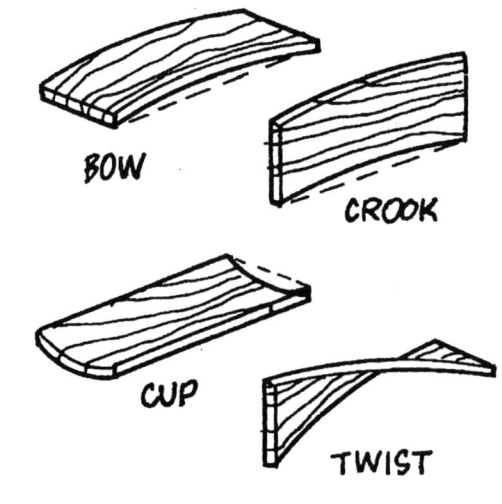

TYPES OF WARPAGE

GRADING LUMBER

As products of nature, no two pieces of wood are alike; they have varying properties of strength, appearance, size, and physical characteristics. In order to establish reasonable standards of uniformity, lumber must be graded for quality. Grading is usually a visual evaluation process based on criteria established by various lumber manufacturer associations.

The grade of a piece of lumber is based on the number, location, and type of imperfection that lowers the strength, durability or use of the lumber. Some of the most common defects include knots, warps, splits,

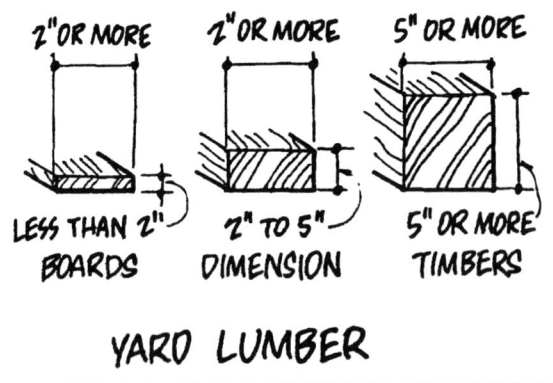

YARD LUMBER

stains, and undesirable grain configurations. The best grades of lumber are practically free from imperfections, while in each lower grade, the imperfections increase in quantity.

Softwood Grades - Established in accordance with the American Lumber Standards on the basis of use, size, and manufacturing characteristics. The classification of principal uses is as follows:

Yard lumber is used in general light frame construction.

Structural lumber is dimension lumber and timbers graded for strength. Factory and shop lumber is used for wood products such as sash and doors.

Yard lumber is further classified by dimension as follows:

<u>Boards</u>: are less than 2 inches thick and 2 inches or more in width. They are graded for appearance and used as siding, subflooring, and trim.

<u>Dimension lumber</u>: is between 2 and 5 inches thick and 2 inches or more in width. It is graded for strength and used for general construction.

<u>Timbers</u>: are 5 x 5 inches and larger, graded for strength, and generally used structurally.

Yard lumber is also classified on the basis of quality as follows:

<u>Select lumber</u>: is the finest appearance grade; A and B grades are suitable for natural finishes, while C and D are considered paint grades.

<u>Common lumber</u>: contains more blemishes than select, and is broken down into four grades of descending quality, from number 1 to number 4.

All yard lumber has grade stamp markings located at the end or side of the individual pieces. These markings indicate where the wood was processed, its type, grade, and strength. During construction, lumber is easily verified by simply checking the grade markings.

Structural lumber is classified by size and use as
- Joists and Planks
- Beams and Stringers
- Posts and Timbers.

Factory and Shop lumber is special purpose lumber machined from common boards into various patterns, some of which are shown below.

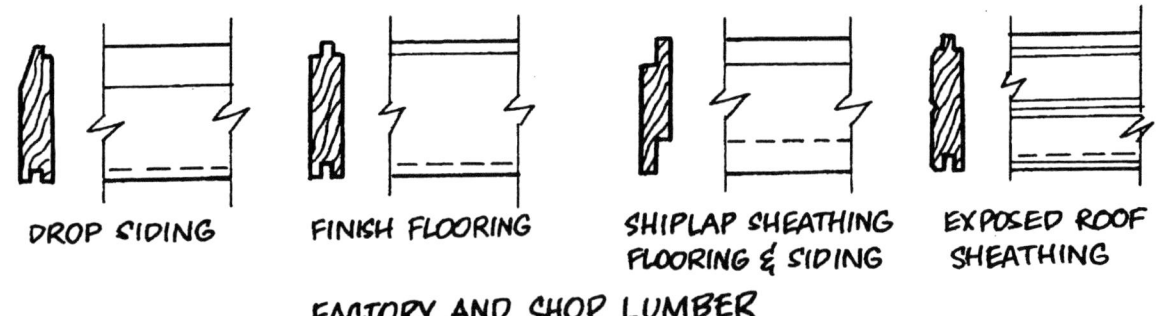

FACTORY AND SHOP LUMBER

Hardwood Grades: These are based on the amount of clear, usable lumber in a piece. Standard lengths vary from 4 to 16 feet, and the standard grades are firsts, seconds, selects, sound wormy, and number 1, 2, 3A and 3B common.

Board Foot: All lumber is specified according to its nominal dimensions, which is the rough or unfinished size. The dressed, surfaced, or finished size is always smaller due to the seasoning and surfacing of lumber before its use. As an example, a nominal 2" x 4" is actually 1-1/2 by 3-1/2 inches in size.

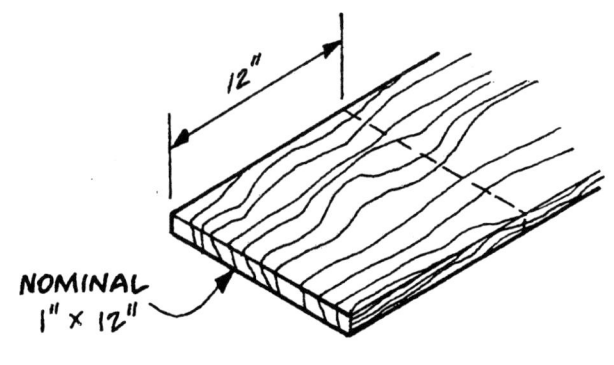

BOARD FOOT MEASURE

Lumber is measured, computed, and priced in board-feet. This is a conventional, standard unit in which a board foot is defined as a nominal 1" x 12" board one foot in length.

Lesson #3 of this "Wood Lecture" is dedicated to the West Coast Lumber Grading Standard 17. This publication is the standard that is used in the California Building Code. You will be instructed on how to use the book at a rudimentary level.

PLYWOOD

Plywood is a laminated panel consisting of thin wood sheets (plies) that are permanently bonded together. The plies are generally arranged with their grains at 90 degrees to one another. The center ply is known as the core, while the outside plies are called face and back. When there are five or more plies, the additional

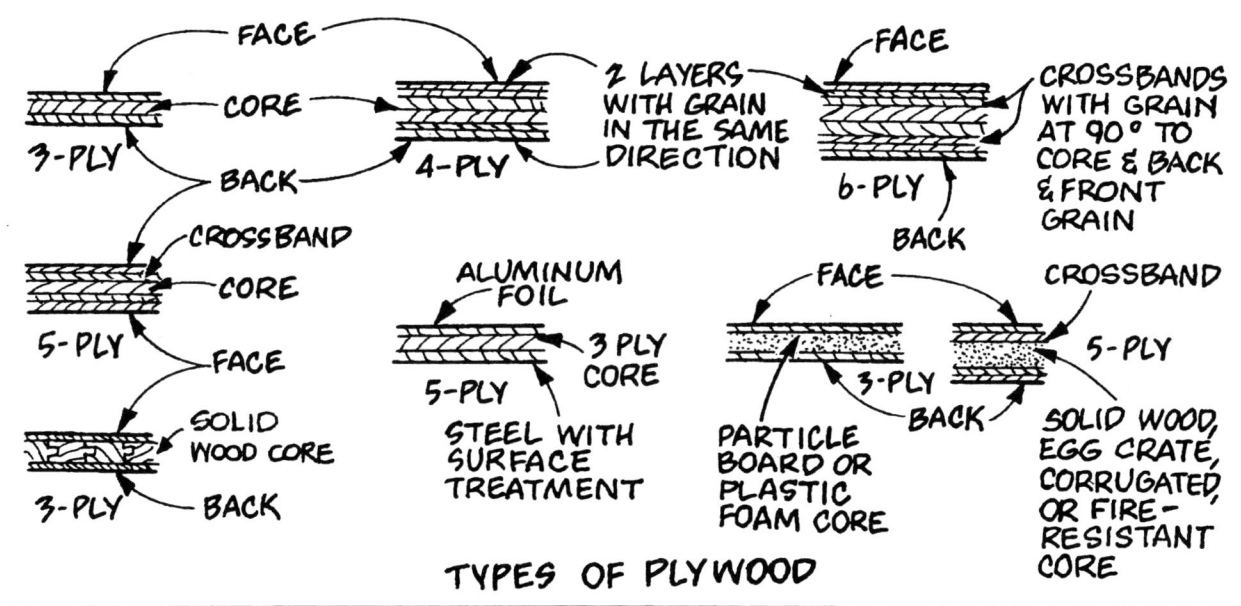

TYPES OF PLYWOOD

sheets, called cross-bands, are located between, and placed 90 degrees to, the core and the outside plies.

Plywood is used in construction whereever a combination of structural and enclosure qualities are required, as for example in formwork, sheathing, roof diaphragms, etc.

The advantages of plywood over sawn lumber are its great strength in two directions, greater resistance to shrinking and splitting, and less warpage. In addition, a sheet of plywood covers a large surface area with relatively few pieces of material.

Plywood is classified as interior or exterior, depending on the type of adhesive used: moisture-resistant for interior use and waterproof for exterior use. Plywood is also classified as softwood or hardwood, depending on the species of the face veneers. All plywood is graded according to the quality of the face veneers, with A being the best and D the poorest.

© Professional Study Inc. 2003

Plywood veneers are produced by slicing or by rotary cutting, depending on the required use or desired appearance. Plywood is manufactured in an odd number of plies and in some special even-ply sheets, ranging from 1/8 to 1-1/4 inches in thickness, and in a variety of sheet sizes, the most common being the standard 4 x 8 foot sheet.

In addition to normal construction plywood, other types include overlaid (covered with resin-impregnated paper), marine (special glue), prefinished (stained and ready to use), and patterned sheets (grooved, roughsawn, etc.) The major uses of these special plywoods are for furniture, cabinets, flooring, exterior siding, and interior wall finishes.

MISCELLANEOUS PANELS

There is an increasingly wider use today of engineered sheet materials, which have been developed for the construction industry. For the most part, these materials are processed combinations of natural materials generally intended for non-structural or decorative purposes. They are commonly used for concrete forms, cabinets, doors, wall paneling, partitions, decking, and insulation.

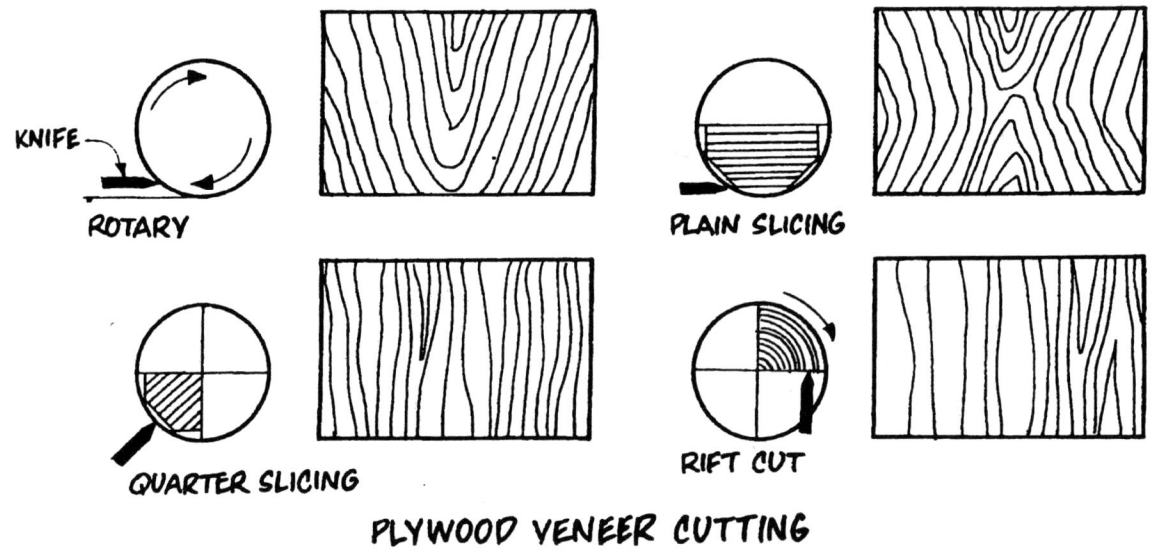

PLYWOOD VENEER CUTTING

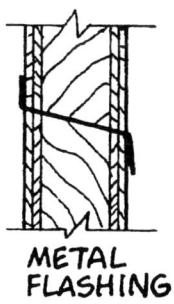

HORIZONTAL PLYWOOD JOINTS

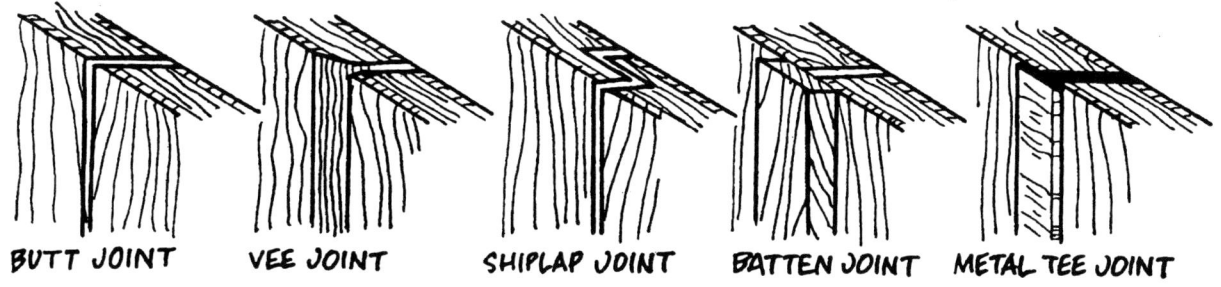

VERTICAL PLYWOOD JOINTS

Hardboard: is made from wood paper pulp which has been compressed under heat and pressure. It is available in two categories: basic and prefinished, and in three types: tempered, standard, and service standard. These are available in 4' x 8' sheets, which are 1/8" to 3/8" thick.

Prefinished hardboard: is available in a variety of patterns, textures, and finishes, such as baked enamels, plastic laminates, etc.
Prefinished hardboard is used for exterior siding, soffits, interior walls, ceilings, cabinet work, pegboards, and acoustical treatment.

Fiberboard is manufactured from waste paper, wood pulp, and fibers. It is used for acoustical tile, sheathing, and interior wall finishes. Standard sizes are 4'-0" x 8'-0" and in thicknesses from 2" to 1". Fiberboard roof insulation and laminated fiberboard decking are manufactured in standard sizes of 2' x 4'.

Flakeboard is composed of large wood flakes bonded together with synthetic resins under pressure. Flakeboard is lightweight and has a good R factor and acoustical properties, but its surface is easily damaged. Its main use is as an insulating back-up material or as an acoustical material on upper walls and ceilings.

Particleboard is dry-formed of wood particles bonded together with synthetic resin. It is used primarily as core stock for plastic laminate or hardwood veneers. As such, it is used in the manufacture of furniture, cabinets, countertops, wall paneling, and doors of all types.

Beadboard is an insulating board consisting of a core of small, foam plastic beads with heavy paper laminated to both sides. The major use of beadboard is as an insulating material, such as perimeter insulation on foundation walls. Its R factor is less than that of rigid foam insulation of the same thickness.

Plastic laminates : consist of a base of phenolic-resin impregnated Kraft paper over which a patterned sheet is applied. Over all this is laid a sheet of melamine resin. When a thin sheet of aluminum is placed under the decorative sheet, it dissipates heat quickly, making the laminate flameresistant. These layers are then cured with intense heat and pressure to fuse the material. Popularly known by trade names such as Formica, the material has found popular acceptance for counter tops, wall coverings, and furniture.

Asbestos-cement boards are formed from a mixture of portland cement and asbestos fiber that has been wetted and then pressed into a sheet. The material is strong, permanent, and resistant to fire, water, acid, rot, fungus, and insects. Asbestos-cement panels may be used inside or out, and are available in a variety of textures, colors, and with perforations. In recent years, the use of asbestos has diminished, because of health hazards associated with that material.

GLUED LAMINATED (GLULAM) LUMBER

Laminated structural members are fabricated from layers of wood that are bonded with adhesives, and which have the grain of all layers running approximately parallel. The usual thickness of laminations is 1-1/2 inches, although 3/4 inch laminations are used to achieve small radius curves; and members are produced in several standard widths and a great range of depths.

Laminated members are factory produced under rigidly controlled manufacturing conditions, resulting in members that are superior to sawn lumber in several ways. For the same sized member, they can span greater distances and support heavier loads, they are more weather resistant, they are consistent in size, appearance, and strength, and they are more dimensionally stable than solid timber.

Remember that as the inspector your are responsible for making sure that any glulam members that are brought to your site are stamped, and identified as inspected by a DSA approved inspector. The laboratory of record usually sets this up, however you must verify that is has taken place.

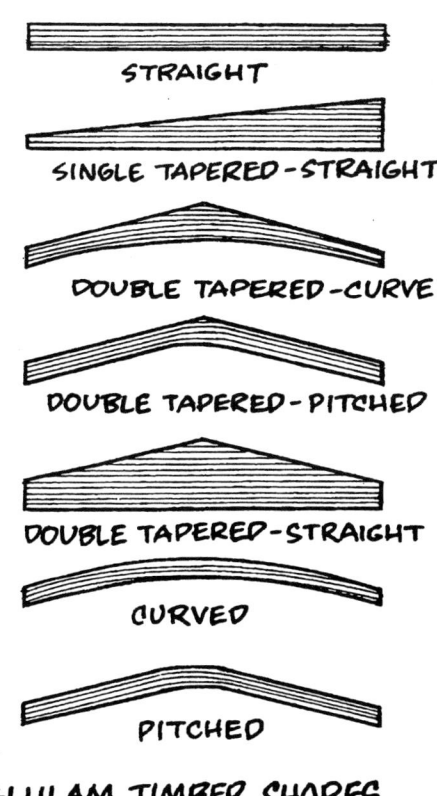

GLULAM TIMBER SHAPES

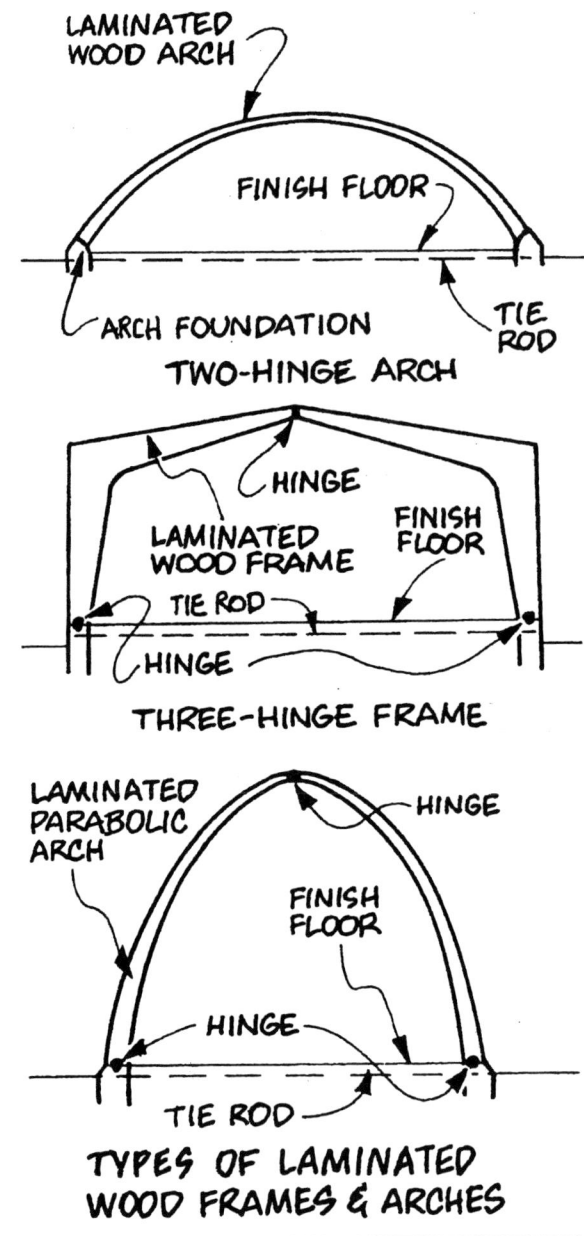

TYPES OF LAMINATED WOOD FRAMES & ARCHES

Glulam members are available in three grades based on appearance:

Industrial is the grade used where appearance is not a prime concern.

Architectural is the grade used where appearance is an important requirement.

Premium is the top grade, specified where the finest natural finish is desired.

In specifying laminated timbers, one must designate the type of adhesive, the stress grade required, and the apearance grade desired.

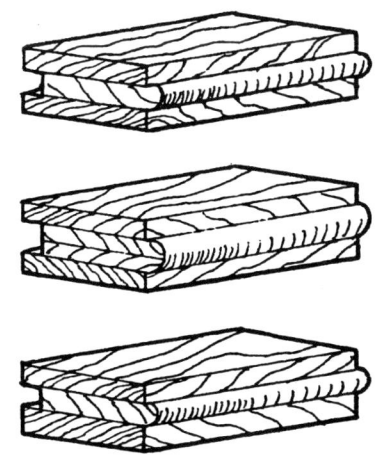

LAMINATED WOOD DECKING

Laminated decking is manufactured from layers of kiln-dried lumber that are bonded with adhesives. It is available in 2-1/4" to 4" thicknesses and in various standard lengths. The interior surface of the decking is intended to be exposed and is available smooth, grooved, prefinished, or stained.

WOOD PRESERVATION

Insects, decay, and fire represent continual threats to wood. To some degree, proper seasoning reduces some of these threats, but in most cases, wood must be treated to prevent (or delay) destruction from these causes.

Insects that attack wood include a variety of wood-eating termites which bore from within, so that a may appear sound but actually is eaten away inside and ready to fail. Carpenter ants, bees, and beetles also consume wood, not for food, but to develop a shelter. And marine organisms destroy wood located in salt or brackish water.

In many areas today, a wood-framed structure cannot be sold or mortgaged unless it has received certification from a state-approved termite inspection company.

Termites can be controlled by using termite shields, which are metal strips used to prevent the insects from reaching the wood, by poisoning the ground adjacent to the building, or by pressure-treating the wood close to the earth. Since termites attack from within, surface coatings are generally ineffective, and preservatives which completely penetrate the wood should be used instead.

Decay in wood is caused by fungi which feed on the cell walls. The development of any fungus depends on mild temperatures, moisture, and air. Without all three conditions, decay cannot occur. In fact, even in dry rot, some moisture is present. Decay can be avoided if wood is kept dry and well ventilated, or if it is kept completely submerged in water so that air is excluded. In the latter case, some timbers have lasted for centuries.

Chemical preservatives that protect wood from fungi, as well as insects and marine organisms, are of two types: oil-borne solutions, such as creosote; and water-borne solutions, such as chromated zinc chloride. Preservatives may be brushed, sprayed, or dipped, but for maximum effectiveness, pressure is required for deeper penetration of the solution. Some preservatives cause discoloration or an oily surface that is difficult to paint.

Fire is an ever-present danger to wood, with the exception of heavy timbers which burn very slowly. Wood can be made fire resistant by either impregnating with chemical solutions, such as ammonium phosphate, or by the use of a surface treatment. Surface applications, such as an intumescent paint, retard the increase of temperature and thereby reduce the rate of flame spread.

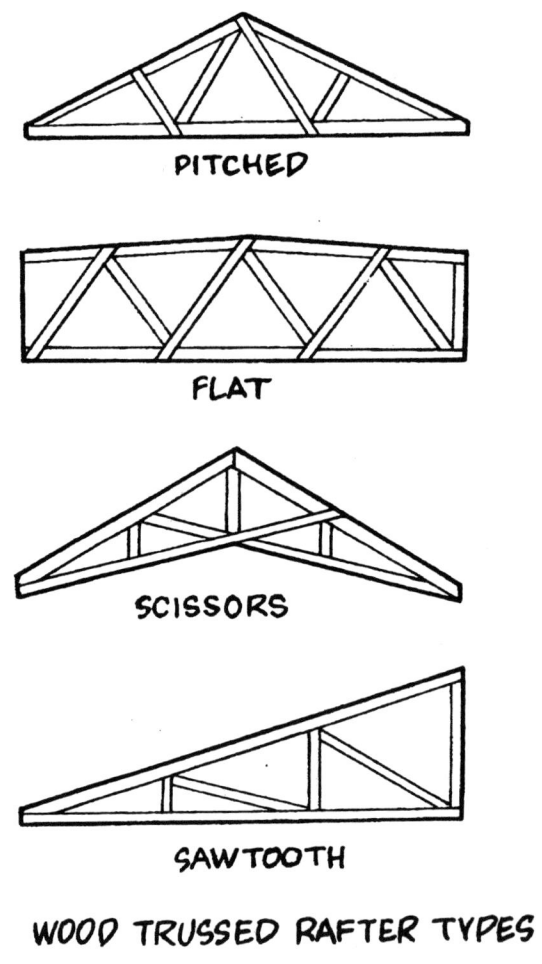

WOOD TRUSSED RAFTER TYPES

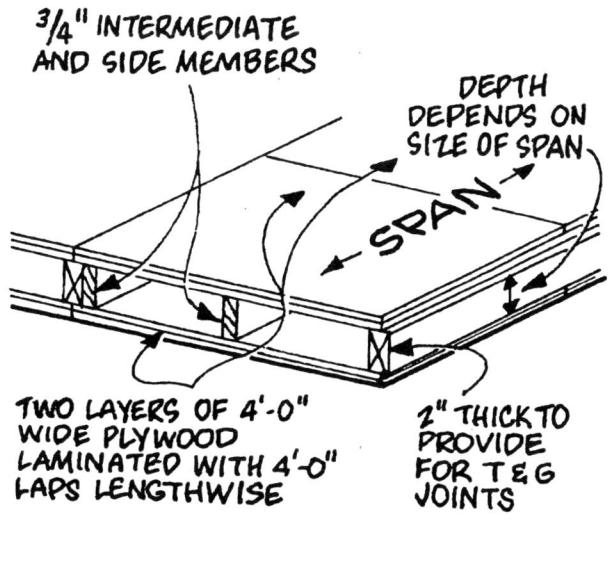

STRESSED SKIN PLYWOOD PANEL

WOOD FRAMING

Years ago, when tall trees, and hence large timbers, were plentiful, a designer faced with a 50-foot span would call for 50-foot-long sawn girders which were placed at intervals across the structure. Here was roof framing at its simplest - little engineering, no fabrication, no assembly, and a minimum of small members to be concerned about.

Today, such large timbers are costly and difficult to obtain. Instead, wood framing utilizes trusses, rigid frames, built-up girders, and glued laminated beams. Since the beginning of this century, when grading rules and working stresses were established, wood framing has become relatively standarized and refined.

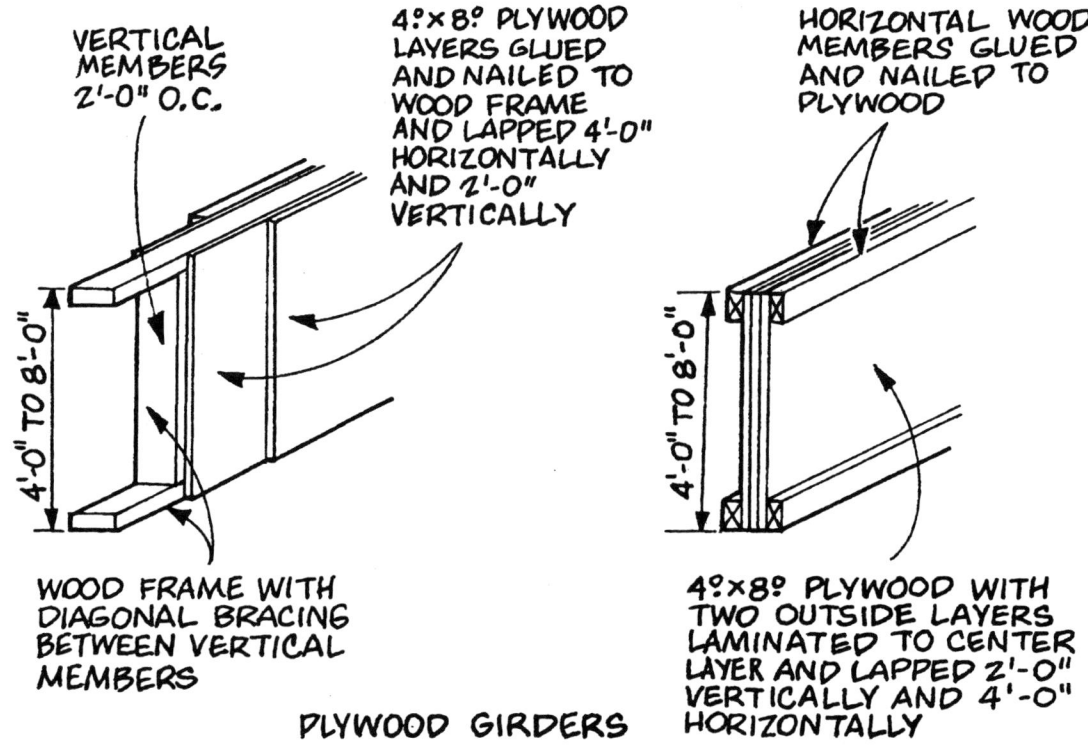

PLYWOOD GIRDERS

There are two types of wood wall framing systems commonly used for dwellings and other small structures; the platform frame (often called western framing) and the balloon frame. The basic difference in these two systems is that in platform framing there are separate studs for each floor, whereas the balloon frame exterior wall studs extend continuously through two stories, from the foundation to the top plate.

Wood post and beam systems employ beams, rather than joists or rafters, to support floors and roofs. The supporting beams in turn rest on posts or columns, rather than studs, which transfer the building loads to the foundation. The resulting skeleton frame forms a three-dimensional modular grid of spaces which is often left exposed. Lateral stability is provided by rigid connecting joints, as well as enclosing exterior wall panels.

CONCLUSION

As a DSA inspector you will be expected to know quite a lot about wood and wood structural systems and grading processes. Unlike masonry an steel you will also not receive any assistance from a special inspector. It is for this reason that DSA devotes such a high number of questions on the certification exams.

It is important for any inspector candidate to understand the above information in order to have a full understanding of this material. The lessons that follow in this wood lecture are specifically geared toward the information that you will need for the exam.

© Professional Study Inc. 2003

Chapter 10: Wood
LESSON 10.2

(Title 24, Part 2, Volume 2, Chapter 23A)

Along with concrete wood is the most common construction material there is. It is for this reason that this subject is represented so prominently in the DSA certification exams. The Class 2 and 3 exams are heavily weighted toward wood since Class 2 and 3 projects are almost exclusively made of wood structural systems.

The following is a brief summary of the highpoints in Chapter 23A (Wood)

WOOD
(Title 24, Part 2, Volume 2, Chapter 23A)

Take out your code book and highlight the code sections as they appear on this list in either red or yellow.

The "**Commentary**" on the right is broken down into four categories and they are as follows:

TEST QUESTION (Highlight in Red)
(Indicates that this material is very likely to be specifically referenced on the DSA exams)

REMEMBER (Highlight in Yellow)
(Indicates that you should know this material and that it is relevant to your work as an inspector)

BEWARE (Highlight in Yellow)
(Indicates that there is something that may not be apparent at first but that the inspector will have to deal with)

SEE ALSO (Highlight in Yellow)
(Indicates that there is another code section that affects this information)

Highlighting List
Highlight List (T-24, Part 2, Ch.23A)
Chapter 23A [For DSA/SS & OSHPD 1 & 4]
WOOD

Division I. GENERAL DESIGN REQUIREMENTS

SECTION 2301A. GENERAL

2301A.1 Scope. The quality and design of wood members and their fastenings shall conform to the provisions of this chapter.

2301A.2.2 Conventional light-frame construction...........

shall be in accordance with the applicable requirements of Section 2305A.

SECTION 2302A. DEFINITIONS

GRADE (Lumber) is the classification of lumber in regard to strength and utility in accordance with UBC Standard 23-1 and the grading rules of an approved lumber grading agency.

> **Comment:** SEE ALSO WCLG Book Lesson #4

WOOD OF NATURAL RESISTANCE TO DECAY OR TERMITES ....

Recognized species are:

Decay resistant: Redwood, Cedars, Black Locust
Termite resistant: Redwood, Eastern Red Cedar

SECTION 2304A. MINIMUM QUALITY

2304A.1 Quality and Identification. All lumber, *plywood*, structural glued-laminated timber, end-jointed lumber, ...
piles and poles regulated by this chapter shall conform to the applicable standards and grading rules specified in this code and shall be so identified by the grade mark or certificate of inspection issued by an approved agency.

All preservatively treated wood required to be treated under Section 2306A shall be identified by the quality mark of an inspection agency which has been accredited by an accreditation body which complies with the requirements of the American Lumber Standard Committee Treated Wood Program, or equivalent.

> **Comment:** TEST QUESTION
> Lumber Grading Stamp Example:
>
> **Interpreting Grade Stamps**
>
> Most grade stamps, except those for rough lumber or heavy timbers, contain five basic elements:
>
> (b)12 STAND (c)
> ABC   S-DRY /D\
> (a)   (e)   /F I R\ (d)
>
> a. The tra quality
> b. Mill ide brand
> c. Grade name,
> d. Specie cates combi
> e. Condit of surf
>   S-D
>   MC
>   S-G

2304A.2 Minimum Capacity or Grade.

Plywood used for structural purposes shall be of *one of* the grades specified in UBC Standard 23-2. ...

End-jointed wood products shall not be used for structural purposes unless specifically approved by the enforcement agency.

2304A.3 Timber Connectors and Fasteners.

The number and size of nails connecting wood members shall not be less than that set forth in Tables 23A-II-B-1 and 23A-II-B-2. Other connections shall be fastened to provide equivalent strength. End and edge distances and nail penetrations shall be in accordance with the applicable provisions of Division III, Part III.

> **Comment:** REMEMBER
> Refer to Table 23A-11-B for # of nails & size for Typical Connections

Fasteners for pressure-preservative treated and fire-retardant treated wood shall be of hot-dipped zinc coated galvanized, stainless steel, silicon bronze or copper.

> **Comment:** TEST QUESTION
> Always use galvanized (or corrosion resistant) nails in treated wood.

2304A.4.3 Structural glued-laminated timber.
The manufacture and fabrication of structural glued-laminated timber shall be under the supervision of qualified personnel.

2304A.5 Dried Fire-retardant-treated Wood.
Approved fire-retardant-treated wood shall be dried, following treatment, to a maximum moisture content as follows: solid-sawn lumber 2 inches (51 mm) in thickness or less to 19 percent, and plywood to 15 percent.

2304A.8 Rejection..........................

Wood members which are required to carry design loads and which the project architect, engineer or inspector judge to be misgraded shall be reinspected by a qualified lumber grading inspector to verify the proper grading of the material.

Wood members which have permissible grade characteristics or defects in such combination as to affect the serviceability of the member shall be rejected by the project inspector with the concurrence of the responsible architect or structural engineer.

SECTION 2305A. DESIGN AND CONSTRUCTION REQUIREMENTS

2305A.5 The design and construction of conventional light-frame wood structures shall be in accordance with Division IV.

2305A.5 The design and construction of conventional light-frame wood structures shall be in accordance with Division IV.

2305A.11 Testing and inspections shall be in accordance with Division IX.

Division II.GENERAL REQUIREMENTS

Part I.REQUIREMENTS APPLICABLE TO ALL DESIGN METHODS

SECTION 2306A . DECAY AND TERMITE PROTECTION

2306A.3 Under-floor Clearance. When wood joists or the bottom of wood structural floors without joists are located closer than 18 inches (457 mm) or wood girders are located closer than 12 inches (305 mm) to exposed ground in crawl spaces or unexcavated areas located within the periphery of the building foundation, the floor assembly, including posts, girders, joists and subfloor, shall be approved wood of natural resistance to decay as listed in Section 2306A.4 or treated wood.

When the above under-floor clearances are required, the under floor area shall be accessible. Accessible under-floor areas shal be provided with a minimum 18-inch-by-24-inch (457mm by 610 mm) opening unobstructed by pipes, ducts and similar construc tion.

> **Comment:** TEST QUESTION
> 18" Min Clear Joists @ crawl space
> 12" Min. Clear Girders @ crawl space

2306A.4 Plates, Sills and Sleepers. All foundation plates or sills and sleepers on a concrete or masonry slab, which is in direct contact with earth, and sills that rest on concrete or masonry foundations, shall be treated wood or Foundation redwood, all marked or branded by an approved agency.

Bottoms of sills and plywood, unless the plywood is treated in accordance with Section 2306A.8 on exterior foundation walls shall not be less than 12 inches (305 mm) above outside finished earth grade. On exterior walls where the earth is paved with an asphalt or concrete slab at least 18 inches (457 mm) wide and draining away from the building, the bottom of sills may be 6 inches (152 mm) above the top of such slab. Other means of termite and decay protection may be accepted by the enforcement agency.

> **Comment:** TEST QUESTION
> Sills & Plywood 12" above finished earth gra
> exterior 6" above paved grade.

Stud walls or partitions around shower or toilet rooms with more than two fixtures, and stud walls adjacent to unroofed paved areas, shall rest on concrete curbs extending at least 6 inches (152 mm) above finished floor or paving level.

> **Comment:** REMEMBER
> Walls @ toilet rooms w/ more than (2) fixture
> must have 6" curbs.

2306A.5 Columns and Posts...............

.... In areas exposed to water splash and in exterior locations, wood columns and posts shall be supported by piers projecting at least 2 inches (51 mm) above the finished floor, and shall bear on a metal base plate or a foundation plate or sill as specified in Section 2306A.4. Posts or columns of treated wood or of foundation-grade redwood or cedar may be placed directly on concrete, solid masonry or grouted masonry.

> **Comment:** REMEMBER
> Columns Min. 2" above finished floor

2306A.6 Girders Entering Masonry or Concrete Walls. Ends of wood girders entering masonry or concrete walls shall be provided with a 1/2-inch (12.7 mm) air space on tops,

> **Comment:** REMEMBER
> 1/2" airspace on top of wood beams entering concrete or masonry.

2306A.8 Wood and Earth Separation. Protection of wood against deterioration as set forth in the previous sections for specified applications is required. In addition, wood used in construction of permanent structures and located nearer than 6 inches (152 mm) to earth shall be treated wood or wood of natural resistance to decay, as defined in Section 2302A.1. Where located on concrete slabs placed on earth, wood shall be treated wood or wood of natural resistance to decay.

2306A.10 Moisture Content of Treated Wood.....................

....................moisture content of 19 percent or less be-

> **Comment:** TEST QUESTION
> All lumber to have maximum 19% moisture content not just treated lumber.

2306A.12 Weather Exposure.

All *plywood* structural panels *used in applications exposed to eather shall be classified for Exterior usage. All plywood structural panels used in locations not exposed to weather shall be assified for either Exterior or Exposure 1 usage.*

2306A.13 Water Splash. Where wood-frame walls and partitions are covered on the interior with plaster, tile or similar materials and are subject to water splash, the framing shall be protected with approved waterproof paper conforming to Section 1402.1.

SECTION 2307A . WOOD SUPPORTING MASONRY OR CONCRETE

Wood members shall not be used to permanently support the dead load of any masonry or concrete.

> **EXCEPTIONS:** 1. Masonry or concrete nonstructural floor or roo surfacing not more than 4 inches (102 mm) thick may be supported by wood members.
>
> 2. Any structure may rest upon wood piles constructed in accord ance with the requirements of Chapter 18A.
>
> 3. Veneer of brick, concrete or stone applied as specified in Sectio 1403.6.2 may be supported by approved treated wood foundatio when the maximum height of veneer does not exceed 30 feet (914 mm) above the foundations. Such veneer used as an interior wall fini may also be supported on wood floors that are designed to support t additional load and designed to limit the deflection and shrinkage 1/600 of the span of the supporting members.
>
> 4. Glass block masonry having a

SECTION 2309A . FLOOR FRAMING

Wood-joisted floors shall be framed and constructed and anchored to supporting wood stud or masonry walls as specified in Chapter 16A.
Fire block and draft stops shall be in accordance with Section 708.

SECTION 2310A . EXTERIOR WALL COVERINGS

2310A.3 Plywood. When plywood is used for covering the exterior of outside walls, it shall be of the exterior type not less than 3/8 inch (9.5 mm) thick.

> **Comment:** REMEMBER Min. 3/8" thick plywood at exterior walls

2310A.7 Nailing. All fasteners used for the attachment of siding shall be of a corrosion-resistant type.

Part II. REQUIREMENTS APPLICABLE TO ENGINEERED DESIGN OF WIND AND EARTHQUAKE LOAD-RESISTING SYSTEMS

SECTION 2315A . WOOD SHEAR WALLS AND DIAPHRAGMS

2315A.3 Wood Diaphragms.

2315A.3.3 *Plywood* **diaphragms**..................

.... except that vertical plywood diaphragms shall be blocked. Plywood shall be applied directly to wood members of at least 2 inches (51 mm) in nominal dimension.

Use of machine nailing is subject to a satisfactory jobsite demonstration for each project and the approval of the project architect or structural engineer and the enforcement agency. The approval is subject to continued satisfactory performance. Machine nailing is not allowed for 5/16-inch (7.9 mm) plywood. If the nail heads penetrate the outer ply more than would be normal for a hand-held hammer, or if minimum allowable edge distances are not maintained, the performance will be deemed unsatisfactory and machine nailing shall be discontinued.

... Casing nails shall not be used in plywood less than one-half inch in thickness.

Plywood diaphragms shall be constructed of plywood sheets, generally not less than 4 feet by 8 feet (1219 mm by 2438 mm) in size, attached to framing members spaced not to exceed the spans set forth in Table 23A-II-E-1 (see also Section 2320A.12), and arranged in the patterns set forth in Table 23A-II-H. In general, panel edges shall bear on the framing members and butt along their center lines. Plywood in shear walls shall be at least 5/16 inch (7.9 mm) thick for studs spaced 16 inches (406 mm) on center and 3/8 inch thick (9.5 mm) where studs are spaced 24 inches (610 mm) on center.

In horizontal plywood diaphragms, no panel less than 24 inches (610 mm) wide shall be used. In vertical plywood diaphragms, no panel less than 12 inches (305 mm) wide shall be used. Nails shall be placed not less than 3/8 inch (9.5 mm) in from the panel edge, shall be spaced not more than 6 inches (152 mm) on center along panel edge bearings, and shall be firmly driven into the framing members. Nails shall be placed not less than 1/2 inch (12.7 mm) in from the panel edge when 3-inch (76 mm) nominal edge members are required per Table 23A-II-H and 23A-II-I-1. No unblocked panels less than 12 inches (305 mm) wide shall be used.

Comment: TEST QUESTION
Min. 24" Wide Panels @ Horiz. Diaphragm
Min. 12" Wide Panels @ Vert. Diaphragm

Comment: REMEMBER
Edge Distance for nailing
- Min. 3/8" for 2x
- Min. 1/2" for 3x and higher

TABLE 23A-II-B-1—NAILING SCHEDULE

CONNECTION	NAILING[1]
1. Joist or rafters to sides of studs	
8-inch joist or less	3-16d
For each additional 4 inches in depth of joist	1-16d
2. Bridging to joist, toenail each end	2-8d
a. Blocking between joists or rafters—	
To joist or rafters—Toenails each side, each end	2-10d[12]
b. Blocking between studs, each end	2-10d toenails or 2-16d
3. 1" × 6" (25 mm × 152 mm) subfloor or less to each joist, face nail	2-8d
4. Wider than 1" × 6" (25 mm × 152 mm) subfloor to each joist, face nail	3-8d
5. 2" (51 mm) subfloor to joist or girder, blind and face nail	2-16d
6. Sole plate to joist or blocking, typical face nail	16d at 16" (406 mm) o.c.
Sole plate to joist or blocking, at braced wall panels	3-16d per 16" (406 mm)
7. Top plate to stud, end nail	2-16d
8. Stud to sole plate	4-8d, toenail or 2-16d, end nail
9. Double studs, face nail	16d at 24" (610 mm) o.c.
10. Doubled top plates, typical face nail	16d at 16" (406 mm) o.c.
Double top plates, lap splice	8-16d
11. Blocking between joists or rafters to top plate, toenail	3-8d
12. Rim joist to top plate, toenail	8d at 6" (152 mm) o.c.
13. Top plates, laps and intersections, face nail	2-16d
14. Continuous header, two pieces	16d at 16" (406 mm) o.c. along each edge
15. Ceiling joists to plate, toenail	3-8d
16. Continuous header to stud, toenail	4-8d
17. Ceiling joists, laps over partitions, face nail	3-16d
18. Ceiling joists to parallel rafters, face nail	3-16d
19. Joist or rafters at all bearings—toenails, each side	2-10d
20. 1" (25 mm) brace to each stud and plate, face nail	2-8d
21. 1" × 8" (25 mm × 203 mm) sheathing or less to each bearing, face nail	2-8d
22. Wider than 1" × 8" (25 mm × 203 mm) sheathing to each bearing, face nail	3-8d
23. Built-up corner studs	16d at 24" (610 mm) o.c.
24. Built-up girder and beams	20d at 32" (813 mm) o.c. at top and bottom and staggered 2-20d at ends and at each splice
25. 2" (51 mm) planks	2-16d at each bearing
26. Wood structural panels and particleboard:[2]	
Subfloor and wall sheathing (to framing):	
$1/2$" (12.7 mm) and less	6d[3]
$19/32$"-$3/4$" (15 mm-19 mm)	8d[4] or 6d[5]
$7/8$"-1" (22 mm-25 mm)	8d[3]
$1 1/8$"-$1 1/4$" (29 mm-32 mm)	10d[4] or 8d[5]
Combination subfloor-underlayment (to framing):	
$3/4$" (19 mm) and less	6d[5]
$7/8$"-1" (22 mm-25 mm)	8d[5]
$1 1/8$"-$1 1/4$" (29 mm-32 mm)	10d[4] or 8d[5]
27. Panel siding (to framing)[2]:	
$1/2$" (12.7 mm) or less	6d[6]
$5/8$" (16 mm)	8d[6]
28. Fiberboard sheathing:[7]	
$1/2$" (12.7 mm)	No. 11 ga.[8]
	6d[4]
	No. 16 ga.[9]
$25/32$" (20 mm)	No. 11 ga.[8]
	8d[4]
	No. 16 ga.[9]
29. Interior paneling	
$1/4$" (6.4 mm)	4d[10]
$3/8$" (9.5 mm)	6d[11]

[1]Common or box nails may be used except where otherwise stated.
[2]Nails spaced at 6 inches (152 mm) on center at edges, 12 inches (305 mm) at intermediate supports except 6 inches (152 mm) at all supports where spans are
48 inches (1219 mm) or more. For nailing of wood structural panel and particleboard diaphragms and shear walls, refer to Sections 2315A.3.3 and 2315A.4.
Nails for wall sheathing may be common, box or casing.
[3]Common or deformed shank.
[4]Common.
[5]Deformed shank.
[6]Corrosion-resistant siding or casing nails conforming to the requirements of Section 2304A.3.
[7]Fasteners spaced 3 inches (76 mm) on center at exterior edges and 6 inches (152 mm) on center at intermediate supports.
(Continued)

TABLE 23A-II-H—ALLOWABLE SHEAR IN POUNDS PER FOOT FOR HORIZONTAL WOOD STRUCTURAL PANEL DIAPHRAGMS WITH FRAMING OF DOUGLAS FIR-LARCH OR SOUTHERN PINE[1]

					BLOCKED DIAPHRAGMS				UNBLOCKED DIAPHRAGMS	
					Nail spacing (in.) at diaphragm boundaries (all cases), at continuous panel edges parallel to load (Cases 3 and 4) and at all panel edges (Cases 5 and 6)				Nails spaced 6" (152 mm) max. at supported edges	
					× 25.4 for mm					
		MINIMUM NAIL PENETRATION IN FRAMING (inches)	MINIMUM NOMINAL PANEL THICKNESS (inches)	MINIMUM NOMINAL WIDTH OF FRAMING MEMBER (inches)	6	4	2½	2[2]	Case 1 (No unblocked edges or continuous joints parallel to load)	All other configurations (Cases 2, 3, 4, 5 and 6)
					Nail spacing (in.) at other panel edges					
					× 25.4 for mm					
PANEL GRADE	COMMON NAIL SIZE				6	6	4	3		
		× 25.4 for mm			× 0.0146 for N/mm					
Structural I	6d	1¼	5/16	2	185	250	375	420	165	125
				3	210	280	420	475	185	140
	8d	1½	3/8	2	270	360	530	600	240	180
				3	300	400	600	675	265	200
	10d[3]	1⅝	15/32	2	320	425	640	730	285	215
				3	360	480	720	820	320	240
C-D, C-C, Sheathing, and other grades covered in UBC Standard 23-2 or 23-3	6d	1¼	5/16	2	170	225	335	380	150	110
				3	190	250	380	430	170	125
			3/8	2	185	250	375	420	165	125
				3	210	280	420	475	185	140
	8d	1½	3/8	2	240	320	480	545	215	160
				3	270	360	540	610	240	180
			7/16	2	255	340	505	575	230	170
				3	285	380	570	645	255	190
			15/32	2	270	360	530	600	240	180
				3	300	400	600	675	265	200
	10d[3]	1⅝	15/32	2	290	385	575	655	255	190
				3	325	430	650	735	290	215
			19/32	2	320	425	640	730	285	215
				3	360	480	720	820	320	240

[1]These values are for short-*duration* loads due to wind or earthquake and must be reduced 25 percent for normal loading *such as for folded plate or boxed girder design*. Space nails 12 inches (305mm) *maximum* on center *for floors* and 12 inches (305 mm) *maximum on center for floors* along intermediate framing members.

Allowable shear values for *common* nails in framing members of other species set forth in *Table 12A, ANSI/NFoPA NDS-91*...shall be calculated for all other grades by multiplying the *above tabulated* shear capacities for *common nails and the panel grade* by the following factors: 0.82 for species with specific gravity greater than or equal to 0.42 but less than 0.49, and 0.65 for species with a specific gravity less than 0.42.

[2]Framing *and blocking* at adjoining panel edges shall be 3-inch (76 mm) nominal or wider and nails shall be staggered where nails are spaced *3 inches (76 mm) or less*.

[3]Plywood joints shall occur at the center of framing members or blocking. The minimum edge distance for nails in the receiving members and the plywood shall be 3/8 inch (9.5 mm) for 2-inch (51 mm) nominal receiving members and 1/2-inch (13 mm) for 3-inch (76 mm) nominal receiving members. Flat blocking receiving 10d nails shall be 3-inch by 4-inch nominal (76 by 102 mm) or larger.

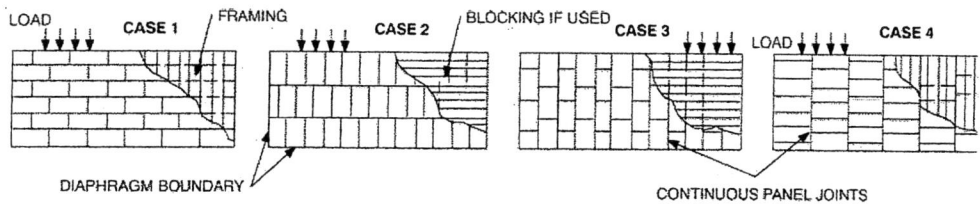

Division III. DESIGN SPECIFICATIONS FOR ALLOWABLE STRESS DESIGN OF WOOD BUILDINGS

4.4.1.4 Bridging for Floor Joists and Roof Joists or Rafters. Roof joists or rafters of more than 8-inch (203 mm) depth and floor joists of more than 4-inch (102 mm) depth which are spaced 32 inches (813 mm) on center or less shall be provided with bridging to distribute superimposed loads. Floor joists shall be bridged every 8 feet (2438 mm) and roof joists or rafters every 10 feet (3048 mm) by solid blocking 2 inches (51 mm) thick and the full depth of the joist or rafter, or by wood cross bridging of not less than 1 inch by 3 inches (25 mm by 76 mm) or nailed metal cross bridging of equal strength. Where cross bridging is used, the lower ends of such cross bridging shall be driven up and nailed after the floor, subfloor or roof has been nailed.

> **Comment:** REMEMBER
> Bridging required for Joists w/ 32" or less spacing
> Roof Joists > 8" deep brace @ 10'-0" o.c.
> Floor Joists > 4" deep brace @ 8'-0" o.c.
>
> Blocking Min. 2" Thick
>
> Cross Bridging Min. 1x3
>
> * Cross Bridging should be nailed after the horizontal diaphr[agm] has been nailed.

Part II. PLYWOOD STRUCTURAL PANELS
SECTION 2317A . PLYWOOD STRUCTURAL PANELS

Part III. FASTENINGS
SECTION 2318A . TIMBER CONNECTORS AND FASTENERS

2318A.3.1 Allowable lateral loads

.... Pilot holes shall have a diameter approximately 90 percent of the nail shank diameter.

> **Comment:** REMEMBER
> Pilot Holes for nails to be 90% of the shank diameter in timber connectors and fasteners.

2318A.3.3 Spacing and penetration. Common wire nails shall have penetration into the piece receiving the point as set forth in Tables 23A-III-C-1 and 23A-III-C-2. Nails or spikes for which the gages or lengths are not set forth in Tables 23A-III-C-1 and 23A-III-C-2 shall have a required penetration of not less than 11 diameters, and allowable loads may be interpolated.

Nails in plywood shall not be overdriven such that the nail heads penetrate the face ply by more than the thickness of the nail head or break the face-ply wood fibers.

2318A.3.4 [For DSA/SS, OHSPD] Corrosion resistance. *Nails and spikes used in wet or exterior locations, such as exterior wall*

.... shall have a hot-dipped or tumbled galvanized coating of not less than 1.5 ounces of zinc per square foot (458 gm/m2) or be fabricated of copper, stainless steel or brass.

TABLE 23A-III-C-1—BOX NAIL DESIGN VALUES (Z) FOR SINGLE SHEAR (Two Member) CONNECTIONS[1,2,3]
(With both members of identical species)

SIDE MEMBER THICKNESS t_s (inches)	NAIL LENGTH L (inches)	NAIL DIAMETER D (inches)	PENNY-WEIGHT	G=0.55 SOUTHERN PINE Z lbs.	G=0.50 DOUGLAS-FIR LARCH Z lbs.	G=0.42 SPRUCE-PINE-FIR Z lbs.
	× 25.4 for mm			× 4.45 for N		
1/2	2	0.099	6d	55	48	38
	2 1/2	0.113	8d	67	59	47
	3	0.128	10d	82	73	59
	3 1/4	0.128	12d	82	73	59
	3 1/2	0.135	16d	89	79	65
	4	0.148	20d	101	90	73
	4 1/2	0.148	30d	101	90	73
	5	0.162	40d	117	105	87
3/4	2	0.099	6d	61	55	47
	2 1/2	0.113	8d	79	72	57
	3	0.128	10d	101	87	68
	3 1/4	0.128	12d	101	87	68
	3 1/2	0.135	16d	108	94	74
	4	0.148	20d	121	105	83
	4 1/2	0.148	30d	121	105	83
	5	0.162	40d	138	121	96
1	2 1/2	0.113	8d	79	72	61
	3	0.128	10d	101	93	79
	3 1/4	0.128	12d	101	93	79
	3 1/2	0.135	16d	113	103	86
	4	0.148	20d	128	118	96
	4 1/2	0.148	30d	128	118	96
	5	0.162	40d	154	141	109
1 1/2	3 1/4	0.128	12d	101	93	79
	3 1/2	0.135	16d	113	103	88
	4	0.148	20d	128	118	100
	4 1/2	0.148	30d	128	118	100
	5	0.162	40d	154	141	120

TABLE 23A-III-C-2—COMMON WIRE NAIL DESIGN VALUES (Z) FOR SINGLE SHEAR (Two Member) CONNECTIONS[1,2,3]
(with both members of identical species)

SIDE MEMBER THICKNESS t_s (inches)	NAIL LENGTH L (inches)	NAIL DIAMETER D (inches)	PENNY-WEIGHT	G=0.55 SOUTHERN PINE Z lbs.	G=0.50 DOUGLAS-FIR LARCH Z lbs.	G=0.42 SPRUCE-PINE-FIR Z lbs.
	× 25.4 for mm			× 4.45 for N		
1/2	2	0.113	6d	67	59	47
	2 1/2	0.131	8d	85	76	61
	3	0.148	10d	101	90	73
	3 1/4	0.148	12d	101	90	73
	3 1/2	0.162	16d	117	105	87
	4	0.192	20d	137	124	103
	4 1/2	0.207	30d	148	134	112
	5	0.225	40d	162	147	123
	5 1/2	0.244	50d	166	151	127
	6	0.263	60d	188	171	144
3/4	2 1/2	0.131	8d	104	90	70
	3	0.148	10d	121	105	83
	3 1/4	0.148	12d	121	105	83
	3 1/2	0.162	16d	138	121	96
	4	0.192	20d	157	138	111
	4 1/2	0.207	30d	166	147	119
	5	0.225	40d	178	158	129
	5 1/2	0.244	50d	182	162	132
	6	0.263	60d	203	181	149
1	3	0.148	10d	128	118	96
	3 1/4	0.148	12d	128	118	96
	3 1/2	0.162	16d	154	141	109
	4	0.192	20d	183	159	124
	4 1/2	0.207	30d	192	167	131
	5	0.225	40d	202	177	140
	5 1/2	0.244	50d	207	181	143
	6	0.263	60d	227	199	159
1 1/2	3 1/2	0.162	16d	154	141	120
	4	0.192	20d	185	170	144
	4 1/2	0.207	30d	203	186	158
	5	0.225	40d	224	205	172
	5 1/2	0.244	50d	230	211	175
	6	0.263	60d	262	240	191

[1] Tabulated lateral design values (Z) for nailed connections shall be multiplied by all applicable adjustment factors (see Division III. Part I).

[2] Tabulated lateral design values (Z) are for common wire nails inserted in side grain with nail axis perpendicular to wood fibers and with the following nail bending

Division IV. CONVENTIONAL LIGHT-FRAME CONSTRUCTION

SECTION 2320A . CONVENTIONAL LIGHT-FRAME CONSTRUCTION DESIGN PROVISIONS

2320A.6 Foundation Plates or Sills. *Sills under bearing, exterior or shear walls shall be bolted to the masonry or concrete with not smaller than 5/8-inch by 12-inch (16 mm by 305 mm) bolts spaced not more than 4 feet (1219 mm) on center with a minimum of two bolts for each piece of sill plate. There shall be a bolt within 9 inches (229 mm) of each end of each piece of sill. The effective embedment length in concrete of bolts designed to resist overturning or uplift forces shall not include the embedment in 6-inch (152 mm) or narrower concrete curbs. Where sills are bored or notched...*

> **Comment:** TEST QUESTION
> Bearing Walls:
> • Min. Size A-Bolts 5/8"
> • Spacing: 4'-0" oc. Max
> • Min. (2) Per Plate Piece
> • Anchor within 9" of the end of the plate

Sills under nonbearing interior partitions on concrete floor slabs shall be anchored at not more than 4 feet (1219 mm) on center to resist a shear of not less than 50 pounds per linear foot (0.7 kN/m) acting either parallel or normal to the wall.

> **Comment:** TEST QUESTION
> Non-Bearing Walls
> • Min. Size A-Bolts 1/2"
> • Spacing 4'-0" Max.

Treated wood sills where cut, drilled or notched shall be treated with a preservative and approved by the architect and the enforcement agency on all exposed surfaces from which preservative treatment has been removed.

2320A.8.3 Framing details.

Notches on the ends of joists shall not exceed one fourth the joist depth. Holes bored in joists shall not be within 2 inches (51 mm) of the top or bottom of the joist, and the diameter of any such hole shall not exceed one third the depth of the joist. Notches in the top or bottom of joists shall not exceed one *tenth* the depth and shall not be located in the middle third of the span. *Notches or holes shall not be placed in joists unless fully detailed in the approved plans.*

> **Comment:** TEST QUESTION
> Max Notch @ Ends of Joists
> • 1/4" of Joist Depth
> • No Holes in joists within top or bottom 2"
> • Diameter of above holes Max. 1/3 depth of joist in any location
> • Notches in top or bottom of joist Max 1/10 depth and no mid 1/3 of span
> • Notches or holes must be detailed in plans.

Joist framing from opposite sides of a beam, girder or partition shall be lapped at least 3 inches (76 mm) or the opposing joists shall be tied together in an approved manner.

> **Comment:** REMEMBER
> Opposite side Joists must be lapped Min. 3"

Ledger strips applied to the sides of girders for support of joists shall not be less than 2 inches by 4 inches (51 mm by 102 mm).

> **Comment:** REMEMBER
> Min. Ledger Strips on sides of joists 2 x 4

2320A.8.7 Bridging. *Floor joists more than 4 inches (102 mm) in depth shall be provided with bridging in accordance with the provisions of Section 2316A.2, Item 22, 4.4.1.4.*

2320A.9.2 *Plywood*.........................

When wood structural panel floors are glued to joists with an adhesive in accordance with the adhesive manufacturer.s directions, fasteners may be spaced a maximum of 12 inches (305 mm) on center at all supports.

2320A.11 Wall Framing.

2320A.11.1 Size, height and spacing. . . .

2320A.11.1.2 Height. Unless supported laterally by adequate framing, the maximum allowable height for studs shall be 10 feet (3048 mm) for 2-inch by 3-inch (51 mm by 76 mm) studs, 14 feet (4267 mm) for 2-inch by 4-inch (51 mm by 102 mm) and 3-inch by 4-inch (76mmby 102 mm) studs, and 20 feet (6096 mm) for 2-inch by 6-inch (51 mm by 152 mm) studs.

> **Comment:** REMEMBER
> Maximum Height for 2 x 3 = 10'-0"
> Maximum Height for 2 x 4 = 14'-0"
> Maximum Height for 3 x 4 = 14'-0"
> Maximum Height for 2 x 6 = 20'-0"

.... *When used in bearing walls, utility studs shall support not more than a roof and ceiling load.*

2320A.11.1.3 Spacing. Studs supporting floors shall be spaced not more than 16 inches (406 mm) on center.

> **Comment:** REMEMBER
> Max. Stud Spacing for bearing walls 24" o.c.

2320A.11.2 Framing details. Studs shall be placed with their wide dimension perpendicular to the wall. Not less than three studs shall be installed at each corner of an exterior wall. Openings in stud walls or partitions shall have headers and a minimum of two studs at jambs, one stud of which may be cut to support the header in bearing.

> **Comment:** REMEMBER
> Minimum number of studs at each corner = 3

NOTE: See Section 2320A.11.6.

Where wood and masonry or concrete walls intersect, the end stud shall be fastened with bolts or other devices at top, bottom and midheight, with at least the equivalent of one bolt of 1/2-inch (13 mm) diameter passing through the end stud and embedded in the masonry or concrete a minimum of 4 inches (102 mm). If the wall intersection is calculated to transfer loads greater than the capacity of the above requirement, the fastening shall be completely detailed on the approved drawings. All studs shall be capped with double top plates, except at interior nonstructural partitions. End joints in double top plates shall be offset at least 48 inches (1219 mm).

> **Comment:** REMEMBER
> Stud to Masonry / Concrete connections;
> (1) @ Top of Stud
> (1) @ Middle of Stud
> (1) @ Bottom of Stud

> **Comment:** TEST QUESTION
> End Joints in Double Top Plates to be offset 4'-0" minimum

2320A.11.3 Bracing ....

All exterior walls and main cross-stud partitions which are not part of the lateral load-resisting system ....

1. Nominal 1-inch by 4-inch (25 mm by 102 mm) continuous diagonal braces let into top and bottom plates and intervening studs, placed at an angle not more than 60 degrees or less than 45 degrees from the horizontal, and attached to the framing in conformance with Table 23A-II-B-1.

2. Wood boards of 5/8-inch (16 mm) net minimum thickness applied diagonally on studs spaced not over 24 inches (610 mm) on center.

3. Wood structural panel sheathing with a thickness not less than 5/16 inch (7.9 mm) for 16-inch (406 mm) stud spacing and not less than 3/8 inch (9.5 mm) for 24-inch (610 mm) stud spacing in accordance with Tables 23A-II-A-1 and 23A-IV-D-1.

4. Fiberboard sheathing 4-foot by 8-foot (1219 mm by 2438 mm) panels not less than 1/2 inch (13 mm) thick applied vertically on studs spaced not over 16 inches (406 mm) on center....

5. Gypsum board [sheathing 1/2 inch (13 mm) thick by 4 feet (1219 mm) wide, wallboard or veneer base] on studs spaced not over 24 inches (610 mm) on center and nailed at 7 inches (178 mm) on center with nails as required by Table 25-I.

2320A.11.7 Pipes in walls
.... *Notches shall not be placed in studs unless fully detailed on the approved plans to restore the structural resistance of the member.*

> **Comment:** REMEMBER
> Notches to be detailed on plans

2320A.11.9 Cutting and notching. *Any cutting and notching shall be detailed on the approved plans.*

2320A.11.10 Bored holes. *Holes exceeding one third of the width of the member being penetrated shall not be placed in studs unless fully detailed on the approved plans. Holes not exceeding*

one third of the stud width shall be neatly bored and shall be located in the center of the member being penetrated.

> **Comment:** TEST QUESTION
> Holes in studs Max 1/3 width of the stud unless approved plans.

2320A.12.8 Blocking. Roof rafters and ceiling joists shall be supported laterally to prevent rotation and lateral displacement when required by Division III, Part I, Section 4.4.1.2. *In addition, rafters of more than 8 inches (203 mm) in depth shall be provided with bridging in accordance with the provisions of Section 2316A.2, Item 22.*

> **Comment:** TEST QUESTION
> Roof Rafters more than 8" deep Need bridging or blocking

Division IX. TESTING AND INSPECTIONS

SECTION 2337A

2337A.1 Glued-laminated Timber. *All structural glued-laminated timber shall be continuously inspected during fabrication by a glue fabrication inspector specially approved for that purpose by the enforcement agency.*

Each structural glued-laminated timber shall be stamped with an identifying mark. The glue fabrication inspector shall make a verified report identifying the timbers by mark and including pertinent data such as the grade and species of lumber, the type of glue, the extremes of moisture content, and such other information as may be required. The glue fabrication inspector.s verified re-

port shall show, of his own personal knowledge, ...

.... The verified report shall either certify the use of official grading bureau marks as required, or that lumber grades were determined by a grader authorized to grade lumber under the provisions of the American

Lumber Standards Committee and who is also trained to grade the tension laminations required and described in ANSI/AITC A190.1 and ASTM D 3737.

2337A.2 Timber Connectors. The installation of all timber connectors shall be continuously inspected by a qualified inspector approved by the enforcement agency. The inspector shall furnish the architect, structural engineer and the enforcement agency with a report ....

2337A.3 Manufactured Trusses. The fabrication of trusses and other assemblages constructed using wood and metal members, or using light metal plate connectors, shall be continuously inspected by a qualified inspector approved by the enforcement agency. The inspector shall furnish the architect, structural engineer and the enforcement agency with a report that the lumber

.... Each inspected truss shall be stamped by the inspector with an identifying mark.

Excerpts from Chapter 35
UNIFORM BUILDING CODE STANDARDS

SECTION 3501 . UBC STANDARDS
The Uniform Building Code standards referred to in various parts of this code, which are also listed in Part II of this chapter, are hereby declared to be part of this code and are referred to in this code as a .UBC standard..

SECTION 3502 . ADOPTED STANDARDS
The standards referred to in various parts of the code, which are listed in Part III of this chapter, are hereby declared to be part of this code.

SECTION 3503 . STANDARD OF DUTY
The standard of duty established for the recognized standards listed in Part IV of this chapter is that the design, construction and quality of materials of buildings and structures be reasonably safe for life, limb, health, property and public welfare.

SECTION 3504 . RECOGNIZED STANDARDS
The standards listed in Part IV of this chapter are recognized standards. Compliance with these recognized standards shall be prima facie evidence of compliance with the standard of duty set forth in Section 3503.

Chapter 10: Wood Grading
LESSON 10.4
West Coast Lumber Grading Rules
"Standard No. 17"

Introduction

Before continuing with this lesson obtain a copy of the West Coast Lumber Grading Rules "Standard No. 17"

The West Coast Lumber Grading Rules are published by the West Coast Lumber Inspection Bureau (WCLIB) which is a private non-profit organization that was organized by the west coast lumber industry to standardize lumber construction grading. These rules are published in a book called the "Standard No. 17" (insert link to picture) and have been adopted by the California Building Code as the Grading Guidelines for school construction projects.

There are a number of questions on the DSA certification exams that pertain to the grading of lumber, and most of them are drawn directly from this book. As a DSA inspector you will be dealing with lumber on a regular basis, and is important that you know how to use the lumber grading book both for the certification exam and for your own use as an inspector.

The following is a brief lesson on using this book and what you need to know for the exam.

Standard No. 17

The book is divided into several chapters many of which are not of any use to the DSA inspector.

There are three basic types of questions that may be asked on the exam.

1. You may be asked to distinguish between different types of members such as studs, planks, joists, stringers etc. These are defined by there nominal dimensions as follows:
    a. Stud 2"-3" thick up to 4" wide
    b. Light Framing (Studs) 2" -4" thick up to 4" wide
    c. Structural Joists and Planks 2" to 4" Thick, 5" and wider
    d. Structural Light Framing 2" to 4" Thick, 2" to 4" Wide
    e. Beams and Stringers 5" and Thicker, Rectangular width more than 2" greater than thickness
    f. Posts and Timbers 5" x 5" and larger, width more than 2" greater than thickness
2. Second you may be asked to identify a grade stamp or an abbreviation that refers to the grade and species. Or perhaps you may be asked to differentiate between to grades and say which one is of a higher quality.
    a. In order to answer these questions look at the type of lumber that they are talking about and compare the defects that are allowed for that category. The larger and more frequent the defects allowed the lower the grade of lumber.
    b. Watch for a comparison between "stud" grade and "No. 2" grade 2x4. "Stud" grade is equivalent in quality to "No. 3" grade lumber and is therefore of a lesser quality than "No. 2"
3. Third you will be asked what the allowable defect is for a given piece of lumber.
    a. Eg. What is the maximum length of a "split" in a 2x10 Structural No. 2 Joist?

For definitions and diagrams of common wood defects see:

Wood Lesson 10.1.

Use the following list of pages and information as a guide for your study materials.

Introduction:
Explains what WCLB is and what they do

- See pg. 9, 10, 11
- Grade Stamps

West Coast Species:
Describes the various lumber species

- See pg. 23, 24, 25
- Species designations and definitions (some species designations are actually terms used to describe several different species under one name eg. Hem-Fir)

See the following excerpt:

HEM-FIR

91. HEM-FIR is a combination species, including Western hemlock (Tsuga heterophylla), California red fir (Abies magnifica), Grand fir (Abies grandis), Noble fir (Abies procera), Pacific silver fir (Abies amabilis), and White fir (Abies concolor). Western hemlock lumber possesses characteristics which rank it among the foremost commercial woods. The true firs found on the Pacific coast often grow in intermingled stands with Western hemlock. Wood of these species is similar in appearance, has similar strength properties and takes similar spans. Therefore, they usually are manufactured and shipped together under identical design values as HEM-FIR. The true firs included in the Hein-Fir grouping may be marketed and grade stamped exclusive of Western hemlock (Tsuga heterophylla) as "White Fir." The assigned design values for Hem-Fir apply to this grouping.

National Grading Rule for Dimension Lumber

- See pg. 70, 71, 72, 73
- Description of Dimension lumber grades and definitions.

See the following excerpt:

120-c. CLASSIFICATION.

The National Grading Rule for Dimension lumber classifies dimension into 3 width categories and 4 use categories. Dimension up to 4" wide is classified as "Structural Light Framing' and "Light Framing." Dimension 2" and wider is classified as "Studs." Dimension 5" and wider is classified as 'Strictural Joists and Planks.

2-4" Thick 2-4" Wide
STRUCTURAL LIGHT FRAMING

Grade Name (and Abbreviation)
Select Structural (Sel Str)'
1
2
3

LIGHT FRAMING
Grade Name (and Abbreviation)
Construction (Const)
Standard (Stand)
Utility (Util)

2-4" Thick 2" & Wider STUDS

Grade Name
Stud

2-4" Thick 5" & Wider
STRUCTURAL JOISTS & PLANKS

Grade Name (and Abbreviation)
Select Structural (Sel Str)
1
2
3

Light Framing
(2" to 4" Thick, 2" to 4" Wide)

- See pg. 76, 77, 78, 79
- Definitions and standards for the following lumber grades
    - Construction
    - Standard
    - Utility
    - Economy
    -

Sample Question: What is the maximum length of a split in a "construction" grade 2x4 stud?

Answer: 3.5" (see the answer below highlighted in red)

See the following excerpt:

**LIGHT FRAMING
ALL WEST COAST SPECIES**
2" to 4" Thick, 2" to 4" Wide
Random Length

122 f There are four grades of Light Framing: "CONcTRUCTION," "STANDARD," "UTILITY" and "ECONOMY." These grades are stress rated except "ECONOMY," with appropriate design values shown in table 6a, Para. 200. Tabulated design values for Utility grade apply to 4" widths only. For widths less than 4", Utility grade design values must be adjusted as indicated in the footnote. For measurement of knots. See Para. 201-b.

12-b "CONSTRUCTION"-LIGHT FRAMING.

Characteristics permitted and limiting provisions shall be:

Checks— - surface seasoning checks, not limited. Through checks at ends are limited as splits.

Knots – sound, firm, encased and pith, must be tight and are permitted in the following sizes or their equivalent displacement:

Nom. Width	Anywhere on Wide Face	Unsound or Loose Knots and Holes (Any cause)	One hole or equivalent smaller holes per 3 lin. w*.
2"	3/4"	5/8"	
3"	1-1/4"	3/4"	
4"	1-1/2"	1"	

Manufacture Standard "E." See Para. 722 (e).
Pitch and pitch streaks - not limited.
Pockets - pitch or bark - not limited.
Shake - If through at ends, limited as splits. Surface shakes up to 2' long.

Skips - hit and miss skips in a maximum of 10% of the pieces. See Para. 720 (f).
Slope of grain - I in 6.
Splits - equal in length to the width of the piece.
Stain - stained sapwood. Firm heart stain or firm red heart.
Wane - 1/4 the thickness and 1/4 the width full length, or equivalent on each face, provided that wane not exceed 1/2 the thickness or 1/3 the width for up to 1/4 the length. See paragraph 750.
Warp - 1/2 of medium. See Para. 752.

122-c "STANDARD" - LIGHT FRAMING.

Characteristics permitted and limiting provisions shall be:

Checks - seasoning checks not limited. Through checks at ends are limited as splits.
Knots - not restricted as to quality and are permitted in the following sizes or their equivalent displacement:

Nom. Width	Anywhere on Wide Face	Holes (Any cause)	One hole or equivalent smaller holes per 2 lin. ft.
2"	1	3/4"	
3"	1-1/2"	1"	
4"	2"	1-1/4"	

Manufacture - Standard "F." See Para. 722(f) . Pitch and pitch streaks - not limited. Pockets - pitch or bark - not limited.
Shake - If through at ends, limited as splits. Away from ends through shakes up to 2' long, well separated. If not through, single shakes shall not exceed 3' long or 1/4 the length, whichever is greater.

* For every grade there is a list of allowed defects and what the maximums are

Structural Joists and Planks
(2" to 4" Thick, 5" and wider)

- See pg. 81, 82, 83, 84, 85
- Definitions and standards for the following lumber grades
    - Dense Select Structural
    - Select Structural
    - Dense No. 1
    - Dense No. 2
    - No. 1
    - Dense No. 2
    - No. 2
    - Dense No. 3

Sample Question: What is the maximum slope of the grain for a Select Structural 2x8 joist?
Answer: 1:12 (see the answer below highlighted in red)

See the following excerpt:

STRUCTURAL JOISTS AND PLANKS
ALL WEST COAST SPECIES
2" to 4" Thick, 5" and Wider

123. There are four grades of Structural Joists and Planks: "SELECT STRUCTURAL," "NO. 1," "NO. 2" and "NO. 3." All of these grades are stress rated with appropriate base design values and width adjustments, shown in tables 4 and 5 (a&b), Para. 200.

For measurement of knots, see Para. 201-b.

123-aa. "DENSE SELECT STRUCTURAL" - JOISTS AND PLANKS (Douglas fir only).

Conforms to all the provisions of Para. 123-a with the additional requirement of density as defined in Para. 204-c.

123-a. "SELECT STRUCTURAL" - JOISTS AND PLANKS.

Characteristics permitted and limiting provisions shall be:

Checks - surface seasoning checks, not limited.
    Through checks at ends are limited as splits.
Knots - sound, firm, encased, and pith knots, if tight and well spaced, are permitted in sizes not to exceed the following, or equivalent displacement:

Nom. Width	At Edge Wide Face	Centerline Wide Face	Unsound or Loose Knots & Holes* (any cause)
5"	1"	1-1/2"	7/8"
6"	1-1/8"	1-7/8"	1"
8"	1-1/2"	2-1/4"	1-1/4"
10"	1-7/8"	2-5/8"	1-1/4"
12"	2-1/4"	3"	1-1/4"
14"	2-3/8"	3-1/4"	1-1/4"
16"	2-3/8"	3-3/8"	1-1/4"
18"	2-1/2"	3-1/2"	1-1/4"

*One hole or equivalent smaller holes per 4 lin. ft.

Manufacture - Standard "E." See Para. 722(e).
Pitch and pitch streaks - not limited. Pockets - pitch or bark - not limited.
Rate of growth - limited to medium grain in Douglas fir only. See Para. 204-a.
Shake - If through at ends, limited as splits. Surface shakes up to 2' long.
Skips - hit and miss skips in a maximum of 10% of the pieces. See Para. 720(f).
Slope of grain - 1 in 12
Splits - equal in length to the width of the piece. Stain - stained sapwood. Firm heart stain or firm red heart limited to 10% of the piece.
Wane - 1/4 the thickness and 1/4 the width full length, or equivalent on each face, provided that wane not exceed 1/2 the thickness or 1/3 the width for up to 1/4 the length. See paragraph 750.
Warp - 1/2 of medium. See Para. 752.

123-bb. "DENSE NO. 1"- STRUCTURAL JOISTS and PLANKS (Douglas fir only).

Conforms to all the provisions of Para. 123-b with the additional requirement of density as defined in Para. 204-c.

123-b. "NO. 1" -STRUCTURAL JOISTS and PLANKS.

For an explanation of No. 1 & Better design values see Para. 754.

Characteristics permitted and limiting provision shall be:

Checks - surface seasoning checks, not limited. Through checks at ends are limited as splits.

Knots - sound, firm, encased, and pith knots, if tight and well spaced, are permitted in sizes not to exceed the following or equivalent displacement:

Nom. Width	At Edge Wide Face	Centerline Wide Face	Unsound or Loose Knots & Holes* (any cause)
5"	1-1/4"	1-7/8"	1-1/8"
6"	1-1/2"	2-1/4"	1-1/4"
8"	2"	2-3/4"	1-1/2"
10"	2-1/2"	3-1/4"	1-1/2"
12"	3"	3-3/4"	1-1/2"
14"	3-1/8"	4"	1-1/2"
16"	3-1/4"	4-1/2"	1-1/2"
18"	3-3/8"	4-5/8"	1-1/2"

tine note or equivalent smaller holes per 3 lin. ft.

Manufacture - Standard "E." Sec Para. 722 (e).
Pitch and pitch streaks - not limited. Pockets - pitch or bark - not limited.
Rate of growth - limited to medium grain in Douglas fir only. See Para. 204-a.
Shake - If through at ends, limited as splits. Surface shakes up to 2' long.
Skips - hit and miss skips in a maximum of 10% of pieces. See Para. 720(f).
Slope of grain - 1 in 10.
Splits - equal in length to width of the piece. Stain - stained sapwood. Firm heart stain or firm red heart.
Wane - 1/4 the thickness and 1/4 the width full length, or equivalent on each face, provided that wane not exceed 1/2 the thickness or 1/3 the width for up to 1/4 the length. See paragraph 750.
Warp - 1/2 of medium. See Para. 752.

123-cc. "DENSE NO. 2"- STRUCTURAL JOIST and PLANKS (Douglas fir only).

Conforms to all the provisions of Para. 123-c with the additional requirement of density as defined in Para. '04-c.

* For every grade there is a list of allowed defects and what the maximums are

Structural Light Framing
(2" to 4" Thick, 2" to 4" Wide)

- See pg. 87, 88, 89
- Definitions and standards for the following lumber grades
  - Dense Select Structural
  - Select Structural
  - Dense No. 1
  - No. 1
  - Dense No. 2
  - No. 2
  - Dense No. 3
  - No. 3

Sample Question: What is the maximum size of a knot on a "Select Structural" 2x4?

Answer: ¾" (look on matrix below the answer is highlighted in red)

See the following excerpt:

STRUCTURAL LIGHT FRAMING ALL WEST COAST SPECIES

2" to 4" Thick, 2" to 4" Wide

124. There are four grades of Structural Light Framing: "SELECT STRUCTURAL," "NO. 1," "NO. 2" and "NO. 3". All of these grades are stress rated, with appropriate base design values and width adjustments shown in tables 4 and 5 (a&b), Para. 200.

For measurement of knots, see Para. 201-b.

124-aa. "DENSE SELECT STRUCTURAL" - STRUCTURAL LIGHT FRAMING (Douglas fir only).

Conforms to all the provisions of 124-a with the additional requirement of density as defined in Para. 204-c.

124-a. "SELECT STRUCTURAL" - STRUCTURAL LIGHT FRAMING.

Characteristics permitted and limiting provisions shall be:

Checks - surface seasoning checks, not limited. Through checks at ends are limited as splits.

Knots - sound, firm, encased, and pith knots, if tight and well spaced, are permitted in sizes not to exceed the following, or equivalent displacement:

Nom. Width	At Edge of Wide Face	Centerline Wide Face	Unsound or Loose Knots & Holes* (any cause)
2"	3/8"	3/8"	3/8"
3"	1/2"	1/2"	1/2"
4"	3/4"	7/8"	3/4"

* For every grade there is a list of allowed defects and what the maximums are

Beams and Stringers
(5" and Thicker, Rectangular width more than 2" greater than thickness)

- See pg. 104, 105, 106, 107, 108, 109
- Definitions and standards for the following lumber grades
    - Select Structural
    - Dense Select Structural
    - Select Structural
    - No. 1 Structural
    - Standard
    - No. 2 Structural
    - Utility

* We have not inserted excerpts for Beams and Stringers. However you should go the above pages in your book and read through the criteria for this type of lumber.

Posts and Timbers
(5" x 5" and larger, width more than 2" greater than thickness)

- See pg. 110, 111, 112, 113, 114, 115
- Definitions and standards for the following lumber grades
    - Dense Select Structural
    - Dense No. 1 Structural
    - No. 1 Structural
    - Standard
    - No. 2 Structural
    - Utility

* We have not inserted excerpts for Beams and Stringers. However you should go the above pages in your book and read through the criteria for this type of lumber.

Chapter 11: Electrical
LESSON 11.1
(Title 24 Part 3)

According to the Title 24 Administrative provisions electrical and mechanical work is to be inspected by either the electrical engineer, a representative of the electrical engineer, or by a special electrical inspector.

4-333. Observation and Inspection of Construction.

(c) Special Inspection.

Where responsibility for observation of construction for mechanical work and electrical work is not delegated to professional engineers registered in these particular branches of engineering [see Section 4-316 (b)], special mechanical and electrical inspection shall be provided.

However the reality of the situation is that electrical work is almost always inspected by the Project Inspector. It is for this reason that it is to your benefit to become familiar with the basics of electrical inspection.

DSA has now changed the testing format for the exams. One of the sections in both the plan reading and code knowledge parts of the exams is on electrical. Therefore it is safe to assume that electrical will be a more prominent part of future DSA exams.

The following is a quick reference guide of electrical code issues. Review the guide carefully and then complete the Section Quiz.

ELECTRICAL QUICK REFERENCE
Title 24 Part 3

WIRE:
The smaller the # the larger the conductor.

EQUIPMENT GROUND
Wire color: green

BRANCH CIRCUT GROUND
Wire color: Grey or neutral color with white stripes.

SIZE OF GROUNDING CONDUCTOR IN SYSTEMS

#2 or smaller:	1/2 electrode	#8 copper
1 or 1/0 :	2/0--3/0	#6 copper
2/0 or 3/0:	4/0—250	#4 copper

SIZE OF GROUNDING CONDUCTOR FOR EQUIPMENT

15 amp	#14 copper
20 amp	#12 copper
30-60 amp	#10 copper
100 amp	#8 copper
200 amp	#6 copper
300 amp	#4 copper

GFCI: Ground Fault Circuit Interupt
Required at all recepticals within 6 ft. 6 in. of water.

CIRCUIT BREAKERS
Used as flourscent light switches: in 120 volt and 277 volt lighting circuits shall be listed and shall be marked "SWD".

© Professional Study Inc. 2003

LIQUID TIGHT / FLEX
 Shall be supported with in 12 in. of termination to box, equipment etc.
 Support not to exceed 4.5 ft.
 6 ft. attacthment to lighting fixtures

SUPPORTS
 EMT Max. 3'-0" from box

WORKING SPACE
 0-150 volts   3 ft.
 151-600 volts
 3 ft. with 1 side hot one no ground
 3.5 ft. with 1 side hot one ground
 4 ft. with 2 sides hot.

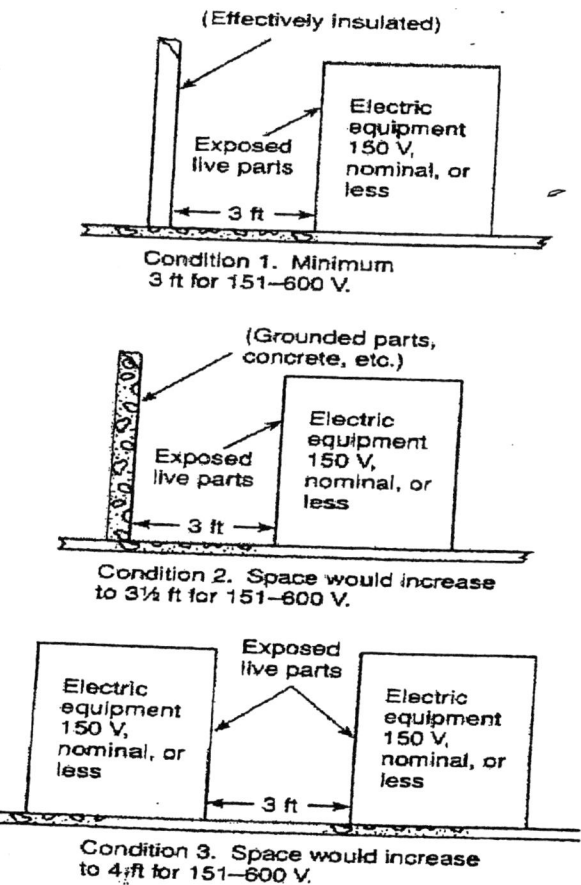

HEADROOM
 6.5 ft. min. or the height of the equipment whichever is greater.

MINIMUM COVER REQUIREMENTS:

Table 300-5. Minimum Cover Requirements, 0 to 600 Volts, Nominal, Burial in Inches
(Cover is defined as the shortest distance measured between a point on the top surface of any direct buried conductor, cable, conduit, or other raceway and the top surface of finished grade, concrete, or similar cover.)

Location of Wiring Method or Circuit	1 Direct Burial Cables or Conductors	2 Rigid Metal Conduit or Intermediate Metal Conduit	3 Nonmetallic Raceways Listed for Direct Burial without Concrete Encasement or Other Approved Raceways	4 Residential Branch Circuits Rated 120 Volts or less with GFCI Protection and Maximum Overcurrent Protection of 20 Amperes	5 Circuits for Control of Irrigation and Landscape Lighting Limited to Not More than 30 Volts and Installed with Type UF or In Other Identified Cable or Raceway
All Locations Not Specified Below	24	6	18	12	6
In Trench Below 2-in. Thick Concrete or Equivalent	18	6	12	6	6
Under a Building	0 (In Raceway Only)	0	0	0 (In Raceway Only)	0 (In Raceway Only)
Under Minimum of 4-in. Thick Concrete Exterior Slab with No Vehicular Traffic and the Slab Extending Not Less than 6 In. Beyond the Underground Installation	18	4	4	6 (Direct Burial) 4 (In Raceway)	6 (Direct Burial) 4 (In Raceway)
Under Streets, Highways, Roads, Alleys, Driveways, and Parking Lots	24	24	24	24	24
One- and Two-Family Dwelling Driveways and Outdoor Parking Areas, and Used Only for Dwelling-Related Purposes	18	18	18	12	18
In or Under Airport Runways, Including Adjacent Areas Where Trespassing Prohibited	18	18	18	18	18

Note 1. For SI units: 1 in. = 25.4 mm.
Note 2. Raceways approved for burial only where concrete encased shall require concrete envelope not less than 2 in. thick.
Note 3. Lesser depths shall be permitted where cables and conductors rise for terminations or splices or where access is otherwise required.
Note 4. Where one of the wiring method types listed in columns 1-3 is used for one of the circuit types in columns 4 and 5, the shallower depth of burial shall be permitted.
Note 5. Where solid rock is encountered, all wiring shall be installed in metal or nonmtallic raceway permitted for direct burial. The raceways shall be covered by a minimum of 2 in. of concrete extending down to rock.

Chapter 11: Plumbing
LESSON 11.2
(Title 24 Part 5)

Unlike electrical as a Project Inspector you are expected to inspect all of the plumbing installations on a project. Therefore after you obtain your DSA certification should take it upon yourself to become educated in the plumbing code.

However plumbing is a subject which is only covered in a very cursory way on the DSA exams. Of the ninety questions on the exam typically less than 5 are related to plumbing issues. It is for this reason that we have prepared the following checklist for your reference. The important DSA related issues with respect to plumbing are those of pipe supports, seismic bracing, and system testing. Study this material and use it as your reference on for the exam.

TRENCHES PARALLEL TO FOOTINGS / PIPES THROUGH FOOTINGS

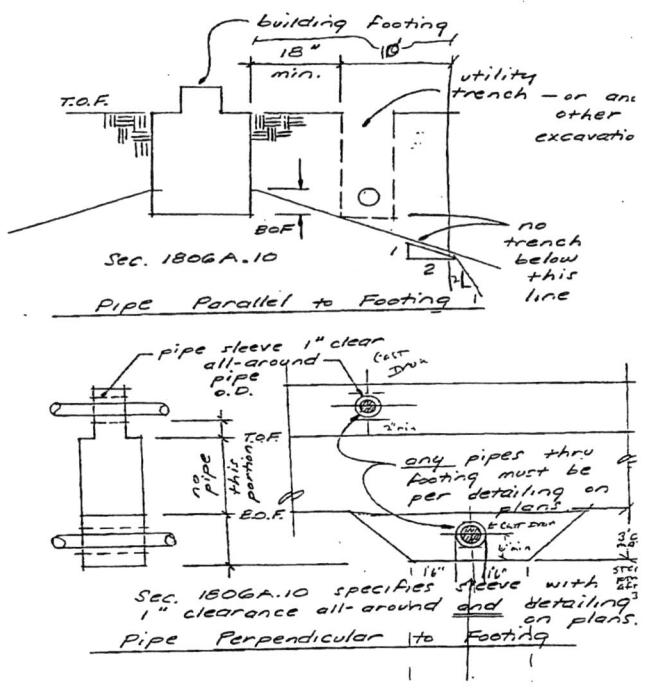

Sleeves:

Sized min. ½" clear around pipe and or insulation.

SEWER MATERIALS

Sewer or other drainage pipe of materials other than approved for use in or under the building shall be within 2 ft. of any building or within 1 ft. of the surface of the ground.

INSTALLATION

Joints: welded or screwed
Welded by: a certified pipe welder for iron and certified for pipe.
Riser connecting to pipe: shall extend horizontally 30 in. before connection with the plastic pipe.

SEWER TESTING

ABS and PVC min. 12" below grade
Water Test
10ft column of water
15 minutes minimum
Air Test
Pump air into system until 5psi
15 minutes w/ out dropping in pressure

EARTH COVERAGE

PE: 18"
Iron: 12"

HANGARS and SUPPORT

ROD SIZE FOR HANGARS AND PIPE

TABLE 3-1

Pipe and Tube Size		Rod Size	
Inches	mm	Inches	mm
1/2 – 4	12.7 – 102	3/8	9.5
5 – 8	127 – 203	1/2	12.7
10 – 12	254 – 305	5/8	15.9

GAS PIPING

Material:
　　Galvanized or black iron pipe or approved piping.

Valves:
　　Approved for gas.

Fittings:
　　Malleable iron, ball, or approved plastic.

1204.0 Gas Testing:
　　All tests in presence of testing authority
　　Testing prior to any appliances

Air, CO_2, or Nitrogen testing
　　Pressurize to 10psi min, or 6" or mercury.
　　Min. 15 minutes
　　Welded pipe or carrying gas w/ more pressure than 14" water column
　　Test 60psi
　　Min. 30 minutes

Pipe Support Minimums:

½"	6'-0" max
¾: or 1"	8'-0" max
1-1/4"+	10'-0" max Horizontal
1-1/4"+	Every Floor Level Vertical

Wrapping:
　　Ferrous gas piping installed underground in exterior locations shall be protected from corrosion by approved coatings or wrapping materials or by any other approved materials or by any other approved manner.
　　All risers shall be wrapped or coated to a point 6 in. above grade or protected in an approved manner.

Tracer wire:
　　An electrically continuous insulated number 18 yellow 0.004 inch (1 mm) diameter copper tracer wire or other approved materials shall be installed with and attached to underground non-metallic gas piping and shall terminate above ground at each end.

PIPE SUPPORT INTERVALS

TABLE 3-2

Materials	Type of Joints	Horizontal	Vertical
Cast Iron Hub and Spigot	Lead and Oakum	5 feet (1524 mm), except may be 10 feet (3048 mm) where 10 foot (3048 mm) lengths are installed [1, 2, 3]	Base and each floor not to exceed 15 feet (4572 mm)
	Compression Gasket	Every other joint, unless over 4 feet (1219 mm), then support each joint [1,2,3]	Base and each floor not to exceed 15 feet (4572 mm)
Cast Iron Hubless	Shielded Coupling	Every other joint, unless over 4 feet (1249 mm), then support each joint [1,2,3,4]	Base and each floor not to exceed 15 feet (4572 mm)
Copper Tube and Pipe	Soldered, Brazed or Welded	1-1/2 inch (38 mm) and smaller, 6 feet (1829 mm), 2 inch (51 mm) and larger, 10 feet (3048 mm)	Each floor, not to exceed 10 feet (3048 mm) [5]
Steel and Brass Pipe for Water or DWV	Threaded or Welded	3/4 inch (19 mm) and smaller, 10 feet (3048 mm), 1 inch (25.4 mm) and larger, 12 feet (3658 mm)	Every other floor, not to exceed 25 feet (7620 mm) [5]
Steel, Brass and Tinned Copper Pipe for Gas	Threaded or Welded	1/2 inch (12.7 mm), 6 feet (1829 mm) 3/4 (19.1 mm) and 1 inch (25.4 mm), 8 feet (2438 mm), 1-1/4 inch (32 mm) and larger, 10 feet (3048 mm)	1/2 inch (12.7 mm), 6 feet (1829 mm), 3/4 (19 mm) and 1 inch (25.4 mm), 8 feet (2438 mm), 1-1/4 inch (32 mm) and larger, every floor level
Schedule 40 PVC and ABS DWV	Solvent Cemented	All sizes, 4 feet (1219 mm). Allow for expansion every 30 feet (9144 mm) [3, 6]	Base and each floor. Provide mid-story guides. Provide for expansion every 30 feet (9144 mm) [6]
CPVC	Solvent Cemented	1 inch (25.4 mm) and smaller, 3 feet (914 mm), 1-1/4 inch (32 mm) and larger, 4 feet (1219 mm)	Base and each floor. Provide mid-story guides [6]
Lead	Wiped or Burned	Continuous support	Not to exceed 4 feet (1219 mm)
Copper	Mechanical	In accordance with standards acceptable to the Administrative Authority	
Steel & Brass	Mechanical	In accordance with standards acceptable to the Administrative Authority	

[1] Support adjacent to joint, not to exceed eighteen (18) inches (457 mm).
[2] Brace at not more than forty (40) foot (12192 mm) intervals to prevent horizontal movement.
[3] Support at each horizontal branch connection.
[4] Hangers shall not be placed on the coupling.
[5] Vertical water lines may be supported in accordance with recognized engineering principles with regard to expansion and contraction, when first approved by the Administrative Authority.
[6] See the appropriate IAPMO Installation Standard for expansion and other special requirements.
Note: [For HCD 1 & HCD 2] See 701.1.2 (w/ CA Amendments)

Chapter 11: Mechanical
LESSON 11.3
(Title 24 Part 4)

According to Title 24 similar to electrical, all mechanical work should be inspected by the mechanical engineer, his representative, or by a special mechanical inspector. Therefore the DSA exams do not cover the subject of mechanical inspection in any great detail.

With the following exception it is our opinion that your study time will be better spent on other subjects. Study the following excerpts from Chapter 16 (Table 16A-O). DSA limits it's questions on the DSA code knowledge exams almost exclusively to seismic bracing issues.

Table 16A-0 (footnotes)

10Equipment includes, but is not limited to, boilers, chillers, heat exchangers, pumps, air-handling units, cooling towers, control panels, motors, switchgear, transformers and life-safety equipment. It shall include major conduit, ducting and piping, which services such machinery and equipment and fire sprinkler systems.
See Section 1632A.2 for additional requirements for determining a_p for non-rigid or flexibly mounted equipment.

Comment: SEE ALSO; Section 7 of this course for futher information on seismic restraint etc.

1632A.6 HVAC Ductwork, Plumbing/Piping and Conduit Systems. All pipes, ducts and conduit shall be braced to resist the forces prescribed in Section 1630A.2. Ductwork shall be constructed in accordance with provisions contained in Part 4, Title 24, California Mechanical Code. Where possible, pipes, conduit, and their connections shall be constructed of ductile materials (copper, ductile iron, steel or aluminum and brazed, welded or screwed connections). Pipes, conduits and their connections, constructed of non-ductile materials (e.g., cast iron, no-hub pipe and plastic), shall have the brace spacing reduced to one-half of the spacing allowed for ductile material in accordance with Section 1630A.5 or other standards approved by the enforcing agency.

Seismic restraints may be omitted for the following conditions, where flexible connections are provided between components and the associated ductwork, piping and conduit:

    1. Fuel piping less than 1 inch (25 mm) inside diameter.

    2. All other piping less than 2.5 inches (64 mm) diameter, except medical gas including vacuum piping, or

        All piping suspended by individual hangers 12 inches (305 mm) or less in length from the top of the pipe to the bottom of the structural support for the hanger, or
        All electrical conduit less than 2.5 inches (64 mm) trade size.

    3. All rectangular air-handling ducts less than 6 square feet (0.56 m2) in cross-sectional area, or
        All round air-handling ducts less than 28 inches (711 mm) in diameter, or

Comment: TEST QUESTION;
You may omit seismic supports under the following:
1. All Pipe < 1" dia.
2. All Pipe < 2.5" dia.
   All Pipe supported < 12" from sturcture
   All Elect Conduit < 2.5" size
3. All Rect Duct < 6 Sq. Ft. in area
   All Round Duct < 28" dia.
   All Duct suspended < 12" from structure

VARIATIONS OF QUESTIONS ON THIS CODE SECTION ARE ASKED ON ALMOST ALL OF THE EXAMS.

All ducts suspended by hangers 12 inches (305 mm) or less in length from the top of the duct to the bottom of the structural support for the hanger, where the hangers are detailed to avoid bending of the hangers and their connections.

Where lateral restraints are omitted, the piping, ducts or conduit shall be installed such that lateral motion of the piping or duct will not cause damaging impact with other systems or structural members, or loss of vertical support.

1632A.6.1 All trapeze assemblies supporting pipes, ducts and conduit shall be braced to resist the forces of Section 1632A.2, considering the total weight of the elements on the trapeze.

Pipes, ducts and conduit supported by a trapeze where none of those elements would individually be braced need not be braced if connections to the pipe/conduit/ductwork or directional changes do not restrict the movement of the trapeze. If this flexibility is not provided, bracing will be required when the aggregate weight of the pipes and conduit exceed 10 pounds/feet (146 N/m). The weight shall be determined assuming all pipes and conduit are filled with water.

Comment: REMEMBER Trapeze should be considered as one for the purpose of seismic bracing. sure you understand this criteria.

Chapter 12: Handicap Access
LESSON 12.1

ACCESS COMPLIANCE
Title 24, PART 1, CH. 11B

Handicap access compliance is one of the most detailed subjects that you as the DSA project inspector will have to deal with. It is practically impossible to predict what access compliance question may be asked on the exams since as you can see there are hundreds of possible questions. This is why we have not prepared a "Highlighting List" for this chapter. Since any question will likely involve recalling and obscure measurement or something similar we believe that it would be unproductive to attempt to memorize all of this information. Instead we have provided this comprehensive "Checklist" that can act as a quick reference. Become familiar with the different subjects and where to locate the necessary information such that you do not waste time needlessly.

Study the materials on this checklist and then take the practice quiz. We recommend that you take the practice quiz several times until you are confident about your speed in this subject. There are approximately 5-10 access compliance questions on the DSA exams. If you are able to find all of the answers in less than 1 minute each then you will have saved 5-10 minutes on your time budget this may mean the difference between passing and not passing.

VAN PARKING

 Application: For each site at an educational facility.
 Required Number: (1) Van (Van accessible)
 Location:
  Route: On shortest accessible route to accessible entrance(s).
  In parking not serving a particular building: On shortest accessible route to closest pedestrian entrance of pedestrian facility.
 Curb cuts & ramps: Provided to pathways.
 Placement: Persons with disabilities must be not compelled to wheel or walk behind parked cars other than their own.
 Dimensions:
  Van: Min 9' wide with min 8' side loading & unloading passenger side aisle, min 18' length.
 Slope: (ADAAG 4.6.3): Max 1:50 (2%) in any direction.
 Surface: Stable, firm & slip resistant.
 Arrangement: Bumper or curb to prevent van encroachment on walkways.
 Signage:
  "Van Accessible" sign for van spaces.
  Reflectorized International Symbol of Accessibility at each space, min 70 sq. ", (min 80" high if in path of travel), & un-obscured by a parked vehicle (ADAAG 4.6.4).
  Tow away sign with telephone # at each entrance to parking area or adjacent to accessible spaces, minimum size: 17" x 22", 1" high letters.
 Accessible Space Surface:
  Painted or outlined space in blue & outlined profile view depicting wheelchair with occupant, or
  36" x 36" outlined profile view of wheelchair with occupant in white on blue background visible to traffic enforcement officer when vehicle occupies space.
 Parking structures (if any): 8'2" min vertical clearance at entrance and within to accessible parking spaces.

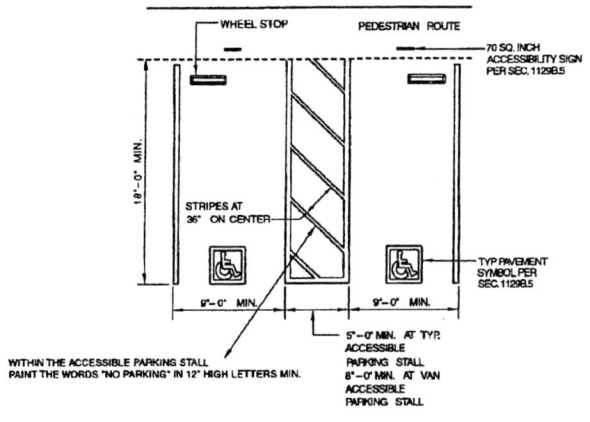

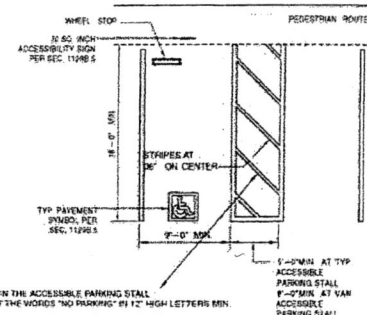

FIGURE 11B-18B—SINGLE PARKING STALLS

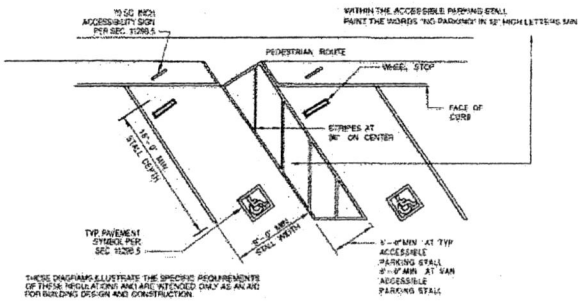

EXTERIOR ROUTES OF TRAVEL,

ENTRANCES & EXITS
Exterior Routes of Travel:
Location:
> From Van parking to accessible toilets, drinking fountain, and all project relocatables
> To each entrance & exterior ground floor exits.
>> Along normal paths of travel.
>> Between all relocatables that are a part of the project

Configuration:
> Most practical direct route from entrance to the site to buildings and facilities.
> Entrances & Exits All new entrances in a relocatable project or those on the accessible route from van parking to accessible toilets and drinking fountain.

Exceptions: Exits not required by State Fire Marshall & if more than 24" above grade.

© Professional Study Inc. 2003

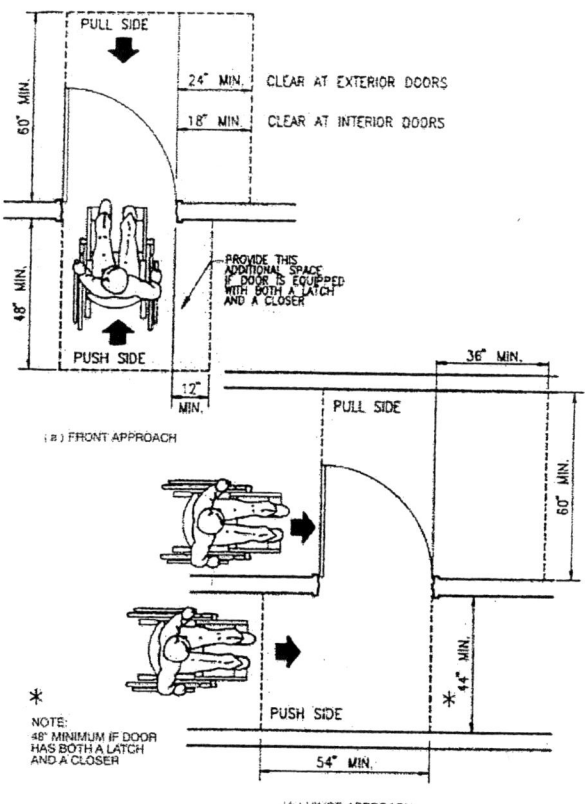

EXTERIOR SIGNS & IDENTIFICATION
Description: International Symbol of Accessibility.
Required Location:
    At every major junction in the accessible route of travel from van parking space to toilets, drinking fountain & relocatables.

    Every accessible entrance on the route involving relocatable buildings or where access is to accessible toilets, drinking fountain.

    As required along route, directing persons to accessible entrance, if building has inaccessible entrances, i.e. remodeled buildings.

Color: White figure on blue background = #1590 in Federal Standard 5996.

CURB RAMPS
Required Location: [1995: 11-19A, B, C & 11-20A, B, C, & D 1.
   At each van accessible parking space unloading area (if not flush to adjacent walk). 2. Where pedestrian way crosses curb.
Width: Min 48"

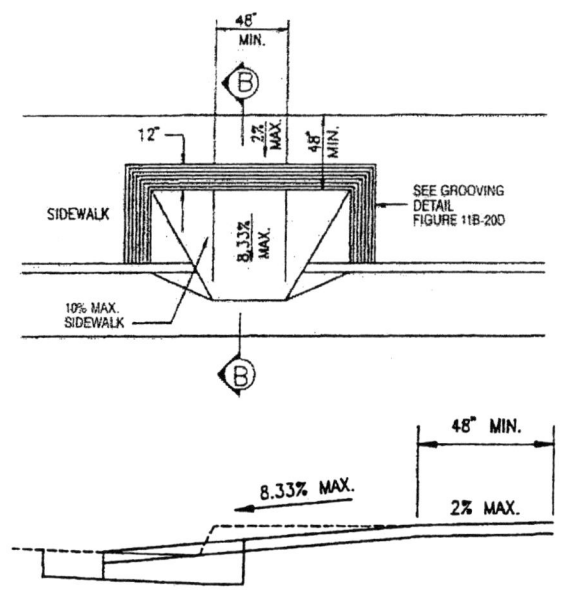

Finish: Stable, firm, slip-resistant contrasting with adjacent sidewalk.
Slope: Max 1:12 (8.3%).
Slope of flared sides (ADAAG 4.7.5): Max 1:10 (10%).
Slope of adjoining gutters, road surfaces, accessible route: 1:50 (2%), for 4 feet at top & bottom of curb ramp. (Text requires 120 [5%] but DSA policy requires compliance with 2% figure)
Top Landing: 4 feet deep over full width or slope of flared sides max 1:12 (8.3%). [1995: Fo.11-22]
Transition: (ADAAG 4.7-2) to walkway or a road or gutter, flush & no abrupt changes. However, Title 24 requires 12" lip beveled at 45 degrees_
Built up Curb Ramps: Shall not project into vehicular traffic lanes or over five feet into parking access aisles.
Space for Parked Vehicles: Must not obstruct use of curb ramps.
   Detectable Warnings:
      Application: At entry to hazardous vehicular areas when curb ramps slopes are less than 1:15 (6.7%S)
Description : Truncated domes:
   Diameter. 0.9" at base to .45" at top.
   height: 02",
   spacing: center-to--center 2.35",
   contrast: light-on-dark or dark-on-light,
   Material: integral part of walking surface.
   Location: full width a 24 inch depth of curb ramp inside grooved border.
   Orientation of domes: In-line pattern preferred over staggered pattern.
Grooved border: [1995: Fig.11-20GH]
   Location: at level surface of sidewalk, along top and each side
   Width: 12"
   Depth: ¼" every 3/4".

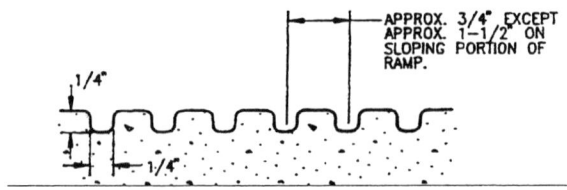

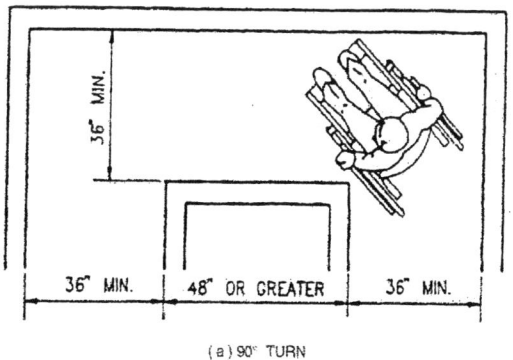

(a) 90° TURN

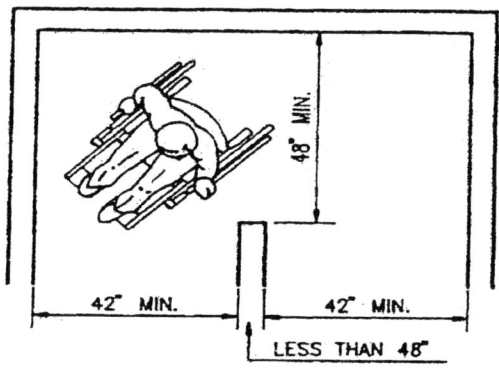

(b) TURNS AROUND AN OBSTRUCTION

WALKS & SIDEWALKS
Width: Min 48". Of right-of-way restriction, natural barriers, or other existing conditions, E.F. = 36".)
   Slope: Max 1:20. Where slope exceeds 1:20 (5%), walkway must meet ramp standards. See Checklist #6 for handrail & other requirements.

Change in level: Max 12", 1/4"-12" beveled 12. Changes > 1/2" must comply with ramp standards. See Checklist #6.

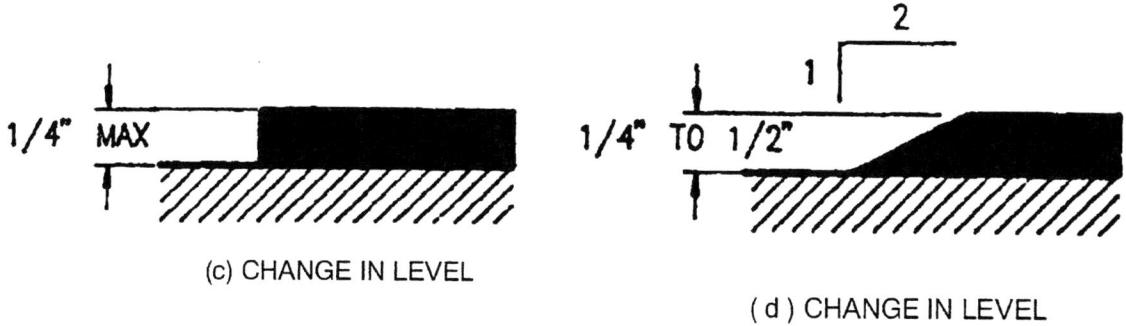

(c) CHANGE IN LEVEL

(d) CHANGE IN LEVEL

Surface: Stable, firm, & slip-resistant.
Surface Slope:
< 6% - medium salted.
6% - slip resistant
   Cross slope: Max 1:50 (2%).
   Gratings: No gratings if possible. Where necessary, max width 12" in direction, of traffic flow.

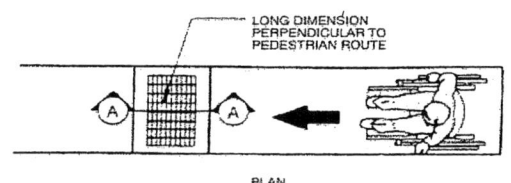

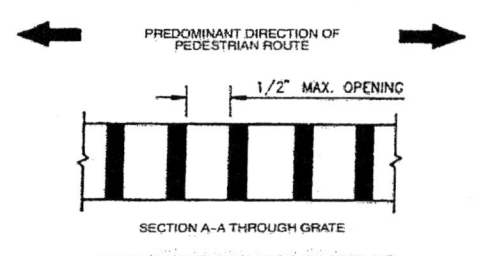

(a) GRATE ORIENTATION TO PATH OF TRAVEL

Level Areas by Doors & Gates:
Swing side: 60" x 60".
Push side: 48" wide x 44" deep.
.3. Swing side Strike Edge Clearance: 24".

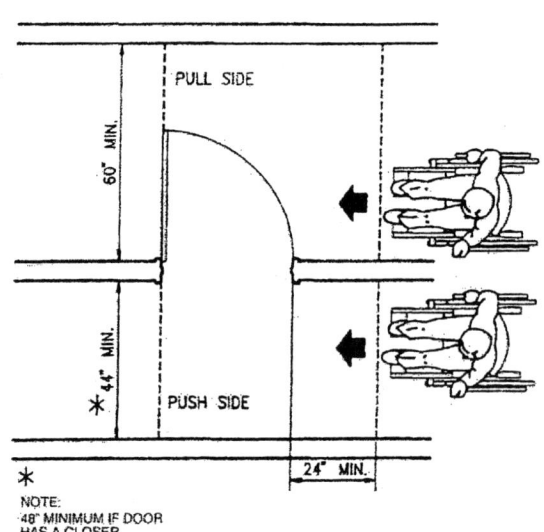

Continuous Gradients: Every 400 feet, 5 foot long level area.
U-Turns: Around an obstacle < 48", width must be minimum 42" on approach & 48" in turn.
Passing spaces: For routes <60", 60" wide x 60" long or intersecting walks at 200 foot intervals.
Hazards:
  Warning Curbs:
  Location: Abrupt changes in level > 4" vertical (planters, fountains, ponds).
  Height 6". Exception allowed: Where guardrail or handrail provided if guide rail centered 2 - 4" above walk, walk
  Overhanging Obstructions: Min 80" above walking surface. 3. Detectable Warnings:
  Location: Where walk crosses or adjoins vehicular way not separated by curb, guardrails, or handrails; and by drop-off at transit boarding platforms.
  Width: 24" - 36"
  Truncated domes
  Color Yellow = Federal Color # 33538 of Standard # 595E. If color value contrast < 7 0% between yellow warning & walk, 1" wide black strip shall separate yellow warning from walk. e. Material: Durable, slip resistant.
  Resiliency: Providing difference in sound on cane contact from surrounding surface. Pedestrian Access Detectable

Directional Texture at Boarding Platforms:
Location: Behind yellow detectable warning texture aligning with all passenger doors of tr2ns~t vehicles.

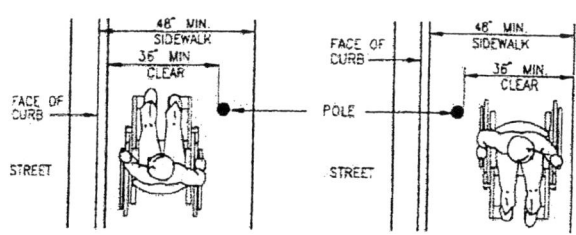

(a) SIDEWALK OBSTRUCTIONS

RAMPS
Width:
To entrances of occupancies serving 300 or less: Min 60".
In Group R (residential) Occupancies serving 50 or less: 36".
All others: 48".

Slope: Max 1:12 (8.3%). (1:14 [7.1%] or less slope preferred.)
Cross Slope: Max 1:50 (2%).
Surface: stable, firm, slip resistant.
Landings:
Location: Top & bottom of each ramp & intermediately at min of every 30" of rise.
Top Landing Dimensions: Min 60" wide & min 60" in direction of ramp run.
Intermediate Landing Dimensions: Width, as required for ramps. Direction of ramp run, min 60". For intermediate landings which change direction > 30 degrees, min 72".
Bottom Landing Dimensions: Width, as required for ramps. Direction of ramp run, min 72".
Encroachment of Doors. Doers In any position can not reduce the min dimensions of landing to < 42", & can reduce width max 3" when fully open.
Strike Edge Extension: Width of landing shall extend 24" past strike edge of any door or gate for exterior doors, & 18" past strike edge for interior doors.
1120A.5.5.1 Location of landings. Landings shall be provided at the top and bottom of each ramp. Intermediate landings shall be provided at intervals not exceeding 30 inches (762 mm) of vertical rise and at each change of direction. Landings are not considered in determining the maximum horizontal distance of each ramp.

SLOPE	MAXIMUM RISE (inches) (× 25.4 for mm)	MAXIMUM HORIZONTAL PROJECTION (feet) (× 304.8 for mm)
1:12	30	30
1:16	30	40
1:20	30	50
1:15	30	37.5

Wheel Guides: For ramps exceeding 10 feet in length, either 2" guide curb on both sides or wheel guide centered 3" + or - 1" above ramp surface.
Drainage (ADAAG 4.8.8): Provided to prevent water collection on ramps & approaches.
Handrails: Required for ramps with slopes 1:12 to 1:20 (8.3% to 5%). (Exceptions: Not required next to fixed seating in assembly areas or on curb ramps.)
Location: On both sides, continuous for full length (including dogleg or switchback), extending 12" beyond top & bottom, with returned ends.
Height 34 - 38" above the surface of ramp.
Mounting Space: 1-12" from wall.
Mounting (ADAAG 4.8.5): Cannot rotate within fittings.
Grip: 1-1/4" to 1-12" & smooth. (1 12T nominal pipe size allowed.)
Edges: Rounded to min radius of 1/8".
Located in a Recess: Recess max 3" deep, extending min 18" clear above top of rail.
Structural Strength (ADAAG 4.8.5 & 4.26.3): Must resist 250 lbf in any direction.

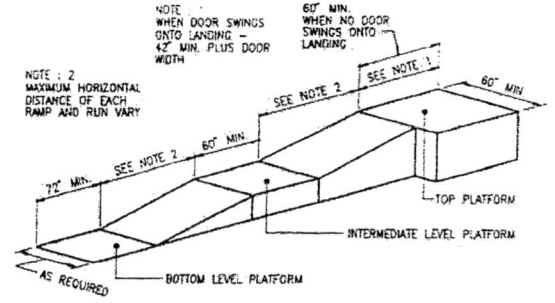

(a) STRAIGHT RAMP RUN

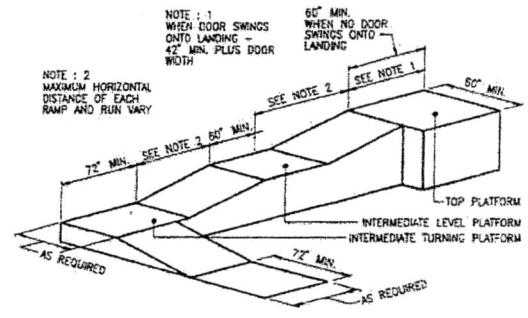

(b) RAMP WITH TURNING PLATFORM

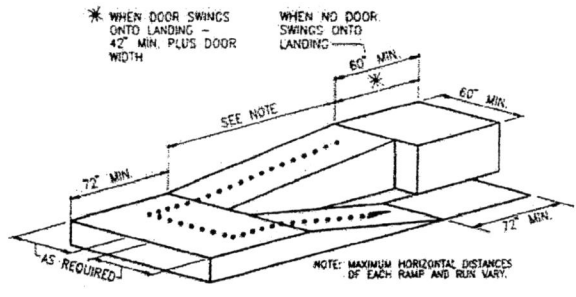

(a) RAMP WITH INTERMEDIATE SWITCH-BACK PLATFORM

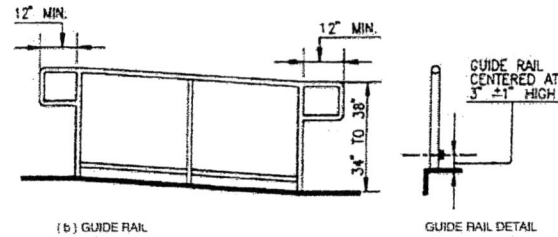

(b) GUIDE RAIL   GUIDE RAIL DETAIL

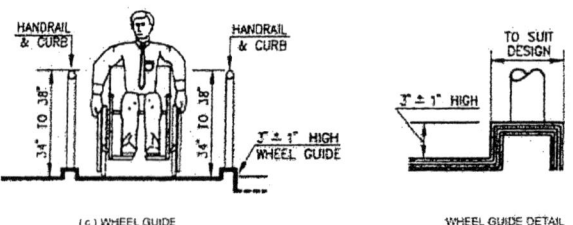

(c) WHEEL GUIDE   WHEEL GUIDE DETAIL

STAIRWAYS

1120A.4.1 Required handrails. Stairways shall have handrails on each side, and every stairway required to be more than 88 inches (2235 mm) in width shall be provided with not less than one intermediate handrail for each 88 inches (2235 mm) of required width. Intermediate handrails shall be located equidistant with the width of the stairway.

1120A.4.2.2 Handrails shall extend a minimum of 12 inches (305 mm) beyond the top nosing and 12 inches (305 mm), plus the tread width, beyond the bottom nosing.

1120A.4.2.5 Handrail projections. Handrails projecting from a wall shall have a space of 1 1/2 inches (38 mm) between the wall and the handrail.

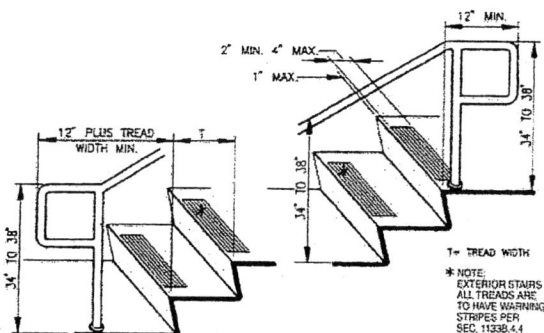

1120A.4.3 Striping for the visually impaired. The upper approach and the lower tread of each stair shall be marked by a strip of clearly contrasting color at least 2 inches (51 mm) wide placed parallel to, and not more than 1 inch (25 mm) from, the nose of the step or landing to alert the visually impaired. The strip shall be of material that is at least as slip resistant as the other treads of the stair. Where stairways occur outside a building, the upper approach and all treads shall be marked by a strip of clearly contrasting color at least 2 inches (51 mm) wide and placed parallel to and not more than 1 inch (25 mm) from the nose of the step or landing to alert the visually impaired. The strip shall be of a material that is at least as slip resistant as the other treads of the stair. A painted strip shall be acceptable.

1120A.4.3.1 Treads. All tread surfaces shall be slip-resistant. Treads shall have smooth, rounded or chamfered exposed edges, and no abrupt edges at the nosing (lower front edge).

1120A.5.5.1 Location of landings. Landings shall be provided at the top and bottom of each ramp. Intermediate landings shall be provided at intervals not exceeding 30 inches (762 mm) of vertical rise and at each change of direction. Landings are not considered in determining the maximum horizontal distance of each ramp.

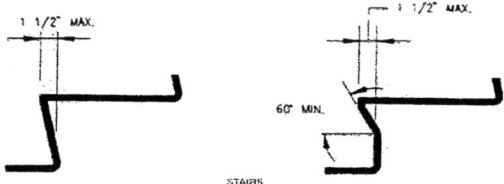

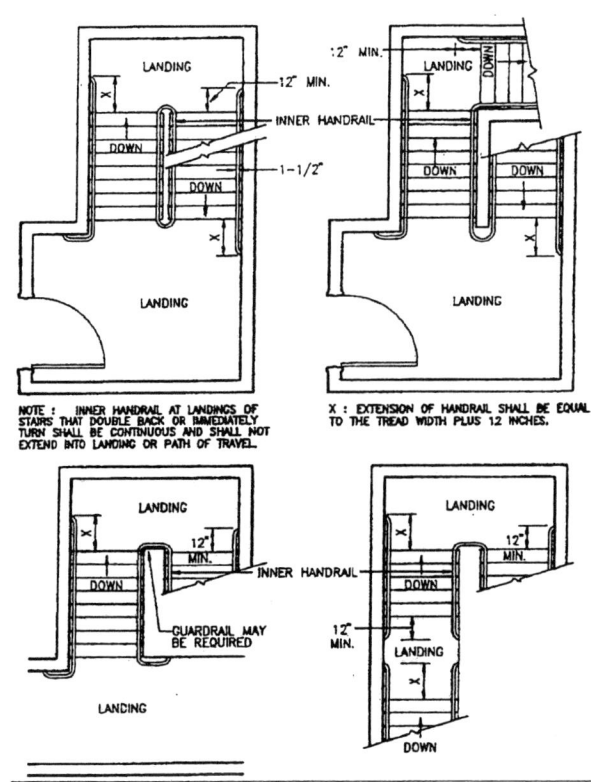

ELEVATORS

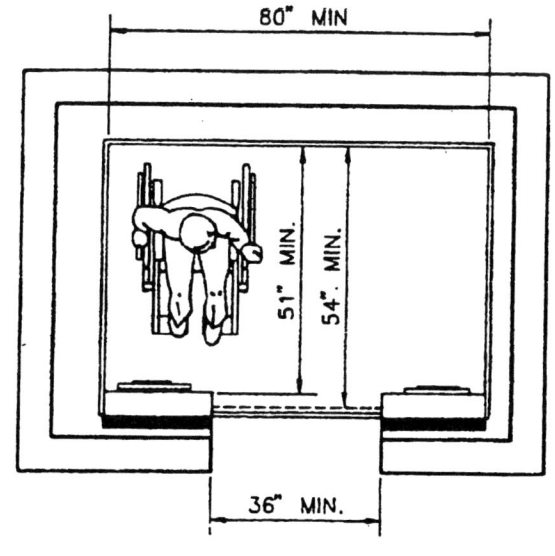

(b) CENTER OPENING DOOR

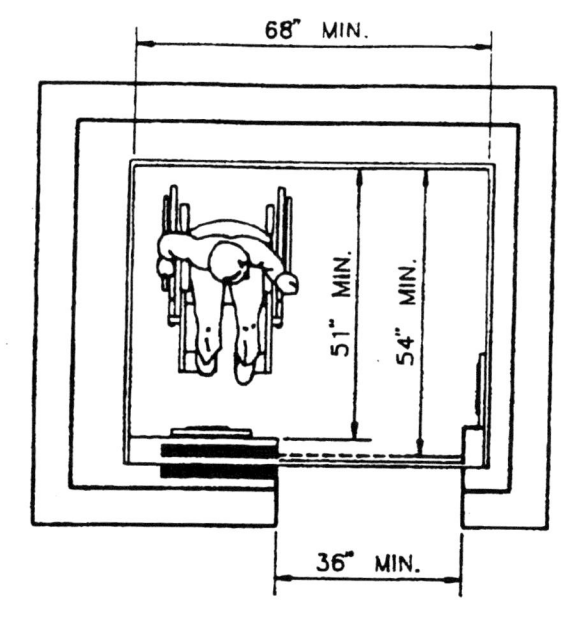

(a) SIDE OPENING DOOR

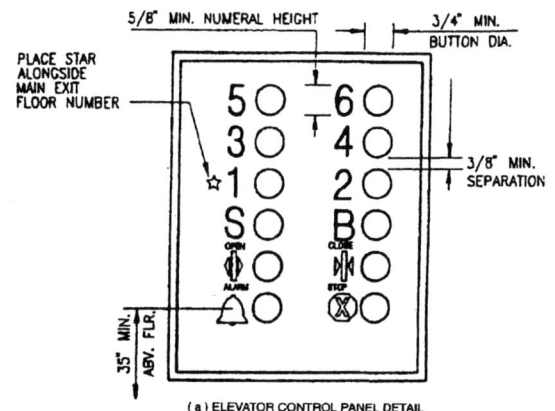

(a) ELEVATOR CONTROL PANEL DETAIL

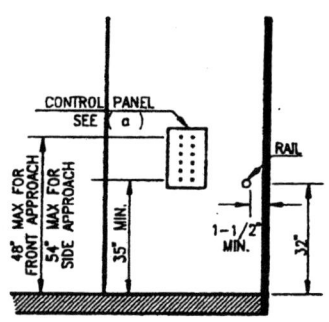

(b) MAXIMUM INSTALLATION HEIGHTS ABOVE CAB FLOOR

DRINKING FOUNTAINS

Application: ADAAG 4.1.3(10)(a) requires 50% of drinking fountains to be accessible in order that the remaining 50% will accommodate people unable to bend to the lower fountain. CA requires all drinking fountains to be accessible. Therefore, to meet requirement of both codes, we recommend the following:
Floors with 1 drinking fountain location: Min 1 accessible & min 1 standard.
Floors with multiple drinking fountain locations: 1 accessible per 1 standard at each location.

Location (ADAAG 4.1.3(10)): On accessible route.

Placement: Completely within alcove or not encroaching into accessible route. (ADAAG allows exception for existing construction & CA True 24 U.H. exception may be used. Therefore in existing buildings, fountain may project beyond alcove if U.H. & E.F. E.F.= (1) 12" textured border on floor beyond edges of fountain, or (2) (preferred) wing walls on each side extending to front of fountain, to min 6" from floor & min 32" clear between walls.)

Alcove Dimensions:
Alcove Width: Min 32".
Alcove Depth: Min 18".

Fixture Dimensions:
Depth: Min 18".
Knee Space: Min 27" high & 8" deep.
Toe Space: Min 9" high & 17" deep.
Bubbler (In existing buildings, U.H. if E.F. U.H. no E.F. if physical constraints determined by enforcing authority.):
 Location: Max 36" above floor & min 6" from front of fixture. (ADAAG 4.15.3: Min 3" from front of fixture in round or oval bowl.)
 Water Flow:
  Direction: Parallel to front edge.
  Height Min 4".
 Controls:
  Location: Max 6" from front edge.
  Operation (ADAAG 4.15.4 & 427.4): Operable with one hand without tight grasping, pinching or twisting of wrist.
  Force To Operate (ADAAG 4.15.4 & 427.4): Max 5 IV.
  Clear Space (ADAAG 4.15.5(1)): 30" x 48" perpendicular to fixture.
  Floor Surface: Stable, firm & slip-resistant.

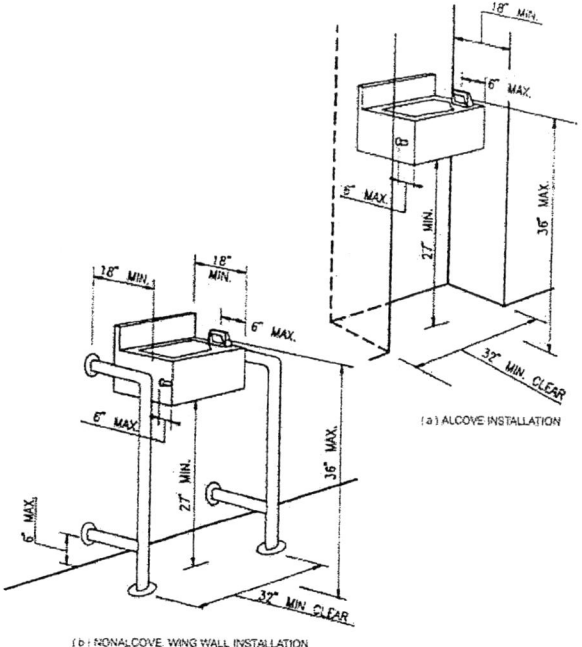

(a) ALCOVE INSTALLATION

(b) NONALCOVE WING WALL INSTALLATION

SIGNS & IDENTIFICATION

Directional & Informational Signs (except menus, directories, temporary signs.):
  Character Proportions:
Width to height = 3:5 to 1:1;
Stroke width to Height = 1:5 to 1:10.
Height of Overhead Symbols (sized for uppercase): Min 3".
Finish: (ADAAG 4.30.5): non-glare.
Contrast Light-on-dark, or dark-on-light.

Permanently Signed Rooms & Spaces (Examples: names of rooms, room numbers, restrooms, exits):
  Requirements: Raised letters & California (not ADA) Braille.
  Location: On wall adjacent to ltch side of door, 60" above floor. (At double doors, on right wall.)
  Raised letter Characteristics:
    5/8" to 2" high, raised 1132'
    sans serif, upper case.
    Non-glare (ADAAG 4.30.4).
    Contrast (ADAAG 4.30.4): t fight-on-dark or dark-on-fight.
  Braille: Grade II, dots = 1/10" on center in each cell with 2/10" space between cells, raised 1/40". 5.
  Obstacles: A person must be able to approach within 3" of signage without encountering protruding objects or standing (sitting) within swing of door.
  Pictograms:
    Location: Where used in permanently signed rooms & spaces, equivalent verbal description placed below in raised letters & Grade II Braille. (Exceptions: International symbol of accessibility, & circles & triangles on restroom doors)
    Border Dimension: Min 6" high.

Remodeled Buildings (Gov't Code 7251): In lobby in building directory, accessible restrooms and elevators indicated.

DOORS

Application: All relocatable doors or path of travel accessible entrances & exits serving toilets, drinking fountain or on the accessible route from van parking.

Hardware:
  Type of Lock or Latch: Cannot require use of key, special knowledge or effort.
  Door-opening Hardware:
    Location: 30" - 44" above floor.
    Type: Operable with single effort without requiring ability to grasp hardware:
  Door Closer (ADAAG 4.13.10): From open position of 70 degrees, door must take min 3 seconds to move 3" from latch (measured from edge).

Door Type: Revolving doors not allowed as required accessible entrance.

Door Size:
  Height Min 68".
  Width: Min 3'.
  Opening Width Min 32' (For hinged doors, measured at angle of 90 degrees from closed position.) Applies to one where) air of doors, manual or automatic. (Note: California exceptions allowing 30" opening cancelled) ADAAG 4.1.6(3) (d): "Where it is technically infeasible... a projection of 5/8" max will be permitted for the latch side stop." Therefore, 31 3/8"only where structural member must be removed.)
  Doorway Depth: Max 24'.

Thresholds:
  Height Max 1/2".
  Bevel: 12 for 1/4 to 12" heights.

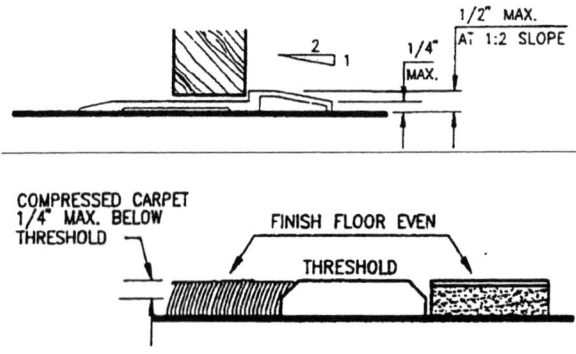

1120A.2.4 Thresholds. The floor or landing shall not be more than 1/2 inch (12.7mm) lower than the threshold of the doorway. Changes in level between 1/4 inch (6 mm) and 1/2 inch (12.7mm) shall be beveled with a slope no greater than 1 unit vertical in 2 units horizontal (50% slope). Changes in level greater than 1/2 inch (12.7 mm) shall be accomplished by means of a ramp.

Clear Areas at Doors:
    Swing Side: Min 60" perpendicular to closed door.
        Doors with no closer & wheelchair approach to latch side: Min 44".
        Doors with no closer, no latch & wheelchair approach to hinge side: Min 44".
        Door with both latch & closer & wheelchair approach to hinge side: Min 48".
    Push Side: 48" perpendicular to closed door.

Strike Side Clearance (width of level area beside door latch side:
    Swing Side:
        Exterior Doors: Min 24".
        Interior Door: Min 18".
        Doors with Hinge Approach Only: Min 36".
    Push Side: Min 12" in doors with closer & latch if corridor 48" wide.
    Consecutive Doors in Vestibule:
        48" perpendicular to door opening + width of door when open 90 degrees.
        Swing: Doors shall swing either in same direction or away from space between doors.

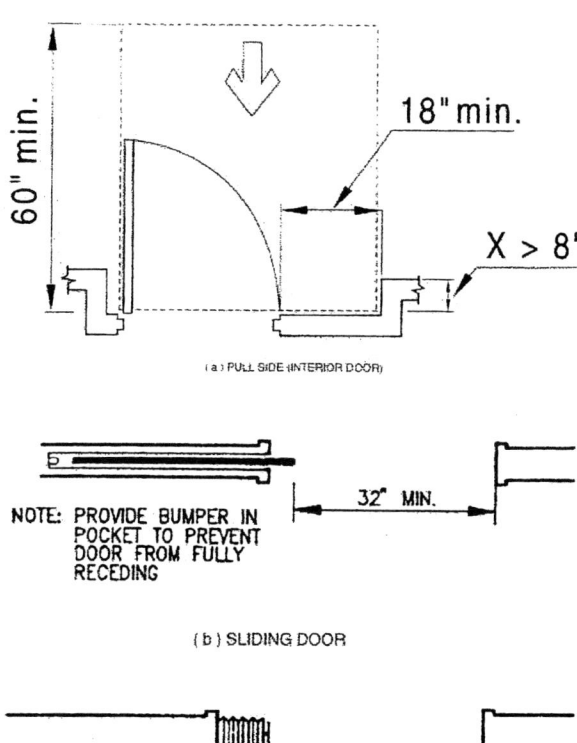

(a) PULL SIDE (INTERIOR DOOR)

(b) SLIDING DOOR

(c) FOLDING DOOR

Bottom: Min 10" high smooth panel on push side of door.

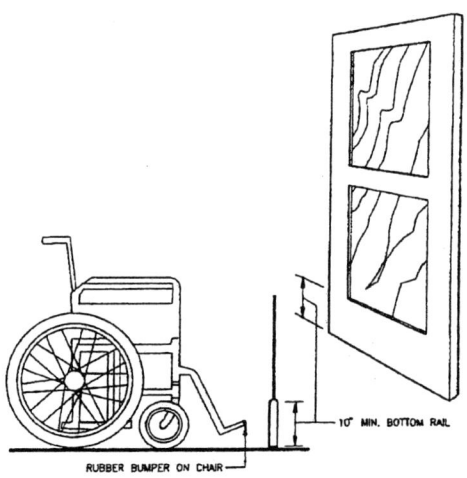

Door pressure
    Exterior doors: Max effort to operate doors = 8-1/2 lbs.
    interior doors: Max effort = 5 lbs
    Fire doors: As above, but may I e increased by fire authority to max 15 lbs only if authorized.

Automatic Doors (ADAAG 4.13.12) See ANSI/BHMA A156.10-1985 (national standard):
Low Powered Doors
    Specifications: Min 3 seconds to open to back check. See ANSI Al 56.19-1984 (national standard.)
    Force To Stop Door Movement: Max 15 lbf.
Power-Assisted Doors (ADAAG Section 4.13.12):
    Opening Force: Max 5 IV.
    Closing: See ANSI A156.19-1984 (national standard).
Signage: See Signage

TOILET ROOMS
Application:
    One pair of Men/Women or Boys/Girls sanitary facilities in an accessible building.
Separate Facilities:
    Required where provided for non-disabled.
Children's Facilities:
    Specific heights may be adjusted for accessibility needs of children.
Doors
    Specifications
    Door Swing (ADAAG 4232): shall not encroach into clear space at fixtures.

Signage:
    Women's Required Symbol: Circle, 1/4" thick, 12" in diameter.
    Men's Required Symbol: Equilateral triangle 1/4" thick, edges 12" long & vertex upward.
    Unisex Required Symbol: Equilateral triangle 1/4" thick superimposed on & within circle 1/4" thick 12" diameter
    Height: Centered 60" above floor.
    Contrast Color different from doc.
    Raised letters & Braille:
        Location: On wall adjacent to latch side of door (at double doors, on right wall.)
        Height 60" above floor.
        Raised letter Characteristics:
5/8' to 2" high raised 1132".
Sans serif, uppercase.
Non-glare (ADAAG 4.30.4).
contrast (ADAAG 4.30.4): Light-on-dark or dark-on-light
    California (NOT ADA) Braille: Grade II, dots= 1/10" on center in each cell with 2110" space between cells, raised 1/40".
Obstacles: A person may approach within 3" of signage without encountering protruding objects.
Pictograms: (It is recommended that pictograms, if provided, be placed on the wall with the raised letters & braille.)
    Equivalency. Where used in permanently signed rooms & spaces, raised letters & Grade II Braille placed below. Exceptions: International symbol of accessibility; & circles and triangles on restroom doors.
    Border dimension = 6" high.

Multiple Accommodation Toilets:
 Common Area Clear space:
  Dimension: 60" circle or space 56" x 63".
  Height From floor to 27" above floor.
  Doors Encroachment: Max 12° into accessible route for all doors except door to accessible stall. Not allowed into fixture clear space (ADAAG 4.222 &4.23.2). 2.
 Accessible Compartments:
  Application: Min 1.
 Entrance Side Clear space:
  All compartments: Min 44' measured at right angle to closed compartment door.
  Accessible compartment: min 48" measured at right angle to closed compartment door

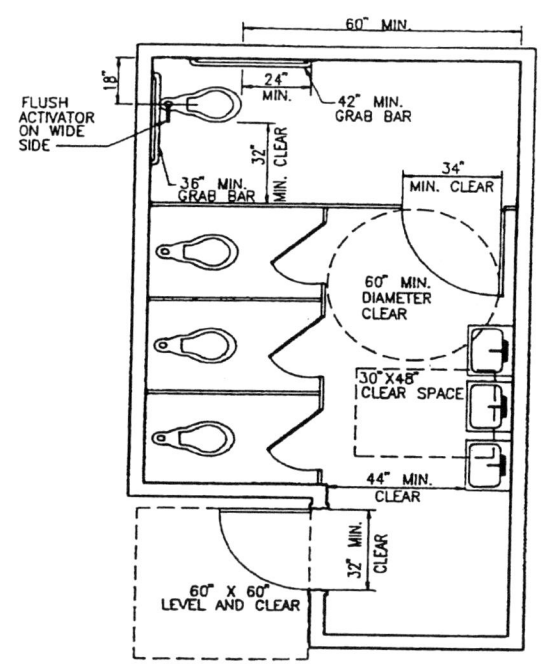

 Doors:
  Clear Opening Width (measured w/door at 90 degrees:
   End location: Min 32".
   Side location: Min 34".
  Strike edge clearance: Min 18". Not required if door has 9" clearance underneath.
  Closure: Self-closing.
  Handle: Loop or u-shaped below latch in flip-over style, sliding or other style not requiring grasping or twisting.
  When Located at End of Aisle: Min 18" strike side clearance.
 Width (ADAAG 4.17.3): Min. 60"
 Interior Clear space:
  From water closet to 1 wall: 18" from centerline of water closet
  In Front of Water Closet
   End opening door Min 48".
   Side opening door Min 60".
 In-Swinging Doors (ADAAG 4.17.5 & 4.13.5):
  Depth: Min 36" extra depth.
  Strike Side Clearance: Min 18".
 Grab Bar Encroachment Max 3".

Minimally Accessible Compartment:
 Application: Min 1 per six total compartments including the fully accessible stall,
 Stall Width: Min 36".
 Doors:
  Swing: Outward.
  Type: Self-closing.
 Grab Bars: Required.

Single Accommodation Toilets:
    Clear Space: Min 60" diameter arch - or T -shaped space.
    Water Closet (WC) Clear Space:
        One Side of WC:
            WC to wall: Min 32".
            WC to lavatory: Min 28".
        Other Side of WC: Center WC to wall 18"
        Front of WC: Min 48".
    Accessible Route:
        Width: Min 36" except at doors.
        Around Obstacle:

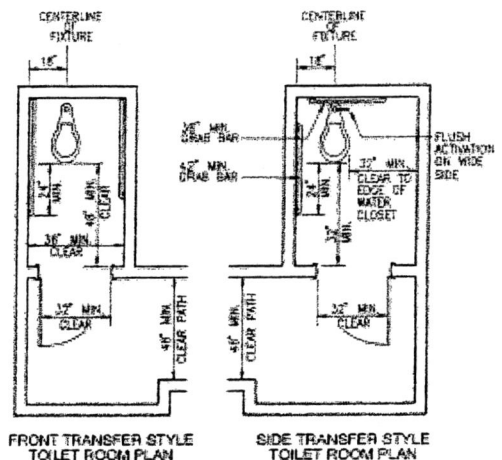

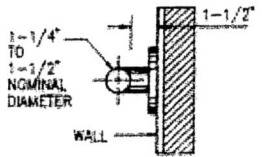

Water Closets

Seat Height Min 17" to max 19"
Flush Controls:
    Type: Operable with 1 hand & not requiring tight grasping, pinching or twisting of wrist.
    Location: Clear side space beside water closet.
    Height Max 44" above floor.
    Force: Max 5 Ibf.
Water Closet Seat Type (AD, AG 4.16.3): Automatic spring to lifted position not allowed.

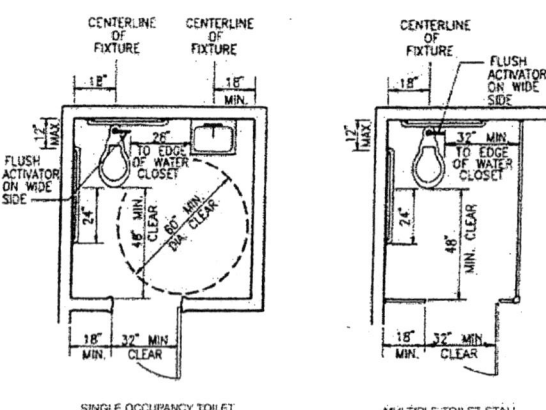

Grab Bars:
- Location: In accessible compartment or accommodation.
- Height: 33" above & parallel to floor 33" - 36" above tank of tank-type toilet.
- Length:
  - Side. Min 42" with 24" in front of water closet stool.
  - Back: Min 36".
- Diameter: 1 114" - 1 112- or equivalent
- Mounting Space: 1 1/2" from wall.
- Recess Mounting (ADAAG 426.3): Recess max 3" deep & extend min 18" above top of rail.
- Structural Strength: Must reset 250 lbf in any direction.
- Rotation in Fittings: Not allowed.
- Surface: Including wall nearby, free of sharp or abrasive element.
- Edges: Min radius= 1/8".

Toilet Tissue Dispensers:
- Height (ADAAG 4.16.6): Min 19" above floor.
- Location: On wall max 12" in front of toilet seat.
- Type: Dispensers that do not permit continuous paper flow not allowed.
- Clearance (ADAAG 4.16.6): Cannot obstruct use of grab bars.

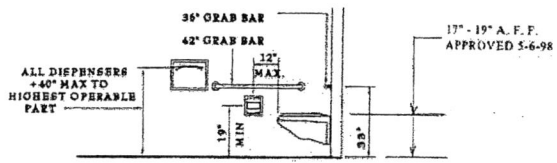

Lavatories:
- Application: Min 1.
- Clear Space:
  - Dimensions (ADAAG 4.19.3 & 42.4): Min 30" x min 48" for front approach.
  - Should adjoin accessible route & may extend max 19" under lav.
  - Surface: Stable, firm, slip-resistant.
- Mounting:
  - Wall-hung: Min 18" from wall to center line
  - Height Max 34" above floor
  - Knee Space: Min 29" high, 30" wide & 8" deep.
  - Toe Clearance: Min 9" high, 30" wide & 17" deep.
- Pipes: Insulated with no sharp or abrasive surfaces,
- Operating mechanisms
  - Type: Operable with 1 hand & not requiring tight grasping, pinching or twisting of the wrist.
  - Force: Max 5 lbf.
  - Self-closing time: Min 10 seconds.

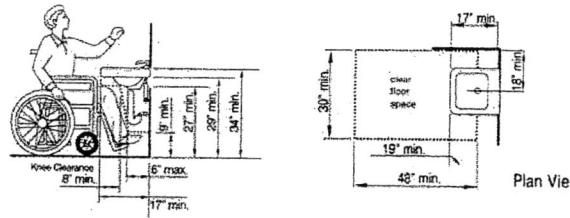

Towel, Sanitary Napkins & Waste Receptacles:
- Application: Min 1 of each type.
- All Operable Parts Height Max 40" above floor.
- Level Clear Space (ADAAG 427.2 & 42.4):
  - Dimensions: Min 30" x min 48" for either front or parallel approach.
  - Surface: Stable, firm, slip-resistant
- Controls (ADAAG 227.4): Operable with 1 hand without tight grasping, pinching or twisting of the wrist

Mirrors:
- Application: Min 1.
- Height Bottom edge max 40" above floor.

Urinals:
- Application: Min 1.
- Clear Space:

Dimensions: Min 30"x min 48" in front & may overlap accessible route.
Surface: Stable, firm, slip-resistant.
Plumbing Specifications (In existing buildings, in existing buildings floor-mounted urinals will be acceptable)
Fixture Extension: Min 14" from wall.
Height Max 17" above floor.
Controls:
Type: Operable with 1 hand & not requiring tight grasping, pinching or twisting of the wrist.
Height: Max 44" above floor.
Force: Max 5 lbf.
Shield (ADQ.AG 4.2.4.3): If provided & do not extend beyond front edge, width between panels min. 29" clr.

TABLE 1115B-1—SUGGESTED DIMENSIONS FOR CHILDREN'S USE

The Division of the State Architect, Office of Regulation Services recommends the following dimensions as adequately serving the needs of children in projects under our jurisdiction. These recommendations are based on the federal "Recommendations for Accessibility for Children in Elementary School" and other recognized publications on access for children:

A = Adult Dimensions (age 12 and over)
E = Elementary Dimensions
K = Kindergarten and Pre-school Dimensions

DIMENSION	SUGGESTED		
	A (Inches)	E (Inches)	K (Inches)
Toilet centering from wall	18	15	12
Toilet seat height/Dimensions to top of seat	17-19	15	10-12
Grab bar height (side)	33	27	20-22
Toilet paper in front of toilet	12 max.	6 max.	6 max.
Napkin disposal in front of toilet	12 max.	12 max.	N/A
Dispenser or mirror height	40 max.	36 max	32 max.
Lavatory/sink top height	34 max.	29 max.	24 max.
Lavatory/sink knee clearance	27 min.	24 min.	19 min.
Urinal lip height	17 max.	15 max.	13 min.
Urinal flush handle height	44 max.	37 max.	32 max.
Drinking fountain bubbler height	36 max.	32 max.	30 max.
Drinking fountain knee clearance	27 min.	24 min.	22 min.
Ramp/stair handrail height	34-38	27	22

Chapter 13: SUSPENDED CEILINGS
LESSON 13.1
IR M-3

The following information pertains to one of the most common inspection conditions that the DSA Inspector runs across. Suspended ceilings are part of almost any school building. Therefore it is a very important subject on the certification exams as well. There are usually about 5 questions pertaining to suspended ceilings on the DSA exams.

Study the following information and highlight your IR manual accordingly.

Highlighting List
Suspended Ceilings
(IR M-3)

Take out your IR manual and highlight the sections as they appear on this list in either red or yellow.

The "**Commentary**" on the right is broken down into four categories and they are as follows:

1. **TEST QUESTION (Highlight in Red)**
   - (Indicates that this material is very likely to be specifically referenced on the DSA exams)

2. **REMEMBER (Highlight in Yellow)**
   - (Indicates that you should know this material and that it is relevant to your work as an inspector)

3. **BEWARE (Highlight in Yellow)**
   - (Indicates that there is something that may not be apparent at first but that the inspector will have to deal with)

4. **SEE ALSO (Highlight in Yellow)**
   - (Indicates that there is another code section that affects this information)

© Professional Study Inc. 2003

IR M-3
DSA IR M-3 – 6-6-03

Purpose: The purpose of this IR is to provide guidelines for the installation of metal suspension systems for lay in ceilings.

1. Ceiling Notes.

1.1 12 ga. (min.) hanger wires may be used for up to and including 4'-0" x 4'-0" grid spacing and shall be attached to main runners.

1.2 Provide 12 ga. hanger wires at the ends of all main and cross runners within eight inches (8") of the support or within one-fourth (1/4) of the length of the end tee, whichever is least, for the perimeter of the ceiling area. End connections for runners which are designed and detailed to resist the applied vertical and horizontal forces may be used in lieu of the 12 ga. hanger wires, subject to Division of the State Architect (DSA) review and approval.

1.3 Provide trapeze or other supplementary support members at obstructions to typical hanger spacing. Provide additional hangers, struts or braces as required at all ceiling breaks, soffits or discontinuous areas. Hanger wires that are more than 1 in 6 out of plumb are to have counter sloping wires.

1.4 Ceiling grid members may be attached to not more than two (2) adjacent walls. Ceiling grid members shall be at least 1/2" free of other walls. If walls run diagonally to ceiling grid system runners, one end of main and cross

> **Comment:** REMEMBER
> Two of the four sides of T-Bar are to be attached and are to be free. ½" clear from wall to allow for movement

© Professional Study Inc. 2003

runners should be free, and a minimum of 1/2" clear of wall.

1.5 At the perimeter of the ceiling area where main or cross runners are not connected to the adjacent wall, provide interconnection between the runners at the free end to prevent lateral spreading. A metal strut or a 16 ga. wire with a positive mechanical connection to the runner may be used. Where the perpendicular distance from the wall to the first parallel runner is 12" or less, this interlock is not required.

1.6 Provide bracing assemblies consisting of a compression strut and four (4) 12 ga. splayed bracing wires oriented 90 degrees from each other (see Figure 1) at the following spacing:

> **Comment:** REMEMBER
> Provide compression struts

1. For school buildings, place bracing assemblies at a spacing not more than 12' by 12' on center.

> **Comment:** TEST QUESTION
> Compression strut spacing at 12' x 12' on schools

2. For Essential Services Buildings, place bracing assemblies not more than 8' by 12' on center.

3. Provide bracing assemblies at locations not more than one half (1/2) the spacings given above, from each perimeter wall and at the edge of vertical ceiling offsets.

> **Comment:** TEST QUESTION
> Compression struts max 6'-0" from walls.

4. Suspended acoustical ceiling systems with a ceiling area of 144 square feet or less, and fire rated suspended acoustical ceiling systems with a ceiling area of 96 square feet or less, surrounded by walls which connect directly to the structure above, do not require bracing assemblies when attached to two adjacent walls.

METAL SUSPENSION SYSTEMS
FOR LAY IN PANEL CEILINGS

The slope of these wires shall not exceed 45 degrees from the plane of the ceiling and shall be taut. Splices in bracing wires are not to be permitted without special DSA approval.

> **Comment:** REMEMBER
> Slope Splay wires at 45 degrees min

1.7 Fasten hanger wires with not less than three (3) tight turns. Fasten bracing wires with four (4) tight turns. Make all tight turns within a distance of 1½" inches. Hanger or bracing wire anchors to the structure should be installed in such a manner that the direction of the wire aligns as closely as possible with the direction of the forces acting on the wire.

> **Comment:** TEST QUESTION
> Hanger wires to have 3 tight turns within 1-1/2"
> Bracing wires to have 4 tight turns within 1-1/2"

> **Note:** Wire turns made by machine where both strands have been deformed or bent in wrapping can waive the 1½" requirement, but the number of turns should be maintained, and be as tight as possible.

1.8 Separate all ceiling hanging and bracing wires at least six inches (6") from all unbraced ducts, pipes, conduit, etc. It is acceptable to attach lightweight items, such as single electrical conduit not exceeding 3/4" nominal diameter, to hanger wires using connectors acceptable to DSA.

1.9 When drilled-in concrete anchors or shot-in anchors are used in reinforced concrete for hanger wires, 1 out of 10 must be field tested for 200 lbs. in tension. When drilled-in concrete anchors are used for bracing wires, 1 out of 2 must be field tested for 440 lbs. in tension. Shot-in

> **Comment:** TEST QUESTION
> Wires into Concrete (Drilled in Anchors)
> • Hangar wires test 10% to 200 lbs. tension
> • Bracing wires test 50% to 444 lbs. tension
>
> * No shot in anchors for bracing wires

anchors in concrete are not permitted for bracing wires. If any shot-in or drilled-in anchor fails,
see CBC, Section 1923A.3.5.

> **Note:** Drilled-in or shot-in anchors require special DSA approval when used in
> prestressed concrete.

1.10 Attach all light fixtures and ceiling mounted air terminals or services, to the ceiling grid runners to resist a horizontal force equal to the weight of the fixtures. Screws or approved fasteners are required.

1.11 Flush or recessed light fixtures and air terminals or services, weighing less than 56 lbs., may be supported directly on the runners of a heavy duty grid system but, in addition, they must have a minimum of two 12 ga. slack safety wires attached to the fixture at diagonal corners and anchored to the structure above. All 4' x 4' light fixtures must have slack safety wires at each corner. All flush or recessed light fixtures and air terminals or services weighing 56 lbs. or more must be independently supported by not less than four (4) taut 12 ga. wires each attached to the fixture and to the structure above regardless of the type of ceiling grid system used.

Comment: TEST QUESTION
- Fixtures < 56 lbs. 2 slack wires 12 ga. Opposite corners
- Fixtures > 56 lbs. 4 taut wires 12 ga. Four corners

The four (4) taut 12 ga. Wires including their attachment to the structure above must be capable
of supporting four (4) times the weight of the unit.

1.12 All fixtures and air terminals or services supported on intermediate duty grid systems must be independently supported by not less than four (4) taut 12 ga. wires each attached to the fixture or terminal, and to the structure above.

1.13 Support surface mounted light fixtures by at least two positive devices which surround the ceiling runner and which are each supported from the structure above by a 12 ga. wire. Spring clips or clamps that connect only to the runner are not acceptable. Provide additional supports when light fixtures are 8'-0" or longer.

1.14 Support pendant mounted light fixtures directly from the structure above with hanger wires or cables passing through each pendant hanger and capable of supporting four (4) times the weight of the fixture. A bracing assembly per Figure 1, is required where the pendant hanger penetrates the ceiling. Special details are required to attach the pendant hanger to the bracing assembly to transmit horizontal forces.

> **Comment:** REMEMBER
> Pendant lights to supported from swinging.

2. Additional Requirements for Fire Rated Ceilings.

2.1 Provide Underwriter Laboratory (U.L.) design number or State Fire Marshal (SFM) listing number. The components and installation details must conform in every respect with the U.L. or SFM approval for the design number specified. Custom designs which combine components from different approved designs but have not been tested as a complete assembly are not acceptable.

© Professional Study Inc. 2003

2.3 Pop rivets, screws, or other attachments are not acceptable unless specifically detailed on the drawings and approved by U.L. and SFM.

3. Additional Requirements for Metal Panels. Metal panels and panels weighing more than 1/2 psf, other than acoustical tile, are to be positively attached to the ceiling suspension runners.

4. Suspended Acoustical Ceilings Below Gypsum Board Ceilings. Where gypsum board or other ceiling finishes are attached to the framing, special details will be required for the vertical hanger wire and lateral bracing wire support connections to the framing.

5. Reuse of Existing Ceiling Hanger Wires and Splay Wires.

5.1 The gage and spacing of the wires must comply with the current applicable codes.

5.2 All existing ceiling hanger wires must be tested to 200 lbs. in tension.

5.3 All existing splayed bracing wires must be field tested to 440 lbs. in tension.

5.4 If a new wire is to be spliced to an existing wire, the following is required:

> 1. The architect or structural engineer in general responsible charge must submit to DSA a detail and specification describing how the splice is to be made.
>
> 2. All new wires, after being spliced to the existing wires, must be field tested per Items 5.2 and 5.3 above.
>
> 3. All field tests must be performed in the presence of the project inspector.
>
> > **Note:** Alternate manufacturers and systems may be submitted for

Comment: REMEMBER
Re-used wires need to be tested per this section.

review and approved by the
Division of the State Architect.

SUSPENDED CEILING BRACING ASSEMBLY
Bracing assemblies are required at spacing indicated in section 1.6 on page 1 of IR 25-2

Compression struts:
Steel section with l/r ratio of 200 maximum. Attach to main runners within 2" of cross runner with 2-#12 self-drilling self-tapping (SDST) screws and to structure with 2-#12 x 2" screws at wood or 3/16" diameter anchor at concrete/steel. Compression strut shall not replace hanger wire.

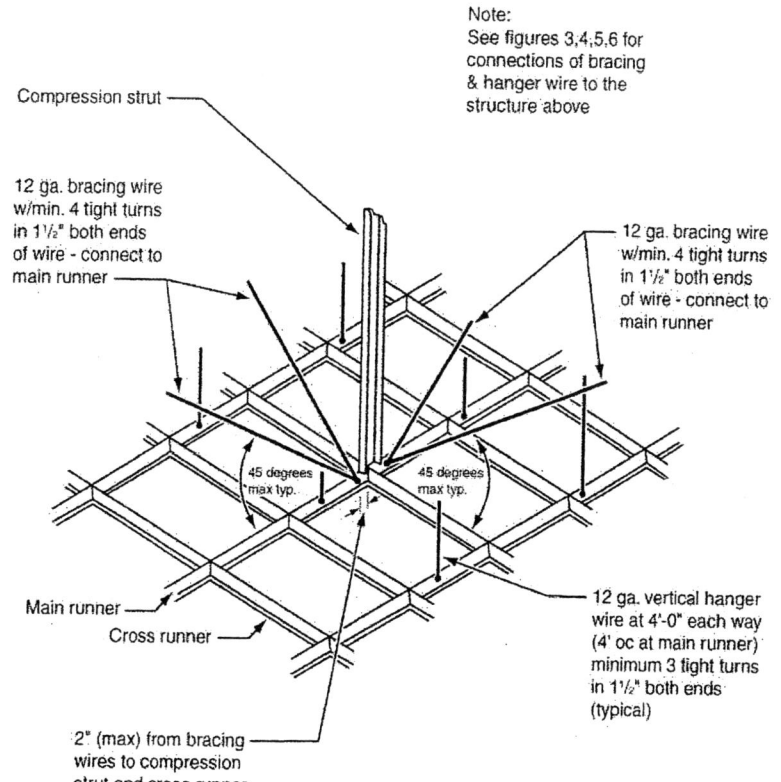

Figure 2
ACCEPTABLE HANGER WIRE CONNECTION TO GRID

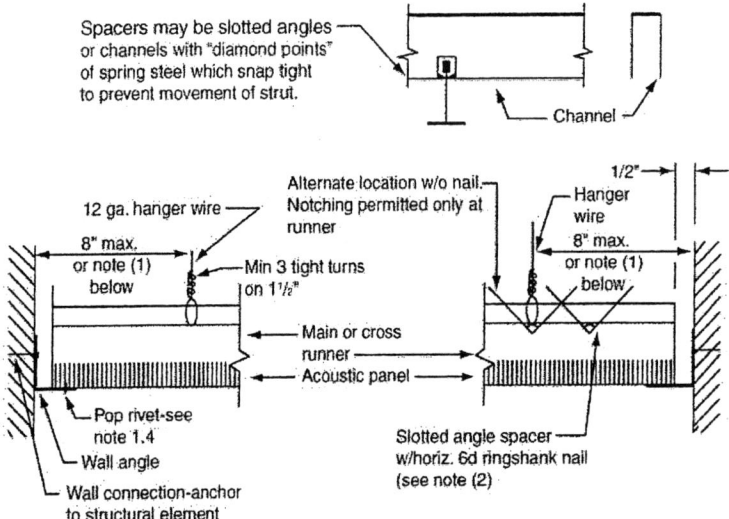

Detail (A) Horizontal strut - typical (see note 1.5)

Notes: (1) 1/4 of the length of the end runner whichever is less.
(2) Nails at the end of horizontal struts are to be placed with nail head toward centerline of span of strut

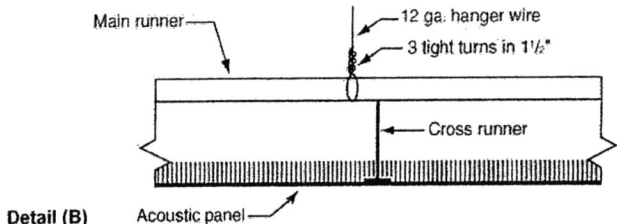

Detail (B)

Figure 3A
ACCEPTABLE DETAILS - WIRE CONNECTIONS TO WOOD FRAMING

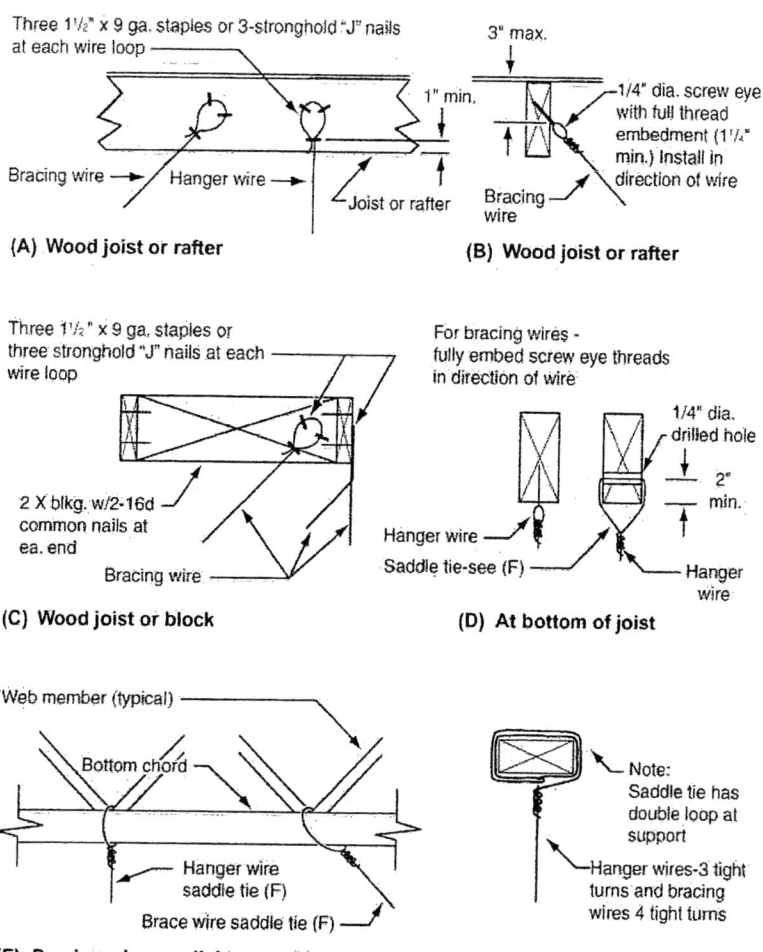

Figure 3B
ACCEPTABLE DETAILS – WIRE CONNECTION AT WOOD FRAMING

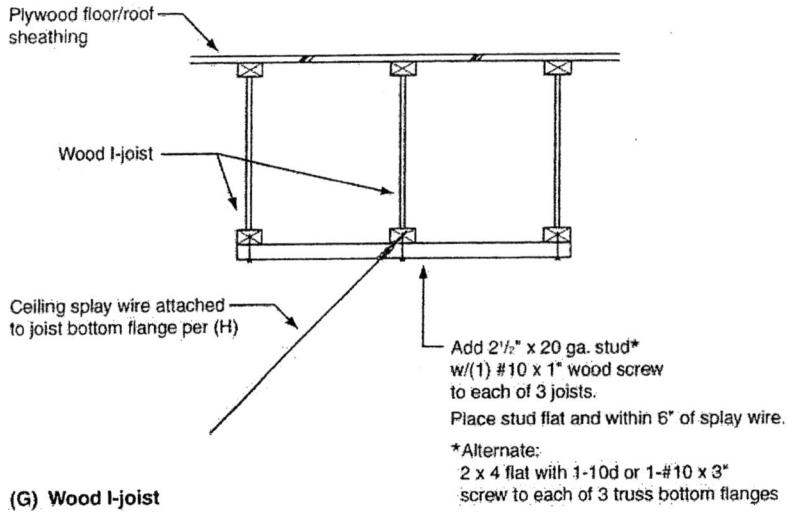

(G) Wood I-joist

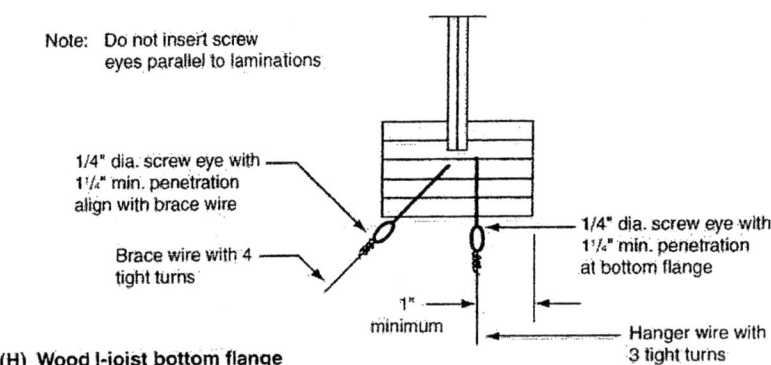

(H) Wood I-joist bottom flange

Figure 4
ACCEPTABLE DETAILS - WIRE CONNECTION TO CAST-IN-PLACE CONCRETE

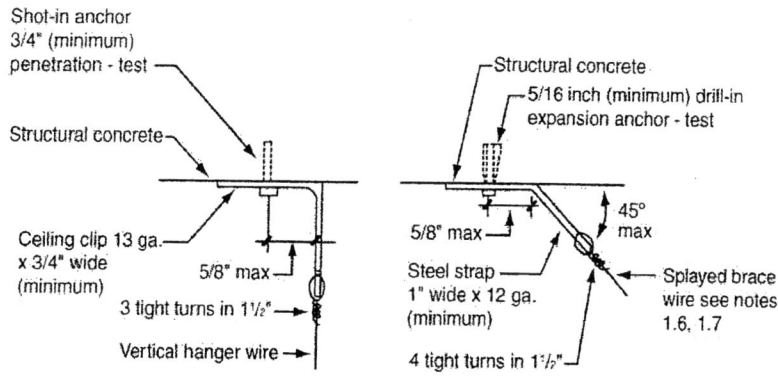

(A) Vertical hanger wire clip attachment (B) Splayed bracing wire clip attachment

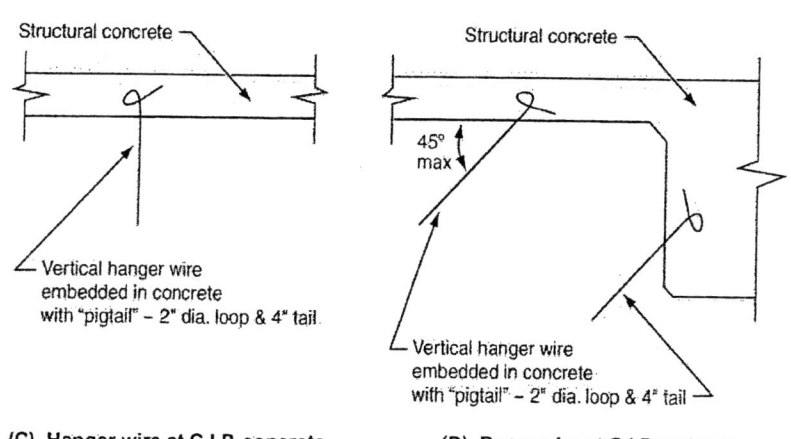

(C) Hanger wire at C.I.P. concrete (D) Brace wire at C.I.P. concrete

Figure 7
ACCEPTABLE LOCATION OF SLIP JOINTS IN ESB EXITWAYS

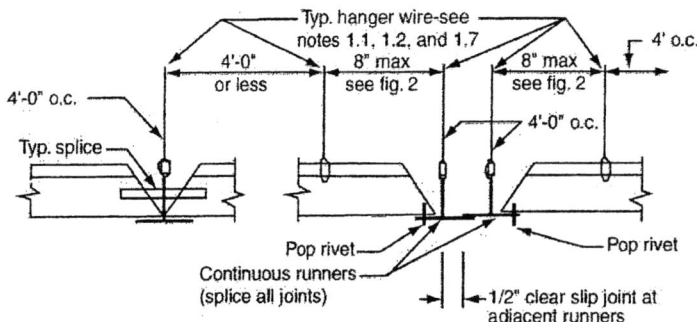

(A) Acceptable slip joint at exitways intersection

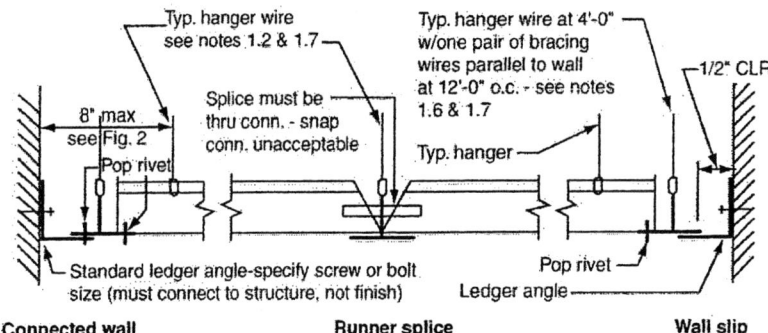

(B) Acceptable exitways details at essential sevices buildings (ESB)

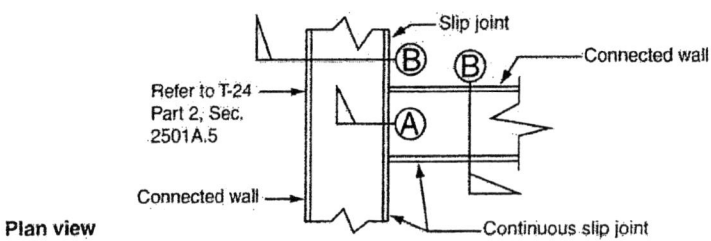

Plan view

DSA Class 1 Certified Inspector - Code Knowledge

Academy » DSA-1A » Quizzes » Book Question Quiz » Attempt 1

Logout

Raw score: 4/40 (10.0 %)

Grade: 10.0/100

Continue

1
Marks: 0/1

Corrosion resistant fasteners are desired but are not mandatory in pressure treated wood.

Answer: ○ True   (●) False

CBC Ch 2304A.2

2
Marks: 0/1

The Minimum anchor bolt size is _____ x _____ inches in a class B shear wall with HD5A's and 6x plate.

Answer:
- a. 1/2" x 12"   2320A.6   CBC
- b. 5/8 x 10"
- (c. 5/8 x 12")
- d. 1/2" x 10"

3
Marks: 0/1

You are inspecting a shear wall where the stud separation is called out to be 16" on center and the plywood is called out to be 2 layers of 1/2" or one layer of 3/4". You notice that some of the plywood panels are between one and six bays wide. You need to determine whether the plywood panels that were installed are acceptable. Which of the answers below would be the best answer?

Answer:
- a. Any 3/4" panel 1 bay wide and any 1/2" panel 2 bay wide is acceptable
- b. Any 1/2" panel 1 bay wide and any 3/4" panel 2 bays wide is unacceptable.   2315A.3.3   CBC
- c. Any 1/2" panel 3 bays wide and any 3/4" panel 2 bays wide is

acceptable
- d. Any 1/2" panel 2 bays wide and any 3/4" panel 2 bays wide is acceptable
- (e. A, C, and D)
- f. A and B

4
Marks: 1/1

2x2 Rectangular ducts are always required to be seismically braced.

Answer: ○ True (● False)

CEC Ch 16A'0'

5
Marks: 0/1

Electric Metal Conduit (EMT) shall be supported at _____ from an electrical box?

Answer:
- (a. 36")
- b. 12" Calif. Elec. Code
- c. 48"
- d. 18"

6
Marks: 0/1

What is the maximum vertical spacing of supports for a hubless cast iron sewer?

Answer:
- a. 10'
- (b. 15')
- c. 12'
- d. 20' Calif. Plumbing. Code Table 3-2

7
Marks: 0/1

Striping shall be provided at the _____ and _____ of each stair inside a building.

Answer:
- a. upper approach, lower tread
- b. Lower approach,

upper approach
- c. Upper approach, Lower tread ⭕
- d. Lower approach, Upper tread   Part 2, Vol. 1, Sec. 1120A.4.3

8 Marks: 0/1

What is the maximum allowable effort required to operate an accesible interior door?

Answer:
- a. 8-1/2 lbs
- b. 5 lbs ⭕
- c. 15 lbs   Part 2, Vol. 1 Ch. 11A
- d. 12 lbs

9 Marks: 0/1

What is the maximum dimension of the gap between parts of a grate along the path of travel?

Answer:
- a. 1/2" ⭕
- b. 1/4"
- c. 3/16"   Part 2, Vol. 1, Ch. 11A
- d. 3/8"

10 Marks: 0/1

What is the minimum number of Van Accessible parking spaces for an elementary school?

Answer:
- a. 1 space ⭕
- b. 2 spaces
- c. 1 per 3 regular HC spaces
- d. 0 spaces   Part 2, Vol. 1, Ch. 11A

11 Marks: 0/1

A recessed light fixture weighing 60 lbs requires 4 taut wires at four corners for proper attachment.

Answer: ○ True ○ False

IRM-3 (1.11)

12
Marks: 1/1

Shot-in anchors are ok for suspended ceiling bracing wires as long as 100% of them are tension tested?

Answer: ○ True (○ False)

IRM-3

13
Marks: 0/1

What is the number of turns required for a tie of a bracing wire?

Answer:
○ a. 3 tight turns
(○ b. 4 tight turns)
○ c. 5 tight turns
○ d. 6 tight turns IRM-3 (1.7)

14
Marks: 0/1

What is the maximum slope for suspended ceiling hangar wires?

Answer:
○ a. 1:4 IRM-3 (1.3)
(○ b. 1:6)
○ c. 1:5
○ d. 1:8

15
Marks: 0/1

You are in charge of inspecting the foundations for a new gymnasium. The foundations have been excavated and will be ready to start forming some stem walls. You have already called and infomed DSA about the work earlier that morning. Concrete will be placed the following day. Is this acceptable.

Answer:
☑ a. Yes
☐ b. No. Because forms need to be inspected
☐ c. Yes as long as the concrete is poured in the

afternoon.
- [x] d. No. Because forms must not be set
- [ ] e. No
- [ ] f. B and C

CBC Part 1 Admin

16 A special inspector is needed for all concrete placements regardless of PSI.
Marks: 0/1

Answer: ○ True ●(False)

CBC Part 1 Admin

17 High strength bolting requires inspection at the beginning and at the end of operations.
Marks: 1/1

Answer: ○ True ●(False)

CBC Part 2 Ch. 17 "Continuous"

18 Addenda pertaining to the structural system must be signed by the following
Marks: 0/1

Answer:
- ○ a. The Architect and DSA
- ●(b. The Architect, Engineer, and DSA)
- ○ c. The Engineer, and DSA
- ○ d. The Architect and Engineer

CBC Part 1 Admin

19 Draft stops in Attics in non-sprinklered school buildings must be installed so that a there is a maximum concealed area of _____ square ft and horizontal dimension between stops of _____ feet.
Marks: 0/1

Answer:
- ●(a. 3000, 60)
- ○ b. 6000, 60   Part 2, Vol. 1 Sec 708.3.1.2
- ○ c. 9000, 60
- ○ d. 9000, 100

DSA-1A: Book Question Quiz

20 What is the maximum area of glazing allowed in a 1-1/2 hr or a 1 hr rateed door is _____ per leaf.
Marks: 0/1

Answer:
- a. 144 sq in.
- b. 96 sq in.
- **c. 100 sq in.** ⊙
- d. 120 sq in. Part 2, Vol. 1 Sec 713.7

21 What is the required mounting height of a strobe light in a room with 10'-0" high ceilings?
Marks: 0/1

Answer:
- **a. 6'-8"** ⊙
- b. 7'-0"
- c. 8'-0"
- d. 9'-6" CFC 1212.0

22 What rating of fire assembly is required for an opening in a 2 hr occupancy separation?
Marks: 0/1

Answer:
- a. 20 min   Part 2, Vol. 1 Sec 302.3 (4)
- b. 1 hr
- **c. 1-1/2 hr** ⊙
- d. 2 hr

23 All electrical conduit greater than 2.5 inches in trade size must be seismically restrained.
Marks: 0/1

Answer: **True** False
Part 2, Vol. 2 Sec 1632A.6 (2)

24 Electrical raceways including cable tray must be suspended by solid threaded rods that are longer than 12" must have seismic restraints.
Marks: 0/1

Answer: (True) False
Table 16A-O Note 12

25
Marks: 0/1

Racks and cabinets taller than 4'-0" must be seismically restrained.

Answer: True (False)
Table 16A-O Note 23 Max 5'-0" tall

26
Marks: 0/1

A special inspector need not be constantly present during the welding of stairs and railings.

Answer: (True) False
1701A.5 (4)

27
Marks: 0/1

The project inspector is required to be constantly present during the placement of reinforced concrete.

Answer: (True) False
1701A.5 (1)

28
Marks: 0/1

What DSA form is the project inspector required to file prior to bringing in a special inspector to perform inspections on a project?

Answer:
- a. DSA6   1701A.2.1
- (b. DSA5)
- c. DSA5A
- d. DSA6A

29
Marks: 1/1

In seismic zone 4, 1/2" bolts are ok in bearing walls but not in shear walls.

DSA-1A: Book Question Quiz

Answer: ○ True ● False

30
Marks: 0/1

It is ok to place concrete into a 30 ft. deep concrete Pile foundation with the use of a _____ as long as the concrete does not drop more than 6 ft.

Answer: **(● a. Tremie)**
● b. Concrete pump
● c. Water reducing agent 1905A.7.1
● d. Plasticising agent
● e. Approved mix design

31
Marks: 0/1

Samples must be taken from concrete placed each _____ at a rate of once for each _____ cubic yards or every _____ square feet of surface area for slabs or walls.

Answer: ● a. Day, 50, 1500
(● b. Day, 50, 2000)
● c. Pour, 75, 1500
● d. Day, 75, 2000 1905A.6.1

32
Marks: 0/1

What is the minimum concrete cover for a #5 wall bar not exposed to earth or weather?

Answer: ● a. 1"
● b. 1-1/2"
(● c. 3/4")
● d. 2" 1907A.7.1 Note 3

33
Marks: 0/1

Mortar samples are to be taken at a rate of one on three successive working days and then at one week intervals there after.

Answer: (**True**) False

2105A

34 What is the Grade of Concrete Masonry Unit that is required for use in school projects?

Marks: 0/1

Answer:
- (a. N-1)
- b. N-2
- c. S
- **d. M-1** 2102A, UBC Standard 21-4

35 What is the maximum projection of mortar into the grout space that is allowable?

Marks: 0/1

Answer:
- a. 1/2" 2104A
- (b. 1/4")
- c. 3/16"
- d. 3/4"

36 You as the inspector are required to submit a DSA Form 5 for any welding inspector you have on your job.

Marks: 0/1

Answer: (**True**) False

Sec. 2231A.5

37 What is the required certification for a welding special inspector?

Marks: 0/1

Answer:
- (a. AWS-CWI)
- b. ICBO-SS
- **c. DSA Struct. Steel** Sec. 2231A.5

DSA-1A: Book Question Quiz

38

Marks: 0/1

Which of the following publications describes the procedures for identifying materials that are delivered on site?

Answer: (a. CBC Vol. 2)
 b. AISC Steel Manual
 c. AWS D1.1   Sec. 2203A
 d. AWS D1.4

39

Marks: 0/1

Anchor bolts shall be spaced no more than _____ inches apart.

Answer: a. 24"
 (b. 48")
 c. 36"   1806A.6
 d. 12"

40

Marks: 0/1

How many rebar tests would be required for 12 tons of #5 rebar that has been satisfactorily identified?

Answer: (a. 2)
 b. 1
 c. 3   1 per 10 tons 1929A.2
 d. 5

Continue

You are logged in as Khurt Geisse (Logout)

DSA-1A

Appendix

1. DSA Certified Inspector Exam Application
2. IR-A8 Duties of a DSA Certified Inspector

© Professional Study Inc. 2003

Appendix #1

DSA Certified Inspector Exam Application

© Professional Study Inc. 2003

DSA Project Inspector Examination Information and Application Package

2004 Exam Dates:

Examination Date	Earliest Postmark Date for Filing	Latest Postmark Date For Filing
Wednesday, **March 17, 2004**	Jan. 5, 2004	Feb. 20, 2004
Wednesday, **June 16, 2004**	Feb. 23, 2004	May 7, 2004
Wednesday, **September 15, 2004**	May 10, 2004	Aug. 6, 2004
Wednesday, **December 8, 2004**	Aug. 9, 2004	Oct. 29, 2004

Contents:

	Page #
Announcement	1
Package Information page	2
General Information	3
Project Classification	4
Application Form	5
Application Instructions	6
Class 1 or 2 Experience Record Form	7
Instructions for Completing Class 1 or 2	8
Class 3 or 4 Experience Record Form	9
Instructions for Completing Class 3 or 4	10
Qualifying Experience Limitations	11
Experience Guidelines	12
Frequently Asked Questions	13

Exam Application Fee:

The exam application fee is $225.00 (non-refundable)

Additional application forms are available on our website: www.dsa.ca.gov. For Project Inspector Application and instructions click on "Inspector Info."

The exams will be based on the 2001 Title 24 codes.

Questions? Call David Sault: 916/327-3459   Email: David.Sault@dgs.ca.gov

DSA Project Inspector Examination
General Information

The Project Inspector examination is designed to determine knowledge in the areas of acceptable construction practice, plan reading, techniques of construction and inspection, as well as understanding of applicable codes and regulations.

Exam Description

Each examination consists of two Parts; a 'Plan Reading Part' in the morning and a 'Code Part' in the afternoon. The 'Plan Reading Part' of the examination includes questions grouped into three subject areas; Structural, Architectural (which includes Access and Fire & Life Safety), and Mechanical/Electrical/Plumbing (MEP). The 'Code Part' of the examination has the same three sections, including a fourth section, Administrative (which includes inspector duties and responsibilities). To pass either part of the examination applicants must obtain a minimum score in each section in addition to an overall minimum score for that part. To become certified applicants must pass both parts of the examination. The passing score for each part of the examination is anticipated to be 65%. The minimum scores to pass the exam are given in the grid below:

	Overall	Sections			
		Admin	Structural	Architectural	MEP
PLAN PART	65%	/////////	60%	60%	55%
CODE PART	65%	60%	60%	60%	55%

DSA may change the minimum scores required to pass at any time without advanced notice.

Exam Duration, Locations, and Notification Dates

Each Part of the exam lasts three hours. There will be 30 minutes allowed prior to the Plan Reading Part to review the drawings provided. One hour is allowed for lunch. Lunch is **not** provided. Examinations will be held in northern and southern California. Qualified applicants will be notified by mail of acceptance to take the examination, and specific times and locations, at least two weeks before the examination date. Candidates will be notified of results approximately 28 days after the examination date.

Fees and Transfers

The fee for the examination is $225.00, **non-refundable**. Applicants who do not qualify to take the exam will **not** receive a refund, but may submit additional information and/or re-apply for a future examination one time (within six months) without submitting an additional fee. Applicants who are accepted and are not able to attend the exam for any reason may transfer to a future examination date one-time (within six months).

Exam Qualification and Re-Application

- Applicants who do not qualify for the examination (or who fail the examination) may apply for the Assistant Inspector Program for no additional fee.
- Applicants who fail one PART of the examination may re-take that PART only.
- Applicants who fail one SECTION in either PART of the exam must re-take that entire PART.
- Applicants who fail one, or both, parts of an examination may re-apply for any subsequent exam date except for the very next scheduled exam date.

Important: Certification does not guarantee that an individual will be approved for any school project. Experience, workload and past performance will be evaluated and considered on each specific project by the DSA field engineer.

Re-Certification

Candidates who pass the examination will be required to re-certify every four years. Re-certification requirements are described on our website at www.dsa.ca.gov. Click on "Inspector Info" and search for "Inspector Re-Certification Information."

Project Classification:

There are four classifications of construction projects as defined below. All projects are "classified" by DSA during plan review. An individual must hold a certificate of the appropriate class to apply for the position of "Project Inspector" for a specific project. Individuals must be evaluated and approved by the owner, project architect, structural engineer, and DSA for each specific project prior to start of construction. The following classification definitions are also used to categorize the experience stated by applicants in their Experience Record Forms.

Class 1:
- Buildings or additions of 2,000 square feet or greater that utilize materials other than wood-frame shear walls (for example: masonry/concrete shear walls, steel brace frames, concrete, or steel moment-resisting frames) as the primary lateral load-resisting system.
- Substantial structural alterations to the gravity and/or lateral load-resisting system of the building types described above.

Class 2:
- Buildings or additions <u>over</u> 2,000 square feet that utilize wood-frame shear walls as the primary lateral load-resisting system. Projects may be single or multi-level. The project may contain incidental masonry, concrete and/or structural steel construction (e.g. gravity load carrying columns and beams). Buildings may have isolated exceptions to the lateral load-resisting system, such as a steel brace frame at one location in the structure.
- Buildings or additions of <u>less than</u> 2,000 square feet in floor area that have primary lateral load-resisting systems utilizing concrete, masonry or steel construction. A single-story masonry building with a regular configuration (see C.B.C. Sec. 1629A.5.2), a floor area of less than 7,000 square feet, and a wood-frame roof structure *may* be considered to be a Class 2 structure.
- Two-story relocatable buildings (on-site construction) utilizing shop-fabricated building frames.
- Alteration, modernization, and reconstruction projects that exceed the limitations of the Class 3 scope of work, but do not include substantial alterations to structural systems of concrete, steel or masonry.
- Non-building structures that exceed the limitations of the Class 3 scope of work (signs, poles, bleachers, walls, fences, retaining walls, etc.).

Class 3:
- Buildings or additions of wood-frame, single-story construction, with conventional (spread footing) concrete foundations and a total floor area less than 2,000 square feet. Structures must utilize wood-frame shear walls as the primary lateral load-resisting system. The project may include isolated steel or concrete elements (e.g. steel or concrete columns).
- Structural alteration projects limited to wood-frame, single-story construction. When deemed appropriate by DSA, alterations to (or addition of) isolated steel, masonry or concrete elements may be included in Class 3 projects. Alteration projects involving significant changes to the lateral load-resisting system may be classified as Class 2 projects.
- Alteration and modernization projects that are primarily non-structural, such as electrical, mechanical, plumbing, disabled access features, and site improvement work.
- Most non-building structures such as signs, poles, bleachers, walls, fences, retaining walls, etc.

Class 4:
- Site installation of premanufactured, single-story, relocatable buildings.

See IR A-7 for a complete definition of Project Classifications

Inspectors who pass the Class 1 examination are qualified to apply for any project. Class 2 inspectors may apply or Class 2, 3, or 4 projects. Class 3 inspectors may apply for Class 3 or 4 projects. Class 4 inspectors may only inspect Class 4 projects.

State of California • Arnold Schwarzenegger, Governor
State and Consumer Services Agency

DEPARTMENT OF GENERAL SERVICES

Division of the State Architect - Headquarters
1102 Q Street, Suite 5100, Sacramento, CA 95814

PROJECT INSPECTOR EXAMINATION APPLICATION

Office Use Only
ID#_____
CK#_____
$_____

PREFERRED EXAMINATION DATE (Check one):

Examination Date	Earliest Postmark Date for Filing	Latest Postmark Date For Filing
☐ Wednesday, **March 17, 2004**	Jan. 5, 2004	Feb. 20, 2004
☐ Wednesday, **June 16, 2004**	Feb. 23, 2004	May 7, 2004
☐ Wednesday, **September 15, 2004**	May 10, 2004	Aug. 6, 2004
☐ Wednesday, **December 8, 2004**	Aug. 9, 2004	Oct. 29, 2004

Which exam are you applying for? ☐ Class 1   ☐ Class 2   ☐ Class 3   ☐ Class 4
Which part are you applying for?   ☐ Both   ☐ Part 1 (Plan Reading)   ☐ Part 2 (Code Knowledge)
Exam Location Preference: ☐ Northern California   ☐ Southern California

FEES: $225.00 (non-refundable)
Please make checks or money orders (no credit cards) payable to:
Division of the State Architect
Mail application and fee to: DSA, 1102 Q Street, Suite 5100, Sacramento, CA 95814

APPLICANT'S NAME: _____
                        Last Name   First Name   MI

Address: _____ Public Contact Phone #: (____) _____

City: _____ State: _____ Zip: _____ Alternate Phone #: (____) _____

County: _____ e-mail address: _____

Date of Birth: _____

CANDIDATES WITH DISABILITIES OR SPECIAL REQUESTS: If you have a disability or special need that restricts your ability to take a test under standard conditions you may request special testing arrangements. **The request must accompany this application.** For disabilities, clarification of both the disability and the need for special accommodations by a licensed medical professional is required.

PREREQUISITES: A copy of one prerequisite certificate, license or diploma (see list on reverse) and/or inspector certifications already held, must be included with this application.

Description: _____ Certificate/License #: _____

EDUCATION:

School/College/University	Degree/Certificate	Date Graduated

See the reverse side of this application form for additional important information

CERTIFICATION: I hereby certify under penalty of perjury that I am the person indicated above, that I meet all the requirements to take this examination, that I have read and understood both sides of this applications form and that all information given is true and complete. I understand that any false statement will be cause for voiding this application and any subsequent certification. I further certify that I will not reveal the contents of the examination to anyone and affirm that I will abide by the rules of the examination. I understand that upon certification, my name and phone number will be available to the public.

Signature: _____ Date: _____

Office Use Only
A _____
P _____
E _____

Form DSA INSP 1   Revised December 2003

PROJECT INSPECTOR EXAMINATION
APPLICATION INSTRUCTIONS

➤ The following four items <u>must</u> be submitted to apply for the examination:

1. **Application:** Fill out the application (do not use old applications for previous exams. Note that applicants must be, per Title 24, at least 25 years old to qualify for the examination.

2. **Fee:** $225.00 non-refundable (checks or money orders only, credit cards are not accepted).

3. **Prerequisite:** One of the following prerequisites is required in addition to the experience requirements. Send a copy of <u>any one</u> of the following prerequisites. Please do not send any certificates that are not listed below.

   a) **Certification of the International Code Council (ICC)** as a <u>UBC Building Inspector</u>.

   b) **Certification of the American Construction Inspectors Association** as a <u>Registered Construction Inspector, Division II (Building)</u>.

   c) **Certification of the Division of the State Architect** as a <u>Relocatable Building Inspector – In-plant</u> (or prior approval as a Project Inspector on a California hospital or public school project).

   d) **A degree in architecture or engineering** from an accredited college or university (submit copies of transcripts and a description of technical classes for foreign colleges or universities only).

   e) **California licensed architect or California registered professional engineer** (civil or structural).

   f) **California State licensed <u>General Building Contractor</u>.** License must be current and active. Applicant must be the "Qualifying Partner" if the license pertains to a partnership.

   g) **Letters of recommendation from two California licensed architects and/or registered structural engineers.** A sample form letter is available on the DSA website: at www.dsa.ca.gov, click on "Inspector Info."

   h) **Proof of employment by the State of California as a building construction inspector.**

4. **Experience Record Forms:** (Read all instructions carefully before filling out Experience Record Forms). The experience requirements are the most important part of your application. <u>Thirty-six (36) months</u> of qualifying experience is required. DSA certified project inspectors see FAQ #8 on page **14** for special experience requirement options. <u>Experience must be gained in the classification of construction appropriate to the examination class for which you are applying</u> (except for prior school Project Inspector experience, see page **14**). Descriptions of project classifications are on page **4**. The maximum amount of experience that qualifies towards the exam is limited for various experience categories (see **Qualifying Experience Limitations** on page **11**). The intent is to require each applicant to have a wide variety of construction experience to qualify. For example, 3 years of special inspection experience will only count for up to 12 months towards Class 1 or 2 exam qualification. Therefore, it is not necessary to document more than 12 months of special inspection experience on your Experience Record Forms unless you are applying for the Class 3 or 4 exam. See **Directions for Completing Experience Record Forms** on pages **8** and **10** for instructions.

➤ Other Useful Information

Keep a copy of your complete application package. You may need to refer to your package to answer questions that DSA might have during the review of your application. DSA will not provide copies of your application package or experience records to you after they are submitted.

Time: The exam requires a full day to administer, broken out approximately as follows:

Check-in	7:30 – 8:30 a.m.
Review plans prior to Part 1	8:30 – 9:00 a.m.
Part 1 (Plan Reading)	9:00 a.m. – noon
Lunch (not provided)	noon – 12:45 p.m.
Check-in for Part 2	12:45 – 1:00 p.m.
Part 2 (Code Knowledge)	1:00 – 4:00 p.m.

Class 1 or 2 Experience Record Form

(Class 3 or 4 applicants may use this 'project based' form also)
Qualifying experience must be submitted on a separate Experience Record Form for <u>each</u> project.
Resumes are not accepted. See back for directions on filling out this form

1) Experience Record Form # _____ (Number <u>each</u> <u>form</u> for easy reference, e.g. 1, 2, 3):

2) Project Name: _____

Project Location (City/State): _____

Employer: _____ Phone # _____

Address of Employer: _____

DSA Use Only
Months _____
Class _____

3) DSA File Number and Application Number (if applicable): _____

4) My duties on this project commenced on _____ (date (mm/yy)) **and ended on** _____ (date (mm/yy)).

5) During this time period _____ **% of my total work time was spent on this project.**

Project Description (Check all that apply and provide area, and % of time spent, on each aspect)

	☐ New Structure	☐ Addition	☐ Relocatable	☐ Alterations (Including seismic upgrades, fire repairs, and rebuilds. Describe below.)
sq. ft.				
% of time				

Project Cost: $_____

Type of building (for new construction or additions only):
☐ Single family (or duplex) residential ☐ Multi-family residential ☐ Commercial Bldgs
☐ School (under DSA jurisdiction) ☐ Hospital Bldgs ☐ Military Bldgs
☐ Other structures: _____

Primary lateral load-resisting system (for new construction and additions only):
☐ Plywood shear wall ☐ Concrete or masonry shear wall
☐ Concrete or steel moment or braced frame ☐ Other: _____

6) Duties and Responsibilities: (Please check one. See page 12 of instructions.)

Construction
☐ General Superintendent in charge of all aspects of construction
☐ Tradesman – CHECK ONE: ☐ Foreman ☐ Journeyman ☐ Apprentice
   INDICATE TRADE: ☐ Carpenter ☐ Concrete ☐ Steel ☐ Mechanical or Plumbing
   ☐ Electrical ☐ Other (describe) _____

Inspection
☐ Special Inspector (describe scope of work inspected below)
☐ Assistant School Inspector (describe scope of work below)
☐ Non-DSA Building Inspector (e.g. local building department inspections etc. – describe below)
☐ DSA Project Inspector (personally inspecting all aspects of the work on a continuous basis)
☐ OSHPD IOR (personally inspecting all aspects of the work on a continuous basis)

Other
☐ Architectural or Engineering Design (Calif. licensed architect, or structural or civil engineer - describe below)
☐ Construction Manager/Administrator (describe duties and responsibilities in detail below)
☐ Other (describe in detail below): _____

Describe your duties and/or provide additional information: _____
_____
_____
_____ (Use back or attach additional sheet if more space is needed)

I certify under penalty of perjury that the information I have entered on this Experience Record Form is true and complete. I further understand that any false, incomplete, or incorrect statements may be cause for voiding this application and any subsequent certification. I authorize the employers identified on this application to release to DSA any requested information.

APPLICANT'S SIGNATURE	DATE SIGNED

Form DSA INSP 2   Revised December 2003

Directions for Completing Experience Record Forms
For the Class 1 or 2 Exam: (Class 3 or 4 applicants may use this form also.)

> See **Qualifying Experience Limitations** and **Experience Guidelines** (pages 11 and 12) for additional important information.

> Only experience submitted on Experience Record Forms will be evaluated. Resumes are not acceptable in lieu of Experience Record Forms.

1. **Experience Record Form #.** Use a separate Experience Record Form for <u>each</u> project. Do not group different projects with the same employer on the same form. Number each form sequentially. The first form should be your most recent project. For large projects that involve buildings of different types, you may elect to split the projects up into "subprojects" in order to describe experience clearly. To record different types of duties and/or different types of construction that occurred on the same project use separate Experience Record Forms labeled 1a, 1b, etc.

2. **Project name, location, employer, etc.** If you were self-employed, use the name of the entity you contracted with as the "Employer." Every effort must be made to obtain all information; DSA reserves the right to disallow experience which is not verifiable or is incompletely documented.

3. **DSA file and application number.** To receive credit for school projects the DSA file and application numbers are required. To receive credit for hospital projects, OSHPD numbers must be reported in this space.

4. **Start/end dates.** Report start/end dates for your involvement in the actual construction time for the project to the nearest month.

5. **Percentage of time spent on project.** Generally, experience will be obtained at the rate of 40 hours per week. Extra time will not be credited for hours worked in excess of 40 hours per week. In many cases some of the time spent on a particular project will not result in productive qualifying experience; this is understood and acceptable. However, if a project is shut down for more than two weeks, is part time, or involves significant (more than 10%) of the time spent on 'non-qualifying' duties, you must enter the percentage of your time spent on 'qualifying' duties only. If you divide a project into "subprojects" this space is used to report the percentage of your time spent on each part of the total project. **The percentage of time indicated on all Experience Record Forms must not exceed 100% during any time period.**

6. **Duties and responsibilities.** Check only one box. If you served in more than one capacity on a project submit separate Experience Record Forms for each type of experience. Attachments may be required to describe your responsibilities clearly for certain categories. See page 12 for descriptions of the duties and responsibilities for each category. Check "Other" if your duties and responsibilities do not match any of the categories described.

Choosing Projects for Your Class 1 or 2 Experience Record:

Choose projects that are relevant to the class of exam for which you are applying. Experience on alterations, or seismic upgrade projects, is generally relevant to the Class 3 exam, not the Class 1 or 2, even if done on Class 1 type buildings.

Choose projects that reflect a variety of experience. You must have a broad range of construction experience to qualify for the exam. Most types of experience are limited as explained in the **Qualifying Experience Limitations** (see page 11). If you were an electrician for ten years you need not document all ten years of electrician experience if you are applying for the Class 1 or 2 exam because only 12 months will count (there is no limit on the amount of electrician experience if you are applying for the Class 3 or 4 exam). Choose projects that reflect your experience in other categories for the remainder of your experience.

Choose projects where your responsibilities included actual "hands-on" construction experience. Estimating, obtaining permits, and drafting do not qualify as experience towards the exam.

Class 3 or 4 Experience Record Form
(This 'employment based' form is to be used by Class 3 or 4 applicants only)

Qualifying experience must be submitted on a separate Experience Record Form for <u>each</u> employer for which experience is to be considered. Resumes are not accepted. See back for directions on filling out this form

DSA Use Only
Months _____
Class _____

1) Experience Record Form # _____ (Number <u>each</u> form for easy reference, e.g. 1, 2, 3)

2) Employer: _____ **Phone #** _____

Address of Employer: _____

My duties with this employer commenced on _____ and ended on _____.
                                                           date (mm/yy)   date (mm/yy)

3) During this time period I worked an average of _____ hours per week for this employer.

Experience: Indicate the types of projects for which you had experience during this time period.
    Project Descriptions (Check all that apply and provide square feet where requested.)
    ☐ New Construction (approx. sq ft: _____) ☐ Addition (approx. sq ft: _____) ☐ Relocatable
    ☐ Alterations (including seismic upgrades, fire repairs and rebuilds – describe below).
    Identify types of buildings for new construction or additions
    ☐ Single family (or duplex) residential   ☐ Multi-family residential   ☐ Commercial Bldgs
    ☐ School (under DSA jurisdiction)   ☐ Hospital Bldgs   ☐ Military Bldgs
    ☐ Other structures: _____

4) Duties and Responsibilities: Indicate duties and responsibilities for which you have had experience during this time period. **(Check all that apply.)**

Construction
☐ General Superintendent in charge of all aspects of construction
☐ Tradesman – CHECK ONE: ☐ Foreman ☐ Journeyman ☐ Apprentice
    INDICATE TRADE: ☐ Carpenter ☐ Concrete ☐ Steel ☐ Mechanical or Plumbing
    ☐ Electrical ☐ Other (describe) _____

Inspection
☐ Special Inspector (describe scope of work inspected below)
☐ Assistant School Inspector (describe scope of work inspected below)
☐ Non-DSA Building Inspector (e.g. local building dept. inspections, etc. – describe below)
☐ DSA Project Inspector (personally inspecting all aspects of the work on a continuous basis)
☐ OSHPD IOR (personally inspecting all aspects of the work on a continuous basis)

Other
☐ Architectural or Engineering Design (Calif. licensed architect, or structural or civil engineer)
☐ Architectural or Engineering Construction Administration
☐ Construction Manager/Administrator (describe responsibilities below)
☐ Other (describe responsibilities below)

Describe your duties: _____
_____
_____
_____
_____
_____ (Use back or attach additional sheet if more space is needed)

I certify, under penalty of perjury, that the information I have entered on this Experience Record Form is true and complete. I further understand that any false, incomplete, or incorrect statements may be cause for voiding this application and any subsequent certification. I authorize the employers identified on this application to release any information they may have concerning my employment to the State of California.

APPLICANT'S SIGNATURE	DATE SIGNED

Form DSA INSP 3   Revised December 2003

Directions for Completing Experience Record Forms for the Class 3 or 4 Exam:

Class 3 or 4 applicants may also use the Class 1 or 2 (project based) Experience Record Forms.

See **Qualifying Experience Limitations** and **Experience Guidelines** (Pages **11** and **12**) for important additional information on how DSA determines eligibility of applicants' experience.

1. **Experience Record Form #.** A separate Experience Record Form will be required for each employment period. Number each form sequentially. The first form should be your most recent job. To record different types of duties and/or different types of construction that occurred with the same employer use separate Experience Record Forms labeled 1a, 1b, etc.

2. **Employer, address, and phone number.** If you were self-employed, use the name of the entity you contracted with as the "Employer." Every effort must be made to obtain all information; DSA reserves the right to disallow experience which is not verifiable or is incompletely documented.

3. **Start/end dates.** Report start/end dates for the time you were employed to the nearest month.

4. **Duties and responsibilities.** Check all boxes that apply; if you served in more than one capacity indicate the approximate percentage of time spent on each type of experience. Describe your responsibilities clearly. See page **12** for descriptions of the duties and responsibilities for each category. Check "Other" if your duties and responsibilities do not match any of the categories described. You may continue on the back of the form, or attach further information to describe your duties and/or the projects that you worked on.

➢ **Education.** Many colleges and universities offer programs specifically for inspectors. Degrees in construction technology, engineering technology, engineering and architecture may also qualify. A copy of a diploma, and course descriptions, are required. Education may count for up to 12 months of experience towards the Class 3 or 4 exam only. Education does not count as experience towards the Class 1 or 2 exams (although a degree in engineering or architecture may qualify as a prerequisite, see page **6**).

Qualifying Experience Limitations

A total of three years (36 months) of qualifying experience is required. The maximum number of months for common types of construction experience is limited, as shown in the table below. (For example: A carpenter who has worked for 3 years *on new (ground-up) commercial building projects* may only count 12 months of carpentry experience towards the Class 2 exam, the other 24 months of experience must be gained in other categories.)

Most qualifying experience will fit into one of the categories shown below. If you have experience of a type that is not shown, that you feel may be qualifying, be sure to describe your duties in detail on the Experience Record Form(s).

Experience must be gained on projects fitting the description of the examination class for which you are applying. See "Experience Guidelines" on the next page for definitions of Experience Categories and other important rules and exceptions.

Qualifying Experience Grid – This table indicates the maximum number of months that may apply toward exam eligibility

Exam Class	Construction			Inspection			Other	
	General Superintendent	Tradesman	Special Inspector	Assistant School Inspector	Non-DSA[1] Building Inspector	Architect or Engineer	Construction Manager/ Administrator[2]
1	No limit	12	12	12 [2,3]	12 [2,5]	No limit	12
2	No limit	12	12	24 [2,3]	12 [2,5]	No limit	12
3[4]	No limit	No limit	No limit	No limit	No limit	No limit	24
4[4]	No limit	No limit	No limit	No limit	No limit	No limit	24

Footnotes:
1. DSA Project Inspector experience is evaluated differently; see FAQ #8 on page **14**.
2. Describe specific day to day duties in detail. Include an average percentage of time spent on each aspect of your duties.
3. Subject to the recommendation of your DSA field engineer; otherwise counts as Class 3 experience only.
4. Education and training from DSA recognized programs may count for up to 12 months of experience towards the Class 3 or Class 4 exam only. See "Education" on page **10**.
5. OSHPD Inspector of Record (IOR) experience is accepted without limit.

Experience Guidelines

General Information

Experience on residential construction only counts towards the Class 3 exam (not the Class 1 or 2).

Building construction experience gained outside of the United States may, at DSA's discretion, be credited to a maximum of 12 months. This limitation applies to the total of <u>all</u> foreign experience.

These guidelines may not be appropriate to every situation. Experience that is not described below will be evaluated on a case by case basis. Applicants will be evaluated based solely on the written information submitted on their Experience Record Form(s). Verification of duties or employment may be requested at the sole discretion of DSA.

Generally, non-building experience (bridges, dams, mechanical plant installations, roads, railways, etc.) is not acceptable. Certain types of non-building experience may be accepted as a supplement to building experience on a case by case basis. Experience not related to building construction (for example, electrical work on automobiles) would not qualify.

Description of Duties and Responsibilities

Construction:

General Superintendent. Supervision of all aspects of the construction and coordination of all crews and/or subcontractors. The general superintendent is the on-site "at risk" person in charge of the entire construction project. He or she is intimately familiar with the plans and specifications and provides quality assurance for the entire project. Administrative duties such as processing change order requests are secondary to the primary duties of the general superintendent (see Construction Manager/Administrator below).

Tradesman. Physically performing the work of carpentry, concrete, steel, electrical, mechanical, or plumbing on buildings. Painting, paving, carpet-laying, and other 'non-safety related' construction experience do not qualify.

Inspection:

Special Inspector. Welding, masonry, and other types of code required special inspection work.

Assistant School Inspector. You <u>must</u> be approved by DSA to be the assistant inspector on a school project. The experience gained by the assistant may vary widely. Generally, experience gained as an assistant will qualify towards the Class 3 examination. More responsible/extensive experience may qualify towards the Class 2 exam while less responsible/extensive experience may only qualify for the Class 4 exam. Verification of responsibilities by your DSA field engineer may be required.

Non-DSA Building Inspector. Residential inspections may qualify towards the Class 3 or 4 examination; commercial, public, and institutional building inspections may qualify towards the Class 1 or Class 2 exam on a case-by-case basis. Plan review or other non-inspection related duties do not qualify. Applicants will need to specify the percentage of time spent inspecting various types of construction and provide detailed information on the types of inspections performed as well as the types of buildings inspected.

DSA Project Inspector. Approved by DSA as the project inspector for an entire project. See FAQ #8 on page 14 for special options for minimum experience required.

OSHPD IOR. Approved as the Inspector of Record (IOR) by the Office of Statewide Health Planning and Development (OSHPD) on hospital projects.

Other:

Architectural or Engineering Design. Building design experience only counts for California licensed Architects, Registered Structural Engineers, or Registered Civil Engineers.

Construction Manager/Administrator. Administrative duties related to organizing, planning and coordinating a construction project. Only experience gained on school projects under DSA jurisdiction qualifies. A Construction Manager (CM) generally cannot claim experience in categories that are the responsibility of others.

DSA Project Inspector Examination
Frequently Asked Questions

1. **What should I bring to the exam?**

   Answer: You should bring the reference books that you would bring to the construction site to perform your inspections. The following is a list of things you <u>may</u> need; it is not meant to be an exhaustive list, nor will all reference books be of value during the exam:

   What you must bring
   - Your Site Admittance Form
   - Your Picture Identification
   - #2 Pencils and erasers

   What you may bring
   - A simple calculator (non-printing, self-contained, silent. Palm top computers are not allowed)
   - The 2001 version of Title 24, Parts 1, 2, 3, 4, 5, 9 and 12
   - West Coast Lumber Inspection Bureau (WCLIB) Lumber Grading Rules
   - American Welding Society (AWS) D1.1, Structural Welding Code
   - American Institute of Steel Construction (AISC), Steel Construction Manual
   - ASTM reports for common construction materials and practices
   - National Fire Protection Association (NFPA) 13, 14, 17, 17-A, 24 and 72
   - All other reference books that you would bring to the jobsite to perform inspections on a project. All commercially published, bound reference books are permitted. Please be aware that you may not have time to look up every question.

   What you should not bring
   - Do not bring seminar or class handouts of any type (including DSA seminar binders).
   - Do not bring the DSA "IR manual" or any other material downloaded from any website.
   - Do not bring ring bound notebooks (ring bound codebooks are allowed), spiral bound books, or loose paper of any kind.
   - Do not bring photocopies of any reference books.
   - Do not insert <u>any</u> additional pages into your codebooks or other reference books.

2. **How should I study for the exam?**

   Answer: The exam is meant to test for practical construction experience as well as knowledge of the code and the ability to read and interpret drawings. It is difficult for a person with no practical field construction experience to learn the detailed construction knowledge necessary to pass the exam from studying books or taking classes. The best teacher is actual experience, either performing construction or assisting another inspector on a large job. Of course, studying the codes and other reference books mentioned in question 1 above is also recommended. Some further resources that may be beneficial include:

   - Classes which may be available at community colleges.
   - Seminars provided by the American Construction Inspector's Association (ACIA), aimed at school inspection as well as more general inspection topics.
   - ACIA monthly meetings where inspectors can share their ideas and experiences.

3. **Does DSA provide training for prospective inspectors?**

   Answer: The inspector training seminars offered by DSA are for DSA certified project inspectors and DSA accepted assistant inspectors. The DSA seminars concentrate on continuing education and code updates. DSA seminars are mandatory for all DSA project inspectors. The seminars are intended to ensure that project inspectors are knowledgeable of the rules, regulations, and standards that apply to the inspection of school construction.

   DSA personnel participate in introductory training seminars provided by the American Construction Inspector's Association (ACIA). These seminars are recommended for individuals who are interested in becoming inspectors. ACIA may be contacted at (888) 867-2242.

4. **If I apply for the Class 1 test but do not qualify, can I change my application to the Class 2 or Class 3 test?**

   Answer: No, you will have to pay an additional fee to be re-evaluated for the Class 2 or Class 3 test.

DSA Project Inspector Examination
Frequently Asked Questions

5. **If I take the Class 1 exam and miss passing by a small margin, will I be certified as a Class 2 (or Class 3) inspector?**

    Answer: No, you must decide which exam you want to apply for and pass it. Even if you miss the passing score by only one point you will have to retest.

6. **What are the cost and cancellation policies?**

    Answer: The cost is $225.00 payable at the time you submit your application.

    - No refunds will be made even if an applicant is not permitted to take the examination due to age, prerequisite, or experience. Read the instructions carefully before sending in your application and fee.
    - Applicants who do not qualify to take the exam may submit additional information and re-apply for a future examination <u>one time</u> (within six months) without submitting an additional fee. Applicants who still do not qualify will have to submit a new application fee to re-apply again.
    - Applicants who do not qualify for the examination but do qualify for the assistant inspector program may apply for the assistant inspector program for no additional fee.
    - Applicants who are accepted but are not able to attend the exam for any reason will receive a <u>one-time transfer</u> to a future examination within six months. No refunds are available for cancellations.

7. **How do I get approved to do in-plant inspection of relocatable buildings?**

    Answer: Relocatable Building Inspector In-Plant (RBIP) Certificates are issued to individuals who pass the RBIP test. The RBIP test is separate from the project inspector tests. The RBIP test is given on an individual, as needed basis. Contact David Sault at (916) 327-3459 for an application and additional information on this program. Class 1 inspectors qualify to apply for "in-plant" inspection work and do not need an RBIP certificate.

8. **I am already a DSA certified Project Inspector. How can I upgrade to a higher class of certification?**

    Answer: You may qualify for the exam class **one step higher** than your current certification level if you meet any of the special experience requirement options in the table below

SPECIAL EXPERIENCE REQUIREMENT OPTIONS FOR DSA PROJECT INSPECTOR UPGRADES				
	<u>CLASS 1</u>	<u>CLASS 2</u>	<u>CLASS 3</u>	<u>CLASS 4</u>
OPTION #1[1]	36 months of combined construction / inspection[2] experience (construction in the appropriate class; inspection[2] in the next lower class)			
OPTION #2	24 months[3] of inspection[2] experience in next lower class			
OPTION #3	48 months[3] of project inspector experience on class 3 projects			

<u>Footnotes:</u> **1**: See table on page 5 for qualifying experience. You may also include DSA project inspector experience in this option

   2: DSA approved project inspector experience on the entire project meeting the class description one step lower than the exam class applied for.

   3: These minimums may be reduced by one half (1/2) with a special recommendation of your DSA field engineer.

DSA Project Inspector Examination
Frequently Asked Questions

9. **What kind of experience do I need to qualify for each class of examination?**

    Answer: Experience requirements are described in detail in this application package.

10. **My construction experience doesn't fit into any of the categories; how do I report it?**

    Answer: Mark "other" and describe your experience in the space provided at the bottom of the Experience Record Form. You may attach additional pages if there isn't enough space.

11. **I received a letter stating that additional information is required to qualify; what should I do?**

    Answer: The boxes that are marked on your letter explain what additional information is required. Most applications are returned for further detail on the applicant's experience. The following suggestions may help to clarify your experience:

    - Fill out the Experience Record Form with detailed information on your experience on a project-by-project basis; attach additional pages as required (resumes are not acceptable).
    - Include pertinent information such as start and finish dates for each project and the percentage of time spent on separate tasks such as 'inspection' versus 'construction management'.
    - Overlapping projects will only count once (if you did ten different projects over a three-month time frame you will be credited with three months of experience, not thirty).
    - Emphasize experience in varying aspects of building construction, additional years of experience (beyond the maximum limits shown in the table on page 11) are not considered qualifying. For example, a carpenter with 20 years of experience will not qualify for the Class 1 exam unless he has experience in other aspects of construction (Steel, electrical, special inspections, etc.). The Project Inspector on even a small school project must have knowledge in many facets of construction.
    - Emphasize your construction experience. Practical field construction experience is generally considered to be at least as important as education in code and plan reading skills.
    - DSA realizes that each applicant's experience and background are unique. If you have experience that is not addressed in the guidelines, or other special circumstances, this will be considered. If you have further questions please call David Sault at (916) 327-3459.

12. **I failed the "plan reading" part of the exam and passed the "code" part. Can I re-apply for the "plan reading" part only?**

    Answer: Yes, but the full fee is required with the application.

13. **I failed the "plan reading" part of the Class 1 exam and passed the "code" part. Can I take only the "plan reading" part of the Class 2 exam or do I have to take both parts of the Class 2 exam?**

    Answer: You must take both parts of an exam class to receive a certificate even if you already passed one part of a more difficult exam.

14. **I passed the test except that I didn't pass one Section. Can I just re-take that one Section?**

    Answer: No, you must re-apply and take the entire Part over again. If you only missed one (or more) Section(s) in one Part then you only need to retake that Part.

DSA Project Inspector Examination
Frequently Asked Questions

15. Do I have to be certified to serve as an inspector?

    Answer: DSA has instituted an assistant inspector program to allow uncertified individuals to assist Project Inspectors under certain conditions. An application must be filed with the DSA headquarters office. If accepted, the individual's name and phone number will be posted on the DSA web site as an acceptable candidate for assistant inspector work. (Form DSA-5A must then be submitted to the DSA regional office describing the specific duties to be performed by the assistant inspector for each project). Further information is provided in IR A-7 and on the DSA website at **www.dsa.ca.gov** under "Inspector Info."

Important:

Certification does not guarantee that an individual will be approved for any school project. Experience, workload and past performance will be evaluated and considered on a case-by-case basis by the DSA field engineer.

IMPORTANT REMINDERS:

- In January of 2004, DSA Headquarters and Sacramento Regional Offices moved to 1102 Q Street, Sacramento 95814

- APPLICANTS: Mail your <u>Exam Application</u> to DSA Headquarters at **Suite 5100**

- CERTIFIED INSPECTORS: Mail your inspector reports to *your* DSA Regional Office

- DSA <u>Sacramento</u> Regional Office is now located at 1102 Q Street, **Suite 5200**, Sacramento 95814

Appendix #2

IR-A8 Duties of a DSA Certified Inspector

California Department of General Services · Division of the State Architect · Interpretation of Regulations Document

PROJECT INSPECTOR & ASSISTANT INSPECTOR
Duties and Performance Rating by DSA

IR A-8

REFERENCE: California Building Standards Administrative Code (Title 24, Part 1)
Sections 4-211, 4-333, 4-334, 4-336, 4-337, 4-342, & 4-343
California Education Code, Sections 17309 & 81141

Revised 1-25-02
Supersedes IR 4-1 (3/90)
See DSA IR A-7

This interpretation is intended for use by the plan review and field engineers of DSA to indicate an acceptable method for achieving compliance with applicable codes and regulations. Its purpose is to promote more uniform statewide criteria for use in plan review and supervision of construction of public schools, community colleges and essential services buildings. Other methods proposed by design professionals to solve a particular problem may be considered by DSA and reviewed for code and regulation compliance.

Purpose: This IR provides clarification of the duties of school construction project inspectors and assistant inspectors as required by the California Building Standards Code (Title 24, Part 1). The IR also describes the performance rating process utilized by DSA to evaluate inspectors for approval on future school construction projects.

Section 1 – REQUIRED DUTIES of the PROJECT INSPECTOR

The project inspector must perform specific duties in accordance with Title 24, Part 1 (Sections 4-333, and 4-342). The project inspector acts under the direction of the design professional in general responsible charge and is subject to supervision by DSA. The project inspector does not have the authority under Title 24 to direct the contractor in the execution of the work, nor to stop the work of construction.

The project inspector's responsibilities include:

- A thorough understanding of all requirements of the construction documents. The inspector must seek direction from the design professional(s) in the event of the inspector's uncertainty in comprehension of the documents.

- Inspection of all portions of the construction for compliance with the requirements of the construction documents.

- Identification, documentation, and reporting of deviations in the construction from the requirements of the construction documents.

- Submittal of verified reports (Form DSA-6). At the conclusion of the project any outstanding deviations must be noted on the Form DSA-6.

Seven Categories of Code-Prescribed Duties of the Project Inspector

The code-prescribed duties of the project inspector have been organized into the following seven categories. The inspector's performance in each of these categories serves as the basis for the DSA field engineer's rating of the inspector (see Section 2 on page 5 of this IR).

1. Inspector's Job File

The inspector must maintain approved (DSA-stamped) construction documents at the job-site in an organized, readily accessible manner. The inspector must also maintain any other construction documents or directives received from the responsible design professional(s). The following list of documents and codes must be maintained at the job-site during construction:

- Approved plans and specifications.
- Test and Inspection List (Form DSA-103-1).
- Building Codes: Title 24, Part 1 (administrative code); Title 24, Part 2, Volumes 1, 2, and 3 (build-

ing code); Title 24, Part 3 (electrical code); Title 24, Part 4 (mechanical code); Title 24, Part 5 (plumbing code) and Title 24, Part 6 (energy code). The code edition must be as referenced on the approved plans and specifications.

- Approved addenda.
- Approved deferred approval documents.
- Approved preliminary change orders.
- Approved change orders.
- A copy of shop drawings, samples, and approved submittals.
- Any other documents or directives received from the responsible design professional(s).

2. Inspector's Comprehension of the Construction Documents

The inspector must study and fully comprehend the requirements of the construction documents in order to provide competent inspection of the work. It is necessary for the inspector to possess a thorough understanding of the requirements of the plans and specifications *before* that portion of the work is performed.

The inspector must:

- Consult the responsible design professional(s) to resolve any uncertainties in the inspector's comprehension of the plans and specifications prior to construction of that portion of the work.
- Readily identify non-compliant work as the construction progresses, to facilitate prompt corrective action.
- Verify code-compliant implementation of the materials testing and special inspection program.

Title 24, Part 1, Section 4-343, specifies that the contractor must direct inquiries regarding document interpretation to the design professional in general responsible charge, through the inspector. This code provision requires the contractor to inform the inspector of all uncertainties in the contractor's comprehension of the construction documents.

3. Continuous Inspection of the Work

Continuous inspection means complete and timely inspection of every part of the work. Title 24, Part 1 requires prompt inspection of the work as it progresses. Title 24, Part 1 also requires that prompt verbal notification be made to the contractor of any deviation, so that the deviation can be immediately corrected.

Work such as concrete work or masonry work which can be inspected only as it is placed requires the constant presence of the inspector. Certain types of work which can be completely inspected after the work is installed may be carried out while the inspector is not present, provided that the inspector promptly identifies and reports all deviations.

The project inspector must have personal knowledge of the construction obtained through the project inspector's own physical inspection of the work in all stages of its progress. When special inspectors or approved assistant inspectors are required on a project, the project inspector's personal knowledge may include that knowledge obtained from these individuals.

4. Records of Inspections

The inspector must maintain detailed records of all inspections. The inspector's records must pro-

vide a comprehensive and timely documentation of the inspected work, promptly identifying all compliant and non-compliant construction. These records must be readily accessible and maintained in an organized manner. The following is a list of the inspection records that must be maintained at the job-site:

- A systematic record of the inspection of all work required by the construction documents. Marking properly completed work on a set of construction documents is a recommended method to verify that the requirements of the plans and specifications have been met. The inspector must also record the resolution of reported deviations.
- Construction Procedure Records per Title 24, Part 1, Section 4-342(6), including but not limited to concrete placement operations, welding operations, pile penetration blow counts, and other records specified on the approved construction documents.
- Log of project inspector's and assistant inspector's time spent on-site. DSA may require verification from the inspector of time spent at the job-site during all phases of the work.

5. Communications Required of the Inspector

The inspector must, during the course of construction, provide specific code-prescribed notices and reports to the responsible design professional(s), DSA, the school district, and the contractor. The inspector must maintain records of all communications. These records must be readily accessible and maintained in an organized manner. The date and recipients of all communications must be clearly indicated.

The inspector is required to provide the following communications during the course of a construction project:

- **Notifications to DSA** as required by Title 24, Part 1, Section 4-342 (b) 5; including start of work, minimum 48 hours prior to completion of foundation trenches, minimum 48 hours prior to first concrete placement, and when work is suspended for more than two weeks.
- **Inspector's Semi-Monthly Reports** (see Title 24, Part 1, Section 4-337). The project inspector must make semi-monthly reports (on the 1st and 15th of every month) on the progress of construction. The semi-monthly report must be submitted to the design professional in general responsible charge and the structural engineer; a copy must be sent to DSA and the school district.

    A semi-monthly report must be prepared in accordance with DSA's *Guideline for Inspector's Semi-Monthly Report*. The guideline is available on-line at www.dgs.ca.gov/dsa (click on "Forms"), or at DSA regional offices.

    Note for single-story relocatable building projects: At the discretion of the responsible design professional(s), the inspector may submit the DSA standard form *Checklist for Site Inspection of Relocatable Buildings* in lieu of semi-monthly reports. The checklist is to be submitted at the completion of the work. The checklist is available on-line at www.dgs.ca.gov/dsa (click on "Forms"), or at DSA regional offices.

- **Deviation Notices** (see Title 24, Part 1, Section 4-342 (b) 7). When the inspector identifies deviations from the approved plans and specifications, the inspector must verbally notify the contractor. If the deviation is not immediately corrected, the inspector is required to promptly issue a written notice of deviation to the contractor, with a copy sent to the responsible design professional(s), and DSA. The resolution of reported deviations must be documented by the inspector.

- **Record of Communications to the Responsible Design Professional(s)** All uncertainties in the inspector's or contractor's comprehension of the documents must be reported in writing to the responsible design professional(s).
- **Verified Reports** (Form DSA-6) (refer to Title 24, Part 1, Section 4-336). The project inspector shall submit verified reports directly to DSA within seven days of any of the following:
    1) Work on the project is suspended for a period of more than one month.
    2) The services of the inspector are terminated for any reason.
    3) DSA requests a verified report.
    4) At the time of occupancy of any building of a project.
    5) The entire project is complete.

    The report shall clearly describe all non-compliant work including work done in accordance with change orders that are pending DSA approval. The report shall state that the inspector knows of his or her own personal knowledge that the construction has, in every material respect, been performed in compliance with the DSA approved documents. The inspector shall declare under penalty of perjury that all information presented on the report is true.

6. Inspector's Monitoring of the Materials Testing & Special Inspection Program

The inspector is responsible, under the direction of the design professional in general responsible charge, for monitoring the work of any special inspectors and materials testing laboratories to ensure that the Materials Testing & Special Inspection Program for the project is satisfactorily completed.

The project inspector must monitor the following aspects of the Materials Testing & Special Inspection Program:

- When DSA approval for special inspectors is required, the project inspector must identify and report any special inspectors on the job-site that are not DSA-approved.
- The project inspector must verify that the materials testing lab has received sufficient advance notification to perform the required material sampling or special inspection.
- The project inspector is responsible for verifying that all required material sampling and special inspections have been performed. The project inspector is also responsible to observe any special inspector's on-site presence and performance of duties, the special inspector's documentation of complying and non-complying work, and issuance of deviation notices.
- The project inspector is responsible for reviewing all materials test and special inspection reports. The project inspector must be aware of deviations reported by any materials testing lab or special inspector. Once the responsible design professional(s) initiate a course of action for the resolution of deviations, the project inspector must verify that the course of action was followed and the deviations resolved.

7. Monitoring of Assistant Inspector(s)

The project inspector must provide technical guidance to assistant inspector(s) and must verify the assistant inspector's comprehension of the construction documents. The project inspector must also monitor the assistant inspector's performance, verifying that the assistant inspector is properly checking the construction, recording inspections, and performing other assigned duties.

The project inspector must ensure that any assistant inspector is performing the duties indicated on the assistant inspector's approved Form DSA-5A.

Section 2 – DSA's RATING of the INSPECTOR'S PERFORMANCE

The DSA field engineer makes site visits at various stages of the project construction, observing the project inspector's and assistant inspector(s) execution of code-prescribed duties. At the final site visit, the DSA field engineer will complete a *Project Inspector's Performance Rating* for the project inspector and an *Assistant Inspector's Performance Rating* for any assistant inspector(s). These forms identify seven categories (six for assistant inspectors) of code-prescribed duties as outlined in Section 1 of this IR.

The performance rating is used by DSA as a basis for approval of the project inspector or assistant inspector on future projects. The scope of the performance rating is limited to the inspector's execution of code-prescribed duties on a specific project. An overall rating of "unsatisfactory" may adversely affect the inspector's qualification for approval by DSA on future projects.

The DSA Field Engineer's Role During Construction - *The Field Trip Note*

The responsibilities of the DSA field engineer include observing the project inspector's execution of code-required duties. During each visit to the job-site, the DSA field engineer will document on the DSA Field Trip Note improper or incomplete execution of the inspector's code-prescribed duties. The field engineer will also provide an acceptable process to correct inadequate execution of the inspector's code-prescribed duties. Copies of the Field Trip Note will be distributed to the inspector, the design professional in general responsible charge, and the school district.

DSA's Rating of the Inspector - *The Project Inspector's Performance Rating Form*

At the final visit to the job-site, the DSA field engineer will complete the *Project Inspector's Performance Rating* (Form DSA-180-5.1) for project inspectors, or the *Assistant Inspector's Performance Rating* (Form DSA-180-5.1a) for assistant inspectors. These forms are available on-line at www.dgs.ca.gov/dsa (click on "Forms") or at DSA regional offices.

RATING THE INSPECTOR'S PERFORMANCE OF CODE-PRESCRIBED DUTIES

The DSA field engineer must make a determination of "satisfactory," "needs improvement," or "unsatisfactory" performance in each of the seven categories (six for assistant inspectors) indicated on the rating form.

The rating in each category is based on the observations documented by the DSA field engineer on the Field Trip Note(s). Documented problems with the inspector's performance that were satisfactorily addressed during the course of construction can result in a rating of "satisfactory." Any documented improper or incomplete execution of code-prescribed duties that have not been satisfactorily addressed may result in an "unsatisfactory" or "needs improvement" rating.

OVERALL RATING OF THE INSPECTOR

The DSA field engineer will also give the inspector an overall rating of "satisfactory," "needs improvement," or "unsatisfactory" performance on the rating form. The overall rating is based on the ratings the inspector received in the seven categories (six for assistant inspectors). An overall rating of "satisfactory" results from satisfactory ratings in each of the categories. An unsatisfactory

rating in one or more of the categories may be justification for an overall rating of "unsatisfactory."

The DSA field engineer will communicate the rating in each category and the overall rating to the inspector. The inspector can, upon request and by scheduled appointment, review the ratings with the DSA supervisor or regional manager at the DSA regional office. "Unsatisfactory" overall ratings require the review and signature of the DSA supervising engineer and DSA regional manager prior to placement in the inspector's personal file.

DSA's Inspector File

The *Inspector's Performance Rating* is confidential and will be maintained in the inspector's personal and confidential file at the DSA regional office that provided construction oversight for the project. Access to these files will only be permitted to DSA personnel and the individual inspector.

An inspector may review this personal file by scheduling an appointment with the appropriate DSA supervising engineer or regional manager. The inspector must present a photo ID. The inspector may not make copies of the file contents, nor at any time will the file be allowed out of the DSA regional office, unless subpoenaed by a court.